Franz Kielhorn

Sanskrit Language Grammar

Franz Kielhorn

Sanskrit Language Grammar

ISBN/EAN: 9783742806734

Manufactured in Europe, USA, Canada, Australia, Japa

Cover: Foto ©Lupo / pixelio.de

Manufactured and distributed by brebook publishing software (www.brebook.com)

Franz Kielhorn

Sanskrit Language Grammar

SANSKRIT GRAMMAR.

BOMBAY:
PRINTED AT THE EDUCATION SOCIETY'S PRESS, BYCULLA.

A GRAMMAR

OF

THE SANSKRIT LANGUAGE.

BY

F. KIELHORN, Ph. D.

SUPERINTENDENT OF SANSKRIT STUDIES IN DECCAN COLLEGE.

Registered under Act **XXV.** of 1867.

Bombay:
GOVERNMENT CENTRAL BOOK DEPOT.

1870.

All Rights Reserved.

PK 666
.K48

WEBER COLLECTION

E1600
'05

TO

PROFESSOR A. F. STENZLER,

WHO FIRST TAUGHT ME SANSKRIT,

IN MEMORY

OF MANY HAPPY HOURS.

PREFACE.

The present Grammar, which is published at the request and under the patronage of Mr. J. B. Peile, the Director of Public Instruction in this Presidency, is intended principally for Indian students. It contains as much of the Sanskrit accidence as is necessary for the ordinary B.A. examination. Those who look higher, I refer to the Siddhânta-Kaumudî and other indigenous works on grammar, without a careful study of which a scholarlike knowledge of the Sanskrit language appears to me unattainable.

My chief aim in composing this grammar has been correctness, and to attain this object I have considered it the safest plan not to give any rules nor to put down any forms without the authority of the best native grammarians. I trust I may not appear presumptuous in maintaining that this has not always been an easy task, and that in many cases much patient labour and weighing of arguments had to be gone through before a certain form could, on the best possible authority, either be accepted as correct or rejected as incorrect. The result of my labour is before the public; and, having done my best, I shall be grateful to every one who will take the trouble to point out to me any errors which insufficient care or reading or want of judgment has allowed me to pass unnoticed.

On the arrangement of my grammar only few words need be said here. I have considered it necessary to separate the roots of the tenth class from those of the other nine classes, and to treat of them under the head of derivative verbal bases. Most scholars will, I hope, approve of this change. Nor will they, I trust, object to the introduction of the subjunctive mood in § 218. That the terms *Radical Aorist* and *S-Aorist* will be generally approved of, I feel less assured, and I shall be ready to give up the *S-Aorist* for any better or more scientific term that may be suggested to me. To introduce into a Sanskrit grammar the expressions *First* and *Second* Aorist at a time when the best Greek grammars try to get rid of them, appears to me little advisable; and I cannot see the appropriateness of the terms *Simple* and *Compound* Aorist when it is far from certain that the letter *s*, which is employed in the formation of the four last varieties of the Aorist, is really the remainder of the root *as* 'to be.'

F. KIELHORN.

Deccan College, March 1870.

TABLE OF CONTENTS.

	PAGE
CHAPTER I.—THE LETTERS §§ 1—14	1
1. The Devanâgarî Alphabet §§ 1—6	1
2. Classification of the Letters §§ 7—14	4
CHAPTER II.—RULES OF EUPHONY §§ 15—59	6
A. Final and Initial Letters of complete words §§ 15—41	6
1. Contact of final and initial vowels §§ 19—26	6
2. Contact of final vowels and consonants with initial vowels and consonants §§ 27—41	8
(a) Changes of final consonants §§ 27—37	8
(b) Changes of initial consonants §§ 38—41	11
B. Changes of Final Letters of nominal and verbal Bases and Initial Letters of Terminations, and of other letters in the interior of words. §§ 42—59	12
CHAPTER III.—DECLENSION OF NOUNS SUBSTANTIVE AND ADJECTIVE §§ 60—169	15
A. Consonantal Bases §§ 71—130	17
1. Unchangeable Bases §§ 71—91	17
Decl. I. Bases in ण् and ऋ §§ 71—72	17
Decl. II. Bases in क्, ख्, ग्, घ्, द्, ठ्, ड्, ढ्, त्, थ्, द्, ध्, प्, फ्, व्, भ्, च्, ज्, श्, ष्, स्, ह्, §§ 73—82.	18

CONTENTS.

  Decl. III. Bases in र् §§ 83—84 23

  Decl. IV. Bases in इन् §§ 85—87 24

  Decl. V. Bases in the affixes अस्, इस्, उस्, §§ 88—91. 25

 2. Changeable Bases §§ 92—130 26

  Decl. VI. Comparative Bases in यस् §§ 97—100 .. 27

  Decl. VII. Participle Bases in अत् §§ 101—108.... 28

  Decl. VIII. Bases in the affixes मत्, वत्, यत्, §§ 109—113 31

  Decl. IX. Bases in the affixes अन्, मन्, वन्, §§ 114—121 32

  Decl. X. Perfect Participle Bases in वस्, §§ 122—125. 35

  Decl. XI. Bases in अच् अञ्च् §§ 126—130 37

B. Vowel-Bases §§ 131—153 38

  Decl. XII. Bases in अ and आ §§ 131—135 38

  Decl. XIII. Bases in इ and उ §§ 136—140 40

  Decl. XIV. Femin. Bases in ई and ऊ §§ 141—144. 43

  Decl. XV. Monosyll. Masc. and Fem. Bases in आ, ई, ऊ at the end of Tatpur. Comp. §§ 145—147 .. 44

  Decl. XVI. Bases in ऋ §§ 148—152.... 45

  Decl. XVII. Bases in ऐ, ओ, औ § 153 47

 Alphabetical list of irregular Bases §§ 154—167 47

 Affixes expressing the meanings of cases § 168 51

CHAPTER IV.—COMPARISON OF ADJECTIVES §§ 170—176. 52

  (a) By means of तर and तम §§ 170—172 52

  (b) By means of ईयस् and इष्ठ §§ 173—175 53

CONTENTS.

PAGE

Chapter V.—PRONOUNS, PRONOMINAL ADJECTIVES, AND THEIR DECLENSION §§ 177—200 .. 55

    1. Personal Pronouns §§ 177—178 55

    2. Demonstrative Pronouns §§ 179—181 56

    3. The Relative Pronoun § 182 58

    4. The Interrogative Pronoun §§ 183—184 59

    5. Indefinite Pronouns §§ 185—186.... 60

    6. Reflexive Pronouns §§ 187—188 60

    7. Possessive Pronouns §§ 189—190 60

    8. Correlative Pronouns §§ 191—192 61

    9. Reciprocal Pronouns § 193 61

    10. Pronominal Adverbs § 194 62

    11. Pronominal Adjectives §§ 195—200 62

Chapter VI.—NUMERALS AND THEIR DECLENSION §§ 201—213 63

    Cardinals and Ordinals §§ 201—203.... 63

    Declension of the Cardinals and Ordinals §§ 204—211 68

    Numeral Adverbs § 212 69

    Other Numeral Derivatives § 213 70

Chapter VII.—CONJUGATION OF VERBS §§ 214—477 70

  I. Conjugation of Primitive Roots § 221—395 72

    1. The Parasmaipada and Âtmanepada §§ 224—377.... 73

        Augment and Reduplication §§ 228—232 75

		PAGE
A.	Special Tenses §§ 234—294....	77
	(a) Special Tenses of Roots with unchangeable special Base (1st, 4th, and 6th Classes) §§ 238—247..	80
	Irregular Roots of the 1st, 4th, and 6th Classes § 247	83
	(b) Special Tenses of Roots with changeable special Base §§ 248—294	85
	Irregular Roots of the 2nd, 3rd, 5th, 7th, 8th and 9th Classes §§ 263—294	98
B.	General Tenses §§ 295—377 ..	103
	1. The Perfect §§ 297—322	104
	(a) The Reduplicated Perfect §§ 299—319	104
	(b) The Periphrastic Perfect §§ 320—322	117
	2. The Aorist §§ 323—358	119
	(a) The Radical Aorist §§ 325—336	119
	(b) The S-Aorist §§ 337—358	122
	3. The two Futures §§ 359—369	130
	(a) The Simple Future §§ 360—364	130
	(b) The Periphrastic Future §§ 365—369	134
	4. The Conditional §§ 370—371	137
	5. The Benedictive §§ 372—377	138
2.	The Passive §§ 378—393	142
	A. The Present and Imperfect §§ 379—382	142
	B. The Perfect, Aorist, Future, Conditional, and Benedictive §§ 383—393	143
	Conjugation of rt. बुध् in Par., Âtm., and Pass. § 394 ..	146
	Alphabetical list of some Irregular Verbs § 395	150

CONTENTS. xiii

	PAGE
II. Conjugation of Derivative Verbal Bases §§ 396—477	159
1. Conjugation of the roots of the tenth class and of the Causal of all roots §§ 396—430	159
(A.) Conjugation of the roots of the tenth class §§ 396—415	159
(B.) The Causal §§ 416—430	169
2. The Desiderative §§ 431—448	178
3. The Frequentative §§ 449—466	190
4. Nominal Verbs §§ 467—477	199
CHAPTER VIII.—PREPOSITIONS AND OTHER VERBAL PREFIXES §§ 478—482	205
CHAPTER IX.—FORMATION OF NOMINAL BASES §§ 483—567.	209
I. Derivative Nominal Bases §§ 486—530	210
1. Participles §§ 490—503	211
(a) Participles of the Present Tense §§ 490—492	211
(b) Participles of the Simple Future § 493	213
(c) Participles of the Perfect §§ 494—496	214
(d) The Past Participles §§ 497—503	215
2. The Gerund §§ 504—517	222
(a) The Gerund in त्वा §§ 505—509	223
(b) The Gerund in य §§ 510—516	227
(c) The Gerund in अम् § 517	229
3. The Infinitive § 518	230
4. Verbal Adjectives §§ 519—529	231
(a) The Verbal Adj. in तव्य § 520	231
(b) The Verbal Adj. in अनीय §§ 521—522	231
(c) The Verbal Adj. in य 523—529	233
5. A list of the most common Taddhita Affixes § 530.	236

		PAGE
II.	Compound Nominal Bases §§ 531—567	239
	1. Tatpurusha or Determinative Comp. §§ 538—552.	244
	(a) Dependent Determinative Comp. §§ 538—543.	244
	(b) Appositional Determ. Comp. (Karmadhâraya) §§ 544—548	248
	(c) Numeral Determ. Comp. (Dvigu) §§ 549—552.	251
	2. Bahuvrîhi or Attributive Compounds §§ 553—559.	253
	3. Dvandva or Copulative Compounds §§ 560—564.	257
	4. Avyayîbhâva or Adverbial Compounds §§ 565—566.	259

ADDITIONS AND CORRECTIONS.

Note on § 373, b, 1, § 379 b, &c.: The following are the most common roots that drop their penultimate nasal in the Benedict. Par. &c: अञ्ज् 'to anoint,' भञ्ज् 'to break,' रञ्ज् 'to colour' &c., सञ्ज् 'to adhere,' ष्वञ्ज् 'to embrace;' ग्रन्थ् 'to string together,' मन्थ् 'to agitate;' उन्द् 'to moisten,' स्कन्द् 'to descend,' स्यन्द् 'to flow;' इन्ध् 'to kindle,' बन्ध् 'to bind;' दम्भ् 'to deceive,' स्तम्भ् 'to support;' दंश् 'to bite,' भ्रंश् or भ्रंस् 'to fall;' ध्वंस् 'to fall,' शंस् 'to praise,' हंस् 'to fall;' तृंह 'to kill.'

Page 22, l. 5, I. D. Ab. Du. आश्रीभ्याम्; D. Ab. Plur. आश्रीभ्यः:—Page 36, l. 19, read जभिवांसौ.—Page 49, l. 9, L. Sing. दिवि.—Page 50, l. 14, N. Plur. पादाः—Page 101, l. 11, read जहि.—Page 101, l. 17 and 18, read इयनि and इयनु.—Page 111, l. 24, 1 Plur. चक्रसिम.—Page 120, l. 12, read अस्कदन्.—Page 152, l. 2, Bened. ऊर्णूयात्.

SANSKRIT GRAMMAR.

CHAPTER I.

THE LETTERS.

1.—*The Devanâgarî Alphabet.*

§ 1. The Devanâgarî alphabet consists of the following letters:—

(a) 14 vowel-signs:— अ *a*, आ *â*, इ *i*, ई *î*, उ *u*, ऊ *û*, ऋ *ṛi*, ॠ *ṛî*, ऌ *ḷi*, ॡ *ḷî*, ए *e*, ऐ *ai*, ओ *o*, औ *au*.

(b) 33 syllabic signs for the various consonants, each followed by the vowel *a*:—

क	*ka*,	ख	*kha*,	ग	*ga*,	घ	*gha*,	ङ	*ṅa*;
च	*cha*,	छ	*chha*,	ज	*ja*,	झ	*jha*,	ञ	*ña*;
ट	*ṭa*,	ठ	*ṭha*,	ड	*ḍa*,	ढ	*ḍha*,	ण	*ṇa*;
त	*ta*,	थ	*tha*,	द	*da*,	ध	*dha*,	न	*na*;
प	*pa*,	फ	*pha*,	ब	*ba*,	भ	*bha*,	म	*ma*;
य	*ya*,	र	*ra*,	ल	*la*,	व	*va*;		
श	*śa*,	ष	*sha*,	स	*sa*,	ह	*ha*.		

(c) Two signs for two nasal sounds, viz. *Anusvâra*, denoted by ं, *i.e.* a dot placed above the letter, after which Anusvâra is pronounced (*e. g.* अंस *aṁsa*), and *Anunâsika*, denoted by ँ, *i.e.* a dot within a semi-circle placed above the letter, after which Anunâsika is pronounced; and one sign for a hard spirant called *Visarga*, denoted by :, *i.e.* two vertical dots placed after the letter, after which Visarga is pronounced (*e. g.* गजः *gajaḥ*).

§ 2. (a) The vowel-signs in § 1 (a) denote only such vowels as are not preceded by a consonant in the same sentence or verse, *i. e.* they denote the vowels which stand at the commencement of a sentence or verse, and those vowels in the middle of a sentence or verse, which are preceded by another vowel, *e.g.* अभवत *abhavata*; स आह *sa âha*.

(b) Short *a* following upon a consonant of the same sentence or verse, is not denoted at all, *e. g.* गजः *gajaḥ*.

(c) The remaining vowels, when following a consonant of the same sentence or verse, are denoted thus:—

	á	i	í	u	ú	ṛi	ṛí	ḷi	ḷí	e	ai	o	au
by	ा	ि	ी	ु	ू	ृ	ॄ	ॢ	ॣ	े	ै	ो	ौ
e.g.	का	कि	की	कु	कू	कृ	कॄ	कॢ	कॣ	के	कै	को	कौ
i.e.	ká	ki	kí	ku	kú	kṛi	kṛí	kḷi	kḷí	ke	kai	ko	kau

Exception: The vowel ṛi is after r denoted by the initial sign ऋ = ṛi; ॠ = ṛṛi. (See § 3 c.)

§ 3. (a) When any of the 33 syllabic signs in § 1 (b) is to denote a consonant which is not followed by any vowel and stands at the end of a sentence or verse, the sign ्, called *Viráma* (*i.e.* 'pause'), is placed under it; *e.g.* ककुप् *kakup*, अभवत् *abhavat*, अयम् *ayam*.

(b) Two or more consonants which are not separated by a vowel or vowels are denoted by combinations of the syllabic signs in § 1 (b). These combinations are formed either by placing the succeeding under the preceding sign, leaving out the horizontal top line of the former, or by placing the signs one after the other, leaving out the vertical stroke of the preceding sign; *e.g.* प्त = *p-ta*; क्न = *k-na*; न्द = *n-da*; च्य = *ch-ya*; त्स्न्य = *t-s-n-ya*. Owing to the difficulty of printing the Viráma is occasionally employed in combinations of consonants; *e.g.* युङ्क्ते instead of युङ्क्ते *yuṅkte*.)

(c) When the consonant r precedes another consonant or the vowel ऋ ṛi, without the intervention of a vowel, it is denoted by the sign ् placed above the letter *before* which it is pronounced; *e.g.* अर्क *arka*, कार्त्स्न्य *kártsnya*. This sign for r is placed to the right of any other signs which may stand above the letter over which it has to be placed; *e.g.* अर्केण *arkeṇa*, अर्को *arko*, अर्कं *arkam*. When r follows another consonant without the intervention of a vowel, it is denoted by the sign ् placed under the consonant after which r is pronounced; *e.g.* वज्र *vajra*, शुक्र *śukra*.

§ 4. The changes which some of the letters in § 1 (b) undergo when they are combined with other letters will appear from the following alphabetical list:—

क्क *k-ka*, क्ख *k-kha*, क्च *k-cha*, क्त *k-ta*, क्त्य *k-t-ya*, क्त्र *k-t-ra*, क्त्व *k-t-va*, क्न *k-na*, क्म *k-ma*, क्य *k-ya*, क्र or क्र *k-ra*, क्ल *k-la*, क्व *k-va* ; क्ष *k-sha*, क्ष्म *k-sh-ma*, क्ष्य *k-sh-ya*, क्ष्व *k-sh-va* ;

ख्य *kh-ya*, ख्र *kh-ra* ;

THE LETTERS.

ग्य *g-ya,* ग्र *g-ra,* ग्र्य *g-r-ya;*

घ्न *gh-na,* घ्म *gh-ma,* घ्र *gh-ra;*

ङ्क *ṅ-ka,* ङ्क्त *ṅ-k-ta,* ङ्क्ष *ṅ-k-sha,* ङ्क्ष्व *ṅ-k-sh-va,* ङ्ख *ṅ-kha,* ङ्ग *ṅ-ga,* ङ्घ *ṅ-gha,* ङ्ञ *ṅ-ña,* ङ्म *ṅ-ma;*

च्च *ch-cha,* च्छ *ch-chha,* च्छ्र *ch-chh-ra,* च्ञ *ch-ña,* च्म *ch-ma,* च्य *ch-ya;*
छ्य *chh-ya,* छ्र *chh-ra;*

ज्ज *j-ja,* ज्झ *j-jha,* ज्ञ *j-ña,* ज्ञ्य *j-ñ-ya,* ज्म *j-ma,* ज्य *j-ya,* ज्र *j-ra,* ज्व *j-va;*
ञ्च *ñ-cha,* ञ्छ *ñ-chha,* ञ्ज *ñ-ja;*

ट्क *ṭ-ka,* ट्ट *ṭ-ṭa,* ट्य *ṭ-ya;*

ठ्य *ṭh-ya,* ठ्र *ṭh-ra;*

ड्ग *ḍ-ga,* ड्म *ḍ-ma,* ड्य *ḍ-ya;*

ढ्य *ḍh-ya,* ढ्र *ḍh-ra;*

ण्ट *ṇ-ṭa,* ण्ठ *ṇ-ṭha,* ण्ड *ṇ-ḍa,* ण्ढ *ṇ-ḍha,* ण्ण *ṇ-ṇa,* ण्म *ṇ-ma,* ण्य *ṇ-ya,* ण्व *ṇ-va;*

त्क *t-ka,* त्त *t-ta,* त्त्य *t-t-ya,* त्त्र *t-t-ra,* त्त्व *t-t-va,* त्थ *t-tha,* त्न *t-na,* त्प *t-pa,* त्म *t-ma,* त्य *t-ya,* त्र or त्र *t-ra,* त्र्य *t-r-ya,* त्व *t-va,* त्स *t-sa,* त्स्न *t-s-na,* त्स्न्य *t-s-n-ya,* त्स्य *t-s-ya;*

थ्य *th-ya;*

द्ग *d-ga,* द्द *d-da,* द्द्य *d-d-ya,* द्ध *d-dha,* द्ध्व *d-dh-va,* द्न *d-na,* द्ब *d-ba,* द्भ *d-bha,* द्भ्य *d-bh-ya,* द्म *d-ma,* द्य *d-ya,* द्र *d-ra,* द्र्य *d-r-ya,* द्व *d-va,* द्व्य *d-v-ya;*

ध्न *dh-na,* ध्म *dh-ma,* ध्य *dh-ya,* ध्र *dh-ra,* ध्व *dh-va;*

न्त *n-ta,* न्त्य *n-t-ya,* न्त्र *n-t-ra,* न्द *n-da,* न्द्र *n-d-ra,* न्ध *n-dha,* न्ध्र *n-dh-ra,* न्न *n-na,* न्म *n-ma,* न्य *n-ya,* न्र *n-ra;*

प्त *p-ta,* प्न *p-na,* प्प *p-pa,* प्म *p-ma,* प्य *p-ya,* प्र *p-ra,* प्ल *p-la,* प्व *p-va,* प्स *p-sa;*

ब्ज *b-ja,* ब्द *b-da,* ब्ध *b-dha,* ब्न *b-na,* ब्ब *b-ba,* ब्भ *b-bha,* ब्य *b-ya,* ब्र *b-ra;*

भ्न *bh-na,* भ्य *bh-ya,* भ्र *bh-ra,* भ्व *bh-va;*

म्न *m-na,* म्प *m-pa,* म्ब *m-ba,* म्भ *m-bha,* म्म *m-ma,* म्य *m-ya,* म्र *m-ra,* म्ल *m-la,* म्व *m-va;*

य्य *y-ya,* य्व *y-va;*

रु *r-u,* रू *r-ū;* र्क *r-ka,* र्ध *r-dha,* र्ध्न *r-dh-na;*

ल्क *l-ka,* ल्प *l-pa,* ल्म *l-ma,* ल्य *l-ya,* ल्ल *l-la,* ल्र *l-ra;*

व़ v-na, व्य v-ya, व्र v-ra, व्व v-va;

शु or शु́ ś-u, शू or शू́ ś-û, शृ or शृ́ ś-ṛi, शॄ or शॄ́ ś-ṛî, श्च ś-cha, श्च्य ś-ch-ya, श्न ś-na, श्य or श्य ś-ya, श्र ś-r-a, श्र्य ś-r-ya, श्ल ś-la, श्व ś-va, श्व्य ś-v-ya, इश ś-śa;

ष्ट sh-ṭa, ष्ट्य sh-ṭ-ya, ष्ट्र sh-ṭ-ra, ष्ट्र्य sh-ṭ-r-ya, ष्ट्व sh-ṭ-va, ष्ठ sh-ṭha, ष्ठ्य sh-ṭh-ya, ष्ण sh-ṇa, ष्ण्य sh-ṇ-ya, ष्प sh-pa, ष्म sh-ma, ष्य sh-ya, ष्व sh-va;

स्क s-ka, स्ख s-kha, स्त s-ta, स्त्य s-t-ya, स्त्र s-t-ra, स्त्व s-t-va, स्थ s-tha, स्न s-na, स्प s-pa, स्फ s-pha, स्म s-ma, स्म्य s-m-ya, स्य s-ya, स्र s-ra, स्व s-va, स्स s-sa;

हू h-û, हृ h-ṛi, ह्ण h-ṇa, ह्न h-na, ह्म h-ma, ह्र h-ra, ह्ल h-la, ह्व h-va.

§ 5. The sign ऽ, called *Avagraha*, is in many texts employed to indicate the elision of short अ *a* after preceding ए *e* and ओ *o*; *e. g.* गजोऽस्ति *gajo 'sti*, तेऽभवन् *te 'bhavan*.

§ 6. The numerical figures are:—

१ २ ३ ४ ५ ६ ७ ८ ९ ०
1 2 3 4 5 6 7 8 9 0

१० 10; १५ 15; १४३ 143; २६८ 268; १८६९ 1869.

2.—*Classification of the Letters.*

§ 7. (*a*) Vowels are divided into:—

 (1.) *Simple* Vowels, अ, आ, इ, ई, उ, ऊ, ऋ, ॠ, ऌ, ॡ; and
 (2.) *Diphthongs*, ए, ऐ, ओ, औ.

(*b*) They are also divided into:—

 (1.) *Short* vowels, अ, इ, उ, ऋ, ऌ; and
 (2.) *Long* vowels, आ, ई, ऊ, ॠ, ॡ; ए, ऐ, ओ, औ.

§ 8. Short vowels which are not followed by any consonant or are followed by only one consonant, are *prosodially short* (*laghu*); short vowels followed by combinations of two or more consonants, and all long vowels are *prosodially long* (*guru*).

§ 9. Vowels which differ in nothing but their quantity are called *homogeneous* vowels; *e. g.* अ and आ are homogeneous; इ and ई; उ and ऊ &c.

§ 10. *Guṇa* and *Vṛiddhi.* The vowels अ, ए, ओ and the syllables अर् and अल् are called Guṇa; the vowels आ, ऐ, औ, and the syllables आर् (and आल्) are called Vṛiddhi. The relation of the Guṇa and Vṛiddhi vowels and syllables to the simple vowels appears from the following table:—

Simple V.	अ	इ & ई	उ & ऊ	ऋ & ॠ	ऌ
Guṇa.	अ	ए	ओ	अर्	अल्
Vṛiddhi.	आ	ऐ	औ	आर्	(आल्)

§ 11. The vowel ऌ appears only in the one verbal root कॢप्; the long vowel ॡ is found nowhere in the real language.

§ 12. (*a*) The classification of the consonants will appear from the following table:—

	HARD OR SURD.			SOFT OR SONANT.			
	Unaspirate.	Aspirate.	Sibilant.	Unaspirate.	Aspirate.	Nasal.	Semi-vowel.
Gutturals..	क	ख	:	ग	घ	ङ	ह
Palatals ..	च	छ	श	ज	झ	ञ	य
Linguals..	ट	ठ	ष	ड	ढ	ण	र
Dentals ..	त	थ	स	द	ध	न	ल
Labials ..	प	फ	:	ब	भ	म	व

(*b*) The letter ह is properly speaking not a semi-vowel but a soft spirant.

(*c*) All vowels are likewise soft or sonant.

§ 13. (*a*) Anusvâra when preceding one of the consonants श, ष, स, ह, य, र, ल, व, is always pronounced with the nose only.

(*b*) When standing at the end of a word and followed by one of the consonants क्, ख्, ग्, घ्, (ङ्), च्, छ्, ज्, झ्, (ञ्), ट्, ठ्, ड्, ढ्, (ण्), त्, थ्, द्, ध्, न्, प्, फ्, ब्, भ्, म्, it may be pronounced either with the nose only, or like the nasal of that class to which the following consonant belongs.

(*c*) In some texts Anusvâra is written in the interior of a simple word for any of the five nasals ङ्, ञ्, ण्, न्, म्, when these nasals are followed by a hard or soft unaspirate or aspirate consonant of their own class; e. g. भङ्क is written अंक, अन्त is written अंत, &c.; this (graphic) Anusvâra must always be pronounced like the special nasal for which it has been written.

§ 14. The sign for Anunâsika, ̐, is commonly only used to distinguish the nasalized यँ, लँ, and वँ, from the unnasalized य, ल, and व.

CHAPTER II.

RULES OF EUPHONY (*Sandhi*).

A.—FINAL AND INITIAL LETTERS OF COMPLETE WORDS.

§ 15. A complete word (which ought to be carefully distinguished from a verbal root or a nominal base), when standing alone or at the end of a sentence or verse, may end in any vowel—except ऋ, ऌ, and ॡ,— or in one of the consonants क्, ट्, त्, प्, ङ्, ण्, न्, म्, ल्, or Visarga.

§ 16. Words are not allowed to end in more than one consonant except that they may end in one of the conjunct consonants क्कँ, ट्टँ, त्तँ and प्पँ, provided both elements of these conjuncts are radical letters or substitutes for radical letters; e. g. Nom. Sing. of the base ऊर्ज् = ऊर्क्; 3. Sing. Imperf. Par. of rt. मृज् = अमार्ट्.

§ 17. A word, when standing alone or at the commencement of a sentence or verse, may begin with any vowel or consonant—except ऋ, ऌ, ॡ, ङ्, ञ्, ण्, Anusvâra or Visarga.

§ 18. When complete words are joined together so as to form a sentence or verse, their final and initial letters remain in some instances unchanged, but in the majority of cases the final of the preceding or the initial of the following word, or both, must undergo certain changes which are intended to facilitate the pronunciation. The rules which teach these changes are called the *Rules of Euphony*, or *Rules of Sandhi*.

1.—*Contact of Final and Initial Vowels.*

§ 19. Final simple vowels, short or long, unite with homogeneous initial simple vowels, short or long, and form the corresponding long vowels *i. e.*—

अ or आ + अ or आ = आ; *e. g.* अत्र + अस्ति = अत्रास्ति; अत्र + आसीन् = अत्रासीन्; यदा + अस्ति = यदास्ति.

इ or ई + इ or ई = ई; e. g. अस्ति + इह = अस्तीह; अपि + ईक्षते = अपीक्षते; नदी + इह = नदीह.

उ or ऊ + उ or ऊ = ऊ; e. g. साधु + उक्तम् = साधूक्तम्; साधु + ऊचुः = साधूचुः.

ऋ + ऋ = ऋ; e. g. कर्तृ + ऋजु = कर्तॄजु.

§ 20. Final अ and आ unite with initial इ or ई to ए, with initial उ or ऊ to ओ, with initial ऋ to अर्, with initial ए or ऐ to ऐ, and with initial ओ or औ to औ; e.g.—

तव + इच्छा = तवेच्छा; यदा + इच्छा = यदेच्छा; यथा + ईक्षते = यथेक्षते; सा + उवाच = सोवाच; तदा + ऊचुः = तदोचुः; यथा + ऋषिः = यथर्षिः; तव + एव = तवैव; नव + ऐश्वर्यम् = नवैश्वर्यम्; सा + ओषधिः = सौषधिः; तव + औत्सुक्यम् = तवौत्सुक्यम्.

§ 21. Final simple vowels, short or long (except अ and आ), before initial vowels not homogeneous to them, are changed into the corresponding semi-vowels : i. e.—

इ or ई before अ, आ, उ, ऊ, ऋ, ए, ऐ, ओ, औ into य्; e. g. इति + आह = इत्याह; इति + उक्तम् = इत्युक्तम्; नदी + एव = नद्येव.

उ or ऊ before अ, आ, इ, ई, ऋ, ए, ऐ, ओ, औ into व्; e. g. मधु + अस्ति = मध्वस्ति; मधु + इह = मध्विह.

ऋ before अ, आ, इ, ई, उ, ऊ, ए, ऐ, ओ, औ, into र्; e. g. कर्तृ + अस्ति = कर्त्रस्ति; कर्तृ + इह = कर्त्रिह.

§ 22. Final ए and ओ before initial अ remain unchanged, but the initial अ is dropped; e. g.—

ते + अत्र = तेऽत्र; प्रभो + अत्र = प्रभोऽत्र.

§ 23. Final ए and ओ before any other initial vowel than अ are changed to अय् and अव्, or more commonly both to अ; the initial vowel is not changed; e.g.—

ते + आसन् = तयासन् or more commonly त आसन्.
ते + इह = तयिह   ,,   ,,   ,,   त इह.
प्रभो + एहि = प्रभवेहि   ,,   ,,   ,,   प्रभ एहि.

§ 24. Final ऐ and औ are before all initial vowels changed to आय् and आव्, or both to आ; the usual practice of printed books is to change ऐ to आ, and औ to आव्. The initial vowel remains unchanged; e.g.—

तस्मै + अदात् = तस्मायदात्, or usually तस्मा अदात्.
तस्मै + उक्तम् = तस्मायुक्तम्, ,,   ,,   तस्मा उक्तम्.
तौ + इह = ताविह, sometimes ता इह.
नौ + एव = नावेव,   ,,   ,,   ता एव.

Exceptions.

§ 25. (a) Final अ or आ of a preposition unites with the initial ऋ of a verbal form to आर्; *e. g.* प्र + ऋच्छति = प्रार्च्छति.

(b) Final अ or आ of a preposition unites with an initial ए and ओ of a verbal form (except with the initial ए of forms derived from इ 'to go,' and एध् 'to grow') to ऐ and औ; *e. g.*—

प्र + एजते = प्रैजते; प्र + ओखति = प्रौखति.—But अप + एति = अपैति.

§ 26. (a) ई, ऊ, and ए, when final in dual forms and in अमी (Nom. Plur. Masc. of अदस्) remain unchanged (*pragṛihya*) before all initial vowels, and all initial vowels remain unchanged after them; *e. g.*—

गिरी + इह = गिरी इह "two hills here."
गिरी + एतौ = गिरी एतौ "these two hills."
अमी + अश्वाः = अमी अश्वाः "those horses."

भानू + आस्ताम् = भानू आस्ताम्; साधू उचतुः; लते इह; लते अत्र.

(b) The final vowel of monosyllabic interjections and the final ओ of particles remain unchanged, and initial vowels remain unchanged after them; *e. g.*—

अ + अपेहि = अ अपेहि; इ इन्द्रः; हे इन्द्र; अहो अपेहि.

2.—*Contact of Final Vowels and Consonants with Initial Vowels and Consonants.*

(a.) *Changes of Final Consonants.*

§ 27. Final क्, ट्, and प्—

(a) Before initial hard consonants remain unchanged; *e. g.* सम्यक् + तृप्तम् = सम्यक्तृप्तम्; परिव्राट् + तिष्ठति = परिव्राट्तिष्ठति; ककुप्+शुष्का = ककुप्शुष्का.

(b) Before initial vowels and soft consonants are changed to ग्, ड्, and ब्; *e. g.* सम्यक् + उक्तम् = सम्यगुक्तम्; सम्यक् + वदति = सम्यग्वदति; परिव्राट् + गच्छति = परिव्राड्गच्छति; ककुप् + दृष्टा = ककुब्दृष्टा.

(c) Before initial nasals are changed to ग्, ड्, न्, or more commonly to ङ्, ण्, म्, respectively; *e. g.* सम्यक् + मिलित: = सम्यग्मिलित: or सम्यङ्मिलित:; परिव्राट् + न = परिव्राड्न or परिव्राण्न; ककुप् + न = ककुब्न or ककुम्न.

§ 28. Final त्—

(a) Before initial क्, ख्, त्, थ्, प्, फ्, प्, and स्, remains unchanged: *e. g.* तन् + करोति = तत्करोति; तन् + तिष्ठति = तत्तिष्ठति; तन् + फलम् = तत्फलम्; तद् + सहते = तत्सहते.

(b) Before initial vowels, ग्, घ्, द्, ध्, ब्, भ्, य्, र्, व्, and ह्, final त् is changed to द्; *e. g.* तन् + अर्हति = तदर्हति; तन् + गच्छति = तद्गच्छति; तन् + भूतम् = तद्भूतम्; तन् + रमते = तद्रमते.

(c) Before initial nasals final त् is changed to द्, or more commonly to न्: *e. g.* तन् + नृत्यति = तद्नृत्यति or तन्नृत्यति; तन् + मुखम् = तद्मुखम् or तन्मुखम्.

(d) Before initial च्, छ्, final त् is changed to च्; before ज्, झ्, to ज्; before ट्, ठ्, to ट्; before ड्, ढ्, to ड्; before ल् to ल्; *e. g.* तन् + च = तच्च; तन् + छिनत्ति = तच्छिनत्ति; तन् + जातम् = तज्जातम्; तन् + टङ्कम् = तट्टङ्कम्; तन् + उयते = तड्उयते; तन् + लुब्धम् = तल्लुब्धम्.

(e) Before initial श् final त् is changed to च्, after which the initial श् is commonly changed to छ्; *e. g.* तन् + शास्त्रम् = तच्शास्त्रम् or तच्छास्त्रम्.

§ 29. Final ङ् and ण्—

(a) Remain unchanged before all initial vowels and consonants except when they are preceded by a short vowel and followed by an initial vowel; *e. g.* प्राङ् + अस्ति = प्राङस्ति; प्राङ् + तिष्ठति = प्राङ्तिष्ठति; प्राङ् + स: = प्राङ्स:; सुगण् + गच्छति = सुगण्गच्छति; सुगण् + च = सुगण्च; सुगण् + पट्रम् = सुगण्पट्रम्.

(b) Are doubled when preceded by a short vowel and followed by any initial vowel; *e. g.* प्रत्यङ् + आस्ते = प्रत्यङ्ङास्ते; सुगण् + इति = सुगण्णिति.

§ 30. Final न्—

(a) Is doubled when preceded by a short vowel and followed by any initial vowel; *e. g.* तुदन् + इह = तुदन्निह.

(b) Before initial vowels (except where (a) is applicable) and before Gutturals, Labials, द्, ध्, न्, य्, र्, व्, ष्, स् and ह्, final न् remains unchanged; e.g. तान् + आह = तानाह; तान् + पालयति = तान्पालयति; तान् + भर्तॄन् = तान्भर्तॄन्; तान्+धत्ते=तान्धत्ते; तान् + न = तान्न; तान् + यानि = तान्यानि; तान्+षट् =तान्षट्; तान् + सः = तान्सः; तान् + ह = तान्ह.

(c) Before initial ज्, झ्, and श्, final न् is changed to ञ्; before initial ड् and ढ्, to ण्; and before initial ल् to the nasalized ल् i.e., to ँ. After ञ् the initial श् may be changed to छ् e.g. तान् + जनान् = ताञ्जनान्; तान् + शत्रून् = ताञ्शत्रून् or ताञ्छत्रून्; तान् + डम्बरान् = ताण्डम्बरान्; तान् + लोकान् = ताँल्लोकान्.

(d) Between final न् and initial च् or छ्, ट् or ठ्, and त् or थ्, the corresponding sibilants श्, ष् and स् are inserted (i. e. श् before च् or छ्, ष् before ट् or ठ्, स् before त् or थ्), before which the final न् is changed to Anusvâra, e. g. तान् + च = तांश्च; तान् + टङ्कान् = तांष्टङ्कान्; तान् + तु = तांस्तु.

§ 31. Final म्—

(a) Before initial vowels *must* remain unchanged, e. g. तम् + आह = तमाह; तम् + एव = तमेव.

(b) Before initial sibilants, and before ह् and र्, *must* be changed to Anusvâra, e. g. तम् + शत्रुम् = तं शत्रुम्; तम् + सः = तं सः; तम् + ह = तं ह; तम् + रक्षति = तं रक्षति.

(c) Before any other initial consonant final म् may be changed to Anusvâra, or it may be changed into the nasal of the class to which the initial consonant belongs (to यं, लं, वं before य, ल, व.) *The usual practice is to change* म् *before all consonants to Anusvâra*, e. g. अहम् + करोमि = अहं करोमि (or अहङ्करोमि); अहम् + च = अहं च (or अहञ्च); अहम् + तिष्ठामि = अहं तिष्ठामि (or अहन्तिष्ठामि); अहम् + पिबामि = अहं पिबामि (or अहम्पिबामि); अहम् + वच्मि = अहं वच्मि (or अहव्वच्मि).

§ 32. Final ल् remains unchanged before all initial letters; e. g. कमल् + अस्ति = कमलस्ति; कमल् + करोति = कमलकरोति.

§ 33. Final *Visarga*, preceded by any vowel—

(a) Before initial hard Gutturals and Labials (क्, ख्, प्, फ्), must remain unchanged, e.g. रामः + करोति = रामः करोति; पुनः + करोति = पुनः करोति; रविः + करोति = रविः करोति.

(b) Before initial sibilants, may remain unchanged or may be assimilated to the following sibilant; e.g. रामः + षट् = रामः षट् or रामष्षट्; रामः + सहते = रामः सहते or रामस्सहते; पुनः + सः = पुनः सः or पुनस्सः.

(c) Before initial च् or छ्, ट् or ठ्, and त् or थ्, must be changed to ज्, ष्, and स् respectively, e.g. रामः + च = रामश्च; रामः + तु = रामस्तु; पुनः + तु = पुनस्तु; रविः + तु = रविस्तु.

§ 34. Final *Visarga*, not preceded by अ or आ, is changed to र्, before any initial vowel or soft consonant; but it is dropped before an initial र्, and a preceding short vowel is lengthened; e.g. रविः + उदेति = रविरुदेति; मनुः + गच्छति = मनुर्गच्छति; रविः + रुढः = रवी रुढः.

Exception: The final Visarga of भोः: 'O, Ho,' is dropped before all soft letters.

§ 35. Final अः, when standing for original अस्—

(a) Is changed to ओ before all initial soft consonants, e.g. रामः (for रामस्) + गच्छति = रामो गच्छति; रामः + हसति = रामो हसति.

(b) Is changed to ओ before initial अ; the initial अ itself is dropped; e. g. रामः + अस्ति = रामो स्ति.

(c) Is changed to अ before all other initial vowels than अ; e.g. रामः + इह = राम इह; रामः + उवाच = राम उवाच.

§ 36. Final आः, when standing for original आस्, is changed to आ before all initial vowels and soft consonants; e. g. अश्वाः (for अश्वास्) + अत्र = अश्वा अत्र; अश्वाः + इह = अश्वा इह; अश्वाः + धावन्ति = अश्वा धावन्ति.

§ 37. The final Visarga of अः and आः, when standing for original र्, is changed to र् before all initial vowels and soft consonants; before an initial र् it is dropped and a preceding अ is lengthened, e.g. पुनः (for पुनर्) + अत्र = पुनरत्र; पुनः + इह = पुनरिह; पुनः + गच्छति = पुनर्गच्छति; पुनः + रमते = पुना रमते; द्वाः (for द्वार्) + अत्र = द्वारत्र; द्वाः + दृष्टा = द्वादृष्टा; द्वाः + रिक्ता = द्वा रिक्ता.

(b.) *Changes of Initial Consonants.*

§ 38. Initial छ—

(a) After a final short vowel and after the particles मा and आ, *must* be changed to च्छ; e. g. तव + छाया = तव च्छाया; मा + छिदत् = मा च्छिदत्; आ + छादयति = आच्छादयति.

(b) After a final long vowel छ may optionally be changed to च्छ; e.g. सा + छिनत्ति = सा च्छिनत्ति or सा छिनत्ति.

§ 39. Initial ह after final ग्, ड्, द् and ब्, being substitutes for क्, ट्, त्, and प् according to § 27 (b) and § 23 (b), is commonly changed to घ, ढ, ध and भ respectively; e.g. सम्यक् + ह = सम्यग्घ or commonly सम्यग्ध; तत् + ह = तद्दह or तद्ध; परिव्राट् + ह = परिव्राड्ढ or परिव्राड्ढ; ककुप् + ह = ककुब्भ or ककुब्भ.

§ 40. (a) The initial न् of verbal roots is generally changed to ण् after the prepositions अन्तः, निः, परा, परि, प्र and after दुः; e.g. परि + नयति = परिणयति; प्र + नेनुम् = प्रणेतुम्; प्र + नेता = प्रणेता.

(b) The initial न् of नृत् 'to dance,' नन्दू 'to rejoice,' and of some other less common roots remains unchanged; e.g. प्र + नृत्यति = प्रनृत्यति.

(c) The initial न् of नश् 'to perish,' remains unchanged, when the final श् is changed to ष्; e.g. प्र + नश्यति = प्रणश्यति; but प्र + नष्टः = प्रनष्टः.

§ 41. (a) The initial स् of many verbal roots is changed to ष् after prepositions ending in इ and उ, and after निः and दुः; e.g. नि + सीदति = निषीदति; अभि + सिञ्चति = अभिषिञ्चति; अभि + स्तौति = अभिष्टौति; नि + सेवते = निषेवते.

(b) The initial स् of roots which contain a ऋ, ॠ or र्, remains generally unchanged, e.g. वि + स्मरन् (from root स्मृ) = विस्मरन्; वि + स्रवति (from root स्रु) = विस्रवति; वि + स्तोर्णम् (from root स्तृ) = विस्तोर्णम्.

B.—Changes of Final Letters of Nominal and Verbal Bases and Initial Letters of Terminations, and of other Letters in the Interior of Words.

§ 42. The special rules for the changes which take place when final letters of nominal and verbal bases come into contact with initial letters of terminations will be given under the heads of Declension, Conjugation, &c. Here only the most general rules are noticed.

§ 43. In the interior of a simple word no hiatus (i.e. the succession of two vowels without an intervening consonant) is allowed, except in तिरइ 'a sieve.'

§ 44. The rules laid down in §§ 19—24 apply generally also to the final letters of bases and the initial letters of terminations; e.g. कान्त + अः = कान्ताः; कान्ता + अः = कान्ताः; कान्त + ई = कान्ते; कान्त + औ = कान्तौ; मति + ए = मत्ये; नदो + अः = नद्वः.

§ 45. Final इ, ई, and उ, ऊ, especially when they are radical vowels are sometimes changed to इय् and उव् before terminations commencing with vowels; e.g. थी + अन्ति = वियन्ति; भी + इ = भिये; यु + अन्ति = युवन्ति; भू + इ = भुवि.

§ 46. Radical इ and उ followed by radical र् or व् are generally lengthened when र् or व् are followed by another consonant; e.g. दिव् + यामि = दीव्यामि; गिर् + भिः = गीर्भिः; पुर् + भिः = पूर्भिः.

§ 47. Final radical ऋ is sometimes changed to रि, or, when preceded by more than one consonant, to अर्; *e. g.* कृ + यते = क्रियते; स्मृ + यते = स्मर्यते.

§ 48. Final radical ऋ before terminations beginning with vowels is generally changed to इर्, before terminations beginning with consonants to ईर्; when ऋ is preceded by a labial letter, it is changed to उर् and ऊर् respectively; *e. g.* कृ + अति = किरति; कृ + यते = कीर्यते; पिपृ + अति = पिपुरति; पिपृ + याम् = पिपूर्याम्.

§ 49. Final ए, ऐ, ओ, and औ, before terminations commencing with vowels or य्, are mostly changed to अय्, आय्, अव्, and आव् respectively; *e. g.* ने + अन = नयन; रै + अः = रायः; गो + इ = गवि; नौ + अः = नावः; गो + य = गव्य.

§ 50. Before initial vowels, semivowels, and nasals of terminations, final consonants of nominal and verbal bases remain generally unchanged; *e. g.* दुह् + ए = दुहे; दोह् + मि = दोह्मि; दुह् + यते = दुह्यते; वच् + मि = वच्मि; मरुत् + आ = मरुता.

§ 51. When a termination begins with any other consonant than a semivowel or nasal, the following rules apply:—

(*a*) Final hard consonants before initial soft consonants become soft; *e. g.* मरुत् + भिः = मरुद्भिः; सर्वदृक् + भ्याम् = सर्वदृग्भ्याम्.

(*b*) Final soft consonants before initial hard consonants become hard; *e. g.* तमोनुद् + सु = तमोनुत्सु; अद् + ति = अत्ति.

(*c*) Final aspirate consonants are changed to the corresponding hard unaspirates before initial hard consonants, and to the corresponding soft unaspirates before initial soft consonants; *e. g.* सुयुध् + सु = सुयुत्सु; अग्निमथ् + भिः = अग्निमद्भिः.

(*d*) Final palatal consonants (including श्), प्, and ह्, are commonly changed to क्, ग्, or to ट्, ड्; *e.g.* वाच् + भिः = वाग्भिः; र्‌ज् + भिः = र्‌ग्भिः; सदृश् + भिः = सदृग्भिः; सम्राज् + भिः = सम्राड्भिः; लिह् + भिः = लिड्भिः; लिह् + सु = लिट्सु.

(*e*) Final स् is changed to Visarga, or to र्, or it is dropped; अस् is changed to ओ before soft consonants; *e. g.* मनस् + सु = मनःसु or मनस्सु; ज्योतिस् + भिः = ज्योतिर्भिः; आस् + ध्वे = आध्वे; मनस् + भिः = मनोभिः.

§ 52. Of two or more conjunct consonants which meet at the end of a word, generally (see § 16) only the first is retained, the others being dropped; *e. g.* मरुन्त् + स् = मरुन्त्; सुयुध् + स् = सुयुत् + स् (by § 51 c) = सुयुत्; अदन्त् + स् = अदन्; but ऊर्ज् + स् = ऊर्क् + स् (by § 51 d and b) = ऊर्क्.

§ 53. When the final soft aspirates घ्, द्, ध्, भ्, or ह् are changed to unaspirate letters, and when the syllable which originally ended with घ्, द्, ध्, भ्, or ह्, commences with one of the soft unaspirate letters ग्, ज्, ड्, or न्, the latter are changed to घ्, द्, ध्, or भ् respectively; *e. g.* भुध् + सु = भुत् + सु (by § 51 c) = भुस्सु; दुह् + स् = दुक् + स् = धुक् + स् = धुक्.

§ 54. छ् standing in the interior of a simple word between two vowels is changed to च्छ्; *e. g.* rt. छिद्, Imperf. अच्छिनत्, Perf. चिच्छेद; rt. प्रछ्, Perf. पप्रच्छ.

§ 55. Initial त् and थ् of terminations after soft aspirates are changed to ध्; *e. g.* लभ् + त = लभ् + ध, = लब्ध (§ 51 c); हन्ध् + थः = हन्ध् + धः = हन्द्धः.

§ 56. Initial dentals of terminations after final linguals of bases are changed to the corresponding linguals; *e. g.* ईड् + ते = ईड्डे (§ 51 b); द्विष् + धि = द्विड् + धि (§ 51 d) = द्विड्ढि; इष् + त = इष्ट; मृड् + नाति = मृड्णाति.

§ 57. न् when immediately preceded by च् or ज्, is changed to ञ्; *e. g.* याच् + ना = याच्ञा; यज् + न = यज्ञ.

§ 58. Dental न्, provided it be followed by a vowel or by one of the consonants न्, म्, य्, व्, is changed to lingual ण्, when it is preceded by ऋ, ॠ, र् or ष्, either immediately or separated from these letters by vowels, Gutturals, Labials, य्, व्, ह्, or Anusvâra, *e.g.* कर्तृ + नाम् = कर्तॄणाम्; कर् + अन = करण; कर्मन् + आ = कर्मणा; ब्रह्मन् + आ = ब्रह्मणा; राम, Instr. Sing. रामेण; द्वेष, Instr. Sing. द्वेषेण; पुष् + नाति = पुष्णाति; गृह् + नाति = गृह्णाति. But गर्त + नाम् = गर्तानाम्; अर्ध, Instr. Sing. अर्धेन &c.

§ 59. The sibilant स्, provided it be followed by a vowel or by a dental consonant, or by म्, or य्, or व्, is changed to ष्, when it is preceded by क्, र्, ल्, or by any vowel except अ and आ, either immediately or separated from it by Anusvâra or Visarga, *e. g.* कमल् + सु = कमलषु; वाच् + सु = वाक् + सु = वाक्षु; अग्नि + सु = अग्निषु; भानु + सु = भानुषु; ज्योतिस् + आ = ज्योतिषा; धनुस्, Nom. Plur. धनूंषि; सर्पिः + सु = सर्पिःषु or सर्पिष्षु; वच् + स्यति = वक् + स्यति = वक्ष्यति &c.

CHAPTER III.

DECLENSION OF NOUNS SUBSTANTIVE AND ADJECTIVE.

§ 60. The Declension of Adjectives does not, in general, differ from that of Substantives.

§ 61. Nouns substantive and adjective have *three Genders*, a *masculine* gender, a *feminine* gender, and a *neuter* gender. The gender of substantives must be learnt from the dictionary. Adjectives assume the gender of the substantives which they qualify.

§ 62. Nouns substantive and adjective are given in the dictionary in their *base* or *crude form*. Whenever an adjective assumes in the Feminine a base different from that which it has in the masculine gender, its masculine base is given in the dictionary, and the feminine base is derived from the masculine base by the addition to the latter of a feminine affix; *e.g.* कान्त 'beloved,' Fem. base कान्त + आ = कान्ता; धनिन् 'wealthy,' Fem. base धनिन् + ई = धनिनी. The neuter base of adjectives is generally the same as the masculine base.

§ 63. Declension consists in the addition to the base of certain terminations which denote the various cases in the different numbers.

§ 64. Nouns substantive and adjective have *three Numbers*, a *singular* number, a *dual* number, and a *plural* number. The dual number denotes 'two,' *e.g.* Base अश्व 'horse,' Sing. अश्व: 'a horse,' Dual अश्वौ 'two horses.'

§ 65. There are *eight Cases* in each number; viz. *Nominative* (N.), *Accusative* (Ac.), *Instrumental*, (I.) *Dative* (D.), *Ablative* (Ab.), *Genitive* (G.), *Locative* (L.), and *Vocative* (V.). The meaning of the Instrumental is in English expressed by such prepositions as 'by, with, by means of;' the meaning of the Ablative by such prepositions as 'away from, from;' the meaning of the Locative is generally expressed by 'in,' or 'at.'

§ 66. Table of Case-terminations added to masculine and feminine bases :—

	Sing.	Dual.	Plur.
N.	ः (*i.e.* सु),	औ	अः (*i.e.* अस्).
Ac.	अम्	औ	अः (*i.e.* अस्).
I.	आ	भ्याम्	भिः (*i.e.* भिस्).
D.	ए	भ्याम्	भ्यः (*i.e.* भ्यस्).
Ab.	अः (*i.e.* अस्)	भ्याम्	भ्यः (*i.e.* भ्यस्).
G.	अः (*i.e.* अस्)	ओः (*i.e.* ओस्)	आम्
L.	इ	ओः (*i.e.* ओस्)	सु.

The termination of the N. Sing. is always dropped after bases ending in consonants (see § 52). The Vocative is generally like the Nominative.

§ 67. The same terminations are added to neuter bases except in the N. Ac. and V. of all numbers. *No* termination is added to neuter bases (except those in अ) in the N., Ac. and V. Sing.; in the N., Ac. and V. Dual ई is added instead of औ; in the N., Ac. and V. Plur. इ is added instead of अः and a nasal is inserted before the final of bases ending in consonants, except those that end in a nasal or semivowel.

§ 68. The above terminations undergo various changes, especially when added to bases ending in vowels; these changes are best learned from the paradigms given under the various declensions.

§ 69. Terminations beginning with consonants may for convenience' sake be called *consonantal terminations,* terminations beginning with vowels *vowel-terminations.*

§ 70. According to the final letter of the base the Declension of nouns substantive and adjective is divided into :—

A.—Declension of bases ending in consonants or Declension of *Consonantal Bases* (Decl. I.-XI.), and

B.—Declension of bases ending in vowels or Declension of *Vowel-Bases* (Decl. XII.—XVII.).

Consonantal Bases are subdivided into—

1. *Unchangeable Bases, i.e.* Bases which either undergo no change at all (Decl. I), or undergo generally only such changes as are required by the rules of Sandhi (Decl. II.-V.); and

2. *Changeable Bases, i.e.* Bases which in their declension show a strong, and a weak form, or a strong, a middle, and a weakest form; (Decl. VI.–XI.).

A.—CONSONANTAL BASES.

1.—Unchangeable Bases.

DECLENSION I.

Bases ending in ण् *and* ल्.

§ 71. *Sandhi*:—

1. ट् may optionally be inserted between the final ण् of a base and the termination सु of the L. Plur.

2. After final ल् the termination सु of the L. Plur. is changed to जु. (§ 59).

§ 72. *Paradigms*: सुगण् *m. f. n.* 'counting well,' कमल् *m. f. n.* 'naming the goddess Lakshmî or the lotus.'

| Base: | सुगण् | *sugaṇ* | कमल् | *kamal* |

Masc. and Fem.

Singular.

N. V.	सुगण्	*sugaṇ*	कमल्	*kamal*
Ac.	सुगणम्	*sugaṇ-am*	कमलम्	*kamal-am*
I.	सुगणा	*sugaṇ-â*	कमला	*kamal-â*
D.	सुगणे	*sugaṇ-e*	कमले	*kamal-e*
Ab. G.	सुगणः	*sugaṇ-aḥ*	कमलः	*kamal-aḥ*
L.	सुगणि	*sugaṇ-i*	कमलि	*kamal-i*

Dual.

N. V. Ac.	सुगणौ	*sugaṇ-au*	कमले	*kamal-au*
I. D. Ab.	सुगण्भ्याम्	*sugaṇ-bhyâm*	कमल्भ्याम्	*kamal-bhyâm*
G. L.	सुगणोः	*sugaṇ-oḥ*	कमलोः	*kamal-oḥ*

Plural.

N. V. Ac.	सुगण:	sugaṇ-aḥ	कमल:	kamal-aḥ
I.	सुगण्भि:	sugaṇ-bhiḥ	कमलिभ:	kamal-bhiḥ
D. Ab.	सुगण्भ्य:	sugaṇ-bhyaḥ	कमल्भ्य:	kamal-bhyaḥ
G.	सुगणाम्	sugaṇ-ām	कमलाम्	kamal-ām
L.	सुगण्सु or सुगण्ट्सु	sugaṇ-su or sugaṇ-ṭ-su	कमल्सु	kamal-shu

Neuter.

Sing. N. V. Ac.	सुगण्	sugaṇ	कमल्	kamal
Dual. N. V. Ac.	सुगणी	sugaṇ-i	कमली	kamal-i
Plur. N. V. Ac.	सुगणि	sugaṇ-i	कमलि	kamal-i

The remaining cases are like those of the Masc. and Fem; *e. g.* I. सुगणा, कमला; D. सुगणे, कमले &c.

DECLENSION II.

Bases ending in

(a) क्, ख्, ग्, घ्, ट्, ठ्, ड्, ढ्, त्, थ्, द्, ध्, प्, फ्, ब्, भ्;
(b) च्, ज्, श्, ष्, छ्;
(c) ह्;

(a.)—*Bases ending in* क्, ख्, ग्, घ्, ट्, ठ्, ड्, ढ्, त्, थ्, द्, ध्, प्, फ्, ब्, भ्;

§ 73. *Sandhi* :—

1. Before vowel-terminations the final of the base remains unchanged (§ 50.)

2. In the N. and V. Sing. Masc. and Fem., and in the N., V. and Ac., Sing. Neut. final क्, ख्, ग्, घ् become क्, final ट्, ठ्, ड्, ढ् become ट्, final त्, थ्, द्, ध् become त्, and final प्, फ्, ब्, भ् become प्. (§ 51.)

3. In the L. Plur. finals are treated as in the N. Sing. (§ 51); subsequently the termination सु is after क् changed to षु (§ 59), and त् may optionally be inserted between final ट् and the termination सु.

4. Before the terminations भि:, भ्य:, and याम् final क्, ख्, ग्, घ् become ग्, final ट्, ठ्, ड्, ढ् become ड्, final त्, थ्, द्, ध् become द्, and final प्, फ्, ब्, भ् become ब्. (§ 51.)

DECLENSION OF NOUNS.

5. When final ग्, ड्, भ् or भ् by rules 2, 3, and 4 are changed to क्, ट्, न्, प्, or to ग्, ड्, द्, ब्, § 53 must be observed.

§ 74. *Paradigms*: हरित् *m. f. n.* 'green;' अग्निमथ् *m. f. n.* 'kindling fire;' तमोनुद् *m. f. n.* 'dispelling darkness;' सुयुध् *m. f. n.* 'fighting well;' धर्मबुध् *m. f. n.* 'knowing the law;' सर्वशक् *m. f. n.* 'almighty.'

Base: हरित्   अग्निमथ्   तमोनुद्   सुयुध्   धर्मबुध्   सर्वशक्

Masc. and Fem.

Singular.

N.V.	हरित्	अग्निमन्	तमोनुन्	सुयुन्	धर्मभुन्	सर्वशक्
Ac.	हरितम्	अग्निमथम्	तमोनुदम्	सुयुधम्	धर्मबुधम्	सर्वशकम्
I.	हरिता	अग्निमथा	तमोनुदा	सुयुधा	धर्मबुधा	सर्वशका
D.	हरिते	अग्निमथे	तमोनुदे	सुयुधे	धर्मबुधे	सर्वशके
Ab.G.	हरितः	अग्निमथः	तमोनुदः	सुयुधः	धर्मबुधः	सर्वशकः
L.	हरिति	अग्निमथि	तमोनुदि	सुयुधि	धर्मबुधि	सर्वशकि

Dual.

N.V.Ac.	हरितौ	अग्निमथौ	तमोनुदौ	सुयुधौ	धर्मबुधौ	सर्वशकौ
I.D.Ab.	हरिद्भ्याम्	अग्निमद्भ्याम्	तमोनुद्भ्याम्	सुयुद्भ्याम्	धर्मभुद्भ्याम्	सर्वशग्भ्याम्
G.L.	हरितोः	अग्निमथोः	तमोनुदोः	सुयुधोः	धर्मबुधोः	सर्वशकोः

Plural.

N.V.Ac.	हरितः	अग्निमथः	तमोनुदः	सुयुधः	धर्मबुधः	सर्वशकः
I.	हरिद्भिः	अग्निमद्भिः	तमोनुद्भिः	सुयुद्भिः	धर्मभुद्भिः	सर्वशग्भिः
D.Ab.	हरिद्भ्यः	अग्निमद्भ्यः	तमोनुद्भ्यः	सुयुद्भ्यः	धर्मभुद्भ्यः	सर्वशग्भ्यः
G.	हरिताम्	अग्निमथाम्	तमोनुदाम्	सुयुधाम्	धर्मबुधाम्	सर्वशकाम्
L.	हरित्सु	अग्निमत्सु	तमोनुत्सु	सुयुत्सु	धर्मभुत्सु	सर्वशक्षु

Neuter.

Sing.N.V.Ac.	हरित्	अग्निमन्	तमोनुन्	सुयुन्	धर्मभुन्	सर्वशक्
Dual.N.V.Ac.	हरितो	अग्निमथी	तमोनुदी	सुयुधी	धर्मबुधी	सर्वशकी
Plur.N.V.Ac.	हरिन्ति	अग्निमान्थि	तमोनुन्दि	सुयुन्धि	धर्मबुन्धि	सर्वशाङ्कि

The rest like Masc. and Fem.

§ 75. Decline मरुत् *m.* 'wind,' like हरित् in Masc.; दृषद् *f.* 'a stone,' like तमोनुद् in Fem.; ककुभ् *f.* 'a region.'

(*b.*)—*Bases ending in* च्, ज्, श्, ष्, छ्.

§ 76. *Sandhi:*—

1. Before vowel-terminations the final of the base remains unchanged (§ 50); but final छ् may optionally be changed to श्.

2. In all the remaining cases

(*a*) Final च् is changed to क्, and the base is then declined as a base ending in क्.

(*b*) Final ज् is changed to क्; but when the final ज् forms part of the roots सृज् 'to create' (except in स्रज् *f.* 'a garland,' Sing. N. स्रक् &c.), मृज् 'to cleanse,' यज् (contracted into इज्) 'to sacrifice,' (except in ऋत्विज्, *m.* 'an officiating priest,' Sing. N. ऋत्विक् &c.), राज् 'to shine, to govern,' भ्राज् (दुभ्राज्) 'to shine,' and as the final of परिव्राज् *m.* 'a religious mendicant,' it is changed to ट्. Afterwards the bases are declined as bases ending in क् and ट् respectively.

(*c*) Final श् is changed to ट्; but when forming part of the roots दिश् 'to point,' दृश् 'to see,' स्पृश् 'to touch,' and मृश् 'to stroke,' it is changed to क्; and when forming part of the root नश् 'to perish,' it is changed optionally either to ट् or to क्. Afterwards the bases are declined as bases ending in ट् or in क्.

(*d*) Final ष् is changed to ट्, except in दभ्रुष् *m. f. n.* 'bold,' where it is changed to क्. The bases are afterwards declined as bases ending in ट् and क् respectively.

(*e*) Final छ् is changed to ट्, and the base is then declined as a base ending in ट्.

§ 77. *Examples*: The N., V., and Ac. Sing. and the I. and L. Plur. of the Masc. and Fem., and the N. V. Ac. Sing., Dual, and Plur. of the Neuter of the following paradigms: सत्यवाच् *m. f. n.* 'speaking the truth;' शेषभुज् *m. f. n.* 'eating the rest;' विश्वसृज् *m. f. n.* 'creating the universe;' विश् *m. f. n.* 'entering;' सुदृश् *m. f. n.* 'well-looking;' नश् *m. f. n.* 'perishing;' द्विष् *m. f. n.* 'hating;' दभ्रुष् *m. f. n.* 'bold;' शब्दप्राछ् or शब्दप्राश् *m. f. n.* 'inquiring about a word.'

DECLENSION OF NOUNS.

Base:	सत्यवाच्	शेषभुज्	विश्वसृज्	विश्	सुदृश्	नश्

Masc. and Fem.

Sing. N.V.	सत्यवाक्	शेषभुक्	विश्वसृट्	विट्	सुदृक्	नट् or नक्
Sing. Ac.	सत्यवाचम्	शेषभुजम्	विश्वसृजम्	विशम्	सुदृशम्	नशम्
Plur. I.	सत्यवाग्भिः	शेषभुग्भिः	विश्वसृड्भिः	विड्भिः	सुदृग्भिः	नड्भिः or नग्भिः
Plur. L.	सत्यवाक्षु	शेषभुक्षु	विश्वसृट्सु	विट्सु	सुदृक्षु	नट्सु or नक्षु
			or विश्वसृट्त्सु	or विट्त्सु		or नट्त्सु

Base:	द्विष्		दधृष्		शब्दमाछ् or शब्दमाश्	

Masc. and Fem.

Sing. N.V.	द्विट्		दधृक्		शब्दमाट्	
Sing. Ac.	द्विषम्		दधृषम्		शब्दमाच्छम् or शब्दमाशम्	
Plur. I.	द्विड्भिः		दधृग्भिः		शब्दमाड्भिः	
Plur. L.	द्विट्सु or द्वित्सु	दधृक्षु		शब्दमाट्सु or शब्दमाट्त्सु	

| Base: | सत्यवाच् | शेषभुज् | विश्वसृज् | विश् | सुदृश् | नश् |

Neuter.

Sing. N.V.Ac.	सत्यवाक्	शेषभुक्	विश्वसृट्	विट्	सुदृक्	नट् or नक्
Dual. N.V.Ac.	सत्यवाची	शेषभुजी	विश्वसृजी	विशी	सुदृशी	नशी
Plur. N.V.Ac.	सत्यवाञ्चि	शेषभुञ्जि	विश्वसृञ्जि	विंशि	सुदृंशि	नंशि

| Base: | द्विष् | दधृष् | शब्दमाछ् or शब्दमाश् |

Neuter.

Sing. N.V.Ac.	द्विट्	दधृक्	शब्दमाट्
Dual. N.V.Ac.	द्विषी	दधृषी	शब्दमाच्छी or शब्दमाशी
Plur. N.V.Ac.	द्विंषि	दधृंषि	शब्दमाञ्छि or शब्दमांशि

§ 78. Decline: वाच् f. 'speech,' like सत्यवाच् in Fem.;
रुज् f. 'a disease,' like शेषभुज् in Fem.;
सम्राज् m. 'a king', like विश्वसृज् in Masc.;
दिश् f. 'space', like सुदृश् in Fem.;
त्विष् f. 'splendour', like द्विष् in Fem.

§ 79. *Irregular bases:* आशिष् f. 'a blessing,' and सजुष् m. 'a companion.'

	Singular.	Dual.	Plural.
N. V.	आशीः सर्जूः	आशिषौ सर्जुषौ	आशिषः सर्जुषः
Ac.	आशिषम् सर्जुषम्		
I.	आशिषा सर्जुषा	आशीर्भ्याम् सर्जूभ्याम्	आशीर्भिः सर्जूभिः
D.	आशिषे सर्जुषे		आशीर्भ्यः सर्जूभ्यः
Ab.	आशिषः सर्जुषः		
G.	आशिषः सर्जुषः	आशिषोः सर्जुषोः	आशिषाम् सर्जुषाम्
L.	आशिषि सर्जुषि		आशीःषु सर्जूःषु or आशीषु सर्जूषु

(c.)—*Bases ending in* ह्.

§ 80. *Sandhi* :—

1. Before vowel-terminations the final ह् remains unchanged. (§ 50.)

2. In all the remaining cases (*a*) ह् is changed to ट्; (*b*) but when forming part of a root which ends with ह् and commences with द्, and in उष्णिह् *f.* a particular kind of metre, ह् is changed to घ्; (*c*) when forming part of the roots दुह् 'to hate,' मुह् 'to faint,' स्निह् 'to love,' and स्नुह् 'to spue,' ह् may optionally be changed to ट् or to घ्; (*d*) and when forming part of the root नह् 'to bind,' it is changed to ध्. Afterwards the bases are declined as bases originally ending in ट्, घ्, or ध्.

§ 81. *Examples:* The N., V. and Ac. Sing., and the I. and L. Plur. of the Masc. and Fem., and the N. V. Ac. Sing., Dual and Plur. of the Neuter of the following paradigms: लिह् *m. f. n.* 'licking;' गुह् *m. f. n.* 'covering;' दुह् *m. f. n.* 'milking;' द्रुह् *m. f. n.* 'hating;' उपानह् *f.* 'a shoe.'

Base :	लिह्	गुह्	दुह्	द्रुह्	उपानह्
		Masc. and Fem.			Fem.
Sing. N. V.	लिट्	घुट्	धुक्	ध्रुट् or ध्रुक्	उपानत्
Sing. Ac.	लिहम्	गुहम्	दुहम्	द्रुहम्	उपानहम्
Plur. I.	लिड्भिः	घुड्भिः	धुग्भिः	ध्रुड्भिः or ध्रुग्भिः	उपानद्भिः
Plur. L.	लिट्सु or लिट्त्सु	घुट्सु or घुट्त्सु	धुक्षु	ध्रुट्सु or ध्रुट्त्सु	उपानत्सु
	Neuter.				
Sing.N.V.Ac.	लिट्	घुट्	धुक्	ध्रुट् or ध्रुक्	
Dual.N.V.Ac.	लिही	गुही	दुही	द्रुही	
Plur.N.V.Ac.	लिंहि	गुंहि	दुंहि	द्रुंहि	

§ 82. *Irregular base*: नुरासाह् m., a name of Indra, changes its स् to ष् whenever its final ह् is changed; *e.g.* N. V. नुराषाट्, but Ac. नुरासाहम्, I. नुरासाहा &c.

DECLENSION III.

Bases ending in र्.

§ 83. *Sandhi* :—

1. The final र् is changed to Visarga in the N. and V. Sing. Masc. and Fem. and in the N., V. and Ac. Sing. Neut.

2. In all other cases it remains unchanged. (§ 50.)

3. Penultimate इ and उ are lengthened in the N. and V. Sing. Masc. and Fem. and in the N., V. and Ac. Sing. Neut., and before all consonantal terminations. (§ 46.)

4. The termination सु of the L. Plur. is changed to षु. (§ 59.)

§ 84. *Paradigms*: गिर् *f.* 'speech;' पुर् *f.* 'a town;' वार् *n.* 'water.'

Base :	गिर्	पुर्	वार्
		Singular.	
N. V.	गीः	पूः	वाः
Ac.	गिरम्	पुरम्	वाः
I.	गिरा	पुरा	वारा
D.	गिरे	पुरे	वारे
Ab.G.	गिरः	पुरः	वारः
L.	गिरि	पुरि	वारि
		Dual.	
N.V.Ac.	गिरौ	पुरौ	वारी
I.D.Ab.	गीर्भ्याम्	पूर्भ्याम्	वार्भ्याम्
G.L.	गिरोः	पुरोः	वारोः
		Plural.	
N.V.Ac.	गिरः	पुरः	वारि
I.	गीर्भिः	पूर्भिः	वार्भिः
D. Ab.	गीर्भ्यः	पूर्भ्यः	वार्भ्यः
G.	गिराम्	पुराम्	वाराम्
L.	गीर्षु	पूर्षु	वार्षु

DECLENSION IV.

Bases ending in इन् (*Masc. and Neut.*)

§ 85. *Sandhi* :—

1. Before vowel-terminations the final न् of the base remains unchanged (§ 50), except when it is changed to ण् by § 58.

2. Before consonantal terminations final न् is dropped; the termination सु of the L. Plur. becomes यु. (§ 59.)

3. The final न् is dropped in the N. Sing. Masc. and the N. and Ac. Sing. Neut., and optionally in the V. Sing. Neut.

4. The penultimate इ is lengthened in the N. Sing. Masc. and in the N., V. and Ac. Plur. Neut.

§ 86. *Paradigms*: धनिन् *m. n.* 'possessing riches;' स्रग्विन् *m. n.* 'wearing a garland.'

Base	धनिन्	स्रग्विन्	धनिन्	स्रग्विन्
	Masculine.		**Neuter.**	

Singular.

N.	धनी	स्रग्वी	धनि	स्रग्वि
Ac.	धनिनम्	स्रग्विणम्		
I.	धनिना	स्रग्विणा		
D.	धनिने	स्रग्विणे	............like Masc.	
Ab.G.	धनिनः	स्रग्विणः		
L.	धनिनि	स्रग्विणि		
V.	धनिन्	स्रग्विन्	धनि or धनिन्	स्रग्वि or स्रग्विन्

Dual.

N.V.Ac.	धनिनौ	स्रग्विणौ	धनिनी	स्रग्विणी
I.D.Ab.	धनिभ्याम्	स्रग्विभ्याम्	............like Masc.	
G.L.	धनिनोः	स्रग्विणोः		

Plural.

N.V.Ac.	धनिनः	स्रग्विणः	धनीनि	स्रग्वीणि
I.	धनिभिः	स्रग्विभिः		
D.Ab.	धनिभ्यः	स्रग्विभ्यः	............like Masc.	
G.	धनिनाम्	स्रग्विणाम्		
L.	धनिषु	स्रग्विषु		

§ 87. The Feminine base of nouns which follow this declension is formed by the addition of the feminine affix ई to the masculine base, e. g. धनिन्, Fem. base धनिनी; स्रग्विन्, Fem. base स्रग्विणी; it is declined like नदी (§ 141).

DECLENSION V.

Bases ending in the affixes अस्, इस्, उस्.

§ 88. *Sandhi* :—

1. The final स् is changed to Visarga in the N. and V. Sing., Masc. and Fem., and the N., V. and Ac. Sing. Neut.

2. Before vowel-terminations the स् of अस् remains unchanged (§ 50), but the स् of इस् and उस् becomes ष् (§ 59).

3. Before भिः, भ्यः and भ्याम्, अस् is changed to ओ, इस् to इर्, and उस् to उर्.

4. The termination सु of the L. Plur. remains unchanged after अस्, while the स् of अस् may optionally either remain स् or be changed to Visarga. After इस् and उस् the termination सु must be changed to षु (§ 59), and the स् of इस् and उस् must be changed, either to ष् or to Visarga.

5. The अ of अस् is lengthened in N. Sing. Masc. and Fem.; and अ, इ, उ of अस्, इस्, उस् are lengthened in the N., V. and Ac. Plur. Neut.

§ 89. *Paradigms*: सुमनस् *m. f. n.* 'well-minded;' उदर्चिस् *m. f. n.* 'flaring upwards;' सधनुस् *m. f. n.* 'armed with a bow.'

Base : सुमनस्   उदर्चिस्   सधनुस्   सुमनस्   उदर्चिस्   सधनुस्

	Masc. and Fem.			Neuter.		
		Singular.				
N.	सुमनाः	उदर्चिः	सधनुः	सुमनः	उदर्चिः	सधनुः
Ac.	सुमनसम्	उदर्चिषम्	सधनुषम्			
I.	सुमनसा	उदर्चिषा	सधनुषा			
D.	सुमनसे	उदर्चिषे	सधनुषे	like Masc. and Fem.		
Ab.G.	सुमनसः	उदर्चिषः	सधनुषः			
L.	सुमनसि	उदर्चिषि	सधनुषि			
V.	सुमनः	उदर्चिः	सधनुः	सुमनः	उदर्चिः	सधनुः

Dual.

N.V.Ac.	सुमनसौ	उदर्चिषौ	सधनुषौ	सुमनसी	उदर्चिषी	सधनुषी
I.D.Ab.	सुमनोभ्याम्	उदर्चिर्भ्याम्	सधनुर्भ्याम्	} like Masc. and Fem.		
G.L.	सुमनसोः	उदर्चिषोः	सधनुषोः			

Plural.

N.V.Ac.	सुमनसः	उदर्चिषः	सधनुषः	सुमनांसि	उदर्चींषि	सधनूंषि
I.	सुमनोभिः	उदर्चिर्भिः	सधनुर्भिः			
D.Ab.	सुमनोभ्यः	उदर्चिर्भ्यः	सधनुर्भ्यः	} like Masc. and Fem.		
G.	सुमनसाम्	उदर्चिषाम्	सधनुषाम्			
L.	सुमनस्सु	उदर्चिष्षु	सधनुष्षु			
	or	or	or			
	सुमनःसु	उदर्चिःषु	सधनुःषु			

§ 90. Decline: चन्द्रमस् *m.* 'the moon,' like सुमनस् in Masc.;
अप्सरस् *f.* 'a nymph,' like सुमनस् in Fem.;
पयस् *n.* 'water,' like सुमनस् in Neut.;
ज्योतिस् *n.* 'light,' like उदर्चिस् in Neut.;
यजुस् *n.* 'the Yajurveda,' like सधनुस् in Neut.

§ 91. *Irregular bases:* अनेहस् *m.* 'time,' and पुरुदंशस् *m.*, a name of Indra, drop Visarga in the N. Sing : अनेहा, पुरुदंशा. उशनस् *m.*, a proper name, does the same (N. Sing. उशना); and forms the V. Sing. either उशनः or उशन or उशनन्.

2.—Changeable Bases.

§ 92. In the first five declensions the base remains, so far as it is not affected by the rules of Sandhi, nearly always one and the same throughout all cases. In the remaining declensions of consonantal bases, the base has generally two forms, a *strong base* and a *weak base*. The weak base is usually that which is given in the dictionary; the strong base is formed from it by lengthening of the penultimate vowel, or by the insertion of a nasal before the final consonant &c.; *e. g.*

Weak base राजन् भवत् महत् &c.
Strong base राजान् भवन्त् महान्त् &c.

§ 93. Some nouns have three bases, a *strong base*, a *middle base*, and a *weakest base*. Here usually the middle base is given in the dictionary. If we strengthen it, *e. g.* by lengthening its penultimate vowel, we obtain the strong base; if we weaken it, *e. g.* by contracting two of its letters into one, we obtain the weakest base; *e. g.*

Middle base	श्वन्	युवन्	मत्यच्	&c.
Strong base	श्वान्	युवान्	मत्यञ्च्	&c.
Weakest base	शुन्	यून्	मतीच्	&c.

§ 94. *Nouns with two bases*, i.e. a strong base and a weak base: The strong base is used in the *strong cases*, the weak base in the *weak cases*.

(*a*) The strong cases are the Nom. and Acc. Sing., the Nom. and Acc. Dual, and the Nom. (*not the Acc.*) Plur. in Masc. and Fem., and the Nom. and Acc. Plur. in Neut.

(*b*) All the remaining cases (except the Vocatives) in Masc. Fem. and Neut. are weak.

§ 95. *Nouns with three bases, i. e.* a strong base, a middle base, and a weakest base: The strong base is used in the *strong cases*, the middle base in the *middle cases*, and the weakest base in the *weakest cases*.

(*a*) The strong cases are, as before, the Nom. and Acc. Sing., the Nom. and Acc. Dual, and the Nom. (*not the Acc.*) Plur. in Masc. and Fem., and the Nom. and Acc. Plur. in Neut.

(*b*) Of the remaining cases those the terminations of which begin with consonants (*i. e.* the I. D. Ab. Dual and the I. D. Ab. and Loc. Plur. in Masc. Fem. and Neut.), and the Nom. and Acc. Sing. Neut. are middle cases.

(*c*) All the remaining cases (except the Vocatives) are weakest cases.

§ 96. The Voc. Dual and Plur. in Masc., Fem. and Neut. are always like the Nominatives. The Voc. Sing. is sometimes like the Nom. Sing. and has sometimes a peculiar form of its own. It can neither be called strong, nor middle, nor weak.

DECLENSION VI.

Comparative bases in यस् (*Masc. and Neut*).

§ 97. *Two bases:* strong base ending in यांस्; weak base ending in यस्.

§ 98. *Sandhi* :—

1. In the N. Sing. Masc. यांस् becomes यान्, in all other strong cases it remains unchanged.

2. In the weak cases the base in यस् is treated like a base in अस् of Declension V.

3. In the V. Sing. Masc. यस् becomes यन्. The V. Sing. Neut. is like the N. Sing. Neut.

§ 99. *Paradigm:* गरीयस् *m. n.* 'heavier.'

Strong Base: गरीयांस्
Weak Base: गरीयस्

Masculine.

	Singular.	Dual.	Plural.
N.	गरीयान्	गरीयांसौ	गरीयांसः
Ac.	गरीयांसम्	गरीयांसौ	गरीयसः
I.	गरीयसा	गरीयोभ्याम्	गरीयोभिः
D.	गरीयसे	गरीयोभ्याम्	गरीयोभ्यः
Ab.	गरीयसः	गरीयोभ्याम्	गरीयोभ्यः
G.	गरीयसः	गरीयसोः	गरीयसाम्
L.	गरीयसि	गरीयसोः	गरीयस्सु or गरीयःसु
V.	गरीयन्	गरीयांसौ	गरीयांसः

Neuter.

N.V.Ac.	गरीयः	गरीयसी	गरीयांसि

The rest like Masc.

§ 100. The Feminine base is formed by the addition of the feminine affix ई to the weak base, *e. g.* गरीयस्, Fem. base गरीयसी; it is declined like नदी. (§ 141.)

DECLENSION VII.

Participle bases in अत् (*Masc. and Neut.*)

§ 101. *Two bases:* strong base ending in अन्त्; weak base ending in अत्.

§ 102. *Sandhi:—*

1. In the N. Sing. Masc. अन्त् becomes अन् (§ 52), in all other strong cases it remains unchanged.

2. In the weak cases the base in अत् is treated like a base in न् of Declension II.

3. The V. Sing. Masc. and Neut. is like the N.

§ 103. *Insertion of* न् *before the final* त् *of the base in the Nom., Acc. and Voc. Dual Neut.*:

1. न् must be inserted before the final त् of the base in Participles of the Present tense Par. of roots of the I., IV., and X. classes and of causal and desiderative verbs, *e. g.* बोधन्ती; दीव्यन्ती; चोरयन्ती; बोधयन्ती; बुबोधिषन्तो.

2. न् may optionally be inserted before the final त् of the base in Participles of the Present tense Par. of roots of the VI. class, and of roots in आ of the II. class; and in Participles of the Fut. Par. in स्यत् or ष्यत्; *e. g.* तुदतो or तुदन्तो; याती or यान्तो; दास्यती or दास्यन्तो; करिष्यती or करिष्यन्तो.

3. न् is *never inserted* in the remaining Participles of the Pres. tense Par. *e.g.* अदतो; ददतो; सुन्वतो; युञ्जतो; कुर्वतो; क्रीणती.

§ 104. *Paradigms:* बोधत् *m. n.* 'knowing;' अदत् *m. n.* 'eating;' यात् *m. n.* 'going;' दास्यत् *m. n.* 'one who will give.'

Strong B.	बोधन्त्	अदन्त्	यान्त्	दास्यन्त्
Weak B.	बोधत्	अदत्	यात्	दास्यत्

Masculine.

Singular.

N.V.	बोधन्	अदन्	यान्	दास्यन्
Ac.	बोधन्तम्	अदन्तम्	यान्तम्	दास्यन्तम्
I.	बोधता	अदता	याता	दास्यता
D.	बोधते	अदते	याते	दास्यते
Ab.G.	बोधतः	अदतः	यातः	दास्यतः
L.	बोधति	अदति	याति	दास्यति

Dual.

N.V.Ac.	बोधन्तौ	अदन्तौ	यान्तौ	दास्यन्तौ
I.D.Ab.	बोधद्भ्याम्	अदद्भ्याम्	याद्भ्याम्	दास्यद्भ्याम्
G. L.	बोधतोः	अदतोः	यातोः	दास्यतोः

Plural.

N.V.	बोधन्तः	अदन्तः	यान्तः	दास्यन्तः
Ac.	बोधतः	अदतः	यातः	दास्यतः
I.	बोधद्भिः	अदद्भिः	याद्भिः	दास्यद्भिः
D.Ab.	बोधद्भ्यः	अदद्भ्यः	याद्भ्यः	दास्यद्भ्यः
G.	बोधताम्	अदताम्	याताम्	दास्यताम्
L.	बोधत्सु	अदत्सु	यात्सु	दास्यत्सु

Neuter.

Sing. N.V.Ac.	बोधत्	अदत्	यात्	दास्यत्
Du. N.V.Ac.	बोधन्ती	अदती	यातीor यान्ती	दास्यतीor दास्यन्ती
Pl. N.V.Ac.	बोधन्ति	अदन्ति	यान्ति	दास्यन्ति

The rest like Masc.

§ 105. The Feminine base of these Participles is formed by the addition of the fem. affix ई, न् being inserted as in the N. Ac. V. Dual of the Neut. (§ 103), e. g. बोधत्, Fem. base बोधन्ती; अदत्, Fem. base अदती; यात्, Fem. base याती or यान्ती; दास्यत्, Fem. base दास्यती or दास्यन्ती. The Fem. base is declined like नदी (§ 141).

§ 106. Participles of the Present tense Par. of roots of the 3rd class (*juhotyâdi*) and the five Participles जक्षत् 'eating,' जाग्रत् 'waking,' दरिद्रत् 'being poor,' चकासत् 'shining,' and शासत् 'commanding,' have no strong base, and are therefore declined exactly like nouns in त् of Decl. II. The insertion of न् before the final त् in N. V. Ac. Plur. Neut. is, however, *optional*; e. g. ददत् m. n. 'giving;' जाग्रत् m. n. 'waking.'

Masculine.

	Singular.	Dual.	Plural.
N.V.	ददत् जाग्रत्	ददतौ जाग्रतौ	ददतः जाग्रतः
Ac.	ददतम् जाग्रतम्		

Neuter.

N.V.Ac.	ददत् जाग्रत्	ददती जाग्रती	ददन्ति जाग्रन्ति or ददति जाग्रति

Fem. base ददती, जाग्रती &c.

§ 107. बृहत् m. n. 'great,' and पृषत् m. 'a deer,' n. 'a drop of water,' are declined like अदत्; e.g., Masc. Sing. N. V. बृहन् Ac. बृहन्तम् I. बृहता &c. Fem. base बृहती.

§ 108. महत् m. n. 'great,' differs in its declension from अदत् only by lengthening its penultimate अ in the strong cases; e. g. Masc. Sing. N. महान्, V. महन्, Ac. महान्तम्, I. महता &c.; Neut. N. V. Ac. Sing. महत्, Du. महती, Pl. महान्ति. Fem. base महती.

DECLENSION VIII.

Bases ending in the affixes मन्, वन्, *and* यन् (*Masc. and Neut.*)

§ 109. *Two bases*: strong base ending in मन्न्, वन्न्, यन्न्; weak base ending in मन्, वन्, यन्.

§ 110. *Sandhi*:—

1. In the N. Sing. Masc. मन्न्, वन्न्, and यन्न् become मान्, वान्, and यान् (§ 52); in all other strong cases they remain unchanged.

2. In the weak cases the bases in मन्, वन्, and यन् are treated like अदन् (Decl. VII.).

3. The V. Sing. Masc. ends in मन्, वन्, यन्; the V. Sing. Neut. is like the N. Sing. Neut.

§ 111. *Paradigms*: धीमन् *m. n.* 'intelligent;' विद्यावन् *m. n.* 'possessed of knowledge;' कियत् *m. n.* 'how much?'

	Masculine			Neuter		
Strong B.	धीमन्त्	विद्यावन्त्	कियन्त्	धीमत्	विद्यावत्	कियत्
Weak B.	धीमत्	विद्यावत्	कियत्	धीमत्	विद्यावत्	कियत्

Singular.

	Masculine			Neuter		
N.	धीमान्	विद्यावान्	कियान्	धीमत्	विद्यावत्	कियत्
Ac.	धीमन्तम्	विद्यावन्तम्	कियन्तम्			
I.	धीमता	विद्यावता	कियता			
D.	धीमते	विद्यावते	कियते	like Masc.		
Ab.G.	धीमतः	विद्यावतः	कियतः			
L.	धीमति	विद्यावति	कियति			
V.	धीमन्	विद्यावन्	कियन्	धीमत्	विद्यावत्	कियत्

Dual.

N.V.Ac.	धीमन्तौ	विद्यावन्तौ	कियन्तौ	धीमती	विद्यावती	कियती
I.D.Ab.	धीमद्भ्याम्	विद्यावद्भ्याम्	कियद्भ्याम्	like Masc.		
G.L.	धीमनोः	विद्यावतोः	कियतोः			

Plural.

N.V.	धीमन्तः	विद्वावन्तः	कियन्तः	⎫ धीमन्ति विद्वावन्ति कियन्ति
Ac.	धीमतः	विद्वावतः	कियतः	⎭
I.	धीमद्भिः	विद्वावद्भिः	कियद्भिः	⎫
D.A.	धीमद्भ्यः	विद्वावद्भ्यः	कियद्भ्यः	⎬ like Masc.
G.	धीमताम्	विद्वावताम्	कियताम्	⎪
L.	धीमत्सु	विद्वावत्सु	कियत्सु	⎭

§ 112. The Fem. base is formed by the addition of the fem. affix ई to the weak base; *e. g.* धीमन्, Fem. base धीमती; विद्वावन्, Fem. base विद्वावती; कियन्, Fem. base कियती; it is declined like नदी (§ 141).

§ 113. भवत् used as an honorific pronoun in the sense of 'your honour,' is declined like विद्वावत्, and differs therefore in the N. Sing Masc. and the N. V. Ac. Dual Neut. from the participle भवत् 'being,' which follows बोभत् (Decl. VII).

N. Sing. Masc.   भवान् 'your honour;' भवन् 'being.'
N. V. Ac. Du. Neut. भवती   „   „   ; भवन्ती   „

The feminine base of भवत् 'your honour' is भवती, of भवत् 'being,' भवन्ती; both are declined like नदी (§ 141).

DECLENSION IX.

Bases ending in the affixes अन्, मन्, *and* वन् (*Masc. and Neut.; rarely Fem.*)

§ 114. *Two bases:* strong base ending in आन्, मान्, वान्; weak base, ending in अन्, मन्, वन्.

§ 115. *Sandhi:*—

1. In the N. Sing. Masc. and Fem. आन्, मान्, and वान् become आ, मा, and वा; in all other strong cases they remain unchanged, except when न् is changed to ण् by § 59.

2. In the N. and Ac. Sing. Neut. the final न् of अन्, मन्, and वन् is dropped.

3. The final न् is also dropped before all consonantal terminations.

4. Before vowel-terminations of weak cases the penultimate अ of अन्, मन्, वन्, is dropped; it may be dropped optionally in the Loc. Sing.

DECLENSION OF NOUNS.

Masc., Fem. and Neut. and in the N. V. Ac. Dual Neut. The final न् of the base is liable to be changed to ण् and to ञ् by the influence of preceding letters. (§§ 58, 57.)

5. When the affixes मन् and वन् are immediately preceded by a consonant, their penultimate अ is not dropped; their final न् is liable to be changed into ण् (§ 58).

6. The Voc. Sing. Masc. and Fem. is like the weak base; the Voc. Sing. Neut. may be like the weak base or like the Nom. Sing. Neut.

§ 116. *Paradigms:* राजन् *m.* 'a king;' तक्षन् *m.* 'a carpenter;' आत्मन् *m.* 'soul;' यज्वन् *m.* 'a sacrificer;' सोमन् *f.* 'a boundary;' नामन् *n.* 'a name;' ब्रह्मन् *n.* 'the Supreme Being;' पर्वन् *n.* 'a joint.'

St. B.	राजान्	तक्षान्	आत्मान्	यज्वान्	सीमान्	नामान्	ब्रह्मान्	पर्वान्
W. B.	राजन्	तक्षन्	आत्मन्	यज्वन्	सीमन्	नामन्	ब्रह्मन्	पर्वन्

	Masc.				Fem.	Neut.		

Singular.

N.	राजा	तक्षा	आत्मा	यज्वा	सीमा	नाम	ब्रह्म	पर्व
Ac.	राजानम्	तक्षाणम्	आत्मानम्	यज्वानम्	सीमानम्			
I.	राज्ञा	तक्ष्णा	आत्मना	यज्वना	सीम्ना	नाम्ना	ब्रह्मणा	पर्वणा
D.	राज्ञे	तक्ष्णे	आत्मने	यज्वने	सीम्ने	नाम्ने	ब्रह्मणे	पर्वणे
Ab.G.	राज्ञः	तक्ष्णः	आत्मनः	यज्वनः	सीम्नः	नाम्नः	ब्रह्मणः	पर्वणः
L.	राज्ञि	तक्ष्णि	आत्मनि	यज्वनि	सीम्नि	नाम्नि	ब्रह्मणि	पर्वणि
	or	or			or	or		
	राजनि	तक्षणि			सीमनि	नामनि		
V.	राजन्	तक्षन्	आत्मन्	यज्वन्	सीमन्	नामन्	ब्रह्मन्	पर्वन्
						or	or	or
						नाम	ब्रह्म	पर्व

Dual.

N.V.Ac.	राजानौ	तक्षाणौ	आत्मानौ	यज्वानौ	सीमानौ	नामनी	ब्रह्मणी	पर्वणी
						or		
						नाम्नी		
I.D.Ab.	राजभ्याम्	तक्षभ्याम्	आत्मभ्याम्	यज्वभ्याम्	सोमभ्याम्	नामभ्याम्	ब्रह्मभ्याम्	पर्वभ्याम्
G.L.	राज्ञोः	तक्ष्णोः	आत्मनोः	यज्वनोः	सीम्नोः	नाम्नोः	ब्रह्मणोः	पर्वणोः

Plural.

N.V.	राजानः	तक्षाणः	आत्मानः	यज्वानः	सीमानः	नामानि	ब्रह्माणि	पर्वाणि
Ac.	राज्ञः	तक्षणः	आत्मनः	यज्वनः	सीम्नः			
I.	राजभिः	तक्षभिः	आत्मभिः	यज्वभिः	सीमभिः	नामभिः	ब्रह्मभिः	पर्वभिः
D.Ab.	राजभ्यः	तक्षभ्यः	आत्मभ्यः	यज्वभ्यः	सीमभ्यः	नामभ्यः	ब्रह्मभ्यः	पर्वभ्यः
G.	राज्ञाम्	तक्षणाम्	आत्मनाम्	यज्वनाम्	सीम्नाम्	नाम्नाम्	ब्रह्मणाम्	पर्वणाम्
L.	राजसु	तक्षसु	आत्मसु	यज्वसु	सीमसु	नामसु	ब्रह्मसु	पर्वसु

§ 117. The Feminine base of simple nouns in अन् is, where it exists, formed by the addition of the fem. affix ई, before which the अ of अन् is dropped; *e. g.* राजन्, Fem. base राज्ञी 'a queen,' declined like नदी (§ 141). Some nouns in मन् have an optional base in आ; *e. g.*, besides सीमन् there exists also सीमा, declined like कान्ता (§ 131). Some nouns in वन् form their feminine base by the addition of the fem. affix ई, before which the final न् is changed to र् *e. g.*, अतिसुत्वन्, Fem. base अतिसुत्वरी, declined like नदी (§ 141).

Irregular bases.

§ 118. पूषन् *m.*, अर्यमन् *m.*, two proper names, and bases ending in हन् 'slaying' (derived from, and in form identical with, the root हन् 'to slay'), which also follow this declension, form only the N. Sing. Masc. Fem. and the N. V. Ac. Plur. Neut. from the strong base in आन्, all the other cases from the weak base. Whenever the penultimate अ of हन् is dropped, ह is changed to घ् *e. g.*

	Masc.			Neut.
Sing.N.	पूषा	अर्यमा	वृत्रहा	वृत्रह
Sing.Ac.	पूषणम्	अर्यमणम्	वृत्रहणम्	वृत्रह
Sing.I.	पूष्णा	अर्यम्णा	वृत्रघ्ना	वृत्रघ्ना
Plur. N.	——	——	वृत्रहणः	वृत्रहाणि
Plur.Ac.	——	——	वृत्रघ्नः	वृत्रहाणि
Plur.I.	——	——	वृत्रहभिः	वृत्रहभिः

§ 119. अर्वन् *m.* 'a horse,' forms the Nom. Sing. regularly अर्वा; all other cases are formed from अर्वत्, declined like अदत् (Decl. VII.) *e. g.* Sing. Ac. अर्वन्तम्, I. अर्वता, D. अर्वते &c.

Nouns with three bases.

§ 120. श्वन् *m.* 'a dog,' मघवन् *m.*, a name of Indra, and युवन् *m. n.* 'young,' form their strong and middle cases regularly from the strong bases श्वान्, मघवान्, युवान्, and from the middle bases श्वन्, मघवन्, युवन्; their weakest cases are formed from the weakest bases शुन्, मघोन्, यून्; *e. g.*

Dual.N.V.Ac.	श्वानौ युवानौ *m.*	यूनी *n.*
I.D.Ab.	श्वभ्याम्	युवभ्याम्
G.L.	शुनोः	यूनोः

Sing.N. मघवा; Ac. मघवानम्; I. मघोना &c.

The optional base मघवन् is declined regularly like विद्वान्. (Decl. VIII.) The Fem. bases of श्वन् and मघवन् are शुनी and मघोनी, declined like नदी (§ 141); that of युवन् is युवति declined like मति (§ 136) or युवती declined like नदी (§ 141).

§ 121. अहन् *n.* 'a day;' strong base अहान्; middle base अहर् or अहस्; weakest base अहन्.

Sing. N.V.Ac. अहः *i. e.* (अहर्) I. अह्ना D. अह्ने Ab. G. अह्नः L. अह्नि or अहनि
Dual N.V.Ac. अह्नी or अहनी I. D. Ab. अहोभ्याम् G. L. अह्नोः
Plural N.V.Ac. अहानि I. अहोभिः D. Ab. अहोभ्यः G. अह्नाम् L. अहस्सु or अहःसु

DECLENSION X.

Perfect-Participle bases in वस् (*Masc.* and *Neut.*).

§ 122. *Three bases:* strong base ending in वांस्; middle base ending in वत्; weakest base ending in उष्.

§ 123. *Sandhi:*—

1. In the N. Sing. Masc. वांस् becomes वान्; in all other strong cases it remains unchanged before the terminations.

2. The middle base in वत् is treated like a base in त् of Decl. II.

3. In the weakest cases उष् remains unchanged before the terminations. If the affix वस् was added by means of the intermediate इ, this इ is dropped before उष्; if final म् of a root was changed to न् before वस्, this न् becomes again म् before उष्. Final and medial radical vowels are treated before उष् just as they are treated before the terminations अयुः, अनुः of the Perfect.

4. The Voc. Sing. Masc. ends in वन्; the Voc. Sing. Neut. is like the Nom. Sing. Neut.

§ 124. *Paradigms*: विद्वस् *m. n.* 'knowing;' जग्मिवस् *m. n.* or जगन्वस् *m. n.* 'one who has gone;' निनीवस् *m. n.* 'one who has led;' शुश्रुवस् *m. n.* 'one who has heard.'

Strong B.	विद्वांस्	जग्मिवांस्	जगन्वांस्	निनीवांस्	शुश्रुवांस्
Middle B.	विद्वत्	जग्मिवत्	जगन्वत्	निनीवत्	शुश्रुवत्
Weakest B.	विदुष्	जग्मुष्	जग्मुष्	निन्युष्	शुश्रुवुष्

Masculine.
Singular.

N.	विद्वान्	जग्मिवान्	जगन्वान्	निनीवान्	शुश्रुवान्
Ac.	विद्वांसम्	जग्मिवांसम्	जगन्वांसम्	निनीवांसम्	शुश्रुवांसम्
I.	विदुषा	जग्मुषा	जग्मुषा	निन्युषा	शुश्रुवुषा
D.	विदुषे	जग्मुषे	जग्मुषे	निन्युषे	शुश्रुवुषे
Ab.G.	विदुषः	जग्मुषः	जग्मुषः	निन्युषः	शुश्रुवुषः
L.	विदुषि	जग्मुषि	जग्मुषि	निन्युषि	शुश्रुवुषि
V.	विद्वन्	जग्मिवन्	जगन्वन्	निनीवन्	शुश्रुवन्

Dual.

N.V.Ac.	विद्वांसौ	जग्मिवांसौ	जगन्वांसौ	निनीवांसौ	शुश्रुवांसौ
I.D.Ab.	विद्वद्भ्याम्	जग्मिवद्भ्याम्	जगन्वद्भ्याम्	निनीवद्भ्याम्	शुश्रुवद्भ्याम्
G.L.	विदुषोः	जग्मुषोः	जग्मुषोः	निन्युषोः	शुश्रुवुषोः

Plural.

N.V.	विद्वांसः	जग्मिवांसः	जगन्वांसः	निनीवांसः	शुश्रुवांसः
Ac.	विदुषः	जग्मुषः	जग्मुषः	निन्युषः	शुश्रुवुषः
I.	विद्वद्भिः	जग्मिवद्भिः	जगन्वद्भिः	निनीवद्भिः	शुश्रुवद्भिः
D.Ab.	विद्वद्भ्यः	जग्मिवद्भ्यः	जगन्वद्भ्यः	निनीवद्भ्यः	शुश्रुवद्भ्यः
G.	विदुषाम्	जग्मुषाम्	जग्मुषाम्	निन्युषाम्	शुश्रुवुषाम्
L.	विद्वत्सु	जग्मिवत्सु	जगन्वत्सु	निनीवत्सु	शुश्रुवत्सु

Neuter.

Sg. N.V.Ac.	विद्वत्	जग्मिवत्	जगन्वत्	निनीवत्	शुश्रुवत्
Du. N.V.Ac.	विदुषी	जग्मुषी	जग्मुषी	निन्युषी	शुश्रुवुषी
Pl. N.V.Ac.	विद्वांसि	जग्मिवांसि	जगन्वांसि	निनीवांसि	शुश्रुवांसि

The rest like Masc.

§ 125. The Feminine base is formed by the addition of the fem. affix ई to the weakest base; e. g. विद्वस्, Fem. base विदुषी; जग्मिवस्, Fem. base जग्मुषी; it is declined like नदी (§ 141).

DECLENSION XI.

Bases ending in अच्, derived from, and formally identical with, the root अच्, or अञ्च् 'to move' (Masc. and Neut.).

§ 126. *Three bases*: strong base ending in अञ्च्; middle base ending in अच्. The weakest base is formed by dropping the अ of अच् and substituting for a preceding semivowel its corresponding long vowel, e. g. प्रत्यच्, weakest base प्रतीच्; अन्वच्, weakest base अनूच्; if अच् is not preceded by a semivowel, it is changed into ईच् in the weakest base, e. g. उदच्, weakest base उदीच्. प्राच् and अवाच् remain unchanged in the weakest base; तिर्यच् forms तिरश्.

§ 127. *Sandhi* :—

1. In the N. Sing. Masc. अञ्च् becomes अङ् (§ 51, d; § 52); in all other strong cases it remains unchanged before the terminations.

2. The middle and weakest bases are treated like bases in च् of Decl. II. b (§ 76).

3. The Voc. Sing. Masc. and Neut. is like the Nom.

§ 128. *Paradigms* : प्रत्यच् m. n. 'western;' अन्वच् m. n. 'following;' उदच् m. n. 'northern;' प्राच् m. n. 'eastern;' तिर्यच् m. n. 'moving awry.'

Strong B.	प्रत्यञ्च्	अन्वञ्च्	उदञ्च्	प्राञ्च्	तिर्यञ्च्
Middle B.	प्रत्यच्	अन्वच्	उदच्	प्राच्	तिर्यच्
Weakest B.	प्रतीच्	अनूच्	उदीच्		तिरश्

Masculine.

Singular.

N.V.	प्रत्यङ्	अन्वङ्	उदङ्	प्राङ्	तिर्यङ्
Ac.	प्रत्यञ्चम्	अन्वञ्चम्	उदञ्चम्	प्राञ्चम्	तिर्यञ्चम्
I.	प्रतीचा	अनूचा	उदीचा	प्राचा	तिरश्चा
D.	प्रतीचे	अनूचे	उदीचे	प्राचे	तिरश्चे
Ab.G.	प्रतीचः	अनूचः	उदीचः	प्राचः	तिरश्चः
L.	प्रतीचि	अनूचि	उदीचि	प्राचि	तिरश्चि

Dual.

N.V.Ac.	प्रत्यञ्चौ	अन्वञ्चौ	उदञ्चौ	प्राञ्चौ	तिर्यञ्चौ
I.D.Ab.	प्रत्यग्भ्याम्	अन्वग्भ्याम्	उदग्भ्याम्	प्राग्भ्याम्	तिर्यग्भ्याम्
G.L.	प्रतीचोः	अनूचोः	उदीचोः	प्राचोः	तिरश्चोः

Plural.

N.V.	प्रत्यञ्चः	अन्वञ्चः	उदञ्चः	प्राञ्चः	तिर्यञ्चः
Ac.	प्रतीचः	अनूचः	उदीचः	प्राचः	तिरश्चः
I.	प्रत्यग्भिः	अन्वग्भिः	उदग्भिः	प्राग्भिः	तिर्यग्भिः
D.Ab.	प्रत्यग्भ्यः	अन्वग्भ्यः	उदग्भ्यः	प्राग्भ्यः	तिर्यग्भ्यः
G.	प्रतीचाम्	अनूचाम्	उदीचाम्	प्राचाम्	तिरश्चाम्
L.	प्रत्यक्षु	अन्वक्षु	उदक्षु	प्राक्षु	तिर्यक्षु

Neuter.

Sing.N.V.Ac.	प्रत्यक्	अन्वक्	उदक्	प्राक्	तिर्यक्
Dual.N.V.Ac.	प्रतीची	अनूची	उदीची	प्राची	तिरश्ची
Plur.N.V.Ac.	प्रत्यञ्चि	अन्वञ्चि	उदञ्चि	प्राञ्चि	तिर्यञ्चि

The rest like Masc.

§ 129. The Feminine base is formed by the addition of the fem. affix ई to the weakest base, *e. g.* प्रत्यच्, Fem. base प्रतीची; अन्वच्, Fem. base अनूची; उदच्, Fem. base उदीची; प्राच्, Fem. base प्राची; तिर्यच्, Fem. base तिरश्ची; it is declined like नदी (§ 141).

§ 130. Decline: समयच् 'right;' न्यच् 'low;' विष्वच् 'all-pervading;' अवाच् 'downward.'

B.—VOWEL BASES.

DECLENSION XII.

Bases ending in अ *(Masc. and Neut.) and* आ *(Fem.).*

§ 131. *Paradigm:* कान्त *m. n.* कान्ता *f.* 'beloved.'

	Masc.	Neut.	Fem.
Base:	कान्त	कान्त	कान्ता

Singular.

	Masc.	Neut.	Fem.
N.	कान्तः	कान्तम्	कान्ता
Ac.	कान्तम्		कान्ताम्
I.	कान्तेन		कान्तया
D.	कान्ताय		कान्तायै
Ab.	कान्तात्		कान्तायाः
G.	कान्तस्य		कान्तायाः
L.	कान्ते		कान्तायाम्
V.	कान्त		कान्ते

Dual.

	Masc.	Neut.	Fem.
N.V.Ac.	कान्तौ	कान्ते	कान्ते
I.D.Ab.	कान्ताभ्याम्		कान्ताभ्याम्
G.L.	कान्तयोः		कान्तयोः

Plural.

	Masc.	Neut.	Fem.
N.V.	कान्ताः	कान्तानि	कान्ताः
Ac.	कान्तान्	कान्तानि	कान्ताः
I.	कान्तैः		कान्ताभिः
D.Ab.	कान्तेभ्यः		कान्ताभ्यः
G.	कान्तानाम्		कान्तानाम्
L.	कान्तेषु		कान्तासु

§ 132. Decline: राम *m.* 'Râma,' like कान्त in Masc.;
ज्ञान *n.* 'knowledge,' like कान्त in Neut.;
भार्या *f.* 'a wife,' like कान्ता in Fem.

§ 133. *Irregular base*: अम्बा *f.* 'mother,' forms its Voc. Sing. अम्ब 'O mother!'

§ 134. Several adjectives in अ, आ, follow the pronominal declension; § 195.

§ 135. The Feminine base of adjectives ending in अ, and of substantives in अ which admit of a feminine, is most commonly formed by the addition of the fem. affix आ to the masculine base; *e.g.* प्रिय 'dear,' Fem. प्रिया; अज 'a goat,' Fem. अजा 'a she-goat,' declined like कान्ता Fem. (§ 131.) But in many instances the feminine base is formed by the addition of the fem. affix ई to the masculine base; *e.g.* गौर 'yellow,' Fem. गौरी; पुत्र 'a son,' Fem. पुत्री 'a daughter,' declined like नदी (§ 141). Some nouns in अक change the अ which precedes the penultimate क्, to इ, either necessarily, or optionally; *e.g.* सर्वक 'all, every,' Fem. सर्विका; पुलक 'a son,' Fem. पुलका or पुलिका; but क्षिपक 'throwing,' Fem. only क्षिपका. इन्द्र 'Indra' and भव 'S'iva' form इन्द्राणी 'the wife of Indra,' and भवानी 'the wife of S'iva,' declined like नदी (§ 141). Other particulars must be learnt from the dictionary.

DECLENSION XIII.

Bases ending in इ and उ (Masc., Fem. and Neut.).

(a)—Substantives.

§ 136. *Paradigms :*—अग्नि *m.* 'fire;' मति *f.* 'opinion;' वारि *n.* 'water;' वायु *m.* 'wind,' धेनु *f.* 'a cow;' मधु *n.* 'honey.'

	Masc.	Fem.	Neut.	Masc.	Fem.	Neut.
Base:	अग्नि	मति	वारि	वायु	धेनु	मधु

Singular.

	Masc.	Fem.	Neut.	Masc.	Fem.	Neut.
N.	अग्निः	मतिः	वारि	वायुः	धेनुः	मधु
Ac.	अग्निम्	मतिम्	वारि	वायुम्	धेनुम्	मधु
I.	अग्निना	मत्या	वारिणा	वायुना	धेन्वा	मधुना
D.	अग्नये	मत्यै or मतये	वारिणे	वायवे	धेन्वै or धेनवे	मधुने
Ab.G.	अग्नेः	मत्याः or मतेः	वारिणः	वायोः	धेन्वाः or धेनोः	मधुनः
L.	अग्नौ	मत्याम् or मतौ	वारिणि	वायौ	धेन्वाम् or धेनौ	मधुनि
V.	अग्ने	मते	वारि or वारे	वायो	धेनो	मधु or मधो

Dual.

N.V.Ac.	अमी	मती	वारिणी	वायू	धेनू	मधुनी
I.D.Ab.	अग्निभ्याम्	मतिभ्याम्	वारिभ्याम्	वायुभ्याम्	धेनुभ्याम्	मधुभ्याम्
G.L.	अग्न्योः	मत्योः	वारिणोः	वाय्वोः	धेन्वोः	मधुनोः

Plural.

N.V.	अग्नयः	मतयः	वारीणि	वायवः	धेनवः	मधूनि
Ac.	अग्नीन्	मतीः	वारीणि	वायून्	धेनूः	मधूनि
I.	अग्निभिः	मतिभिः	वारिभिः	वायुभिः	धेनुभिः	मधुभिः
D.Ab.	अग्निभ्यः	मतिभ्यः	वारिभ्यः	वायुभ्यः	धेनुभ्यः	मधुभ्यः
G.	अग्नीनाम्	मतीनाम्	वारीणाम्	वायूनाम्	धेनूनाम्	मधूनाम्
L.	अग्निषु	मतिषु	वारिषु	वायुषु	धेनुषु	मधुषु

(b.)—Adjectives.

§ 137. Adjectives ending in इ and उ (Masc., Fem. and Neut.) are declined like masculine, feminine, and neuter substantives in इ and उ; but in the D., Ab., G., L. Sing. and in the G. and L. Dual of the Neuter they admit the corresponding forms of the Masculine; *e.g.* शुचि *m. f. n.* 'pure,' गुरु *m. f. n.* 'heavy.'

	Masc.	Fem.	Neut.	Masc.	Fem.	Neut.
Sing.N.	शुचिः	शुचिः	शुचि	गुरुः	गुरुः	गुरु
Sing.Ac.	शुचिम्	शुचिम्	शुचि	गुरुम्	गुरुम्	गुरु
Sing.I.	शुचिना	शुच्या	शुचिना	गुरुणा	गुर्वा	गुरुणा
Sing.D	शुचये	शुच्यै	शुचिने	गुरवे	गुर्वै	गुरुणे
		or शुचये	or शुचये		or गुरवे	or गुरवे

§ 138. Adjectives in उ preceded by only one consonant may form a new feminine base by the addition of the feminine affix ई, *e.g.* लघु 'light,' Fem. लघु declined according to § 137, or लघ्वी declined like नद्री in § 141. Some adjectives in उ lengthen their final उ in the Fem.; *e.g.* पङ्गु 'lame,' Fem. पङ्गू, declined like वधू (§ 141.)

Irregular bases.

§ 139. सखि *m.* 'a friend,' and पति *m.* 'a lord, a husband:'

	Sing.		Dual.		Plur.	
N.	सखा	पतिः	सखायौ	पती	सखायः	पतयः
Ac.	सखायम्	पतिम्	सखायौ	पती	सखीन्	पतीन्
I.	सख्या	पत्या	सखिभ्याम्	पतिभ्याम्	सखिभिः	पतिभिः
D.	सख्ये	पत्ये	सखिभ्याम्	पतिभ्याम्	सखिभ्यः	पतिभ्यः
Ab. G.	सख्युः	पत्युः	सख्योः	पत्योः	सखीनाम्	पतीनाम्
L.	सख्यौ	पत्यौ	सख्योः	पत्योः	सखिषु	पतिषु
V.	सखे	पते	सखायौ	पती	सखायः	पतयः

At the end of compounds पति is declined regularly, like अग्नि (§ 136); *e.g.* भूपति *m.* 'a lord of the earth, a king,' L. Sing. भूपतौ. The Fem. of पति is पत्नी 'a wife,' that of सखि is सखी 'a female friend,' declined like नदी § 141.

§ 140. अक्षि *n.* 'an eye,' अस्थि *n.* 'a bone,' दधि *n.* 'curds,' and सक्थि *n.* 'a thigh,' form their weakest cases (except the N. V. Ac. Du.) from अक्षन्, अस्थन्, दधन् and सक्थन् according to Decl. IX.; *e.g.*

	Sing.	Dual.	Plur.
N. Ac.	अस्थि	अस्थिनी	अस्थीनि
I.	अस्थ्ना	अस्थिभ्याम्	अस्थिभिः
D.	अस्थ्ने	अस्थिभ्याम्	अस्थिभ्यः
Ab. G.	अस्थ्नः	अस्थ्नोः	अस्थ्नाम्
L.	अस्थ्नि or अस्थनि	अस्थ्नोः	अस्थिषु
V.	अस्थि or अस्थे	अस्थिनी	अस्थीनि.

DECLENSION XIV.

Feminine Bases ending in ई and ऊ.

(a) *Bases of more than one syllable.*

§ 141. *Paradigms:* नदी *f.* 'a river;' वधू *f.* 'a woman.'

	Sing.		Dual.		Plur.	
N.	नदी	वधूः	नद्यौ	वध्वौ	नद्यः	वध्वः
Ac.	नदीम्	वधूम्			नदीः	वधूः
I.	नद्या	वध्वा	नदीभ्याम्	वधूभ्याम्	नदीभिः	वधूभिः
D.	नद्यै	वध्वै			नदीभ्यः	वधूभ्यः
Ab.	नद्याः	वध्वाः			नदीभ्यः	वधूभ्यः
G.			नद्योः	वध्वोः	नदीनाम्	वधूनाम्
L.	नद्याम्	वध्वाम्			नदीषु	वधूषु
V.	नदि	वधु	नद्यौ	वध्वौ	नद्यः	वध्वः

§ 142. *Irregular bases:* लक्ष्मी *f.* 'Lakshmî,' तरी *f.* 'a boat,' and तन्त्री *f.* 'the string of a lute,' form in the Nom. Sing. लक्ष्मीः, तरीः, and तन्त्रीः.

(b) *Bases of only one syllable.*

§ 143. *Paradigms:* धी *f.* 'understanding;' भू *f.* 'the earth.'

	Sing.		Dual.		Plur.	
N.V.	धीः	भूः	धियौ	भुवौ	धियः	भुवः
Ac.	धियम्	भुवम्				
I.	धिया	भुवा	धीभ्याम्	भूभ्याम्	धीभिः	भूभिः
D.	धिये or धियै	भुवे or भुवै			धीभ्यः	भूभ्यः
Ab.	धियः or धियाः	भुवः or भुवाः	धियोः	भुवोः	धीभ्यः	भूभ्यः
G.					धियाम् or धीनाम्	भुवाम् or भूनाम्
L.	धियि or धियाम्	भुवि or भुवाम्			धीषु	भूषु

§ 144. *Irregular base*: स्त्री *f.* 'a woman.'

	Sing.	*Dual.*	*Plur.*
N.	स्त्री	स्त्रियौ	स्त्रियः
Ac.	स्त्रियम् or स्त्रीम्	स्त्रियौ	स्त्रियः or स्त्रीः
I.	स्त्रिया	स्त्रीभ्याम्	स्त्रीभिः
D.	स्त्रियै	स्त्रीभ्याम्	स्त्रीभ्यः
Ab.	स्त्रियाः	स्त्रीभ्याम्	स्त्रीभ्यः
G.	स्त्रियाः	स्त्रियोः	स्त्रीणाम्
L.	स्त्रियाम्	स्त्रियोः	स्त्रीषु
V.	स्त्रि	स्त्रियौ	स्त्रियः

DECLENSION XV.

Monsyllabic Masc. and Fem. bases in आ, ई, ऊ, (*derived from roots without the addition of any visible affix,*) *when used at the end of Tatpurusha compounds.*

§ 145. These bases take the same terminations that are added to consonantal bases; before vowel terminations the final आ is dropped (except in strong cases), and final ई and ऊ are changed to य् and व्, when immediately preceed by one radical consonant, and to इय् and उव् when preceded by more than one radical consonant. The Voc. Sing. is like the Nom. Sing.

§ 146. *Paradigms*: विश्वपा *m. f.* 'protecting the universe;' जलपी *m. f.* 'one who drinks water;' खलपू *m. f.* 'a sweeper;' यवक्री *m. f.* 'one who buys grain.'

Masc. and Fem.

Base:	विश्वपा	जलपी	खलपू	यवक्री
		Singular.		
N.V.	विश्वपाः	जलपीः	खलपूः	यवक्रीः
Ac.	विश्वपाम्	जलप्यम्	खलप्वम्	यवक्रियम्
I.	विश्वपा	जलप्या	खलप्वा	यवक्रिया
D.	विश्वपे	जलप्ये	खलप्वे	यवक्रिये
Ab.G.	विश्वपः	जलप्यः	खलप्वः	यवक्रियः
L.	विश्वाप	जलपि	खलप्वि	यवक्रियि

Dual.

N.V.Ac.	विश्वपौ	जल्प्यौ	खलप्वौ	यवक्रियौ
I.D.Ab.	विश्वपाभ्याम्	जल्पीभ्याम्	खलपूभ्याम्	यवक्रीभ्याम्
G.L.	विश्वपोः	जल्प्योः	खलप्वोः	यवक्रियोः

Plural.

N.V.	विश्वपाः	} जल्प्यः	खलप्वः	यवक्रियः
Ac.	विश्वपः			
I.	विश्वपाभिः	जल्पीभिः	खलपूभिः	यवक्रीभिः
D. Ab.	विश्वपाभ्यः	जल्पीभ्यः	खलपूभ्यः	यवक्रीभ्यः
G.	विश्वपाम्	जल्प्याम्	खलप्वाम्	यवक्रियाम्
L.	विश्वपासु	जल्पीषु	खलपूषु	यवक्रीषु

§ 147. *Irregular bases:* Bases ending with नी 'leading,' take in the L. Sing. the termination आम् instead of इ, *e. g.* ग्रामणी 'one who leads a village, a chief,' L. Sing. ग्रामण्याम्.

DECLENSION XVI.

Bases ending in ऋ (*Masc. and Neut., rarely Fem.*)

(*a*) ऋ *changeable to* आर्.

§ 148. Nouns derived from roots by means of the affix तृ and denoting an agent, like कर्तृ *m.* 'a maker,' and नप्तृ *m.* 'a grandson', स्वसृ *f.* 'a sister', भर्तृ *m.* 'a husband' (etymologically 'a supporter') change their final ऋ in the Ac. Sing., the N. Ac. V. Dual, and the N. V. Plur. of the Masc. and Fem. to आर्.

§ 149. *Paradigms:* कर्तृ *m. n.* 'a maker;' स्वसृ *f.* 'a sister.'

	Masc.	Neut.	Fem.
		Singular.	
N.	कर्ता	कर्तृ	स्वसा
Ac.	कर्तारम्		स्वसारम्
I.	कर्त्रा	कर्तृणा	स्वस्रा
D.	कर्त्रे	कर्तृणे	स्वस्रे
Ab.G.	कर्तुः	कर्तृणः	स्वसुः
L.	कर्तरि	कर्तृणि	स्वसरि
V.	कर्तः (i.e. कर्तर्)	कर्तृ or कर्तः (i.e. कर्तर्)	स्वसः (i.e. स्वसर्)

Dual.

N.V.Ac.	कर्तारौ	कर्तृणी	स्वसारौ
I.D.Ab.	कर्तृभ्याम्	कर्तृभ्याम्	स्वसृभ्याम्
G.L.	कर्त्रोः	कर्तृणोः	स्वस्रोः

Plural.

N.V.	कर्तारः ⎱	कर्तृणि	स्वसारः
Ac.	कर्तॄन् ⎰		स्वसॄः
I.	कर्तृभिः	कर्तृभिः	स्वसृभिः
D.Ab.	कर्तृभ्यः	कर्तृभ्यः	स्वसृभ्यः
G.	कर्तॄणाम्	कर्तॄणाम्	स्वसॄणाम्
L.	कर्तृषु	कर्तृषु	स्वसृषु

§ 150. The Feminine base of the nouns in ऋ which denote an agent is formed by the addition of the feminine affix ई to the masculine base, *e.g.* कर्तृ, Fem. base, कर्त्री; it is declined like नदी. (§ 141.)

(b) ऋ changeable to अर्.

§ 151. Nouns expressive of relationship like पितृ *m.* 'a father,' मातृ *f.* 'a mother,' देवृ *m.* 'a husband's brother,' &c. (except those mentioned in § 148) change their final ऋ in the Ac. Sing., the N. V. Ac. Dual, and the N. V. Plur. to अर् ; *e. g.* पितृ *m.* 'a father;' मातृ *f.* 'mother.'

	Sing.		*Dual.*		*Plur.*	
N.	पिता	माता ⎫	पितरौ	मातरौ ⎫	पितरः	मातरः
V.	पितः (i. e. पितर्)	मातः ⎬		⎬		
Ac.	पितरम्	मातरम् ⎭		⎭	पितॄन्	मातॄः
I.	पित्रा	मात्रा	पितृभ्याम्	मातृभ्याम्	पितृभिः	मातृभिः

The remaining cases like those of कर्तृ *m.*, and स्वसृ.

§ 152. *Irregular base:* नृ *m.* 'a man,' which is otherwise declined like पितृ, forms in the G. Plur. नृणाम् or नॄणाम्.

DECLENSION XVII.

Bases ending in ऐ, ओ *and* औ.

§ 153. *Paradigms:* रै *m.* 'wealth;' गो *m.f.* 'a bull' or 'a cow;' नौ *f.* 'a ship.'

Base:	रै	गो	नौ

Singular.

N.V.	राः	गौः	नौः
Ac.	रायम्	गाम्	नावम्
I.	राया	गवा	नावा
D.	राये	गवे	नावे
Ab.G.	रायः	गोः	नावः
L.	रायि	गवि	नावि

Dual.

N.V.Ac.	रायौ	गावौ	नावौ
I.D.Ab.	राभ्याम्	गोभ्याम्	नौभ्याम्
G.L.	रायोः	गवोः	नावोः

Plural.

N.V	रायः	गावः	नावः
Ac.	रायः	गाः	नावः
I.	राभिः	गोभिः	नौभिः
D.Ab.	राभ्यः	गोभ्यः	नौभ्यः
G.	रायाम्	गवाम्	नावाम्
L.	रासु	गोषु	नौषु.

Alphabetical list of some irregular bases not mentioned in the preceding paragraphs.

§ 154. अनडुह् *m.* 'an ox,' forms the strong cases (except the N. Sing.) from अनडुाह्, the middle cases from अनडुत्, and the weakest cases from अनडुह्.

	Sing.	Dual.	Plur.
N.	अनड्वान्	अनड्वाहौ	अनड्वाहः
Ac.	अनड्वाहम्		अनडुहः
I.	अनडुहा		अनडुद्भिः
D.	अनडुहे	अनडुद्भ्याम्	अनडुद्भ्यः
Ab.			
G.	अनडुहः		अनडुहाम्
L.	अनडुहि	अनडुहोः	अनडुत्सु
V.	अनड्वन्	अनड्वाहौ	अनड्वाहः

§ 155. अप् *f.* 'water,' is declined only in the Plural: N. V. आपः, Ac. अपः, I. अद्भिः, D. Ab. अद्भ्यः, G. अपाम्, L. अप्सु.

§ 156. क्रोष्टु *m.* 'a jackal,' has two bases, क्रोष्टु and क्रोष्टृ; the base क्रोष्टु is used in all except the strong cases, and declined like वायु (§ 136); the base क्रोष्टृ is used in all strong cases, and in the weakest cases of the Sing. and Dual, and declined like कर्तृ *m.* (§ 149).

	Sing.	Dual.	Plur.
N.	क्रोष्टा	क्रोष्टारौ	क्रोष्टारः
Ac.	क्रोष्टारम्		क्रोष्टून्
I.	क्रोष्टुना or क्रोष्ट्रा		क्रोष्टुभिः
D.	क्रोष्टवे or क्रोष्ट्रे	क्रोष्टुभ्याम्	क्रोष्टुभ्यः
Ab.	क्रोष्टोः or क्रोष्टुः		
G.	क्रोष्टोः or क्रोष्टुः	क्रोष्ट्रोः or क्रोष्ट्रोः	क्रोष्टूनाम्
L.	क्रोष्टौ or क्रोष्टरि		क्रोष्टुषु
V.	क्रोष्टो	क्रोष्टारौ	क्रोष्टारः

§ 157. जरा *f.* 'old age,' is declined regularly throughout, like कान्ता *f.* (§ 131); but it may also optionally form all cases the terminations of which begin with a vowel, from the base जरस्, declined like सुमनस् *f.* (§ 89); *e. g.* Sing. N. only जरा; Ac. जराम् or जरसम्; Plur. I. only जराभिः; G. जराणाम् or जरसाम् &c.

DECLENSION OF NOUNS.

§ 158. दिव् *f.* 'the sky.'

	Sing.	Dual.	Plur.
N.V.	द्यौः	दिवौ	दिवः
Ac.	दिवम्		
I.	दिवा	द्युभ्याम्	द्युभिः
D.	दिवे		द्युभ्यः
Ab.	दिवः		
G.		दिवोः	दिवाम्
L.	दिवि		द्युषु

§ 159. दोस् *n.* (rarely *m.*) 'an arm,' is declined regularly throughout, its final स् being changed to Visarga in the N. Ac. V. Sing. (or, when Masc., only in the N. and V.), to ष् before vowel-terminations, to र् before the terminations भिः, भ्यः and भ्याम्, and to Visarga or to ष् in the L. Plur.; but it may also optionally form all cases except the N. Sing. Du. Plur., and the Ac. Sing. Du. from दोषन्, declined according to Decl. IX.; *e.g.*

	Sing.	Dual.	Plur.
N.	दोः (*n.* and *m.*)	दोषी *n.* दोषौ *m.*	दोंषि *n.* दोषः *m.*
Ac.	दोः *n.* दोषम् *m.*		= N., or दोष्णः *m.*
I.	दोषा or दोष्णा	दोर्भ्याम् or दोषभ्याम्	दोर्भिः or दोषभिः
L.	दोषि or दोष्णि or दोषणि	दोषोः or दोष्णोः	दोःषु or दोष्षु or दोषसु

§ 160. पथिन् *m.* 'a road,' forms the strong cases (except the N. Sing.) from पन्थान्, the middle cases from पथि, and the weakest cases from पथ्.

	Sing.	Dual.	Plur.
N.V.	पन्थाः	पन्थानौ	पन्थानः
Ac.	पन्थानम्		पथः
I.	पथा	पथिभ्याम्	पथिभिः
D.	पथे		पथिभ्यः
Ab.	पथः		
G.		पथोः	पथाम्
L.	पथि		पथिषु

§ 161. पाद् *m.* 'foot,' used as the last member of compounds, forms the weakest cases from पद्, *e.g.* सुपाद् *m.* 'one who has good feet.'

	Sing.	*Dual.*	*Plur.*
N.V.	सुपात्	सुपादौ	सुपादः
Ac.	सुपादम्	सुपादौ	सुपदः
I.	सुपदा	सुपाद्भ्याम्	सुपद्भिः &c.

The Fem. is either like the Masc., or a new Fem. base is formed by the addition of the fem. affix ई to the weakest base, *e.g.* Fem. base सुपदी, declined like नदी (§ 141).

§ 162. पाद *m.* 'foot,' is declined regularly throughout, like कान्त *m.* (§ 131); but it may also form optionally all weak cases (§ 94, *b.*) from पद्; *e. g.*

	Sing.	*Dual.*	*Plur.*
N.	पादः	पादौ	पादः
Ac.	पादम्	पादौ	पादान् or पदः
I.	पादेन or पदा	पादाभ्याम् or पद्भ्याम्	पादैः or पद्भिः &c.

§ 163. पुंस् *m.* 'a man,' forms the strong cases from पुमांस्, the middle cases from पुम्, and the weakest cases from पुंस्.

	Sing.	*Dual.*	*Plur.*
N.	पुमान्	पुमांसौ	पुमांसः
Ac.	पुमांसम्	पुमांसौ	पुंसः
I.	पुंसा	पुम्भ्याम्	पुंभिः
D.	पुंसे	पुम्भ्याम्	पुम्भ्यः
Ab. G.	पुंसः	पुंसोः	पुंसाम्
L.	पुंसि	पुंसोः	पुंसु
V.	पुमन्	पुमांसौ	पुमांसः

§ 164. पुनर्भू *f.* 'a widow remarried,' is declined like वधू (§ 141) except in the Ac. Sing., where it forms पुनर्भ्वम्, and in the Ac. Plur. which is पुनर्भ्वः; G. Plur. पुनर्भूणाम्.

§ 165. सुधी *m. f.* 'a person possessed of good intellect, an intelligent person,' and सुभ्रू *m. f.* 'a person with beautiful eye-brows,' are declined thus:—

Singular.

	Masc.		Fem.	
N.V.	सुधीः	सुभूः	सुधीः	सुभूः
Ac.	सुधियम्	सुभुवम्	सुधियम्	सुभुवम्
I.	सुधिया	सुभुवा	सुधिया	सुभुवा
D.	सुधिये	सुभुवे	सुधिये or सुधियै	सुभुवे or सुभ्रुवै
Ab. G.	सुधियः	सुभुवः	सुधियः or सुधियाः	सुभुवः or सुभुवाः
L.	सुधियि	सुभुवि	सुधियि or सुधियाम्	सुभुवि or सुभुवाम्

Dual.

Masc. and Fem.

N.V.Ac.	सुधियौ	सुभुवौ
I.D.Ab.	सुधीभ्याम्	सुभूभ्याम्
G.L.	सुधियोः	सुभुवोः

Plural.

	Masc.		Fem.	
N.V.Ac.	सुधियः	सुभुवः	सुधियः	सुभुवः
I.	सुधीभिः	सुभूभिः	सुधीभिः	सुभूभिः
D. Ab.	सुधीभ्यः	सुभूभ्यः	सुधीभ्यः	सुभूभ्यः
G.	सुधियाम्	सुभुवाम्	सुधियाम् or सुधीनाम्	सुभुवाम् or सुभूणाम्
L.	सुधीषु	सुभूषु	सुधीषु	सुभूषु

§ 166. स्वयंभू *m.* 'the self-existent one,' a name of Brahman, &c., is declined like खलपू *m.* (§ 146), except that it changes its final उ before vowel-terminations not to व्, but to उव्; *e.g.* Sing. N. V. स्वयंभूः, Ac. स्वयंभुवम्, I. स्वयंभुवा &c.

§ 167. हृदय *n.* 'heart,' is declined regularly throughout, like कान्त *n.* (§ 131); but it may also optionally form all cases except the N. Sing. Du. Plur., and the Ac. Sing. Du., from हृद्, declined according to Decl. II., *e.g.* Sing. N. V. Ac. हृदयम्; I. हृदयेन or हृदा; D. हृदयाय or हृदे; &c.

§ 168. *Affixes added to nominal bases to express the meanings of cases.*

(*a*) The affix तस् is sometimes added to the base of a noun to express the sense of the Ablative case; *e.g.* ग्रामतः 'from the village;' वस्तुतः 'from the real state of the case, in reality;' अज्ञानतः 'from ignorance.'

(b) Similarly the affix ल is added to the bases of nouns to denote the meaning of the Locative case: e. g. देवला 'amongst the gods;' पुरुषला 'among men.'

§ 169. A few nouns, such as स्वर् 'heaven,' संवत् 'a year of Vikramáditya's era,' &c. are *indeclinable*.

CHAPTER IV.

COMPARISON OF ADJECTIVES.

(a)—*By means of the affixes* तर *and* तम.

§ 170. The *Comparative* degree of adjectives is formed by the addition to their masculine base of the affix तर (Masc. and Neut. base; तरा Fem. base), the *Superlative* degree by the addition to their masculine base of the affix तम (Masc. and Neut. base; तमा Fem. base); e. g.

प्रिय 'dear;' Comp. प्रियतर 'dearer;' Superl. प्रियतम 'dearest.'
शुचि 'pure;' ,, शुचितर 'purer;' ,, शुचितम 'purest.'
गुरु 'heavy;' ,, गुरुतर 'heavier;' ,, गुरुतम 'heaviest.'

§ 171. Adjectives which follow Decl. II. change their final consonant before तर and तम as they change it in the N. Sing.; the final न् of adjectives in इन् is dropped; final अस् remains unchanged; final इस् and उस् are changed to इष् and उष्, after which the त् of तर and तम becomes ट्; e.g.

हरित्;	Comp.	हरित्तर;	Superl.	हरित्तम.
अग्निमथ्;	,,	अग्निमत्तर;	,,	अग्निमत्तम.
तमोनुद्;	,,	तमोनुत्तर;	,,	तमोनुत्तम.
सुयुध्;	,,	सुयुत्तर;	,,	सुयुत्तम.
धर्मबुध्;	,,	धर्मभुत्तर;	,,	धर्मभुत्तम.
सत्यवाच्;	,,	सत्यवाक्तर;	,,	सत्यवाक्तम.
धनिन्;	,,	धनितर;	,,	धनितम.
सुमनस्;	,,	सुमनस्तर;	,,	सुमनस्तम.
उदर्चिस्;	,,	उदर्चिष्टर;	,,	उदर्चिष्टम.

§ 172. Adjectives which in their declension show two bases, assume before तर and तम their weak base; those with three bases assume before

नर and नम their middle base; in both cases their final consonant undergoes before नर and नम the same changes which it undergoes before the termination सु of the L. Plur.; *e.g.*

धीमत्;	Comp.	धीमत्तर;	Superl.	धीमत्तम.
विद्वस्;	,,	विद्वत्तर;	,,	विद्वत्तम.
प्राच्;	,,	प्राक्तर;	,,	प्राक्तम.
प्रत्यच्;	,,	प्रत्यक्तर;	,,	प्रत्यक्तम.

(*b*)—*By means of the affixes* ईयस् *and* इष्ठ.

§ 173. Many adjectives may optionally form their *Comparative* degree by the addition of the affix ईयस् (Masc. and Neut. base; ईयसी Fem. base) and their *Superlative* degree by the addition of the affix इष्ठ (Masc. and Neut. base; इष्ठा Fem. base). The difference between नर, तम and ईयस्, इष्ठ is this, that whereas नर and तम are *added to the masculine base* of the adjective, ईयस् and इष्ठ are commonly *added to the root* from which the adjective has been derived, the vowel of the root being gunated; *e.g.*

क्षिप्र	'quick' (from rt. क्षिप्);	Comp. क्षेपीयस्;	Superl.	क्षेपिष्ठ.
स्थिर	'firm' (from rt. स्था);	,, स्थेयस्;	,,	स्थेष्ठ.
उरु	'wide' (from rt. वृ);	,, वरीयस्;	,,	वरिष्ठ.

Optionally क्षिप्रतर, क्षिप्रतम; स्थिरतर, स्थिरतम; उरुतर, उरुतम.

§ 174. The following are some special rules for the addition of ईयस् and इष्ठ :

(*a*) The final vowel of a masculine base which contains more than one syllable, or its final consonant together with the vowel preceding it, are dropped. *e.g.*

पाप	'wicked;'	Comp. पापीयस्;	Superl.	पापिष्ठ.
पटु	'clever;'	,, पटीयस्;	,,	पटिष्ठ.
महत्	'great;'	,, महीयस्;	,,	महिष्ठ.

(*b*) The possessive affixes मत्, वत्, विन् &c. are dropped; when the remainder of the base thereupon consists of only one syllable, it undergoes no change, except that its final resumes its original form; but when the remainder of the base contains more than one syllable, rule (*a*) is applicable to it; *e. g.*

स्रग्विन् (*i.e.* स्रज् + विन्) 'wearing a garland;' Com. स्रजीयस्; Superl. स्रजिष्ठ.
धनवत् (*i.e.* धन + वत्) 'possessed of wealth;' ,, धनीयस्; ,, धनिष्ठ.
वसुमत् (*i.e.* वसु + मत्) 'possessed of wealth;' ,, वसीयस्; ,, वसिष्ठ.

(c) र *i.e. ra* is substituted for the vowel ऋ of a base, when ऋ is preceded by an initial consonant, and immediately followed by only one consonant, *e. g.*

	कृश	'lean;'	Comp. क्रशीयस्;	Superl.	क्रशिष्ठ.
	दृढ	'hard;'	,, द्रढीयस्;	,,	द्रढिष्ठ.
	पृथु	'broad;'	,, प्रथीयस्;	,,	प्रथिष्ठ.
	भृश	'much;'	,, भ्रशीयस्;	,,	भ्रशिष्ठ.
	मृदु	'soft;'	,, म्रदीयस्;	,,	म्रदिष्ठ.
but	ऋजु	'straight;'	,, ऋजीयस्;	,,	ऋजिष्ठ.

§ 175. Alphabetical list of some irregular Comparatives and Superlatives :—

अन्तिक	'near;'	Comp. नेदीयस्;	Superl. नेदिष्ठ.		
अल्प	'small;'	,, अल्पीयस्;	,,	अल्पिष्ठ; or	
		कनीयस्;	,,	कनिष्ठ. *	
क्षुद्र	'mean;'	,, क्षोदीयस्;	,,	क्षोदिष्ठ.	
गुरु	'heavy;'	,, गरीयस्;	,,	गरिष्ठ.	
दीर्घ	'long;'	,, द्राघीयस्;	,,	द्राघिष्ठ.	
दूर	'far;'	,, दवीयस्;	,,	दविष्ठ.	
प्रशस्य	'praiseworthy;'	,, श्रेयस्;	,,	श्रेष्ठ ; or	
		ज्यायस्;	,,	ज्येष्ठ.	
प्रिय	'dear;'	,, प्रेयस्;	,,	प्रेष्ठ.	
बहु	'much;'	,, भूयस्;	,,	भूयिष्ठ. †	
बहुल	'manifold;'	,, बंहीयस्;	,,	बंहिष्ठ.	
युवन्	'young;'	,, यवीयस्;	,,	यविष्ठ; or	
		कनीयस्;	,,	कनिष्ठ.	
वाढ	'firm;'	,, साधीयस्;	,,	साधिष्ठ.	

---

* Compare कन्या.   † Compare भूरि.

वृद्ध	'old;'	Comp. वर्षीयस्;	Superl. वर्षिष्ठ ; or
		,, ज्यायस्;	,, ज्येष्ठ.
वृन्दारक	'great;'	,, वृन्दीयस्;	,, वृन्दिष्ठ.
स्थूल	'great;'	,, स्थवीयस्;	,, स्थविष्ठ.
स्फिर	'large;'	,, स्फेयस्;	,, स्फेष्ठ.
ह्रस्व	'short;'	,, ह्रसीयस्;	,, ह्रसिष्ठ.

§ 176. The affixes तर and तम are sometimes added to comparatives and superlatives in ईयस् and इष्ठ, *e. g.* पापीयस्, पापीयस्तर; पापिष्ठ, पापिष्ठतर, पापिष्ठतम; श्रेष्ठ, श्रेष्ठतम 'the very best.'

CHAPTER V.

PRONOUNS, PRONOMINAL ADJECTIVES, AND THEIR DECLENSION.

1.—*Personal Pronouns.*

§ 177. Bases :—

1. अस्मद् 'I;' special base for the Singular, मद्.

2. युष्मद् 'thou;' special base for the Singular, त्वद्.

The declension of these two pronouns is the same in all the three genders.

Singular.

N.	अहम् 'I;'	त्वम् 'thou.'
Ac.	माम् or मा	त्वाम् or त्वा
I.	मया	त्वया
D.	मह्यम् or मे	तुभ्यम् or ते
Ab.	मत्	त्वत्
G.	मम or मे	तव or ते
L.	मयि	त्वयि

Dual.

N.	आवाम् 'we two;'	युवाम् 'you two.'
Ac.	आवाम् or नौ	युवाम् or वाम्
I.	आवाभ्याम्	युवाभ्याम्
D.	आवाभ्याम् or नौ	युवाभ्याम् or वाम्
Ab.	आवाभ्याम्	युवाभ्याम्
G.	आवयोः or नौ	युवयोः or वाम्
L.	आवयोः	युवयोः

Plural.

N.	वयम् 'we;'	यूयम् 'you.'
Ac.	अस्मान् or नः	युष्मान् or वः
I.	अस्माभिः	युष्माभिः
D.	अस्मभ्यम् or नः	युष्मभ्यम् or वः
Ab.	अस्मत्	युष्मत्
G.	अस्माकम् or नः	युष्माकम् or वः
L.	अस्मासु	युष्मासु

§ 178. The optional shorter forms मा, त्वा, मे, ते, नौ, वाम् and नः, वः are never used at the beginning of a sentence or of a verse. Moreover the fuller forms माम्, त्वाम् &c. *only* are used before the particles च, वा, ह, अह and एव, *e. g.* त्वा मा च 'thee and me,' (not त्वा मा च).

2.—*Demonstrative Pronouns.*

§ 179. Bases:—

1. तद् 'that' or 'he, she, it' (who or which has been mentioned);
2. एतद् 'this' (who or which is very near to the speaker);
3. इदम् 'this' (referring to what is near);
4. अदस् 'that' (referring to what is remote).

Base:	तद्	एतद्	इदम्	अदस्

Masculine.

Singular.

N.	सः	एषः	अयम्	असौ
Ac.	तम्	एतम् or एनम्	इमम् or एनम्	अमुम्
I.	तेन	एतेन or एनेन	अनेन or एनेन	अमुना
D.	तस्मै	एतस्मै	अस्मै	अमुष्मै
Ab.	तस्मात्	एतस्मात्	अस्मात्	अमुष्मात्
G.	तस्य	एतस्य	अस्य	अमुष्य
L.	तस्मिन्	एतस्मिन्	अस्मिन्	अमुष्मिन्

Dual.

N.	तौ	एतौ	इमौ	अमू
Ac.	तौ	एतौ or एनौ	इमौ or एनौ	अमू
I.D.Ab.	ताभ्याम्	एताभ्याम्	आभ्याम्	अमूभ्याम्
G.L.	तयोः	एतयोः or एनयोः	अनयोः or एनयोः	अमुयोः

Plural.

N.	ते	एते	इमे	अमी
Ac.	तान्	एतान् or एनान्	इमान् or एनान्	अमून्
I.	तैः	एतैः	एभिः	अमीभिः
D.Ab.	तेभ्यः	एतेभ्यः	एभ्यः	अमीभ्यः
G.	तेषाम्	एतेषाम्	एषाम्	अमीषाम्
L.	तेषु	एतेषु	एषु	अमीषु

Feminine.

Singular.

N.	सा	एषा	इयम्	असौ
Ac.	ताम्	एताम् or एनाम्	इमाम् or एनाम्	अमूम्
I.	तया	एतया or एनया	अनया or एनया	अमुया
D.	तस्यै	एतस्यै	अस्यै	अमुष्यै
Ab.G.	तस्याः	एतस्याः	अस्याः	अमुष्याः
L.	तस्याम्	एतस्याम्	अस्याम्	अमुष्याम्

Dual.

N.	ते	एते	इमे	अमू
Ac.	ते	एते or एने	इमे or एने	अमू
I.D.Ab.	ताभ्याम्	एताभ्याम्	आभ्याम्	अमूभ्याम्
G.L.	तयोः	एतयोः or एनयोः	अनयोः or एनयोः	अमुयोः

Plural.

N.	ताः	एताः	इमाः	अमूः
Ac.	ताः	एताः or एनाः	इमाः or एनाः	अमूः
I.	ताभिः	एताभिः	आभिः	अमूभिः
D.Ab.	ताभ्यः	एताभ्यः	आभ्यः	अमूभ्यः
G.	तासाम्	एतासाम्	आसाम्	अमूषाम्
L.	तासु	एतासु	आसु	अमूषु

Neuter.
Singular.

N.	तत्	एतत्	इदम्	अदः
Ac.	तत्	एतत् or एनत्	इदम् or एनत्	अदः

I. and the following cases like the Masc.

Dual.

N.	ते	एते	इमे	अमू
Ac.	ते	एते or एने	इमे or एने	अमू

I. and the following cases like the Masc.

Plural.

N.	तानि	एतानि	इमानि	अमूनि
Ac.	तानि	एतानि or एनानि	इमानि or एनानि	अमूनि

I. and the following cases like the Masc.

§ 180. The final Visarga of the N. Sing. Masc. सः and एषः is dropped before words beginning with any other letter than short अ; before words beginning with short अ, अः is changed to ओ and the initial अ dropped; *e.g.* सः + आह becomes स आह, सः + गच्छति becomes स गच्छति, but सः + अब्रवीत् = सोऽब्रवीत्.

§ 181. The optional forms एनम्, एनेन &c. in the Accusatives Sing. Du. and Plur., the Instr. Sing. and the Gen. and Loc. Du. of एतद् and इदम् are used instead of एतम्, एतेन &c. and इमम्, अनेन &c. in a subsequent clause when the persons or things denoted by them have in a preceding clause been denoted by forms of एतद् and इदम्; *e. g.* अनेन व्याकरणमधीतमेनं छन्दो ऽध्यापय 'he has studied grammar, teach him prosody.'

3.—*The Relative Pronoun.*

§ 182. Base :— यद् 'who, which.'

	Masc.	Fem.	Neut.
		Singular.	
N.	यः	या	यत्
Ac.	यम्	याम्	यत्
I.	येन	यया	येन
D.	यस्मै	यस्यै	यस्मै
Ab.	यस्मात्	यस्याः	यस्मात्
G.	यस्य	यस्याः	यस्य
L.	यस्मिन्	यस्याम्	यस्मिन्

Dual.

N. Ac.	यौ	ये	ये
I. D. Ab.	याभ्याम्	याभ्याम्	याभ्याम्
G. L.	ययोः	ययोः	ययोः

Plural.

N.	ये	याः	यानि
Ac.	यान्	याः	यानि
I.	यैः	याभिः	यैः
D. Ab.	येभ्यः	याभ्यः	येभ्यः
G.	येषाम्	यासाम्	येषाम्
L.	येषु	यासु	येषु

4.—*The Interrogative Pronoun.*

§ 183. Base:— किम् 'who? which? what?'

	Masc.	Fem.	Neut.
		Singular.	
N.	कः	का	किम्
Ac.	कम्	काम्	किम्
I.	केन	कया	केन
D.	कस्मै	कस्यै	कस्मै
Ab.	कस्मात्	कस्याः	कस्मात्
G.	कस्य	कस्याः	कस्य
L.	कस्मिन्	कस्याम्	कस्मिन्
		Dual.	
N. Ac.	कौ	के	के
I. D. Ab.	काभ्याम्	काभ्याम्	काभ्याम्
G. L.	कयोः	कयोः	कयोः
		Plural.	
N.	के	काः	कानि
Ac.	कान्	काः	कानि
I.	कैः	काभिः	कैः
D. Ab.	केभ्यः	काभ्यः	केभ्यः
G.	केषाम्	कासाम्	केषाम्
L.	केषु	कासु	केषु

§ 184. कतर 'who or which of two?' and कतम 'who or which of many?' are in all the three genders declined regularly like तद् (§ 179.)

5.—*Indefinite Pronouns.*

§ 185. Indefinite pronouns are formed by the addition of चित्, or of चन or of अपि, to the interrogative pronoun किम् in all its cases: किंचित् or किंचन, or किमपि 'some one, something; any one, anything.'

Masc. Sing. N. कश्चित्, कश्चन, कोऽपि;
    Ac. कंचित्, कंचन, कमपि;
    I. केनचित्, केनचन, केनापि; &c.

§ 186. चित्, चन, and अपि are in the same manner added to derivatives of किम्; *e. g.* कति 'how many?' कतिचित् 'some;' कदा 'when? कदाचित्, or कदाचन, or कदापि 'sometime, any time,' &c.

6.—*Reflexive Pronouns.*

§ 187. The meaning of the reflexive pronoun is in Sanskrit expressed by the noun आत्मन् 'soul, self' (§ 116); though itself always masculine, it denotes all the three genders, and it is used only in the Singular, even when referring to several persons: *e.g.* न शोचाम्यहमात्मानम् 'I (*i.e.* Damayantî) do not sorrow for myself;' गोपायन्ति कुलस्त्रिय आत्मानम् 'noble women protect themselves.'

§ 188. The indeclinable स्वयम् is employed, like the English 'self,' to express emphasis or distinction; *e. g.* स्वयमहमवसम् 'I myself dwelt.'

7.—*Possessive Pronouns.*

§ 189.				
मदीय	masc. neut.,	मदीया	fem.	⎫
मामक	masc. neut.,	मामिका	fem.	⎬ 'my, mine.'
मामकीन	masc. neut.,	मामकीना	fem.	⎭
त्वदीय	masc. neut.,	त्वदीया	fem.	⎫
तावक	masc. neut.,	तावकी	fem.	⎬ 'thy, thine.'
तावकीन	masc. neut.,	तावकीना	fem.	⎭
अस्मदीय	masc. neut.,	अस्मदीया	fem.	⎫
आस्माक	masc. neut.,	आस्माकी	fem.	⎬ 'our, ours.'
आस्माकीन	masc. neut.,	आस्माकीना	fem.	⎭

युष्मदीय masc. neut.,	युष्मदीया	fem.	⎫	
यौष्माक masc. neut.,	यौष्माकी	fem.	⎬	'your, yours.'
यौष्माकीण masc. neut.,	यौष्माकीणा	fem.	⎭	
तदीय masc. neut.,	तदीया	fem.		'his, her, hers, its, their, theirs.'
एतदीय masc. neut.,	एतदीया	fem.		'belonging to this' (person or thing).
स्व masc. neut.,	स्वा	fem.		'one's own.'

§ 190. All these possessive pronouns, except स्व, are declined regularly like कान्त (§ 131), and नदी (§ 141). स्व follows § 199.

8.—*Correlative Pronouns.*

§ 191. Correlative pronouns are derived from the bases of the pronouns तद्, एतद्, इदम्, यद् and किम्.

Base:	तद्		एतद्		इदम्	
	तावत्	'so much.'	एतावत्	'so much.'	इयत्	'so much.'
	तति	'so many.'	—		—	
	तादृश ⎫ तादृश ⎭	'such like.'	एतादृश ⎫ एतादृश ⎭	'such like.'	ईदृश ⎫ ईदृश ⎭	'such like.'
Base:	यद्		किम्			
	यावत्	'as much.'	कियत्	'how much?'		
	यति	'as many.'	कति	'how many?'		
	यादृश ⎫ यादृश ⎭	'what like.'	कीदृश ⎫ कीदृश ⎭	'what like?'		

§ 192. तावत्, एतावत्, इयत्, यावत् and कियत्, follow Declension VIII. (§ 109). तति, यति and कति are declined only in the Plural; they take no termination in the N. and Ac., in the remaining cases they follow अग्नि (§ 136); *e.g.* N. and Ac. तति, I. ततिभिः &c. तादृश, एतादृश &c. follow Decl. II. (§ 76); *e.g.* Masc. Sing. N. तादृक्, Ac. तादृशम् &c. तादृश, एतादृश &c. are in the Masc. and Neut. declined like कान्त (§ 131); in the Fem. the affix ई is added, *e. g.* तादृश, Fem. base तादृशी, and the base then declined like नदी (§ 141).

9.—*Reciprocal Pronouns.*

§ 193. The reciprocal pronouns अन्योन्य, इतरेतर, परस्पर 'each other, one another,' appear commonly only in the Accusative or adverbial form

अन्योन्यम्, इतरेतरम्, परस्परम्, or as first members of compounds, e.g. अन्यो-न्यसंयोग, इतरेतरयोग, परस्परसंबन्ध 'mutual union.' But other forms occur occasionally, e.g. Sing. I. अन्योन्येन; G. अन्योन्यस्य; L. अन्योन्यस्मिन्. Ab. परस्परात् G. परस्परस्य.

10.—*Pronominal Adverbs.*

§ 194. The pronominal adverbs which are most commonly used, are derived from the bases of the pronouns तद्, इदम् (special base for several forms, अ), यद्, and किम् (in some adverbs कु):

Bases:	तद्,	इदम् (अ)	यद्	किम् (कु).
1.	ततः 'thence, thereupon, therefore.'	इतः) 'hence, अतः) therefore.'	यतः 'whence, since, because.'	कुतः 'whence? why? how?'
2.	तत्र 'there.'	अत्र 'here.'	यत्र 'where.'	कुत्र } 'where?' क्व }
3.	तथा 'thus.'	इत्थम् 'thus.'	यथा 'as.'	कथम् 'how?'
4.	तदा } 'then, at तदानीम् } that time.	इदानीम् 'now.'	यदा 'when.'	कदा 'when?'
5.	तर्हि 'then, therefore.'		यर्हि 'when.'	कर्हि 'when?'

11.—*Pronominal Adjectives.*

§ 195. अन्य 'another,' अन्यतर 'either of two,' इतर 'other,' and एकतम 'one of many,' are in all the three genders declined like तद् (179); e.g.

Sing. N. Masc. अन्यः, Fem. अन्या; Neut. अन्यत्.
    D. ,, अन्यस्मै; ,, अन्यस्यै; ,, अन्यस्मै.
Plur. N. ,, अन्ये; ,, अन्याः; ,, अन्यानि. &c.

अन्यतम 'one of many' is declined like कान्त (§ 131).

§ 196. सर्व 'every, all,' विश्व 'every, all,' सम when conveying the sense 'all,' सिम 'all,' एकतर 'one of two,' follow the same declension, except in the N. Ac. Sing. of the neuter gender where they follow कान्त; e.g.

Sing. N. Masc. सर्वः; Fem. सर्वा; Neut. सर्वम्.
    D. ,, सर्वस्मै; ,, सर्वस्यै ,, सर्वस्मै.
Plur. N. ,, सर्वे; ,, सर्वाः; ,, सर्वाणि, &c.

§ 197. उभय 'both' has according to the best authorities no Dual; in the Sing. and Plur. Masc. and Neut. it is declined like सर्व. The Fem. is उभयी, declined like नदी (§ 141).—उभ 'both' is invariably dual, and declined like कान्त (§ 131).

§ 198. नेम 'half,' is declined like सर्व; but the N. Plur. Masc. is नेमे or नेमाः.

§ 199. अधर 'lower, inferior,' अन्तर 'outer,' अपर 'other,' अवर 'posterior, western,' उत्तर 'superior, northern, subsequent,' दक्षिण 'right, southern' (—not दाक्षण 'clever,' which follows कान्त throughout), पर 'subsequent,' पूर्व 'prior, eastern,' and स्व 'own' are declined like सर्व, but they may in the Ab. and L. Sing., and in the N. Plur. optionally follow कान्त (§ 131); *e.g.*

Masc. Sing. D. अधरस्मै; Ab. अधरस्मात् or अधरात्; Plur. N. अधरे or अधराः.

§ 200. अर्ध 'half,' अल्प 'little, few,' कनिपय 'some,' and चरम 'last,' follow कान्त throughout; but they may form the N. Plur. Masc. optionally like सर्व (§ 196); *e.g.*

Masc. Plur. N. अर्धाः or अर्धे.

कनिपय forms its Feminine कनिपया or कनिपयी, the latter declined like नदी.

CHAPTER VI.

NUMERALS AND THEIR DECLENSION

§ 201. *Cardinals and Ordinals:*

1	१	एक 'one.'	प्रथम *m. n.* प्रथमा *f.* 'first.'
2	२	द्वि	द्वितीय, °या
3	३	त्रि	तृतीय, °या
4	४	चतुर्	चतुर्थ, °र्थी
5	५	पञ्चन्	पञ्चम, °मी
6	६	पष्	पष्ठ, °ष्ठी
7	७	सप्तन्	सप्तम, °मी
8	८	अष्टन्	अष्टम, °मी
9	९	नवन्	नवम, °मी
10	१०	दशन्	दशम, °मी

11	११	एकादशन्	एकादश, ॰शी
12	१२	द्वादशन्	द्वादश, ॰शी
13	१३	त्रयोदशन्	त्रयोदश, ॰शी
14	१४	चतुर्दशन्	चतुर्दश, ॰शी
15	१५	पञ्चदशन्	पञ्चदश, ॰शी
16	१६	षोडशन्	षोडश, ॰शी
17	१७	सप्तदशन्	सप्तदश, ॰शी
18	१८	अष्टादशन्	अष्टादश, ॰शी
19	१९	नवदशन् or ऊनविंशति	नवदश, ॰शी; or ऊनविंश, ॰शी; or ऊनविंशतितम, ॰मी
20	२०	विंशति f.	विंश, ॰शी or विंशतितम, ॰मी
21	२१	एकविंशति	एकविंश, ॰शी, or ॰तितम, ॰मी
22	२२	द्वाविंशति	द्वाविंश, ॰शी, or ॰तितम, ॰मी
23	२३	त्रयोविंशति	त्रयोविंश, ॰शी, ,, ,, ,,
24	२४	चतुर्विंशति	चतुर्विंश, ॰शी, ,, ,, ,,
25	२५	पञ्चविंशति	पञ्चविंश, ॰शी, ,, ,, ,,
26	२६	षड्विंशति	षड्विंश, ॰शी, ,, ,, ,,
27	२७	सप्तविंशति	सप्तविंश, ॰शी, ,, ,, ,,
28	२८	अष्टाविंशति	अष्टाविंश, ॰शी, ,, ,, ,,
29	२९	नवविंशति or ऊनत्रिंशत्	नवविंश, ॰शी, or नवविंशतितम, ॰मी, or ऊनत्रिंश, ॰शी, or ऊनत्रिंशत्तम, ॰मी
30	३०	त्रिंशत् f.	त्रिंश, ॰शी or त्रिंशत्तम, ॰मी
31	३१	एकत्रिंशत्	एकत्रिंश ॰शी or एकत्रिंशत्तम, ॰मी
32	३२	द्वात्रिंशत्	
33	३३	त्रयस्त्रिंशत्	
34	३४	चतुस्त्रिंशत्	
35	३५	पञ्चत्रिंशत्	
36	३६	षट्त्रिंशत्	
37	३७	सप्तत्रिंशत्	
38	३८	अष्टात्रिंशत्	
39	३९	नवत्रिंशत् or ऊनचत्वारिंशत्	

40	४०	चत्वारिंशत् *f.*	चत्वारिंश, ॰शी or चत्वारिंशत्तम, ॰मी
41	४१	एकचत्वारिंशत्	
42	४२	द्वाचत्वारिंशत् or	
		द्विचत्वारिंशत्	
43	४३	त्रयश्चत्वारिंशत् or	
		त्रिचत्वारिंशत्	
44	४४	चतुश्चत्वारिंशत्	
45	४५	पञ्चचत्वारिंशत्	
46	४६	षट्चत्वारिंशत्	
47	४७	सप्तचत्वारिंशत्	
48	४८	अष्टाचत्वारिंशत् or	
		अष्टचत्वारिंशत्	
49	४९	नवचत्वारिंशत् or	
		ऊनपञ्चाशत्	
50	५०	पञ्चाशत् *f.*	पञ्चाश, ॰शी or पञ्चाशत्तम, ॰मी
51	५१	एकपञ्चाशत्	
52	५२	द्वापञ्चाशत् or	
		द्विपञ्चाशत्	
53	५३	त्रयःपञ्चाशत् or	
		त्रिपञ्चाशत्	
54	५४	चतुःपञ्चाशत्	
55	५५	पञ्चपञ्चाशत्	
56	५६	षट्पञ्चाशत्	
57	५७	सप्तपञ्चाशत्	
58	५८	अष्टापञ्चाशत् or	
		अष्टपञ्चाशत्	
59	५९	नवपञ्चाशत् or	
		ऊनषष्टि	
60	६०	षष्टि *f.*	षष्टितम, ॰मी
61	६१	एकषष्टि	एकषष्ट, ॰ष्टी or एकषष्टितम, ॰मी
62	६२	द्वाषष्टि or द्विषष्टि	

63	६३	त्रयष्षष्टि or त्रिषष्टि	
64	६४	चतुष्षष्टि	
65	६५	पञ्चषष्टि	
66	६६	षट्षष्टि	
67	६७	सप्तषष्टि	
68	६८	अष्टाषष्टि or अष्टषष्टि	
69	६९	नवषष्टि or ऊनसप्तति	
70	७०	सप्तति f.	सप्ततितम, °मी.
71	७१	एकसप्तति	एकसप्तत, °ती or एकसप्ततितम, °मी.
72	७२	द्वासप्तति or द्विसप्तति	
73	७३	त्रयस्सप्तति or त्रिसप्तति	
74	७४	चतुस्सप्तति	
75	७५	पञ्चसप्तति	
76	७६	षट्सप्तति	
77	७७	सप्तसप्तति	
78	७८	अष्टासप्तति or अष्टसप्तति	
79	७९	नवसप्तति or ऊनाशीति	
80	८०	अशीति f.	अशीतितम, °मी.
81	८१	एकाशीति	एकाशीत °ती, or एकाशीतितम, °मी.
82	८२	द्वयशीति	
83	८३	त्र्यशीति	
84	८४	चतुरशीति	
85	८५	पञ्चाशीति	
86	८६	षडशीति	
87	८७	सप्ताशीति	
88	८८	अष्टाशीति	

89	८९	नवाशीति or ऊननवति	
90	९०	नवति f.	नवतितम, ˚मी
91	९१	एकनवति	एकनवत, ˚ती or एकनवतितम, ˚मी.
92	९२	द्वानवति or द्विनवति	
93	९३	त्रयोनवति or त्रिनवति	
94	९४	चतुर्नवति	
95	९५	पञ्चनवति	
96	९६	षण्णवति	
97	९७	सप्तनवति	
98	९८	अष्टानवति or अष्टनवति	
99	९९	नवनवति or ऊनशत	
100	१००	शत n.	शततम, ˚मी.
200	२००	द्विशत n. or द्वे शते	द्विशततम, ˚मी.
300	३००	त्रिशत n. or त्रीणि शतानि	
400	४००	चतुश्शत n. or चत्वारि शतानि	
500	५००	पञ्चशत n. or पञ्च शतानि	
600	६००	पट्शत n. or पट् शतानि	
700	७००	सप्तशत n. or सप्त शतानि	
800	८००	अष्टशत n. or अष्ट शतानि	
900	९००	नवशत n. or नव शतानि	

1000	१०००	सहस्र n. or दश-	सहस्रतम, मी.
		शत n. or दशशती f.	
10,000	१००००	अयुत n.	
100,000	१०००००	लक्ष n. लक्षा f.	

§ 202. The cardinal numbers between 100 and 200, 200 and 300 &c., are commonly expressed by means of अधिक 'exceeded by,' *e. g.* पञ्चाधिकं शतम् or पञ्चाधिकशतम् '100 exceeded by 5', *i.e.* 105; पञ्चदशाधिकं शतम् or पञ्चदशाधिकशतम् 115; पञ्चाशदधिकं शतम्, or पञ्चाशदधिकशतम्, 150. Similarly ऊन is used to denote 'diminished by,' *e. g.* पञ्चोनं शतम् or पञ्चोनशतम् '100 diminished by 5,' *i. e.* 95.

§ 203. In order to denote the cardinal numbers 111—159, 211—259 &c., one may derive from the cardinals एकादशन् 11, &c. an adjective which is formally the same as the shorter form of the corresponding ordinal, and make it agree with the cardinal for 100, 200 &c. in gender, number, and case; *e. g.* पञ्चदशं शतम् 115; पञ्चाशं शतम् 150; पञ्चदशं द्विशतम् 215 &c.

Declension of the Cardinals and Ordinals.

§ 204. एक 'one' (Plur. 'some') is declined in the Sing. and Plur. in all the three genders, and follows the declension of सर्व (§ 196); *e. g.*

Sing. N.	एकः	*m.*,	एका	*f.*,	एकम्	*n.*
	D.	एकस्मै *m.*,	एकस्यै *f.*,	एकस्मै *n.*		
Plur. N.	एके	*m.*,	एकाः	*f.*,	एकानि	*n.*

§ 205. द्वि 'two' is declined only in the Dual.

N. V. Ac. द्वौ *m.* द्वे *f.* द्वे *n.*
I. D. Ab. द्वाभ्याम् *m. f. n.*
G. L. द्वयोः *m. f. n.*

§ 206. त्रि 'three' and चतुर् 'four' are declined in the Plur. in all the three genders.

	Masc.		Fem.		Neut.	
N.V.	त्रयः	चत्वारः	तिस्रः	चतस्रः	त्रीणि	चत्वारि
Ac.	त्रीन्	चतुरः				
I.	त्रिभिः	चतुर्भिः	तिसृभिः	चतसृभिः	त्रिभिः	चतुर्भिः
D.Ab.	त्रिभ्यः	चतुर्भ्यः	तिसृभ्यः	चतसृभ्यः	त्रिभ्यः	चतुर्भ्यः
G.	त्रयाणाम्	चतुर्णाम्	तिसृणाम्	चतसृणाम्	त्रयाणाम्	चतुर्णाम्
L.	त्रिषु	चतुर्षु	तिसृषु	चतसृषु	त्रिषु	चतुर्षु

DECLENSION OF NUMERALS.

§ 207. पञ्चन् 'five,' सप्तन् 'seven,' नवन् 'nine' and the following cardinals up to नवदशन् have one form only for all the three genders, and are declined in the Plural, thus: N. V. Ac. पञ्च; I. पञ्चभिः; D. Ab. पञ्चभ्यः; G. पञ्चानाम्; L. पञ्चसु.

§ 208. षष् 'six' has one form for all the three genders and is declined in the Plural, thus: N. V. Ac. षट्; I. षड्भिः; D. Ab. षड्भ्यः; G. षण्णाम्; L. षट्सु.

§ 209. अष्टन् 'eight' has one form for all the three genders and is declined in the Plural, thus:—

N. V. Ac. अष्ट or अष्टौ
I. अष्टभिः or अष्टाभिः
D. Ab. अष्टभ्यः or अष्टाभ्यः
G. अष्टानाम्
L. अष्टसु or अष्टासु

§ 210. The cardinals from ऊनविंशति 19, विंशति 20, to नवनवति 99, are feminine substantives, and follow as such Decl. XIII., or II.; *e.g.* N. विंशतिः 20, पञ्चाशत् 50; Ac. विंशतिम्, पञ्चाशतम्; I. विंशत्या, पञ्चाशता &c.—शत 100 &c. follow कान्त (§ 131).

§ 211. The ordinals follow in Masc. and Neut. कान्त (§ 131), in the Feminine either कान्ता, or नदी (§ 141). But प्रथम 'the first' may optionally form the N. Plur. Masc., and द्वितीय and तृतीय may optionally form the D. Ab. and L. Sing. Masc. Fem. Neut., like अन्य (§ 195); *e. g.*

Sing. N. प्रथमः *m.* प्रथमा *f.* प्रथमम् *n.*
  D. प्रथमाय *m.* प्रथमायै *f.* प्रथमाय *n.*
Plur. N. प्रथमाः or प्रथमाः *f.* प्रथमानि *n.*
  प्रथमे *m.*
Sing. N. द्वितीयः *m.* द्वितीया *f.* द्वितीयम् *n.*
  D. द्वितीयाय or द्वितीयायै or द्वितीयाय or
  द्वितीयस्मै *m.* द्वितीयस्यै *f.* द्वितीयस्मै *n.*
Plur. N. द्वितीयाः *m.* द्वितीयाः *f.* द्वितीयानि *n.*

§ 212. *Numeral Adverbs:*

(*a*) सकृत् 'once;' द्विः 'twice;' त्रिः 'thrice;' चतुः 'four times;' पञ्चकृत्वः 'five times;' षट्कृत्वः 'six times,' &c.

(*b*) एकधा 'in one way;' द्विधा or द्वेधा 'in two ways;' त्रिधा or त्रेधा 'in three ways;' चतुर्धा 'in four ways;' पञ्चधा 'in five ways;' षोढा or षड्धा 'in six ways,' &c.

(c) एकशः 'singly, by ones;' द्विशः 'two and two, by twos;' त्रिशः 'three and three, by threes,' &c.

§ 213.   *Other numeral derivatives:*

(a) द्वय *m. n.*, द्वयी *f.* or द्वितय *m. n.*, द्वितयी *f.* 'twofold, consisting of two parts;'

त्रय *m. n.*, त्रयी *f.* or त्रितय *m. n.* त्रितयी *f.* 'threefold, consisting of three parts;'

चतुष्टय *m. n.*, चतुष्टयी *f.* 'fourfold, consisting of four parts;'

पञ्चतय *m. n.*, पञ्चतयी *f.* 'fivefold, consisting of five parts,' &c.

These adjectives are declined regularly in the Masc. and Neut. like कान्त, (§ 131) in the Fem. like नदी (§ 141); but in the N. Plur. Masc. they may optionally follow अन्य (§ 195); *e. g.*

Sing. N. द्वयः *m.*;   द्वयी *f*; द्वयम् *n.*

Plur. N. द्वयाः or द्वये; *m.*; द्वयाः *f*; द्वयानि *n.*

(b)   द्वय *n.* or द्वयी *f.*, or द्वितय, *n.* 'a pair.'

त्रय *n.* or त्रयी *f.* or त्रितय *n.* 'a triad, or collection of three.'

चतुष्टय *n.* 'a collection of four.'

पञ्चत् *f.* 'a pentad, or collection of five.'

षट् *n.* 'a collection of six.'

दशत् *f.* 'a decad, or collection of ten,' &c.

CHAPTER VII.
CONJUGATION OF VERBS.

§ 214.   Verbs are given in the dictionary in the form of *roots*; *e. g.* भू 'to be,' अद् 'to eat,' &c.

§ 215. (a) Conjugation consists in making the verbal root undergo certain modifications and in the addition to it of certain prefixes and terminations, which denote the various persons, numbers, voices, tenses, and moods, and by which primitive verbs are distinguished from derivative verbs.

(b)   Some tenses are formed by means of auxiliary verbs; (*Periphrastic* tenses).

§ 216. (a) Verbs have *three Numbers*, a *singular* number, a *dual* number, and a *plural* number, and in each number *three Persons*, a *first* person, a *second* person, and a *third* person. The dual number denotes, as it does in declension, 'two.'

(b) The terminations which denote the persons in the different numbers are called *personal terminations*.

§ 217. (a) Verbs have *six Tenses*, viz. *Present, Imperfect, Perfect, Aorist, Future,* and *Conditional*. The Perfect, the Aorist, and the Future have each two forms; *Reduplicated* Perfect and *Periphrastic* Perfect; *Radical* Aorist and *S*-Aorist; *Simple* Future and *Periphrastic* Future.

(b) The Aorist denotes time past.

§ 218. (a) The Present tense distinguishes *three Moods*, Present *Indicative* (commonly called *Present*), Present *Potential* or *Optative* (commonly called *Potential* or *Optative*), and Present *Imperative* (commonly called *Imperative*). The Imperfect and the Aorist distinguish each an *Indicative* and a *Subjunctive*. The remaining tenses have only an Indicative. There exists, besides, the *Benedictive*, which, although it might be considered a Potential of the Aorist, it is customary to treat as a separate tense.

(b) The *Subjunctive* of the Imperfect and of the Aorist is, in classical Sanskrit, used only after the prohibitive particle मा and after मा स्म. It differs from the Indicative by the absence of the Augment which is prefixed to the root in the Indicative; e. g.

rt. भू ' to be;' Impf. Ind. अभवत्; Subj. भवत्.
  „   Aor. Ind. अभूत्; Subj. भूत्.
rt. इष् ' to wish;' Impf. Ind. ऐच्छत्; Subj. इच्छत्.

मा भूत्, मा स्म भवत्, 'he should not be.'

In the following it will be unnecessary to treat separately of the Impf. Subj. and Aor. Subj., and the terms Imperfect and Aorist will be used for the Impf. Ind. and Aor. Ind. only.

(c) The *Potential* or *Optative* of the Present denotes possibility, probability, supposition, hope, wish, command, &c., and its meaning may be expressed by such auxiliary verbs as 'may, shall,' &c.; sometimes it may be translated by the English Subjunctive mood. The *Benedictive* is used to express a blessing or wish.

§ 219. A table showing the tenses and moods which are in use in classical Sanskrit :—

	A *Indicative.*	B *Subjunctive.*	C *Potential.*	D *Imperative.*
1.	Present.	———	Present.	Present.
2.	Imperfect.	Imperfect.	———	———
3.	Perfect. (a) Reduplicated. (b) Periphrastic.	———	———	———
4.	Aorist. (a) Radical. (b) S-Aorist.	Aorist.	Benedictive.	———
5.	Future. (a) Simple. (b) Periphrastic.	———	———	———
6.	Conditional.	———	———	———

§ 220. The conjugation of verbs is divided into :—

I.—Conjugation of *Primitive Roots*, and

II.—Conjugation of *Derivative Verbal Bases*.

The conjugation of derivative verbal bases is subdivided into :—

1. Conjugation of *roots of the tenth* (*churâdi*) *class* and of the Causal.
2. Conjugation of the *Desiderative*.
3. Conjugation of the *Frequentative*.
4. Conjugation of *Nominal verbs*.

I.—CONJUGATION OF PRIMITIVE ROOTS.

§ 221. Primitive Roots are the roots contained in the *first nine* classes of the collections of roots compiled by the Native grammarians. They differ from derivative verbal bases in this :—in the case of derivative verbal bases the personal terminations and the characteristic marks of the various tenses and moods cannot, in general, be added to the root before by the addition of certain letters or other modifications which remain throughout in all tenses and moods, a *derivative base* has been derived from it; in the case of primitive roots the personal terminations and the characteristic marks of the various tenses and moods are (with some modifications in the special tenses) combined with the simple and unmodified root; e. g.

Prim. root.	Causal Base.	Desid. Base.	Rt. of cl. X. चुर् 'to steal.'
या 'to go;'	यापि 'to cause to go.'	यियास 'to wish to go.'	Deriv. Base. चोरि.
Pres. Ind. याति yá-ti;	यापयति yápay-a-ti;	यियासति yiyása-ti;	चोरयति choray-a-ti;
Simple Fut. यास्यति yá-sya-ti.	यापयिष्यति, yápay-i-shya-ti.	यियासिष्यति yiyás-i-shya-ti.	चोरयिष्यति choray-i-shya-ti.

§ 222. Primitive roots are conjugated in three voices, viz:—

(a) In the *Parasmaipada* or 'active voice' (literally 'voice for another');

(b) In the *Âtmanepada* or 'reflective voice' (literally 'voice for one's self'); and

(c) In the *Passive* voice.

In the Parasmaipada and Âtmanepada the personal termination denotes the agent of the action which is expressed by the root, e. g. Par. ददाति dadá-ti, give-he i. e. 'he gives,' Âtm. आदत्ते ádat-te, take-he, i. e. 'he takes.' In the Passive voice the personal termination denotes either the object of the action expressed by the root, e. g. दीयते díya-te, given-is-he, i. e. 'he is given,' or it denotes, in the case of intransitive verbs, the action itself which is expressed by the root, e. g. गम्यते (तेन,) it is gone (by him) i. e. he goes.

§ 223. In the Perfect, the Aorist, the two Futures, the Conditional, and the Benedictive, the formation of the Passive voice is generally the same as that of the Âtmanepada or reflective voice. In the three moods of the Present tense, however, and in the Imperfect, the formation of the Âtmanepada differs from that of the Passive, and it is therefore necessary to separate the conjugation of the latter voice from that of the Parasmaipada and Âtmanepada.

1.—THE PARASMAIPADA AND ÂTMANEPADA.

§ 224. Many roots are throughout all tenses and moods conjugated both in Parasmaipada and in Âtmanepada, others only in one voice; others again are conjugated in one voice, but they also form some tenses in the other voice; some are restricted to one voice or the other, as certain prepositions are prefixed to them.

§ 225. The Parasmaipada may be said to be used, when the fruit or consequence of the action expressed by the verb accrues to another person or thing than the agent, whereas the Âtmanepada is employed when the fruit or consequence of the action expressed by the verb accrues to the agent; *e. g.* कृ 'to do;' Pres. Ind. Par. करोति 'he does' (for somebody else), Âtmane. कुरुते 'he does' (for himself). यज् 'to sacrifice;' Pres. Ind. Par. यजति (the priest) sacrifices (for somebody else); Âtmane. यजते (the sacrificer) sacrifices (for himself). दा 'to give;' Pres. Ind. Par. ददाति 'he gives.' आदा 'to take;' Pres. Ind. Âtm. आदत्ते 'he takes.' This rule is, however, by no means universally valid and the right use of the two voices must be learnt from the practice of the best writers or from the dictionary.

§ 226. The Parasmaipada and Âtmanepada are formally distinguished by two sets of *Personal terminations,* one of which is added in the Parasmaipada, whereas the other set is always added in the Âtmanepada.

§ 227. The following table contains the personal terminations which with some modifications, are added in the various tenses and moods in Parasmaipada and Âtmanepada. The first column contains the personal terminations of the Present Indicative and of the Simple Future, the second those of the Imperfect, the Present Potential, the Aorist, the Conditional, and the Benedictive; the third those of the Reduplicated Perfect, and the fourth those of the Present Imperative.

Personal terminations of the various tenses and moods in Parasmaipada and Âtmanepada.

		I. Pres. Ind. & Simple Fut.		II. Imperf., Pres. Pot., Aorist, Condit. & Benedict.		III. Redupl. Perfect.		IV. Pres. Imperat.	
		Parasmai.	Âtmane.	Parasmai.	Âtmane.	Parasmai.	Âtmane.	Parasmai.	Âtmane.
Sing.	1.	मि	ए	अम्	इ	अ	ए	आनि	ऐ
	2.	सि	से	:(स्)	थाः(थास्)	थ	से	धि	स्व
	3.	ति	ते	त्	त	अ	ए	तु	ताम्
Dual.	1.	वः (वस्)	वहे	व	वहि	व	वहे	आव	आवहै
	2.	थः (थम्)	आथे	तम्	आथाम्	अथुः	आथे	तम्	आथाम्
	3.	तः (तस्)	आते	ताम्	आताम्	अतुः	आते	ताम्	आताम्
Plur.	1.	मः (मस्)	महे	म	महि	म	महे	आम	आमहै
	2.	थ	ध्वे	त	ध्वम्	अ	ध्वे	त	ध्वम्
	3.	अन्ति	अन्ते	अन्	अन्त	उः	इरे	अन्तु	अन्ताम्

Augment and Reduplication.

§ 228. In order to save repetition we give here the general rules concerning the Augment and the Reduplication of roots.

§ 229. (a) The *Augment* (i. e. 'increase') consists in the vowel अ, prefixed to the root; *e. g.*

rt. तुद् 'to strike;' Impf. Par. अतुदत् *a-tudat*.

(b) When the augment अ is prefixed to a root commencing with a vowel, the result of the combination of the two vowels is the Vṛiddhi-vowel or the Vṛiddhi-syllable of the radical vowel; *e.g.*

rt. अत्	'to go;' Impf. Par.	आतत्.
rt. आस्	'to sit;' Impf. Âtm.	आस्त.
rt. इष्	'to wish,' Special base इच्छ; Impf. Par. ऐच्छत्.
rt. ईक्ष्	'to see;' Impf. Âtm.	ऐक्षत.
rt. उख्	'to go;' Impf. Par.	औखत्.
rt. ऊह्	'to comprehend;' Impf. Âtm.	औहत.
rt. ऋष्	'to go;' Impf. Par.	आर्षत्.
rt. एध्	'to grow;' Impf. Âtm.	ऐधत.
rt. ओख्	'to dry;' Impf. Par.	औखत्.

(c) When one or more prepositions are prefixed to a root, the augment takes its place after the preposition or prepositions and immediately before the root; *e. g.*

rt. पत् with prep. उद्; Pres. Ind. Par. उत्पतति; Impf. Par. उदपतत् *ud-apatat*.

„ „ „ सम् and उद्; Pres. Ind. Par. समुत्पतति; Impf. Par. समुदपतत् *samud-apatat*.

(d) When the letter स् is prefixed to कृ 'to do,' after the prepositions सम्, परि, उप, or to कृ 'to scatter,' after the prepositions उप or प्रति, the augment and the reduplicative syllable take their place after the prepositions but before the inserted स्; *e. g.* Pres. Ind. Par. संस्करोति; Impf. समस्करोत्; Perf. संचस्कार.

§ 230. *Reduplication* consists in the doubling of the first vowel of a root together with any consonant or consonants that precede it; *e. g.*

rt. तुद् 'to strike;' reduplicated तुतुद्.
rt. दरिद्रा 'to be poor;' „ ददरिद्रा.

That portion of a reduplicated form which is prefixed to the root is called the *reduplicative syllable*, e. g. the first नु in तुनुद, or the first द in ददरिद्रा.

§ 231. (a) An aspirate letter of a root is in the reduplicative syllable represented by the corresponding unaspirate letter; e. g.

    rt. छिद् 'to split;' reduplicated चिच्छिद्. (§ 54).
    rt. धा   'to place;'   ,,   दधा.
    rt. भुज्   'to enjoy;'   ,,   बुभुज्.

(b) A guttural by the corresponding palatal (guttural aspirate by palatal unaspirate); ह by ज्; e. g.

    rt. कम् 'to love;' reduplicated चकम्.
    rt. गम् 'to go;'   ,,   जगम्.
    rt. खन् 'to dig;'   ,,   चखन्.
    rt. घस् 'to eat;'   ,,   जघस्.
    rt. हु   'to sacrifice;' ,,   जुहु.

(c) If a root commences with more consonants than one, only the first (or the letter which according to (a) and (b) ought to be substituted for it) is repeated in the reduplicative syllable; e. g.

    rt. श्रु   'to hear;' reduplicated शुश्रु.
    rt. भ्राज् 'to shine;'   ,,   बभ्राज्.
    rt. क्रम् 'to go;'   ,,   चक्रम्.

(d) But if a root commences with a sibilant which is followed immediately by a hard consonant, this hard consonant or its representative must be repeated in the reduplicative syllable; e. g.

    rt. स्तम्भ् 'to support;' reduplicated तस्तम्भ्.
    rt. स्था   'to stand;'   ,,   तस्था.
    rt. स्कन्द् 'to drop;'   ,,   चस्कन्द्.

(e) Radical अ, आ and ऋ are in the reduplicative syllable represented by अ; radical इ, ई, and radical, *not final,* ए and ऐ by इ; radical उ, ऊ, औ and radical, *not final,* ओ by उ; final ए, ऐ and ओ by अ; e. g.

    rt. भ्राज् 'to shine;' reduplicated बभ्राज्.
    rt. कॢप् 'to be fit;'   ,,   चकॢप्.
    rt. छिद् 'to split;'   ,,   चिच्छिद्.
    rt. क्री 'to buy;'   ,,   चिक्री.
    rt. वेप् 'to tremble;'   ,,   विवेप्.

rt. टीक् 'to approach;' reduplicated डुटीक्.
but rt. धे 'to suck;' ,, दधे.
rt. गै 'to sing;' ,, जगै.
rt. शो 'to sharpen;' ,, शशो.

232. Radical ऋ and ॠ are in the reduplicative syllable of the Redupl. Perf. represented by अ, but in that of the Special tenses of roots of the third (*juhotyādi*) class by इ; *e. g.*

rt. भृ 'to bear ;' Red. Perf. Par. बभार.
but Pres. Ind. Par. बिभर्ति.
rt. तृ 'to cross;' Red. Perf. Par. ततार.

SPECIAL AND GENERAL TENSES.

§ 233. The Present tense in all its three moods (Indicative, Potential, and Imperative) and the Imperfect are called *Special Tenses*; the remaining Tenses and the Benedictive are called *General Tenses*.

This distinction is founded on the circumstance that the general tenses of all primitive roots are formed from the root in one and the same way, whereas in the special tenses *a special base* which may be formed in various ways, has to be derived from the root, before the characteristic marks of the tenses and moods and the personal terminations can be added.

A.—SPECIAL TENSES.

Present (Indicative, Potential, Imperative) and Imperfect.

§ 234. The special base of the special tenses is formed in *nine* different ways. Accordingly all primitive roots have by the native grammarians been divided into *nine classes*, each class being denominated after the root which stands first in it.

§ 235. Formation of the Special Base in the nine classes:—

1. Special base of roots of the *first class* (भ्वादि *i. e.* 'commencing with भू'):

(*a*) अ is added to the root;

(*b*) The vowel of the root is gunated, except when it is short and followed by more than one consonant, or when it is long and followed by one or more consonants (observe § 46); *e. g.*

बुध् 'to know;' special base बोध्.
भू 'to be;' ,, ,, भो + अ = भव. (§ 49.)

नी	'to lead;'	special base	ने + अ	= नय.
ह्वे	'to call;'	,, ,,	ह्वे + अ	= ह्वय.
गै	'to sing;'	,, ,,	गै + अ	= गाय.
वद्	'to speak;'	,, ,,		वद.
but निन्द्	'to blame;'	,, ,,		निन्द.
कूज्	'to sing;'	,, ,,		कूज.
मूर्च्छ्	'to faint;'	,, ,,		मूर्च्छ.

2. Special base of roots of the *second class* (अदादि i.e. 'commencing with अद्'): the root remains unchanged; e.g.

अद् 'to eat;' special base अद्.
दुह् 'to milk;' ,, ,, दुह्.
या 'to go;' ,, ,, या.

3. Special base of roots of the *third class* (जुहोत्यादि i.e. 'commencing with जुहोति i.e. हु'): the root is reduplicated (§ 230); e.g.

हु 'to sacrifice;' special base जुहु.
दा 'to give;' ,, ,, ददा.
भृ 'to bear;' ,, ,, बिभृ.

4. Special base of roots of the *fourth class* (दिवादि i.e. 'commencing with दिव्'): य is added to the root (observe § 46); e.g.

नह् 'to bind;' special base नह्य.
तुष् 'to be pleased;' ,, ,, तुष्य.
दिव् 'to play;' ,, ,, दीव्य.

5. Special base of roots of the *fifth class* (स्वादि i.e. 'commencing with सु'): नु (changeable to णु by § 58) is added to the root; e.g.

सु 'to squeeze out;' special base सुनु.
आप् 'to obtain;' ,, ,, आप्नु.
धृष् 'to dare;' ,, ,, धृष्णु.

6. Special base of roots of the *sixth class* (तुदादि i.e. 'commencing with तुद्'): अ is added to the root; (before this अ, final इ and ई become इय्, final उ and ऊ become उव्, final ऋ becomes रिय्, and final ॠ becomes इर्; § 45, 47, 48); e.g.

तुद् 'to strike;' special base तुद.
रि 'to go;'   ,,   ,, रिय.
नु 'to praise;' ,,   ,, नुव.
मृ 'to die;'   ,,   ,, म्रिय.
कृ 'to scatter;' ,,   ,, किर.

7. Special base of roots of the *seventh class* (रुधादि *i.e.* 'commencing with रुध्'): a nasal homogeneous to the final consonant of the root is inserted between the radical vowel and the final consonant, except in roots the penultimate letter of which is a nasal; *e.g.*

रुध् 'to obstruct;' special base रुन्ध्.
युज् 'to join;'   ,,   ,, युञ्ज्.
पिष् 'to pound;'   ,,   ,, पिंष्.
but उन्द् 'to moisten;' ,,   ,, उन्द्.

8. Special base of roots of the *eighth class* (तनादि *i.e.* 'commencing with तन्'): उ is added to the root; *e.g.*

तन् 'to stretch;' special base तनु.

9. Special base of roots of the *ninth class* (क्र्यादि *i.e.* 'commencing with क्री'): नो (changeable to नी by § 53) is added to the root; before it a penultimate radical nasal is dropped; *e.g.*

यु 'to join;' special base युनी.
क्री 'to buy;' ,,   ,, क्रीणी.
स्तम्भ् 'to support;' ,, ,, स्तभ्नी.

§ 236. Some roots form their special base in two or more ways; *e.g.* यु 'to join,' belongs both to the second (*adâdi*) and to the ninth (*kryâdi*) class; Spec. base यु and युनो. क्रम् 'to go,' belongs to the first (*bhvâdi*) and to the fourth (*divâdi*) class; Spec. base क्राम and क्राम्य (both irregular). To which class or classes a root belongs, must be ascertained from the practice of the best writers or from the dictionary.

§ 237. *Unchangeable special base* and *changeable special base.* The special base of roots of the first (*bhvâdi*), fourth (*divâdi*) and sixth (*tudâdi*) classes remains, with some slight modifications, unchanged throughout all the forms of the special tenses and moods in Parasmaipada and Âtmanepada. The special base of the roots of the remaining six classes has generally two forms, a *strong* base and a *weak* base. Accordingly the conjugation of roots of the first, fourth, and sixth classes differs in the special tenses from that of roots of the second (*adâdi*), third (*juhotyâdi*), fifth (*svâdi*), seventh (*rudhâdi*), eighth (*tanadi*), and ninth (*kryâdi*) classes.

(*a.*)—*Special Tenses of Roots with Unchangeable Special Base.*
(1*st,* 4*th,* and 6*th* classes.)

1.—PRESENT INDICATIVE.

§ 238. The personal terminations given in col. I. of § 227 are added to the special base; *e. g.*

rt. भू 1 cl. spec. B. भव; Pres. Ind. Par. भवति; Âtm. भवते.
rt. दिव् 4 cl. ,, ,, दीव्य; ,, ,, ,, दीव्यति; ,, दीव्यते
rt. तुद् 6 cl. ,, ,, तुद; ,, ,, ,, तुदति; ,, तुदते.

239. (*a*) Before terminations beginning with म् or व् the final अ of the special base is lengthened; *e. g.* 1 Sing. Par. भवामि.

(*b*) The final अ of the special base combines with the अ of the terminations भन्ति and अन्ते to अ, and with the termination ए and the आ of the terminations आथे and आते to ए; *e. g.* 3 Plur. Par. भवन्ति ; Sing. Âtm. भवे; 2 Du. Âtm. भवेथे.

2.—PRESENT POTENTIAL.

§ 240. इ (changeable to इय् before vowel-terminations) is added to the special base, and to the base so modified the personal terminations given in col. II. of § 227 are added ; *e.g.*

rt. भू 1 cl. spec. B. भव; Pot. Par. भव+इ+त्=भवेत्; Âtm. भव +इ+त=भवेत.
rt. दिव्4 cl. ,, ,, दीव्य; ,, ,, दीव्य+इ+त्=दीव्येत्; ,, दीव्य+इ+त=दीव्येत.
rt. तुद् 6 cl. ,, ,, तुद; ,, ,, तुद +इ+त् =तुदेत्; ,, तुद +इ+त=तुदेत.

§ 241. उः is substituted for the termination अन् of the 3 Plur. Par., अ for इ of the 1 Sing. Âtm., and रन् for अन्त of the 3 Plur. Âtm.; *e.g.*

3 Plur. Par. भव + इय् + उः = भवेयुः
1 Sing. Âtm. भव + इय् + अ = भवेय.
3 Plur. Âtm. भव + इ + रन्   भवेरन्.

3.—Present Imperative.

§ 242. The personal terminations given in col. IV. of § 227 are added to the special base; *e.g.*

rt. भू 1 cl. spec. B. भव Imper. Par. भवतु; Ātm. भवताम्
rt. दिव् 4 cl. ,, ,, दीव्य ,, ,, दीव्यतु; ,, दीव्यताम्
rt. तुद् 6 cl. ,, ,, तुद ,, ,, तुदतु; ,, तुदताम्

§ 243. (*a*) The termination सि of the 2 Sing. Par. is dropped; *e. g.* 2 Sing. Par. भव.

(*b*) The final अ of the special base combines, with the अ of the term. अन्तु and अन्ताम् to आ, and with the initial आ of the Ātm. terminations आथाम् and आताम् to ए; *e.g.* 3 Plur. Par. भवन्तु; 2 Du. Ātm. भवेथाम्; 3 Du. Ātm. भवेताम्.

(*c*) तात् may optionally be substituted for the term. सि and तु of the 2 and 3 Sing. Par. when these two forms have a benedictive sense; *e.g.* भव or भवतात् 'may you be!'

4.—Imperfect.

§ 244. The special base receives the augment (§ 229), and the personal terminations given in col. II. of § 227 are added to it; *e. g.*

rt. भू 1 cl. spec. B. भव. Impf. Par. अभवत्; Ātm. अभवत
rt. दिव् 4 cl. ,, ,, दीव्य ,, ,, अदीव्यत्; ,, अदीव्यत
rt. तुद् 6 cl. ,, ,, तुद ,, ,, अतुदत्; ,, अतुदत

§ 245. (*a*) Before terminations beginning with म् or व् the final अ of the special base is lengthened; *e.g.* 1 Du. Par. अभवाव; Ātm. अभवावहि.

(*b*) The final अ of the special base combines with the अ of the term. अम्, अन् and अन्न to आ, and with the initial आ of the Ātm. terminations आथाम् and आताम् to ए; *e.g.* 1 Sing. Par. अभवम्; 2 Du. Ātm. अभवेथाम्.

Paradigms.

§ 246. The Special Tenses of भू cl. 1 'to be;' दिव् cl. 4 (commonly only P.) 'to play;' तुद् cl. 6 'to strike.'

Root. भू दिव् तुद्
Spec. B. भव दीव्य तुद

1.—Present Indicative.

		Parasmai.	Âtmane.	Parasmai.	Âtmane.	Parasmai.	Âtmane.
Sing.	1.	भवामि	भवे	दीव्यामि	दीव्ये	तुदामि	तुदे
	2.	भवसि	भवसे	दीव्यसि	दीव्यसे	तुदसि	तुदसे
	3.	भवति	भवते	दीव्यति	दीव्यते	तुदति	तुदते
Dual.	1.	भवावः	भवावहे	दीव्यावः	दीव्यावहे	तुदावः	तुदावहे
	2.	भवथः	भवेथे	दीव्यथः	दीव्येथे	तुदथः	तुदेथे
	3.	भवतः	भवेते	दीव्यतः	दीव्येते	तुदतः	तुदेते
Plur.	1.	भवामः	भवामहे	दीव्यामः	दीव्यामहे	तुदामः	तुदामहे
	2.	भवथ	भवध्वे	दीव्यथ	दीव्यध्वे	तुदथ	तुदध्वे
	3.	भवन्ति	भवन्ते	दीव्यन्ति	दीव्यन्ते	तुदन्ति	तुदन्ते

2.—Present Potential.

		Parasmai.	Âtmane.	Parasmai.	Âtmane.	Parasmai.	Âtmane.
Sing.	1.	भवेयम्	भवेय	दीव्येयम्	दीव्येय	तुदेयम्	तुदेय
	2.	भवेः	भवेथाः	दीव्येः	दीव्येथाः	तुदेः	तुदेथाः
	3.	भवेत्	भवेत	दीव्येत्	दीव्येत	तुदेत्	तुदेत
Dual.	1.	भवेव	भवेवहि	दीव्येव	दीव्येवहि	तुदेव	तुदेवहि
	2.	भवेतम्	भवेयाथाम्	दीव्येतम्	दीव्येयाथाम्	तुदेतम्	तुदेयाथाम्
	3.	भवेताम्	भवेयाताम्	दीव्येताम्	दीव्येयाताम्	तुदेताम्	तुदेयाताम्
Plur.	1.	भवेम	भवेमहि	दीव्येम	दीव्येमहि	तुदेम	तुदेमहि
	2.	भवेत	भवेध्वम्	दीव्येत	दीव्येध्वम्	तुदेत	तुदेध्वम्
	3.	भवेयुः	भवेरन्	दीव्येयुः	दीव्येरन्	तुदेयुः	तुदेरन्

3.—Present Imperative.

		Parasmai.	Âtmane.	Parasmai.	Âtmane.	Parasmai.	Âtmane.
Sing.	1.	भवानि	भवै	दीव्यानि	दीव्यै	तुदानि	तुदै
	2.	भव or भवतात्	भवस्व	दीव्य or दीव्यतात्	दीव्यस्व	तुद or तुदतात्	तुदस्व
	3.	भवतु or भवतात्	भवताम्	दीव्यतु or दीव्यतात्	दीव्यताम्	तुदतु or तुदतात्	तुदताम्
Dual.	1.	भवाव	भवावहै	दीव्याव	दीव्यावहै	तुदाव	तुदावहै
	2.	भवतम्	भवेथाम्	दीव्यतम्	दीव्येथाम्	तुदतम्	तुदेथाम्
	3.	भवताम्	भवेताम्	दीव्यताम्	दीव्येताम्	तुदताम्	तुदेताम्
Plur.	1.	भवाम	भवामहै	दीव्याम	दीव्यामहै	तुदाम	तुदामहै
	2.	भवत	भवध्वम्	दीव्यत	दीव्यध्वम्	तुदत	तुदध्वम्
	3.	भवन्तु	भवन्ताम्	दीव्यन्तु	दीव्यन्ताम्	तुदन्तु	तुदन्ताम्

4.—Imperfect.

	Parasmai.	Âtmane.	Parasmai.	Âtmane.	Parasmai.	Âtmane.
Sing. 1.	अभवम्	अभवे	अदीव्यम्	अदीव्ये	अतुदम्	अतुदे
Sing. 2.	अभवः	अभवथाः	अदीव्यः	अदीव्यथाः	अतुदः	अतुदथाः
Sing. 3.	अभवत्	अभवत	अदीव्यत्	अदीव्यत	अतुदत्	अतुदत
Dual. 1.	अभवाव	अभवावहि	अदीव्याव	अदीव्यावहि	अतुदाव	अतुदावहि
Dual. 2.	अभवतम्	अभवेयाम्	अदीव्यतम्	अदीव्येयाम्	अतुदतम्	अतुदेयाम्
Dual. 3.	अभवताम्	अभवेताम्	अदीव्यताम्	अदीव्येताम्	अतुदताम्	अतुदेताम्
Plur. 1.	अभवाम	अभवामहि	अदीव्याम	अदीव्यामहि	अतुदाम	अतुदामहि
Plur. 2.	अभवत	अभवध्वम्	अदीव्यत	अदीव्यध्वम्	अतुदत	अतुदध्वम्
Plur. 3.	अभवन्	अभवन्त	अदीव्यन्	अदीव्यन्त	अतुदन्	अतुदन्त

§ 247. *Irregular roots of the* 1st, 4th *and* 6th *classes*: All roots of the 1st, 4th, and 6th classes form their special tenses from their special base exactly like भू, दिव् and तुद्, but some are irregular as far as the formation of their special base is concerned. The following is an alphabetical list of the more common irregular roots of the 1st, 4th, and 6th classes together with their special base and the 3 Sing. of the Pres. Ind. Par. or Âtm.

1. इष् cl. 6. P. 'to wish;' Spec. B. इच्छ. Pres. Par. इच्छति
2. ऋ cl. 1. P. 'to go;' ,, ,, ऋच्छ. ,, ,, ऋच्छति
3. कृत् cl. 6. P. 'to cut;' ,, ,, कृन्त. ,, ,, कृन्तति
4. क्रम् cl. 1. P. ⎫
       cl. 1. Â. ⎬ 'to go;' ,, ,, क्राम. ,, ,, क्रामति
       cl. 4. P. ⎭ ,, ,, क्रम. ,, Âtm. क्रमते
        ,, ,, क्राम्य. ,, Par. क्राम्यति
5. गम् cl. 1. P. Â. 'to go;' ,, ,, गच्छ. ,, ,, गच्छति
6. गुप् cl. 1. P. 'to guard;' ,, ,, गोपाय. ,, ,, गोपायति
7. गुह् cl. 1. P. Â. 'to hide;' ,, ,, गूह. ,, ,, गूहति
8. घ्रा cl. 1. P. 'to smell;' ,, ,, जिघ्र. ,, ,, जिघ्रति
9. चम् cl. 1. P. (with prep. आ) 'to drink;' ,, ,, चाम. ,, ,, आचामति
10. जन् cl. 4. Â. 'to be born;' ,, ,, जाय. ,, Âtm. जायते
11. तम् cl. 4. P. 'to be sad;' ,, ,, ताम्य. ,, Par. ताम्यति
12. दंश् cl. 1. P. 'to bite;' ,, ,, दश. ,, ,, दशति
13. दम् cl. 4. P. 'to tame;' ,, ,, दाम्य. ,, ,, दाम्यति
14. दृश् cl. 1. P. 'to see;' ,, ,, पश्य. ,, ,, पश्यति

15.	धूप्	cl. 1. P. 'to fumigate;'	Spec. B.	धूपाय.	Pres. Par.	धूपायति
16.	ध्मा	cl. 1. P. 'to blow;'	,,	,, धम.	,, ,,	धमति
17.	पा	cl. 1. P. 'to drink;'	,,	,, पिब.	,, ,,	पिबति
18.	प्रच्छ्	cl. 6. P. 'to ask;'	,,	,, पृच्छ.	,, ,,	पृच्छति
19.	भ्रंश्	cl. 4. P. 'to fall;'	,,	,, { भ्रश्य.	,, ,,	भ्रश्यति
20.	भ्रंस्			,, { भ्रस्य.	,, ,,	भ्रस्यति
21.	भ्रज्ज्	cl. 6. P. Â. 'to fry;'	,,	,, भृज्ज.	,, ,,	भृज्जति
22.	भ्रम्	cl. 1. P. } 'to roam;'	,,	,, भ्रम.	,, ,,	भ्रमति
		cl. 4. P.		,, भ्रम्य.	,, ,,	भ्रम्यति
				or भ्राम्य.	,, ,,	भ्राम्यति
23.	मद्	cl. 4. P. 'to be intoxicated;'	,,	,, माद्य.	,, ,,	माद्यति
24.	मुच्	cl. 6. P. Â. 'to loosen;'	,,	,, मुञ्च.	,, ,,	मुञ्चति
25.	मृज्	cl. 1. P. 'to wipe off;'	,,	,, मार्ज.	,, ,,	मार्जति
26.	म्ना	cl. 1. P. 'to record;'	,,	,, मन.	,, ,,	मनति
27.	यम्	cl. 1. P. 'to restrain;'	,,	,, यच्छ.	,, ,,	यच्छति
28.	रञ्ज्	cl. 1. P. Â. } 'to colour;'	,,	,, रज.	,, ,,	रजति
		cl. 4. P. Â.	,,	,, रज्य.	,, ,,	रज्यति
29.	लिप्	cl. 6. P. Â. 'to anoint;'	,,	,, लिम्प.	,, ,,	लिम्पति
30.	लुप्	cl. 6. P. Â. 'to break;'	,,	,, लुम्प.	,, ,,	लुम्पति
31.	विद्	cl. 6. P. Â. 'to find;'	,,	,, विन्द.	,, ,,	विन्दति
32.	व्यध्	cl. 4. P. 'to strike;'	,,	,, विध्य.	,, ,,	विध्यति
33.	शम्	cl. 4. P. 'to be tranquil;'	,,	,, शाम्य.	,, ,,	शाम्यति
34.	शो	cl. 4. P. 'to sharpen;'	,,	,, श्य.	,, ,,	श्यति
35.	श्रम्	cl. 4. P. 'to be weary;'	,,	,, श्राम्य.	,, ,,	श्राम्यति
36.	ष्ठिव्	cl. 1. P. } 'to spue;'	,,	,, { ष्ठीव.	,, ,,	ष्ठीवति
		cl. 4. P.		,, { ष्ठीव्य.	,, ,,	ष्ठीव्यति
37.	सञ्ज्	cl. 1. P. 'to adhere;'	,,	,, सज.	,, ,,	सजति
38.	सद्	cl. 6. P. 'to sit;'	,,	,, सीद.	,, ,,	सीदति
39.	सिच्	cl. 6. P. Â. 'to sprinkle;'	,,	,, सिञ्च.	,, ,,	सिञ्चति
40.	सो	cl. 4. P. 'to finish;'	,,	,, स्य.	,, ,,	स्यति
41.	स्था	cl. 1. P. Â. 'to stand;'	,,	,, तिष्ठ.	,, ,,	तिष्ठति
42.	स्वञ्ज्	cl. 1. Â. 'to embrace;'	,,	,, स्वज	,, Âtm.	स्वजते

(b.)—*Special Tenses of Roots with Changeable Special Base*
(2nd, 3rd, 4th, 7th, 8th, and 9th classes).

§ 248. The special base of roots of the 2nd, 3rd, 5th, 7th, 8th, and 9th classes has generally two forms, a *strong* base and a *weak* base. The strong base is used in the *strong forms*, the weak base in the *weak forms*. The strong forms are—

(a) The three persons of the singular of the Pres. Indic. in Parasmai.
(b) The three persons of the singular of the Imperfect in Parasmai.
(c) All the first persons of the Pres. Imperative in Parasmai. and Ātmane.
(d) The 3rd person singular of the Pres. Imperative in Parasmai.

All the remaining forms are weak.

§ 249. *Formation of the special strong base.* The weak base does not, in general, differ from the special base formed in accordance with the rules laid down in § 235. The strong base is derived from it thus:

(a) In roots of the 2nd and 3rd (*adādi* and *juhotyādi*) classes the radical vowel is gunated (except when it is prosodially long and not final); in roots consisting of two syllables the last vowel is gunated; *e.g.*

rt. इ cl. 2. 'to go;' Spec. weak B. इ. — Strong B. ए
rt. विद् cl. 2. 'to know;' ,, ,, ,, विद्. — ,, ,, वेद्
rt. द्विष् cl. 2. 'to hate;' ,, ,, ,, द्विष्. — ,, ,, द्वेष्
rt. दुह् cl. 2. 'to milk;' ,, ,, ,, दुह्. — ,, ,, दोह्
rt. जागृ cl. 2. 'to wake;' ,, ,, ,, जागृ. — ,, ,, जागर्
rt. भी cl. 3. 'to fear;' ,, ,, ,, बिभी. — ,, ,, बिभे
rt. भृ cl. 3. 'to bear;' ,, ,, ,, बिभृ. — ,, ,, बिभर्
rt. या cl. 2. 'to go;' ,, ,, ,, या. — ,, ,, या
rt. ईश् cl. 2. 'to rule;' ,, ,, ,, ईश्. — ,, ,, ईश्
rt. जन् cl. 3. 'to bring forth;' ,, ,, ,, जजन् — ,, ,, जजन्

(b) Of roots of the 5th and 8th (*svādi* and *tanādi*) classes the final उ of the special base is gunated; *e. g.*

rt. सु cl. 5. 'to squeeze out;' Spec. weak B. सुनु. — Strong B. सुनो
rt. धृष् cl. 5. 'to dare;' ,, ,, ,, धृष्णु. — ,, ,, धृष्णो
rt. तन् cl. 8. 'to stretch;' ,, ,, ,, तनु. — ,, ,, तनो

(c) In roots of the 7th (*rudhâdi*) class न i. e. *na* is substituted for the penultimate nasal of the special base; this न is liable to be changed to ण by § 58; *e. g.*

rt. रुध् cl. 7. 'to obstruct;' Spec. weak B. रुन्ध्.—Strong B. रुणध्
rt. युज् cl. 7. 'to join;'   ,,   ,,   ,, युञ्ज्.—   ,,   ,, युनज्
rt. उन्द् cl. 7. 'to moisten;' ,,   ,,   ,, उन्द्.—   ,,   ,, उनद्

(d) Of roots of the 9th (*kryâdi*) class आ is substituted for the final ई of the special base; *e. g.*

rt. यु   cl. 9. 'to join;'   Spec. weak B. युनी —Strong B. युना
rt. क्री cl. 9. 'to buy;'   ,,   ,,   ,, क्रीणी —   ,,   ,, क्रीणा
rt. स्तभ् cl. 9. 'to support;' ,,   ,,   ,, स्तभ्नी —   ,,   ,, स्तभ्ना

§ 250. *General rules of Sandhi* for the combination of final letters of the special (strong and weak) base with initial letters of terminations:

1. A final vowel of a special base combines with the initial vowel to a termination according to the rules of Sandhi in § 44 &c. Initial consonants of terminations after final vowels of special bases remain unchanged, except that the स् of the terminations सि, से and स्व is changed to ष् after all vowels but आ (§ 59), and that the termination धि of the 2 Sing. Pres. Imperat. Par. is after *all* vowels (and semi-vowels) changed to हि; *e. g.*

या cl. 2. 'to go;'   3 Plur. Pres. Ind. Par. या + अन्ति = यान्ति
                     2 Sing. ,,   ,,   ,, या + सि   = यासि
                     2 ,,   ,, Imper.   ,, या + धि   = याहि
इ cl. 2. 'to go;'   2 ,,   ,, Ind.   ,, ए + सि   = एषि
                     2 ,,   ,, Imper. ,, इ + धि   = इहि
चि cl. 5. 'to collect;' 1 ,, ,,   ,,   ,, चिनो + आनि = चिनवानि

§ 251. (2.) When final consonants of special bases meet with initial vowels, semivowels or nasals of terminations, both the final letters of the bases and the initial letters of the terminations remain unchanged (§ 50); *e. g.*

युज् cl. 7. 'to join;' Strong base युनज्, Weak base. युञ्ज्;
  1 Sing. Pres. Ind. Âtm. युञ्ज् + ए = युञ्जे
  1 Dual. Pres. Ind. Par. युञ्ज् + वः = युञ्ज्वः
  1 Sing. Pres. Ind. Par. युनज् + मि = युनज्मि

§ 252. (3.) When final consonants of special bases meet with initial त्, थ्, ध्, स् or Visarga of terminations the rules laid down in § 51 &c. are observed. The following changes deserve special notice:

(*a*) The terminations : (स्) and त् in the 2 and 3 Sing. Impf. Par. are dropped (§ 52); at the same time—

final च् and ज् of the Spec. B. become क्;
final र्   „   „   „   „   Visarga;
final ड् and घ्   „   „   „   „   ट्;

final ह् of the Spec. B. becomes ट्, but in roots commencing with द it becomes क् (observe § 53);

final न्, (थ्), द्, भ्, and स् of the Spec. B. become न् in the 3 person, and they may optionally become न् or Visarga in the 2 person; *e. g.*

3 Sing. Impf. Par. of वच् cl. 2 = अवक्; of युज् cl. 7 = अयुनक्; of रुध् cl. 7 = अरुणत्; of हन् cl. 2 = अहन्; of भृ cl. 3 (strong B. विभर्) = अविभः (*i. e.* भविभर्); of वह् cl. 2 = भवट्; of द्विष् cl. 2 = अद्वेट्; of लिह् cl. 2 = अलेट्; of दुह् cl. 2 = अधोक्.

3 Sing. Impf. Par. of शास् cl. 2 = अशात्; of भिद् cl. 7 = अभिनत्.

2 Sing. Impf. Par. of शास् = अशात् or अशाः; of भिद् = अभिनत् or अभिनः.

(*b*) Before the स् of the terminations सि, से and स्व—

final च्, ज्, ड्, ष्, क्ष्, and ह् of the Spec. B. are changed to क् (observe § 53), after which the initial स् of the termination becomes ष् (§ 59);

final न्, (थ्), द्, and भ् become न्; (§ 51);

final न् becomes Anusvâra;

final र् and स् remain unchanged, but स् after र् is changed to ष्, *e. g.*

2 Sing. Pres. Ind. Par. of युज् = युनक्षि; of द्विष् = द्वेक्षि; of दुह् = धोक्षि; of रुध् = रुणत्सि; of हन् = हंसि; of भृ = विभर्षि; of शास् = शास्सि.

2 Sing. Pres. Imper. Âtm. of चक्ष् cl. 2 = चक्ष्व.

(*c*) Before terminations commencing with त् and थ्—

final च् and ज् become क्;

final न्, (थ्), and द् become न्; (§ 51); final भ् combines with the initial त् and थ् to ड् (§ 55);

final ड् is changed to ट् (§ 51); and final श्, ष्, क्ष् are changed to ग्; after these ट् and ग्, the initial त् and थ् become ट् and ठ् respectively (§ 56);

final ह् of roots commencing with द् combines with the initial त् and थ् to ग्ध्; final ह् of other roots combines with त् and थ् to द् before which short vowels (except ऋ) are lengthened; *e. g.*

3 Dual. Pres. Ind. Par. of युज् = युङ्क्तः; of विद् cl. 2 'to know' = वित्तः; of रुष् = रुन्द्धः;

3 Sing. Pres. Ind. Par. of हन् = हन्ति; of भृ = बिभर्ति; of शास् = शास्ति; of द्विष् = द्वेष्टि;

3 Sing. Pres. Ind. Âtm. of ईड् cl. 2. = ईट्टे;

2 Dual Pres. Ind. Par. of दुह् = दुग्धः; of लिह् = लीढः.

(*d*) Before terminations commencing with भ्—

final च् and ज् become ग्;

final त्, (थ्), द् and भ् become द् (§ 51);

final ड्, श्, ष् and क्ष् combine with भ् to ड्भ्;

final स् is dropped;

final ह् of roots commencing with द् combines with भ् to ग्भ्; final ह् of other roots combines with भ् to द् before which short vowels (except ऋ) are lengthened; *e. g.*

2 Sing. Pres. Imper. Par. of युज् = युङ्ग्धि; of रुष् = रुन्द्धि; 2 Plur. Pres. Ind. Âtm. of ईड् cl. 2 = ईड्ध्वे; 2 Sing. Pres. Imper. Par. of द्विष् = द्विड्ढि; 2 Plur. Pres. Ind. Âtm. of चक्ष् cl. 2 = चड्ढ्वे; of शास् cl. 2 = आड्ढ्वे; 2 Sing. Pres. Imper. Par. of दुह् = दुग्धि; of लिह् = लीढि.

When क् or ग् are substituted for the final ह् of roots commencing with द् (दिह् and दुह्) before terminations beginning with ध्, the initial द् must be changed to ध्; *e. g.*

दिह् cl. 2, 2 Plur. Pres. Ind. Âtm. धिग्ध्वे. But 2 Sing. Pres. Imper. Par. दिग्धि.

I.—PRESENT INDICATIVE.

§ 253. The personal terminations given in col. I. of § 227 are added to the special strong base in the Sing. Par., to the special weak base in the Du. and Plur. Par. and in the whole Âtm.; *e. g.*

CONJUGATION OF VERBS.

Root.		Spec. Strong B.	1 Sing. Par.	Spec. Weak B.	1 Plur. Par.
द्विष्	cl. 2.	द्वेष;	द्वेष्मि;	द्विष्;	द्विष्मः.
हु	cl. 3.	जुहो;	जुहोमि;	जुहु;	जुहुमः.
सु	cl. 5.	सुनो;	सुनोमि;	सुनु;	सुनुमः.
रुध्	cl. 7.	रुणध्;	रुणधिम;	रुन्ध्;	रुन्ध्मः.
तन्	cl. 8.	तनो;	तनोमि;	तनु;	तनुमः.
क्री	cl. 9.	क्रीणा;	क्रीणामि;	क्रीणी;	क्रीणीमः.

§ 254. (a). अन्ते is substituted for the term. अन्ते of the 3 Plur. Âtm. in all 6 classes, and अति for the term. अन्ति of the 3 Plur. Par. of roots of the 3rd (*juhotyâdi*) class, and of the roots चकास्, जक्ष्, जागृ, दरिद्रा, and शास् of the 2nd class ; *e. g*.

द्विष् 3 Plur. Âtm. द्विषते. हु 3 Plur. Par. जुह्वति. शास् 3 Plur. Par. शासति.

(*b*) Final इ and ई, उ and ऊ, and ऋ of special weak bases of roots of the 2nd class are before vowel-terminations changed to इय्, उव्, and र् respectively; final इ and ई, उ, and ऋ of special weak bases of roots of the third class are before vowel-terminations changed to य्, व्, and र्; ई in ह्री cl. 3 is changed to इय्; *e. g*.

3 Plur. Par. of नू cl. 2 = नुवन्ति; of जागृ cl. 2 = जाग्रति; of भी cl. 3 = बिभ्यति; of ह्री cl. 3 = जिह्रियति.

(*c*) The final उ of the special weak base of roots of the 5th class is before vowel-terminations changed to उव् when it is preceded by more than one consonant; otherwise it is changed to व्; *e. g*.

3 Plur. Par. of आप् = आप्नुवन्ति; of सु = सुन्वन्ति.

(*d*) The final ई of the special weak base of roots of the 9th class is dropped before vowel-terminations; *e. g*.

3 Plur. Par. of क्री = क्रीणन्ति.

(*e*) The final उ of the special weak base of roots of the 5th and 8th classes may optionally be dropped before terminations beginning with व् or म्, provided उ be preceded by only one consonant; *e. g*.

सु 1 Plur. Par. सुनुमः or सुन्मः, but आप् only आप्नुमः.

2.—Present Potential.

§ 255. या is added to the special weak base in Parasmaipada, and ई (changeable to ईय् before vowel-terminations) to the special weak base in Âtmanepada; to the base so modified the personal terminations given in col. II. of § 227 are added. Final vowels of the special weak base undergo before ई the changes specified in § 254 (b), (c), and (d).

§ 256. (a) उः is substituted for the termination अन् of the 3 Plur. Par., भ for the इ of the 1 Sing. Âtm., and रन् for अन्त of the 3 Plur. Âtm.

(b) The आ of the characteristic या is dropped before the termination उः of the 3 Plur. Par.; e. g.

Root.		Spec. Weak B.	1 Sing. Par.	1 Sing. Âtm.
द्विष्	cl. 2.	द्विष्	द्विष्याम्	द्विषीय.
हु	cl. 3.	जुह	जुह्याम्	जुह्वीय.
सु	cl. 5.	सुनु	सुनुयाम्	सुन्वीय.
रुध्	cl. 7.	रुन्ध्	रुन्ध्याम्	रुन्धीय.
तन्	cl. 8.	तनु	तनुयाम्	तन्वीय.
क्री	cl. 9.	क्रीणी	क्रीणीयाम्	क्रीणीय.

3.—PRESENT IMPERATIVE.

§ 257. The personal terminations given in col. IV. of § 227 are added to the special strong base in all first persons and in the 3 Sing. Par., to the special weak base in the remaining forms; e. g.

Root.		Sp. Strong B.	3 Sing. Par.	Spec. Weak B.	3 Sing. Âtm.
द्विष्	cl. 2.	द्वेष् ;	द्वेष्टु.	द्विष् ;	द्विष्टाम्.
हु	cl. 3.	जुहो ;	जुहोतु.	जुह ;	जुहताम्.
सु	cl. 5.	सुनो ;	सुनोतु.	सुनु ;	सुनुताम्.
रुध्	cl. 7.	रुणध् ;	रुणद्धु.	रुन्ध् ;	रुन्द्धाम्.
तन्	cl. 8.	तनो ;	तनोतु.	तनु ;	तनुताम्.
क्री	cl. 9.	क्रीणा ;	क्रीणातु.	क्रीणी ;	क्रीणीताम्.

§ 258. (a) The term. धि of the 2 Sing. Par. is (as stated in § 250) changed to हि after special bases ending in vowels (except in जुहुधि from हु) and semivowels. It is dropped after the special bases of roots of the 5th and 8th classes, when the final उ of these bases is preceded by only one consonant. Roots of the 9th class that end in consonants, substitute in the 2 Sing. Par. आन (or आण) for नोहि (or णोहि); e. g.

या cl. 2, याहि; भू cl. 3, विभृहि;—सु cl. 5, Spec. weak base सुनु, 2 Sing. Par. सुनु; but आप् cl. 5, Spec. weak base आप्नु, 2 Sing. Par. आप्नुहि;—अश् cl. 9, Spec. weak base अश्री, 2 Sing. Par. अशान (not अश्रीहि); but क्री, क्रीणीहि.

(b) अताम् is substituted for the term. अन्ताम् of the 3 Plur. Âtm. in all 6 classes, and अतु for the term. अन्तु of the 3 Plur. Par. of roots of the third (*juhotyâdi*) class, and of the roots चकास्, जक्ष्, जागृ, दरिद्रा and शास् of the 2nd class; *e. g.*

द्विष्, 3 Plur. Âtm. द्विषताम्; हु, 3 Plur. Par. जुह्वतु; शास्, 3 Plur. Par. शासतु.

(c) Final vowels of special weak bases are before vowel-terminations changed according to the rules laid down in § 254 (b), (c), (d).

(d) तात् may optionally be substituted for the term. हि and तु of the 2nd and 3rd Sing. Par. when these two forms have a benedictive sense. In both persons this तात् is added to the spec. weak base; *e. g.* आप् cl. 5 2 or 3 Sing. Par. आप्नुतात्.

4.—IMPERFECT.

§ 259. The personal terminations given in col. II. of § 227 are added to the special strong base in the Sing. Par., to the special weak base in the Du. and Plur. Par. and in the whole Âtm. Besides the special base receives the augment; *e. g.*

Root.		Sp. Strong B.	1 Sing. Par.	Spec. Weak B.	1 Plur. Par.
द्विष्	cl. 2.	द्वेष्;	अद्वेषम्.	द्विष्;	आद्विष्म.
हु	cl. 3.	जुहो;	अजुहवम्.	जुह्;	अजुहुम.
सु	cl. 5.	सुनो;	असुनवम्.	सुनु;	असुनुम.
रुध्	cl. 7.	रुणध्;	अरुणधम्.	रुन्ध्;	अरुन्ध्म.
तन्	cl. 8.	तनो;	अतनवम्.	तनु;	अतनुम.
क्री	cl. 9.	क्रीणा;	अक्रीणाम्.	क्रीणी;	अक्रीणीम.

§ 260. (a) अत is substituted for the term. अन्त of the 3 Plur. Âtm. in all 6 classes, and उः for the term. अन् of the 3 Plur. Par. of roots of the third (*juhotyâdi*) class, and of the roots चकास्, जक्ष्, जागृ, दरिद्रा, शास् and विद् of the 2nd class; optionally also of roots of the second class that end in आ, and of द्विष्. A final vowel of the special base is guṇated before उः; a final आ is dropped; *e. g.*

द्विष् 3 Plur. Âtm. अद्विषत; शास् 3 Plur. Par. अशासुः:; हु 3 Plur. Par. अजुह्वुः; या 3 Plur. Par. अयान् or अयुः.

(b) The rules specified in § 254 (b), (c), (d), (e) apply also in the Imperfect.

Paradigms:

§ 261. The Special Tenses of the roots द्विष् cl. 2 'to hate,' हु cl. 3 'to sacrifice,' सु cl. 5 'to squeeze out,' रुध् cl. 7 'to obstruct,' तन् cl. 8 'to stretch,' क्री cl. 9 'to buy.'

	Root	द्विष् cl. 2.		हु cl. 3.*	
	Spec. St. Base:	द्वेष्		जुहो	
	Spec. W. Base:	द्विष्		जुहु	
		Parasmai.	Âtmane.	Parasmai.	Âtmane.

1.—*Present Indicative.*

		Parasmai.	Âtmane.	Parasmai.	Âtmane.
Sing.	1	द्वेष्मि	द्विषे	जुहोमि	जुह्वे
	2	द्वेक्षि	द्विक्षे	जुहोषि	जुहुषे
	3	द्वेष्टि	द्विष्टे	जुहोति	जुहुते
Dual.	1	द्विष्वः	द्विष्वहे	जुहुवः	जुहुवहे
	2	द्विष्ठः	द्विषाथे	जुहुथः	जुह्वाथे
	3	द्विष्टः	द्विषाते	जुहुतः	जुह्वाते
Plural.	1	द्विष्मः	द्विष्महे	जुहुमः	जुहुमहे
	2	द्विष्ठ	द्विड्ढ्वे	जुहुथ	जुहुध्वे
	3	द्विषन्ति	द्विषते	जुह्वति	जुह्वते

2.—*Present Potential.*

		Parasmai.	Âtmane.	Parasmai.	Âtmane.
Sing.	1	द्विष्याम्	द्विषीय	जुहुयाम्	जुह्वीय
	2	द्विष्याः	द्विषीथाः	जुहुयाः	जुह्वीथाः
	3	द्विष्यात्	द्विषीत	जुहुयात्	जुह्वीत
Dual.	1	द्विष्याव	द्विषीवहि	जुहुयाव	जुह्वीवहि
	2	द्विष्यातम्	द्विषीयाथाम्	जुहुयातम्	जुह्वीयाथाम्
	3	द्विष्याताम्	द्विषीयाताम्	जुहुयाताम्	जुह्वीयाताम्
Plural.	1	द्विष्याम	द्विषीमहि	जुहुयाम	जुह्वीमहि
	2	द्विष्यात	द्विषीध्वम्	जुहुयात	जुह्वीध्वम्
	3	द्विष्युः	द्विषीरन्	जुहुयुः	जुह्वीरन्

---

* The rt. हु is really conjugated only in Parasmaipada. The Âtmanepada-forms have been given here merely in order to show the difference between Par. and Âtm. in one and the same verb.

3.—Present Imperative.

		Parasmai.	Âtmane.	Parasmai.	Âtmane.
Sing.	1	द्वेषाणि	द्वेषै	जुहवानि	जुहवै
	2	द्विड्ढि or द्विष्टात्	द्विक्ष्व	जुहुधि or जुहुतात्	जुहुष्व
	3	द्वेष्टु or द्विष्टात्	द्विष्टाम्	जुहोतु or जुहुतात्	जुहुताम्
Dual.	1	द्वेषाव	द्वेषावहै	जुहवाव	जुहवावहै
	2	द्विष्टम्	द्विषाथाम्	जुहुतम्	जुह्वाथाम्
	3	द्विष्टाम्	द्विषाताम्	जुहुताम्	जुह्वाताम्
Plural.	1	द्वेषाम	द्वेषामहै	जुहवाम	जुहवामहै
	2	द्विष्ट	द्विड्ढ्वम्	जुहुत	जुहुध्वम्
	3	द्विषन्तु	द्विषताम्	जुह्वतु	जुह्वताम्

4.—Imperfect.

		Parasmai.	Âtmane.	Parasmai.	Âtmane.
Sing.	1	अद्वेषम्	अद्विषि	अजुहवम्	अजुह्वि
	2	अद्वेट्	अद्विष्ठाः	अजुहोः	अजुहुथाः
	3	अद्वेट्	अद्विष्ट	अजुहोत्	अजुहुत
Dual.	1	अद्विष्व	अद्विष्वहि	अजुहुव	अजुहुवहि
	2	अद्विष्टम्	अद्विषाथाम्	अजुहुतम्	अजुह्वाथाम्
	3	अद्विष्टाम्	अद्विषाताम्	अजुहुताम्	अजुह्वाताम्
Plural.	1	अद्विष्म	अद्विष्महि	अजुहुम	अजुहुमहि
	2	अद्विष्ट	अद्विड्ढ्वम्	अजुहुत	अजुहुध्वम्
	3	अद्विषन् or अद्विषुः	अद्विषत	अजुह्वुः	अजुह्वत

Root: सु cl. 5. रुध् cl. 7.
Spec. St. Base. सुनो रुणध्
Spec. W. Base. सुनु रुन्ध्

		Parasmai.	Âtmane.	Parasmai.	Âtmane.

1.—Present Indicative.

		Parasmai.	Âtmane.	Parasmai.	Âtmane.
Sing.	1	सुनोमि	सुन्वे	रुणध्मि	रुन्धे
	2	सुनोषि	सुनुषे	रुणत्सि	रुन्त्से
	3	सुनोति	सुनुते	रुणद्धि	रुन्द्धे
Dual.	1	सुनुवः or सुन्वः	सुनुवहे or सुन्वहे	रुन्ध्वः	रुन्ध्वहे
	2	सुनुथः	सुन्वाथे	रुन्द्धः	रुन्धाथे
	3	सुनुतः	सुन्वाते	रुन्द्धः	रुन्धाते
Plural.	1	सुनुमः or सुन्मः	सुनुमहे or सुन्महे	रुन्ध्मः	रुन्ध्महे
	2	सुनुथ	सुनुध्वे	रुन्द्ध	रुन्द्धे
	3	सुन्वन्ति	सुन्वते	रुन्धन्ति	रुन्धते

2.—Present Potential.

Sing.	1	सुनुयाम्	सुन्वीय	रुन्ध्याम्	रुन्धीय
	2	सुनुयाः	सुन्वीथाः	रुन्ध्याः	रुन्धीथाः
	3	सुनुयात्	सुन्वीत	रुन्ध्यात्	रुन्धीत
Dual.	1	सुनुयाव	सुन्वीवहि	रुन्ध्याव	रुन्धीवहि
	2	सुनुयातम्	सुन्वीयाथाम्	रुन्ध्यातम्	रुन्धीयाथाम्
	3	सुनुयाताम्	सुन्वीयाताम्	रुन्ध्याताम्	रुन्धीयाताम्
Plural.	1	सुनुयाम	सुन्वीमहि	रुन्ध्याम	रुन्धीमहि
	2	सुनुयात	सुन्वीध्वम्	रुन्ध्यात	रुन्धीध्वम्
	3	सुनुयुः	सुन्वीरन्	रुन्ध्युः	रुन्धीरन्

3.—Present Imperative.

Sing.	1	सुनवानि	सुनवै	रुणधानि	रुणधै
	2	सुनु or सुनुतात्	सुनुष्व	रुन्द्धि or रुन्द्धात्	रुन्त्स्व
	3	सुनोतु or सुनुतात्	सुनुताम्	रुणद्धु or रुन्द्धात्	रुन्द्धाम्
Dual.	1	सुनवाव	सुनवावहै	रुणधाव	रुणधावहै
	2	सुनुतम्	सुन्वाथाम्	रुन्द्धम्	रुन्धाथाम्
	3	सुनुताम्	सुन्वाताम्	रुन्द्धाम्	रुन्धाताम्
Plural.	1	सुनवाम	सुनवामहै	रुणधाम	रुणधामहै
	2	सुनुत	सुनुध्वम्	रुन्द्ध	रुन्द्धम्
	3	सुन्वन्तु	सुन्वताम्	रुन्धन्तु	रुन्धताम्

4.—Imperfect.

Sing.	1	असुनवम्	असुन्वि	अरुणधम्	अरुन्धि
	2	असुनोः	असुनुथाः	अरुणः or अरुणत्	अरुन्द्धाः
	3	असुनोत्	असुनुत	अरुणत्	अरुन्द्ध
Dual.	1	असुनुव or असुन्व	असुनुवहि or असुन्वहि	अरुन्ध्व	अरुन्ध्वहि
	2	असुनुतम्	असुन्वाथाम्	अरुन्द्धम्	अरुन्धाथाम्
	3	असुनुताम्	असुन्वाताम्	अरुन्द्धाम्	अरुन्धाताम्
Plural.	1	असुनुम or असुन्म	असुनुमहि or असुन्महि	अरुन्ध्म	अरुन्ध्माहि
	2	असुनुत	असुनुध्वम्	अरुन्द्ध	अरुन्द्धम्
	3	असुन्वन्	असुन्वत	अरुन्धन्	अरुन्धत

CONJUGATION OF VERBS.

Root: तन् cl. 8. क्री cl. 9.
Spec. St. Base: तनो क्रीणा
Spec. W. Base: तनु क्रीणी

	Parasmai.	Âtmane.	Parasmai.	Âtmane.
		1.—*Present Indicative.*		
Sing. 1	तनोमि	तन्वे	क्रीणामि	क्रीणे
Sing. 2	तनोषि	तनुषे	क्रीणासि	क्रीणीषे
Sing. 3	तनोति	तनुते	क्रीणाति	क्रीणीते
Dual. 1	तनुवः or तन्वः	तनुवहे or तन्वहे	क्रीणीवः	क्रीणीवहे
Dual. 2	तनुथः	तन्वाथे	क्रीणीथः	क्रीणाथे
Dual. 3	तनुतः	तन्वाते	क्रीणीतः	क्रीणाते
Plural. 1	तनुमः or तन्मः	तनुमहे or तन्महे	क्रीणीमः	क्रीणीमहे
Plural. 2	तनुथ	तनुध्वे	क्रीणीथ	क्रीणीध्वे
Plural. 3	तन्वन्ति	तन्वते	क्रीणन्ति	क्रीणते
		2.—*Present Potential.*		
Sing. 1	तनुयाम्	तन्वीय	क्रीणीयाम्	क्रीणीय
Sing. 2	तनुयाः	तन्वीथाः	क्रीणीयाः	क्रीणीथाः
Sing. 3	तनुयात्	तन्वीत	क्रीणीयात्	क्रीणीत
Dual. 1	तनुयाव	तन्वीवहि	क्रीणीयाव	क्रीणीवहि
Dual. 2	तनुयातम्	तन्वीयाथाम्	क्रीणीयातम्	क्रीणीयाथाम्
Dual. 3	तनुयाताम्	तन्वीयाताम्	क्रीणीयाताम्	क्रीणीयाताम्
Plural. 1	तनुयाम	तन्वीमहि	क्रीणीयाम	क्रीणीमहि
Plural. 2	तनुयात	तन्वीध्वम्	क्रीणीयात	क्रीणीध्वम्
Plural. 3	तनुयुः	तन्वीरन्	क्रीणीयुः	क्रीणीरन्
		3.—*Present Imperative.*		
Sing. 1	तनवानि	तनवै	क्रीणानि	क्रीणै
Sing. 2	तनु or तनुतात्	तनुष्व	क्रीणीहि or क्रीणीतात्	क्रीणीष्व
Sing. 3	तनोतु or तनुतात्	तनुताम्	क्रीणातु or क्रीणीतात्	क्रीणीताम्
Dual. 1	तनवाव	तनवावहै	क्रीणाव	क्रीणावहै
Dual. 2	तनुतम्	तन्वाथाम्	क्रीणीतम्	क्रीणाथाम्
Dual. 3	तनुताम्	तन्वाताम्	क्रीणीताम्	क्रीणाताम्
Plural. 1	तनवाम	तनवामहै	क्रीणाम	क्रीणामहै
Plural. 2	तनुत	तनुध्वम्	क्रीणीत	क्रीणीध्वम्
Plural. 3	तन्वन्तु	तन्वताम्	क्रीणन्तु	क्रीणताम्

4.—*Imperfect.*

Sing.	1 अतनवम्	अतन्वि	अक्रीणाम्	अक्रीणि
	2 अतनोः	अतनुथाः	अक्रीणाः	अक्रीणीथाः
	3 अतनोत्	अतनुत	अक्रीणात्	अक्रीणीत
Dual.	1 अतनुव or अतन्व	अतनुवहि or अतन्वहि	अक्रीणीव	अक्रीणीवहि
	2 अतनुतम्	अतन्वाथाम्	अक्रीणीतम्	अक्रीणाथाम्
	3 अतनुताम्	अतन्वाताम्	अक्रीणीताम्	अक्रीणाताम्
Plural.	1 अतनुम or अतन्म	अतनुमहि or अतन्महि	अक्रीणीम	अक्रीणीमहि
	2 अतनुत	अतनुध्वम्	अक्रीणीत	अक्रीणीध्वम्
	3 अतन्वन्	अतन्वत	अक्रीणन्	अक्रीणत

§ 262. In order to exemplify the rules contained in §§ 250 &c. we proceed to give some forms of the regular verbs या, वी, जागृ, ईर्, चक्ष्, आस्, दुह्, लिह्; ह्री, भृ; शक्; युज्, पिष्, हिंस्; and बन्ध्; the student may conjugate each of these roots in full:

1. या cl. 2. P. 'to go;' Pres. Ind. यामि, यासि, याति; यावः, याथः, यातः; यामः, याथ, यान्ति. Pres. Pot. यायाम्. Pres. Imperat. 2 Sing. याहि. Imperf. 3 Plur. अयान् or अयुः.

2. वी cl. 2. P. 'to go;' Pres. Ind. वेमि, वेषि, वेति; वीवः, वीथः, वीतः; वीमः, वीय, वियन्ति. Pres. Pot. वीयाम्. Pres. Imperat. वयानि, वीहि, वेतु. Imperf. अवयम्; 3 Plur. अवियन् (or, according to some, अव्यन्).

3. जागृ cl. 2. P. 'to wake;' Pres. Ind. जागर्मि, जागर्षि, जागर्ति; जागृवः; 3 Plur. जाग्रति. Pres. Pot. जागृयाम्. Pres. Imperat. जागराणि, जागृहि, जागर्तु; 3 Plur. जाग्रतु. Imperf. अजागरम्, अजागः, अजागः; अजागृव; 3 Plur. अजागरुः.

4. ईर् cl. 2. Â. 'to go;' Pres. Ind. ईरे, ईर्षे, ईर्ते; 3 Plur. ईरते. Pres. Pot. ईरीय. Pres. Imperat. ईरै, ईर्ष्व, ईर्ताम्. Imperf. ऐरि.

5. चक्ष् cl. 2. Â. 'to speak;' Pres. Ind. चक्षे, चक्षे, चष्टे; चक्ष्वहे; 2 Plur. चड्ढे; 3 Plur. चक्षते. Pres. Pot. चक्षीय. Pres. Imperat. चक्षै, चक्ष्व, चष्टाम्. Imperf. अचक्षि, अचष्ठाः, अचष्ट. (This root is conjugated only in the Special tenses, and optionally in the Perfect.)

6. आस् cl. 2. Â. 'to sit;' Pres. Ind. आसे, आस्से, आस्ते; 2 Plur. आध्वे. Imperf. आसि.

CONJUGATION OF VERBS.

7. दुह् cl. 2. P. Â. 'to milk;' Pres. Ind. Par. दोह्मि, धोक्षि, दोग्धि; दुह्वः, दुह्मः, दुह्मः; दुह्मः, दुग्ध, दुहन्ति. Pres. Ind. Âtm. दुहे, धुक्षे, दुग्धे; 2 Plur. धुग्ध्वे; Pres. Imper. Par. दोहानि, दुग्धि, दोग्धु. Imperf. Par. अदोहम्, अधोक्, अधोक्; अदुह.

8. लिह् cl. 2. P. Â. 'to lick;' Pres. Ind. Par. लेह्मि, लक्षि, लेढि; लिह्वः, लीढः, लीढः; लिह्मः, लीढ, लिहन्ति. Pres. Ind. Âtm. लिहे, लिक्षे, लीढे; 2 Plur. लीढ्वे. Pres. Imper. Par. लेहानि, लीढि, लेढु; Imperf. Par. अलेहम्, अलेट्, अलेट्; अलिह्.

9. ह्री cl. 3. P. 'to be ashamed;' Pres. Ind. जिह्रेमि, जिह्रेषि, जिह्रेति; जिह्रिवः; 3 Plur. जिह्रियति. Pres. Pot. जिह्रीयाम्. Pres. Imperat. जिह्रयाणि, जिह्रीहि. Imperf. अजिह्रयम्, अजिह्रेः, अजिह्रेत्; अजिह्रिव; 3 Plur. अजिह्रयुः.

10. भृ cl. 3. P. Â. 'to bear;' Pres. Ind. Par. विभर्मि, विभर्षि, विभर्ति; विभृवः; 3 Plur. विभ्रति. Pres. Ind. Âtm. विभ्रे, विभृषे. Pres. Pot. Par. विभृयाम्. Âtm. विभ्रीय. Pres. Imper. Par. विभराणि, विभृहि; Âtm. विभरै, विभृष्व. Imperf. Par. अविभरम्, अविभः, अविभः; अविभृत; 3 Plur. अविभ्रुः; Âtm. अविभ्रि, अविभृथाः.

11. शक् cl. 5. P. 'to be able;' Pres. Ind. शक्नोमि, शक्नोषि, शक्नोति; शक्नुवः (only); 3 Plur. शक्नुवन्ति. Pres. Pot. शक्नुयाम्. Pres. Imperat. शक्नवानि, शक्नुहि, शक्नोतु; 3 Plur. शक्नुवन्तु. Imperf. अशक्नवम्; 1 Du. अशक्नुव; 3 Plur. अशक्नुवन्.

12. युज् cl. 7. P. Â. 'to join;' Pres. Ind. Par. युनज्मि, युनक्षि, युनक्ति; युञ्ज्वः, युङ्क्थः, युङ्क्तः; युञ्ज्मः, युङ्क्थ, युञ्जन्ति. Pres. Ind. Âtm. युञ्जे; 2 Plur. युङ्ग्ध्वे. Pres. Pot. Par. युञ्ज्याम्; Âtm. युञ्जीय. Pres. Imperat. Par. युनजानि, युङ्ग्धि, युनक्तु; Âtm. युनजै. Imperf. Par. अयुनजम्, अयुनक्, अयुनक्; अयुञ्ज्व; Âtm. अयुञ्जि.

13. पिष् cl. 7. P. 'to pound;' Pres. Ind. पिनष्मि, पिनक्षि पिनष्टि; पिंष्वः, पिंष्ठः, पिंष्टः; पिंष्मः, पिंष्ठ, पिंषन्ति. Pres. Pot. पिंष्याम्. Pres. Imperat. पिनषाणि, पिंड्ढि, पिनष्टु. Imperf. अपिनषम्, अपिनट्, अपिनट्; अपिंष्व.

14. हिंस् cl. 7. P. 'to strike;' Pres. Ind. हिनस्मि, हिनस्सि, हिनस्ति; हिंसः. Pres. Pot. हिंस्याम्. Pres. Imperat. हिनसानि, हिन्धि, हिनस्तु. Imperf. अहिनसम्, अहिनः or अहिनन्, अहिनत्.

15. वन्ध् cl. 9. P. 'to bind;' Pres. Ind. वध्नामि; 1 Plur. वध्नीमः. Pres. Pot. वध्नीयाम्. Pres. Imperat. वध्नानि, बधान, वध्नातु. Imperf. अवध्नाम्; 1 Plur. अवध्नीम.

13 s G

Irregular Roots of the 2nd, 3rd, 5th, 7th, 8th and 9th classes.

Second Class (*Adâdi*).

§ 263. Roots ending in उ substitute Vriddhi instead of Guṇa for their final vowel in strong forms the terminations of which begin with consonants; *e. g.* यु P. 'to join;' Pres. Ind. Par. यौमि, यौषि, यौति; युवः. Pres. Imperat. यवानि, युहि, यौतु; यवाव, युतम्. Pres. Pot. युयाम्. Imperf. अयवम्, अयौः, अयौत्; अयुव.

§ 264. अद् P. 'to eat,' forms the 2 Sing. Imperf. Par. आदः and the 3 Sing. Imperf. Par. आदत् (instead of आः or आत्, and आत्).

§ 265. अन् P. 'to breathe;' जक्ष् P. 'to eat;' रुद् P. 'to weep;' श्वस् P. 'to sigh;' and स्वप् P. 'to sleep,' insert इ between the special base and terminations beginning with consonants, except यु; before the terminations : and त् of the 2nd and 3rd Sing. Imperf. Par. they insert optionally either ई or अ; *e. g.* Pres. Ind. रोदिमि, रोदिषि, रोदिति; रुदिवः; 3 Plur. रुदन्ति. Pres. Pot. रुद्याम्. Pres. Imperat. रोदानि, रुदिहि, रोदितु. Imperf. अरोदम्, अरोदीः or अरोदः, अरोदीत् or अरोदत्; अरुदिव. Rt. जक्ष्, 3 Plur. Pres. Ind. जक्षति &c.

§ 266. अस् P. (and, when used as an auxiliary verb, Â.) 'to be,' drops its radical अ in the weak forms and is otherwise irregular :—

		Pres. Ind.		Pres. Pot.		Pres. Imperat.		Imperf.	
		Par.	Âtm.	Par.	Âtm.	Par.	Âtm.	Par.	Âtm.
Sing.	1	अस्मि	हे	स्याम्	सीय	असानि	असै	आसम्	आसि
	2	असि	से	स्याः	सीथाः	एधि	स्व	आसीः	आस्थाः
	3	अस्ति	स्ते	स्यात्	सीत	अस्तु	स्ताम्	आसीत्	आस्त
Dual.	1	स्वः	स्वहे	स्याव	सीवहि	असाव	असावहै	आस्व	आस्वहि
	2	स्थः	साथे	स्यातम्	सीयाथाम्	स्तम्	साथाम्	आस्तम्	आसाथाम्
	3	स्तः	साते	स्याताम्	सीयाताम्	स्ताम्	साताम्	आस्ताम्	आसाताम्
Plural.	1	स्मः	स्महे	स्याम	सीमहि	असाम	असामहै	आस्म	आस्महि
	2	स्थ	ध्वे	स्यात	सीध्वम्	स्त	ध्वम्	आस्त	आध्वम्
	3	सन्ति	सते	स्युः	सीरन्	सन्तु	सताम्	आसन्	आसत

§ 267. इ P. 'to go,' changes its इ to य् in the 3 Plur. Pres. Ind. and Imperat. Par. When combined with the preposition अधि, in the sense of 'to read, to study,' it is Âtm. and changes its इ before vowel-terminations

§ 272.] CONJUGATION OF VERBS. 99

regularly to इय्; *e. g.* Pres. Ind. Par. एमि, एषि, एति; इव:; 3 Plur. यन्ति. Pres. Pot. इयाम्. Pres. Imperat. अयानि, इहि, एतु; 3 Plur. यन्तु. Imperf. आयम्, ऐः, ऐत्; ऐव.—Âtm. with अधि, Pres. Ind. अधीये, अधीषे, अधीते; अधीवहे, अधीयाथे. Pres. Pot. अधीयीय. Pres. Imperat. अध्ययै, अधीष्व. Imperf. अध्यैयि, अध्यैथाः, अध्यैत; अध्यैवहि, अध्यैयाथाम्, अध्यैयाताम्; अध्यैमहि, अध्यैध्वम्, अध्यैयत.

§ 268. ईश् Â. 'to rule,' and ईड् Â. 'to praise,' insert इ between the root and the terminations से, स्व, ध्वे and ध्वम् of the 2nd Sing. and 2nd Plur. Pres. Indic. and Imperative (*not* the Imperfect); *e. g.* ईश्; Pres. Ind. ईशे, ईशिषे, ईष्टे; 2 Plur. ईशिध्वे. Pres. Pot. ईशीय. Pres. Imperat. ईशै ईशिष्व, ईष्टाम्; 2 Plur. ईशिध्वम्. Imperf. ऐशि; 2 Plur. ऐड्ढुम्.—ईड्; Pres. Ind. ईडे, ईडिषे, ईट्टे; 2 Plur. ईडिध्वे. Pres. Pot. ईडीय. Pres. Imperat. ईडै, ईडिष्व, ईट्टाम्; 2 Plur. ईडिध्वम्. Imperf. ऐड; 2 Plur. ऐड्ढुम्.

§ 269. ऊर्णु P. Â. 'to cover,' may optionally substitute Vṛiddhi for its final उ in strong forms the terminations of which begin with consonants, except in the 2nd and 3rd Sing. Imperf. Par.; *e. g.* Pres. Ind. Par. ऊर्णोमि or ऊर्णौमि, ऊर्णोषि or ऊर्णौषि, ऊर्णोति or ऊर्णौति; ऊर्णुवः; 3 Plur. ऊर्णुवन्ति. Pres. Pot. ऊर्णुयाम्. Pres. Imperat. ऊर्णवानि, ऊर्णुहि, ऊर्णोतु or ऊर्णौतु. Imperf. और्णवम्, और्णोः, और्णोत्; और्णुव. Pres. Ind. Âtm. ऊर्णुवे.

§ 270. नु P. 'to grow,' रु P. 'to sound,' and स्तु P. Â. 'to praise,' optionally prefix इ to all terminations beginning with consonants; observe § 263; *e. g.* Pres. Ind. Par. स्तौमि or स्तवीमि, स्तौषि or स्तवीषि, स्तौति or स्तवीति; स्तुवः or स्तुवीवः; 3 Plur. स्तुवन्ति. Pres. Pot. स्तुयाम् or स्तुवीयाम्. Pres. Imperat. स्तवानि, स्तुहि or स्तुवीहि, स्तौतु or स्तवीतु. Imperf. अस्तवम्, अस्तोः or अस्तवीः. Pres. Ind. Âtm. स्तुवे, स्तुषे or स्तुवीषे. Pres. Pot. स्तुवीय. Pres. Imperat. स्तवै, स्तुष्व or स्तुवीष्व. Imperf. अस्तुवि.

§ 271. दरिद्रा P. 'to be poor,' drops its final आ in weak forms before vowel-terminations and substitutes इ for it in weak forms before consonantal terminations; *e. g.* Pres. Ind दरिद्रामि, दरिद्रासि, दरिद्राति; दरिद्रिवः; 3 Plur. दरिद्रति. Pres. Pot. दरिद्रियाम्. Pres. Imperat. दरिद्राणि, दरिद्रिहि, दरिद्रातु; 3 Plur. दरिद्रतु. Imperf. अदरिद्राम्, अदरिद्राः, अदरिद्रात्; अदरिद्रिव; 3 Plur. अदरिद्रुः.

§ 272. ब्रू P. Â. 'to speak' (used only in the special tenses) prefixes in strong forms ई to consonantal terminations; *e. g.* Pres. Ind. Par. ब्रवीमि,

ब्रवीषि, ब्रवीति; ब्रूवः; 3 Plur. ब्रुवन्ति. Pres. Pot. ब्रूयाम्. Pres. Imperat. ब्रवाणि, ब्रूहि, ब्रवीतु. Imperf. अब्रवम्, अब्रवोः, अब्रवीत्; अब्रूव; 3 Plur. अब्रुवन्. Pres. Ind. Ātm. ब्रुवे. Pres. Pot. ब्रुवीय. Pres. Imperat. ब्रवै. Imperf. अब्रुवि.

§ 273. मृज् P. 'to wipe off,' forms its special strong base by substituting Vriddhi instead of Guṇa for its radical vowel; Vriddhi is optionally substituted also in the 3 Plur. Pres. Ind., Imperat., and Imperf. The final ज् is treated like घ् before terminations beginning with त्, थ्, घ्, and स्; e.g. Pres. Ind. मार्ज्मि, मार्क्षि, मार्ष्टि; मृज्वः, मृष्ठः, मृष्टः; मृज्मः, मृष्ठ, मृजन्ति or मार्जन्ति. Pres. Pot. मृज्याम्. Pres. Imperat. मार्जानि, मृड्ढि, मार्ष्टु; मार्जाव, मृष्टम्, मृष्टाम्; मार्जाम, मृष्ट, मृजन्तु or मार्जन्तु. Imperf. अमार्जम्, अमार्ट्, अमार्ट्; अमृज्व; 3 Plur. अमृजन् or अमार्जन्.

§ 274. वच् P. 'to speak,' is deficient in the 3 Plur. Pres. Ind; according to others in the whole Plural; according to others all third persons of the Plur. are wanting. Otherwise it is regular; e.g. Pres. Ind. वच्मि, वक्षि, वक्ति &c.

§ 275. वश् P. 'to wish,' contracts its radical व to उ in all weak forms; e.g. Pres. Ind. वश्मि, वक्षि, वष्टि; उश्वः, उश्ठः, उश्ठः; उश्मः, उश्ठ, उशन्ति. Pres. Pot. उश्याम्. Pres. Imperat. वशानि, उड्ढि, वष्टु; वशाव, उश्ठम्. Imperf. अवशाम्, अवट्, अवट्; और्श, और्ष्टम्.

§ 276. विद् P. 'to know,' is conjugated regularly (cf. § 260 Imperf. 3 Plur.); e.g. Pres. Ind. वेद्मि, वेत्सि, वेत्ति; विद्वः; 3 Plur. विदन्ति. Pres. Pot. विद्याम्. Pres. Imperat. वेदानि, विद्धि, वेत्तु. Imperf. अवेदम्, अवेः or अवेत्, अवेत्; अविद्व; 3 Plur. अविदुः. But it may in the Pres. Ind. optionally take the terminations given in § 227, col. III.: वेद, वेत्थ, वेद; विद्व, विद्युः, विदतुः; विद्म, विद, विदुः. The Pres. Imperat. may optionally be formed periphrastically by adding the termination आम् to विद् (= विदाम्) and by combining विदाम् with the Pres. Imperat. Par. of rt. कृ (§ 290) e.g. विदांकरवाणि, विदांकुरु, विदांकरोतु &c.

§ 277. शास् P. 'to command,' is changed to शिष् in weak forms before consonantal terminations, except in the 2nd Sing. Pres. Imperat. (cf. § 252, d); e.g. Pres. Ind. शास्मि, शास्सि, शास्ति; शिष्वः, शिष्ठः, शिष्टः; शिष्मः, शिष्ठ, शासति. Pres. Pot. शिष्याम्. Pres. Imperat. शासानि, शाधि, शास्तु; शासाव, शिष्टम्; 3 Plur. शासतु. Imperf. अशासम्, अशाः or अशात्, अशात्; अशिष्व; 3 Plur. अशासुः.

CONJUGATION OF VERBS.

§ 278. श्री Â. 'to lie down, to sleep,' gunates its vowel in all the forms of the special tenses; in the 3 Plur. Pres. Ind., Imperat., and Imperf. र् is prefixed to the terminations; *e. g.* Pres. Ind. श्राये, शेषे, शेते; शेवहे; 3 Plur. शेरते. Pres. Pot. शयीय. Pres. Imperat. श्रयै, शेष्व; 3 Plur. शेरताम्. Imperf. अश्रयि, अशेथाः; 3 Plur. अशेरत.

§ 279. सू Â. 'to bring forth,' does not gunate its vowel in strong forms, but changes it to उव्; *e. g.* Pres. Ind. सुवे, सूषे. Pres. Pot. सुवीय. Pres. Imperat. सुवै, सूष्व, सूताम्; सुवावहे. Imperf. असुवि, असूथाः.

§ 280. हन् P. 'to strike,' drops its final न् in weak forms before terminations commencing with त or थ. In the 3rd Plur. Pres. Ind., Imperat. and Imperf. हन् becomes घ्न. The 2nd Sing. Pres. Imperat. is जहि (instead of हहि); *e. g.* Pres. Ind. हन्मि, हंसि, हन्ति; हन्वः, हथः, हतः; हन्मः, हथ, घ्नन्ति. Pres. Pot. हन्याम्. Pres. Imperat. हनानि, जहि, हन्तु; हनाव, हतम्; 3 Plur. घ्नन्तु. Imperf. अहनम्, अहन्, अहन्; अहन्व, अहतम्; 3 Plur. अघ्नन्.

Third Class (*Juhotyâdi*).

§ 281. ऋ P. 'to go,' forms its special strong base इयर्, its special weak base इयृ; *e. g.* Pres. Ind. इयर्मि, इयर्षि, इयर्ति; इयृवः; 3 Plur. इयृति. Pres. Pot. इयृयाम्. Pres. Imperat. इयराणि, इयृहि, इयर्तु; 3 Plur. इयृतु. Imperf. ऐयरम्, ऐयः, ऐयः; ऐयृव; 3 Plur. ऐयरुः.

§ 282. दा P. Â. 'to give,' and धा P. Â. 'to place,' form their special weak bases दद् and दध्; the final ध् of दध् combines with त् and थ् to त्त and त्थ. Whenever the final ध् of दध् becomes त् or द्, the initial द is changed to ध्. The 2nd Sing. Pres. Imperat. Par. is देहि (of दा) and धेहि (of धा); *e. g.* दा; Pres. Ind. Par. ददामि, ददासि, ददाति; दद्वः, दत्थः, दत्तः; दद्मः, दत्थ, ददति. Pres. Pot. दद्याम्. Pres. Imperat. ददानि, देहि, ददातु. Imperf. अददाम्, अददाः, अददात्; अदद्व; 3 Plur. अदद्युः. Pres. Ind. Âtm. ददे, ददसे, दत्ते. Pres. Pot. ददीय. Pres. Imperat. ददै, दत्स्व. Imperf. अददि, अदत्थाः; 2 Plur. अदद्ध्वम्. धा, Pres. Ind. Par. दधामि; Du. दध्वः, धत्थः, धत्तः; 3 Plur. दधति. Pres. Pot. दध्याम्. Pres. Imperat. दधानि, धेहि, दधातु; दधाव, धत्तम्. Imperf. अदधाम्; Plur. अदध्व, अधत्त, अदधुः. Pres. Ind. Âtm. दधे, धत्से, धत्ते; 2 Plur. धद्धे. Pres. Pot. दधीय. Pres. Imperat. दधै, धत्स्व. Imperf. अदधि, अधत्थाः, अधत्त; 2 Plur. अधद्ध्वम्.

§ 283. निज् P Â. 'to cleanse,' विज् P. Â. 'to separate,' and विद् P. Â. 'to pervade,' gunate the vowel इ of the reduplicative syllable in all special forms, and do *not* gunate their radical vowel in strong forms before vowel-terminations; *e. g.* Pres. Ind. Par. नेनिज्मि, नेनेक्षि, नेनेक्ति; नेनिज्वः. Pres. Pot. नेनिज्याम्. Pres. Imperat. नेनिजानि, नेनिग्धि, नेनेक्तु; नेनिजाव. Imperf. अनेनिजम्, अनेनेक्, अनेनेक्; अनेनिज्व; 3 Plur. अनेनिजुः. Pres. Ind. Átm. नेनिजे. Pres. Pot. नेनिजीय. Pres. Imperat. नेनिजै. Imperf. अनेनिजि.

§ 284. नृ P. 'to fill,' is conjugated regularly like भृ; *e. g.* Pres. Ind. पिपर्मि, पिपर्षि, पिपर्ति; पिपृवः, पिपृथः, पिपृतः; पिपृमः, पिपृथ, पिप्रति. But पृ P. 'to fill,' changes its final ऋ in weak forms before consonantal terminations to उर् and before vowel terminations (except in the 3 Plur. Imperf.) to उर्; *e. g.* Pres. Ind. पिपर्मि, पिपर्षि, पिपर्ति; पिपुर्वः, पिपूर्थः, पिपूर्तः; पिपूर्मः, पिपूर्थ, पिपुरति. Pres. Pot. पिपूर्याम्. Pres. Imperat. पिपरानि, पिपुर्हि, पिपर्तु; पिपराव, पिपूर्तम्; 3 Plur. पिपुरतु. Imperf. अपिपरम्, अपिपः, अपिपः; अपिपूर्व; 3 Plur. अपिपरुः.

§ 285. भी, P. 'to fear,' optionally shortens its radical vowel in weak forms before consonantal terminations; *e. g.* Pres. Ind. बिभेमि; Du. बिभीवः or बिभिवः, बिभीथः or बिभिथः, बिभीतः or बिभितः; 3 Plur. बिभ्यति. Pres. Pot. बिभीयाम् or बिभियाम्. Pres. Imperat. बिभयानि, बिभीहि or बिभिहि. Imperf. अबिभयम्, अबिभेः; 1 Du. अबिभीव or अबिभिव; 3 Plur. आबिभयुः.

§ 286. मा Â. 'to measure,' and हा Â. 'to go,' form their special bases before consonantal terminations मिमी, जिही, before vowel-terminations मिमु, जिह्; *e. g.* मा, Pres. Ind. मिमे, मिमीषे, मिमीते; मिमीवहे, मिमाथे. Pres. Pot. मिमीय, Pres. Imperat. मिमै, मिमीष्व, मिमीताम्; मिमावहै. Imperf. अमिमि, अमिमीथाः, अमिमीत; 3 Plur. अमिमत.—हा, Pres. Ind. जिहे, जिहीषे, जिहीते; जिहीवहे, जिहाथे; 3 Plur. जिहते.

§ 287. हा P. 'to abandon,' forms its special weak base before consonantal terminations, except in the Pres. Pot., जहीं or जहि, before vowel-terminations and in the Pres. Pot. जह्; the 2nd Sing. Pres. Imperat. is जहाहि or जहीहि or जहिहि; *e. g.* Pres. Ind. जहामि, जहासि, जहाति; जहीवः or जहिवः, जहीथः or जहिथः; 3 Plur. जहति. Pres. Pot. जह्याम्. Pres. Imperat. जहानि, जहाहि or जहीहि or जहिहि, जहतु; जहाव, जहीतम् or जहितम्; 3 Plur. जहतु. Imperf. अजहाम्; 1 Plur. अजहीव or अजहिव; 3 Plur. अजहुः.

Fifth Class (*Svádi*).

§ 288. श्रु P. 'to hear,' substitutes in the special base ऋ for उ; *e. g.* Pres. Ind. शृणोमि, शृणोषि, शृणोति; शृणुवः or शृण्वः &c.

Seventh Class (*Rudhádi*).

§ 289. नृह् P. 'to kill,' forms its special strong base before consonantal terminations तृणेह्, before vowel-terminations regularly तृणह्; *e. g.* Pres. Ind. तृणेह्मि, तृणेक्षि, तृणेढि; तृंह्ः, तृण्ढः; 3 Plur. तृंहन्ति. Pres. Pot. तृह्याम्. Pres. Imperat. तृणहानि, तृण्ढि, तृणेढु. Imperf. अतृणहम्, अतृणेट्, अतृणेट्; अतृंद्ध; 3 Plur. अतृंहन्.

Eighth Class (*Tanádi*).

§ 290. कृ P. Â. 'to do,' forms its special strong base करो, its special weak base कुरु; the final उ of the latter is dropped before terminations beginning with व् or म्, and in the Pres. Pot. Par.; *e. g.* Pres. Ind. Par. करोमि, करोषि, करोति; कुर्वः, कुरुथः, कुरुतः; कुर्मः, कुरुथ, कुर्वन्ति. Pres. Pot. कुर्याम्. Pres. Imperat. करवाणि, कुरु, करोतु; करवाव, कुरुतम्. Imperf. अकरवम्, अकरोः, अकरोत्; अकुर्व, अकुरुतम्. Pres. Ind. Âtm. कुर्वे, कुर्ष्वे. Pres. Pot. कुर्वीय. Pres. Imperat. करवै. Imperf. अकुर्वि, अकुरुथाः.

Ninth Class (*Kryádi*).

§ 291. The roots ध्रू P. Â. 'to shake,' पू P. Â. 'to purify,' लू P. Â. 'to cut,' री P. 'to go,' &c., लो P. 'to attain,' ह्री P. 'to go,' &c., and all roots ending in ॠ shorten their radical vowel in the special base; *e. g.* पू, Pres. Ind. Par. पुनामि; Âtm. पुने. स्तृ 'to cover,' Pres. Ind. Par. स्तृणामि; Âtm. स्तृणे.

§ 292. ग्रह् P. Â. to seize,' contracts in the special base its radical र to ऋ, *e. g.* Pres. Ind. Par. गृह्णामि; Pres. Imperat. गृह्णानि, गृहाण, गृह्णातु.

§ 293. ज्ञा P. Â. 'to know,' forms its special strong base जाना, its special weak base जानी; *e. g.* Pres. Ind. Par. 3 Sing. जानाति; Âtm. जानीते.

§ 294. ज्या P. 'to become old,' contracts in the special base its radical या to इ; *e. g.* Pres. Ind. जिनामि, जिनासि, जिनाति &c.

B.—General Tenses.

Perfect, Aorist, Future, Conditional, Benedictive.

§ 295. The rules for the formation of the general tenses apply equally to all primitive roots, *i.e.* to all roots of the first nine classes.

§ 296. (a) Roots ending in ए, ऐ and औ change their final diphthong in all general tenses and derivative forms to आ, and are then treated like roots ending originally in आ.

(b) मि 'to throw,' मी 'to destroy,' and दी 'to perish,' change their final vowel to आ wherever Guṇa or Vṛiddhi ought to be substituted for it, and are then treated like roots originally ending in आ; ली 'to attain,' does the same optionally.

1.—The Perfect.

§ 297. The Perfect is formed either by reduplication (*Reduplicated Perfect*) or by means of certain auxiliary verbs (*Periphrastic Perfect*).

§ 298. (a) The reduplicated Perfect is formed—

1. Of all monosyllabic roots beginning with consonants, except कास् Â. 'to cough,' and दय् Â. 'to pity;'

2. Of all monosyllabic roots beginning with अ and आ, except अय् Â. 'to go,' and आस् Â. 'to sit;'

3. Of all monosyllabic roots beginning with इ, उ, or ऋ, provided these vowels are *prosodially short* (§ 8), and of ऊर्णु P. Â. 'to cover.'

(b) The periphrastic Perfect is formed—

1 Of all roots which contain more than one syllable, except ऊर्णु; *e.g.* of चकास्;

2. Of all roots which commence with a vowel that is *prosodially long*, except अ and आ, and of अय् and आस् (a, 2); *e. g.* of इन्ध्, उन्द्, ईड्, ऊह, ईक्ष्, एध् &c.

3. Of कास् and दय् (a, 1).

(c) Both Perfects may optionally be formed—

1. Of उष् P. 'to burn,' विद् P. 'to know,' जागृ P. 'to wake,' दरिद्रा P. 'to be poor.'

2. Of भी P. 'to fear,' भृ P. Â. 'to bear,' हु P. 'to sacrifice,' and ह्री P. 'to be ashamed;' these four roots take in the Periphrastic Perfect the same reduplicative syllable which they take in the Present tense.

(a.)—*The Reduplicated Perfect.*

§ 299. The *base* is formed by reduplication of the root.

(a) Roots beginning with consonants are reduplicated according to the rules laid down in § 230 &c.; e. g.

rt. बुध्;	Perf. Base	बुबुध्;	3 Plur. P.		बुबुधुः
rt. छिद्;	,,	,,	चिच्छिद्;	,, ,, ,,	चिच्छिदुः
rt. कम्;	,,	,,	चकम्;	3 Sing. Â.	चकमे
rt. क्रम्;	,,	,,	चक्रम्;	3 Plur. P.	चक्रमुः
rt. स्कन्द्;	,,	,,	चस्कन्द्;	,, ,, ,,	चस्कन्दुः
rt. कृ;	,,	,,	चकृ;	1 Plur. P.	चकृम
rt. सिच्;	,,	,,	सिषिच्; (§ 59); 3 Plur. P. सिषिचुः
rt. स्तु;	,,	,,	तुष्टु; (§ 59); 1 Plur. P. तुष्टुम

(b) When roots begin with इ or उ, these vowels are doubled; subsequently इ + इ and उ + उ unite to ई and ऊ; but when the radical इ and उ are changed to any vowel not homogeneous (§ 9) to them, the first इ and उ are changed to इय् and उव् respectively; e. g.

rt. इष्; Perf. Base इ + इष्; 3 Plur. P. इ + इषुः = ईषुः; 3 Sing. P. इ + एष = इयेष.
rt. उख्; ,, ,, उ + उख्; ,, ,, ,, उ + उखुः = ऊखुः; ,, ,, ,, उ + ओख = उवोख.
rt. इ; ,, ,, इ + इ; ,, ,, ,, इ + इयुः = ईयुः; ,, ,, ,, इ + आय = इयाय.

(c) Initial आ remains unchanged; initial अ, when prosodically short, is changed to आ; e. g.

rt. आप्;	Perf. Base	आप्;	3 Plur. P.		आपुः
rt. अस्;	,,	,,	आस्;	,, ,, ,,	आसुः

(d) To roots beginning with अ, prosodically long, and to roots beginning with ऋ, the syllable आन् is prefixed; e. g.

rt. अञ्ज्;	Perf. Base	आनञ्ज्;	3 Plur. P.		आनञ्जुः
rt. ऋज्;	,,	,,	आनृज्;	3 Sing. Â.	आनृजे
rt. ऋछ्;	,,	,,	आनृछ्;	3 Plur. P.	आनृच्छुः (§ 54)

§ 300. *Strong and weak forms*: The base of the redupl. Perf. has often two forms, a *strong* base and a *weak* base. The strong base is used in the strong forms, the weak base in the weak forms. *Strong forms* are the three persons of the Singular in Parasmai.; the remaining forms of the Parasmai. and all the forms of the Âtmane. are *weak*.

§ 301. The *weak* base does generally not differ from the base formed by § 299. The *strong* base is formed from it thus:

(a) For penultimate (prosodially short) इ, उ, and ऋ Guṇa (ए, ओ, and अर्) is substituted; *e. g.*

rt. भिद्; Weak B. बिभिद्; Strong B. बिभेद्; 3 Sing. P. बिभेद.
rt. तुद्; ,, ,, तुतुद्; ,, ,, तुतोद्; ,, ,, ,, तुतोद.
rt. कृष्; ,, ,, चकृष्; ,, ,, चकर्ष्; ,, ,, ,, चकर्ष.
but rt. निन्द्; only Perf. Base निनिन्द्; ,, ,, ,, निनिन्द.
rt. मील्; ,, ,, ,, मिमील्; ,, ,, ,, मिमील.

(b) For final इ, ई, उ, ऊ, ऋ, ॠ, Guṇa or Vṛiddhi is substituted in the 1 Sing., Guṇa in the 2 Sing., and Vṛiddhi in the 3 Sing. Par.; *e. g.*

rt. नी; Weak base निनी; Strong base निने or निनै; 1 Sing. Par. निनय or निनाय; 2 Sing. निनेथ or निनयिथ; 3 Sing. निनाय.

rt. द्रु; Weak base दुद्रु; Strong base दुद्रो or दुद्रौ; 1 Sing. Par. दुद्रव or दुद्राव; 2 Sing. दुद्रोथ; 3 Sing. दुद्राव.

rt. कृ; Weak base चकृ; Strong base चकर् or चकार्; 1 Sing. Par. चकर or चकार; 2 Sing. चकर्थ; 3 Sing. चकार.

(c) Penultimate (prosodially short) अ is in the 1 Sing. Par. optionally changed to आ; in the 2 Sing. it remains unchanged; in the 3 Sing. it *must* be changed to आ; *e. g.*

rt. पच्; 1 Sing. Par. पपच or पपाच; 2 Sing. पपक्थ (or पेचिथ, § 315); 3 Sing. पपाच.

§ 302. The terminations given in col. III. of § 227 are added to the reduplicated (strong or weak) base. In many instances the vowel इ *must* be prefixed to the consonantal terminations (थ, व, म, से, वहे, महे and ध्वे) before they can be added to the base; in other cases इ *may* optionally be prefixed. The special rules for the optional addition of इ to consonantal terminations may be learned from § 304; but for all practical purposes it is sufficient to know that इ is *absolutely prohibited* only after the roots mentioned in the following paragraph and that it therefore may be employed after all other roots.

§ 303. (a). इ is never prefixed to the consonantal terminations when they are added to the eight roots :—

कृ 'to do' (except when it is changed to स्कृ; see § 229, d), भृ 'to bear,' वृ 'to choose,' सृ 'to go,' द्रु 'to run,' श्रु 'to hear,' स्तु 'to praise,' and स्रु 'to flow;' e.g.

rt. कृ; Weak B. चकृ; 1 Plur. P. चकृम; Strong B. चकर्; 2 Sing. चकर्थ.
rt. द्रु; ,, ,, दुद्रु; ,, ,, ,, दुद्रुम; ,, ,, दुद्रो; ,, ,, दुद्रोथ.

(But of संस्कृ 2 Sing. P. संचस्करिथ. वृ likewise forms the 2 Sing. Par. in classical Sanskrit ववरिथ.)

(b) Besides, इ is never prefixed to the termination थ, when it is added to monosyllabic roots ending in ऋ, except ऋ 'to go,' and स्वृ 'to sound;' e.g.

rt. स्मृ; 2 Sing. P. सस्मर्थ.

§ 304. (a) इ may optionally be prefixed to the consonantal terminations when they are added to the roots enumerated in § 366, b, 2 and 3;

rt. सिध्; Weak B. सिषिध्, 1 Plur. P. सिषिध्म or सिषिधिम; Strong B. सिषेध्; 2 Sing. P. सिषेद्ध or सिषेधिथ.

(b) Besides, इ may optionally be prefixed to the termination थ, when it is added to roots ending in vowels (except ऋ), or to roots which contain the vowel अ, provided that after these roots इ is forbidden to be prefixed to the terminations of the Periphrastic Future (§ 366 a); इ is optionally prefixed to थ also after स्तृ and भू; e.g.

rt. नी; Strong B. निने; 2 Sing. P. निनेथ or निनयिथ.
rt. स्तृ; ,, ,, सस्वर्; ,, ,, ,, सस्वर्थ or सस्वरिथ.
rt. हन्; ,, ,, जघन्; ,, ,, ,, जघन्थ or जघनिथ.

Exception. अद् 'to eat,' and व्ये 'to cover,' must insert इ before थ; 2 Sing. P. आदिथ, विव्ययिथ.

§ 305. *Sandhi:*

Before vowel-terminations (including the consonantal terminations when इ is prefixed to them) final vowels of the reduplicated base undergo the following changes :—

(a) इ and ई, when preceded by one consonant, are changed to य्, when preceded by more than one consonant, to इय्; e. g.

rt. चि; Weak B. चिचि; 2 Plur. P. चिच्य; 1 Plur. P. चिचियम.
rt. नी; ,, ,, निनी; ,, ,, ,, निन्य; ,, ,, ,, निनियम.
rt. क्षि; ,, ,, चिक्षि; ,, ,, ,, चिक्षिय; ,, ,, ,, चिक्षियिम.
rt. प्री; ,, ,, पिप्री; ,, ,, ,, पिप्रिय; ,, ,, ,, पिप्रियिम.

(b) उ and ऊ are always changed to उव्; e. g.

rt. दु; Weak B. दुदु; 2 Plur. P. दुदुव; 1 Plur. P. दुदुविम.
rt. पू; ,, ,, पुपू; ,, ,, ,, पुपुव; ,, ,, ,, पुपुविम.

(c) ऋ, when preceded by one consonant, is changed to र्, when preceded by more consonants than one, to अर्; e. g.

rt. धृ; Weak B. दधृ; 2 Plur. P. दध्र; 1 Plur. P. दधिम.
rt. स्मृ; ,, ,, सस्मृ; ,, ,, ,, सस्मर; ,, ,, ,, सस्मरिम.

(d) ॠ is changed to अर्; optionally to र् in दॄ, पॄ, and शॄ; e. g.

rt. कृ; Weak B. चकृ; 2 Plur. P. चकर; 1 Plur. P. चकरिम.
rt. दॄ; ,, ,, ददॄ; ,, ,, ,, ददर or दद्र; ,, ,, ददरिम or दद्रिम.

(e) ए, ऐ, ओ and औ, when they are Guṇa or Vṛiddhi substitutes for final इ, ई, उ, and ऊ, are changed to अय्, आय्, अव् and आव् respectively; e. g.

rt. नी; Strong B. निने or निनै; 1 Sing P. निनय or निनाय.
rt. स्तु; ,, ,, तुष्टो or तुष्टौ; ,, ,, ,, तुष्टव or तुष्टाव.

§ 306. The rules which regulate the euphonic changes which must take place when final consonants of the reduplicated base come into contact with initial letters of terminations apply equally to the finals of roots and to the initial letters of terminations in other general tenses and in the formation of words generally. They are therefore, in order to make them more widely applicable, and to save repetition, given here somewhat more fully than would have been necessary for the Reduplicated Perfect. With some of these rules the student has been made acquainted in § 252.

§ 307. When final consonants of roots meet with initial letters of terminations the rules given in §§ 50—59 must be observed. Moreover—

(a) Final य् and व् are dropped before all initial consonants except य्; e. g.

पूय्+त = पूत; तुर्व्+न = तूर्ण (§ 46; 58).

(b) Final म् is changed to न् before all initial consonants except य् and स्; e. g.

जगम्+वस् = जगन्वस्; गम्+तुम् = गन्तुम्; चक्षम्+ध्वे = चक्षन्ध्वे; चक्षम्+वहे = चक्षण्वहे. (§ 58.)

§ 308. Before initial स्—

(a) Final च्, ध्, छ्, ज्, झ्, श्, ष्, क्ष्, and ह् are changed to क् (observe § 53) after which स् is changed to ष् (§ 59); the final ह् of नह्, however, is changed to त्; e. g.

पच्+स्यति = पक्ष्यति; बध्+स्यति = बक्ष्यति; आनश्+से = आनक्षे; जगाह्+से = जघक्षे; नह्+स्यति = नत्स्यति.

(b) Final न् and म् are changed to Anusvâra; e. g.

चक्षम्+से = चक्षंसे; मन्+स्यते = मंस्यते.

(c) Final स् is changed to to त्; e. g.

वस्+स्यति = वत्स्यति; अवास्+सीत् = अवात्सीत्.

§ 309. Before an initial hard dental (त् or थ्)—

(a) Final च्, ज् (except of the roots mentioned under b) and the final ञ्ज् of लञ्ज् are changed to क्; e. g.

मुच्+त = मुक्त; पपच्+थ = पपक्थ; युज्+त = युक्त; तत्यञ्ज्+थ = तत्यक्थ.

(b) Final ध्, छ्, श्, ष्, क्ष्, the final ज् of भ्राज्, मृज्, यज्, राज्, सृज्, and the final ञ्ज् of भञ्ज् are changed to ष्, after which the initial dental is changed to the corresponding lingual (§ 56); e. g.

बबध्+थ = बबष्ठ; दृश्+त = दृष्ट; ददृश्+थ = ददृष्ठ; आनक्ष्+थ = आनष्ठ; सृज्+त = सृष्ट; सस्नञ्ज्+थ = सस्नष्ठ.

(c) Final ह् of roots beginning with द् combines with initial त् or थ् to ग्ध्; e. g.

दह्+त = दग्ध; ददह्+थ = ददग्ध.

(d) Final ह् of other roots combines with initial त् or थ् to ढ्, before which short अ, इ, and उ are lengthened, except in वह् and सह्, the radical अ of which is changed to ओ; e. g.

लिह् + त = लीढ; ववर्ह् + थ = ववर्ढ; उवह् + थ = उवोढ; वह् + तुम् = वोढुम्.

(e) The final ह् of दुह्, मुह्, स्निह् and स्नुह् may follow either (c) or (d); the final ह् of नह् combines with त् or थ् to द्; e. g.

द्रोह् + तुम् = द्रोग्धुम् or द्रोढुम्; मुह् + त = मुग्ध or मूढ; नह् + त = नद्ध; ननह् + थ = ननद्ध.

§ 310. Before initial ध्व्—

(a) The finals mentioned in § 309 (a) are changed to ग्, those mentioned in § 309 (b) to ड्: after the latter, ध् is changed to द्; e. g.

आनश् + ध्वे = आनड्ड्वे

(b) Final ह् combines with the initial ध् of ध्व् in the same manner in which it combines with an initial hard dental (§ 309 c, d, e); but here § 53 must be observed; e. g.

जगाह् + ध्वे = जघाद्ध्वे.

§ 311. The initial ध् of the termination ध्वे of the 2 Plur. Perf. Âtm.—

(a) *Must* be changed to ढ् when it is preceded by any radical vowel except अ or आ; e. g.

rt. कृ; चकृ + ध्वे = चकृढ्वे.
rt. स्तु; तुष्टु + ध्वे = तुष्टुढ्वे.

(b) *May* optionally be changed to ढ् when the intermediate इ is prefixed to it, provided this इ be preceded by one of the consonants य्, र्, ल्, व्, ह्; e. g.

rt. लू; लुलू + इध्वे (by § 305 b) = लुलुव् + इध्वे = लुलुविध्वे or लुलुविढ्वे.

Paradigms:

§ 312. The Reduplicated Perfect of भिद् P. Â. 'to split,' नुद् P. Â. 'to strike,' निन्द् P. 'to blame,' क्रम् P. Â. 'to go,' अस् P. 'to be' (only used as an auxiliary verb), अञ्ज् P. 'to anoint,' इष् P. 'to wish,' अर्च् P. 'to praise,' नी P. Â. 'to lead,' क्री P. Â. 'to buy,' यु P. Â. 'to join,' स्तु P. Â. 'to praise,' कृ P. Â. 'to do,' स्मृ P. 'to remember,' कॄ P. Â. 'to scatter.'

CONJUGATION OF VERBS.

1 Rt. भिद्   2 Rt. तुद्
Strong B. बिभेद्   Strong B. तुतोद्.
Weak B. बिभिद्   Weak B. तुतुद्.

		Par.	Âtm.	Par.	Âtm.
Sing.	1	बिभेद	बिभिदे	तुतोद	तुतुदे
	2	बिभेदिथ	बिभिदिषे	तुतोदिथ	तुतुदिषे
	3	बिभेद	बिभिदे	तुतोद	तुतुदे
Dual.	1	बिभिदिव	बिभिदिवहे	तुतुदिव	तुतुदिवहे
	2	बिभिदथुः	बिभिदाथे	तुतुदथुः	तुतुदाथे
	3	बिभिदतुः	बिभिदाते	तुतुदतुः	तुतुदाते
Plural.	1	बिभिदिम	बिभिदिमहे	तुतुदिम	तुतुदिमहे
	2	बिभिद	बिभिदिध्वे	तुतुद	तुतुदिध्वे
	3	बिभिदुः	बिभिदिरे	तुतुदुः	तुतुदिरे

3 Rt. निन्द्   4 Rt. क्रम्   5 Rt. अस्

Perf. B. निनिन्द्   Strong B. चक्राम् or चक्रम्.   Perf. B. आस्.
Weak B. चक्रम्.

		Par.	Par.	Âtm.	Par.
Sing.	1	निनिन्द	चक्राम or चक्रम	चक्रमे	आस
	2	निनिन्दिथ	चक्रमिथ	चक्रमिषे	आसिथ
	3	निनिन्द	चक्राम	चक्रमे	आस
Dual.	1	निनिन्दिव	चक्रमिव	चक्रमिवहे	आसिव
	2	निनिन्दथुः	चक्रमथुः	चक्रमाथे	आसथुः
	3	निनिन्दतुः	चक्रमतुः	चक्रमाते	आसतुः
Plural.	1	निनिन्दिम	चक्रमिव	चक्रमिमहे	आसिम
	2	निनिन्द	चक्रम	चक्रमिध्वे	आस
	3	निनिन्दुः	चक्रमुः	चक्रमिरे	आसुः

	6 Rt. अञ्ज्	7 Rt. इष्	8 Rt. ऋच्	9 Rt. नी	
Perf. B.	आनञ्ज्	S. B. इयेष्	S. B. आनर्च्	S. B. निने or निनै	
		W. B. ईष्	W. B. आनृच्	W. B. निनी	

		Par.	Par.	Par.	Par.	Âtm.
Sing.	1	आनञ्ज	इयेष	आनर्च	निनाय or निनय	निन्ये
	2	आनञ्जिथ or आनङ्क्थ	इयेषिथ	आनर्चिथ or निनेथ	निनयिथ	निन्यिषे
	3	आनञ्ज	इयेष	आनर्च	निनाय	निन्ये
Dual.	1	आनञ्जिव or आनञ्ज्व	ईषिव	आनृचिव	निन्यिव	निन्यिवहे
	2	आनञ्जथुः	ईषथुः	आनृचथुः	निन्यथुः	निन्याथे
	3	आनञ्जतुः	ईषतुः	आनृचतुः	निन्यतुः	निन्याते
Plural.	1	आनञ्जिम or आनञ्ज्म	ईषिम	आनृचिम	निन्यिम	निन्यिमहे
	2	आनञ्ज	ईष	आनृच	निन्य	निन्यिध्वे or ॰ढ्वे
	3	आनञ्जुः	ईषुः	आनृचुः	निन्युः	निन्यिरे

	10 Rt. क्री		11 Rt. यु	
Strong B.	चिक्रे or चिक्रै		Strong B. युयो or युयौ	
Weak B.	चिक्री		Weak B. युयु	

		Par.	Âtm.	Par.	Âtm.
Sing.	1	चिक्राय or चिक्रय	चिक्रिये	युयाव or युयव	युयुवे
	2	चिक्रयिथ or चिक्रेथ	चिक्रियिषे	युयविथ	युयुविषे
	3	चिक्राय	चिक्रिये	युयाव	युयुवे
Dual.	1	चिक्रियिव	चिक्रियिवहे	युयुविव	युयुविवहे
	2	चिक्रियथुः	चिक्रियाथे	युयुवथुः	युयुवाथे
	3	चिक्रियतुः	चिक्रियाते	युयुवतुः	युयुवाते
Plural.	1	चिक्रियिम	चिक्रियिमहे	युयुविम	युयुविमहे
	2	चिक्रिय	चिक्रियिध्वे or ॰ढ्वे	युयुव	युयुविध्वे or ॰ढ्वे
	3	चिक्रियुः	चिक्रियिरे	युयुवुः	युयुविरे

12 Rt. स्तु
Strong B. तुष्टो or तुष्टौ
Weak B. तुष्टु

	Par.	Âtm.
Sing. 1.	तुष्टाव or तुष्टव	तुष्टुवे
2.	तुष्टोथ	तुष्टुषे
3.	तुष्टाव	तुष्टुवे
Dual 1.	तुष्टुव	तुष्टुवहे
2.	तुष्टुवथुः	तुष्टुवाथे
3.	तुष्टुवतुः	तुष्टुवाते
Plural 1.	तुष्टुम	तुष्टुमहे
2.	तुष्टुव	तुष्टुध्वे
3.	तुष्टुवुः	तुष्टुविरे

13 Rt. कृ
Strong B. चकर् or चकार्
Weak B. चकृ

	Par.	Âtm.
Sing. 1.	चकार or चकर	चक्रे
2.	चकर्थ	चकृषे
3.	चकार	चक्रे
Dual 1.	चकृव	चकृवहे
2.	चक्रथुः	चक्राथे
3.	चक्रतुः	चक्राते
Plural 1.	चकृम	चकृमहे
2.	चक्र	चकृद्वे
3.	चक्रुः	चक्रिरे

14 Rt. स्मृ
Strong B. सस्मर् or सस्मार्
Weak B. सस्मृ

	Par.
Sing. 1.	सस्मार or सस्मर
2.	सस्मर्थ
3.	सस्मार
Dual 1.	सस्मरिव
2.	सस्मरथुः
3.	सस्मरतुः
Plural 1.	सस्मरिम
2.	सस्मर
3.	सस्मरुः

15 Rt. कृ
Strong B. चकर् or चकार्
Weak B. चकृ

	Par.	Âtm.
Sing. 1.	चकार or चकर	चकरे
2.	चकरिथ	चकरिषे
3.	चकार	चकरे
Dual 1.	चकरिव	चकरिवहे
2.	चकरथुः	चकराथे
3.	चकरतुः	चकराते
Plural 1.	चकरिम	चकरिमहे
2.	चकर	चकरिध्वे or ध्वें
3.	चकरुः	चकरिरे

The Reduplicated Perfect of Roots the reduplicated Base of which is weakened in the weak forms.

§ 313. Roots in आ, ए, ऐ, and औ (cf. § 296, a) drop their final vowel in all weak forms, and in the 2 Sing. Par. before the termination इथ.

In the 1st and 3rd Sing. Par. the final radical आ combines with the termination अ to औ; *e.g.* दा P. Â. 'to give,' गै P. 'to sing.'

	Rt. दा		गै
	Strong B. ददा		जगा
	Weak B. दद्		जग्

		Par.	Âtm.	Par.
Sing.	1.	ददौ	ददे	जगौ
	2.	ददाथ or ददिथ	ददिषे	जगाथ or जगिथ
	3.	ददौ	ददे	जगौ
Dual.	1.	ददिव	ददिवहे	जगिव
	2.	ददथुः	ददाथे	जगथुः
	3.	ददतुः	ददाते	जगतुः
Plur.	1.	ददिम	ददिमहे	जगिम
	2.	दद	ददिध्वे	जग
	3.	ददुः	ददिरे	जगुः

§ 314. The roots गम् 'to go,' हन् 'to strike,' जन् 'to be born,' खन् 'to dig,' and घस् 'to eat,' drop their radical vowel in all weak forms; the ह of हन् is changed to घ् in all reduplicated forms; *e.g.* rt. गम्, Strong B. जगाम् or जगम्, Weak B. जग्म्.

	Par.			Âtm.		
	Sing.	Dual.	Plur.	Sing.	Dual.	Plur.
1.	जगाम or जगम	जग्मिव	जग्मिम	जग्मे	जग्मिवहे	जग्मिमहे
2.	जगमिथ or जगन्थ	जग्मथुः	जग्म	जग्मिषे	जग्माथे	जग्मिध्वे
3.	जगाम	जग्मतुः	जग्मुः	जग्मे	जग्माते	जग्मिरे

Perf. Par. of हन् = जघान or जघन, जघनिथ or जघन्थ, जघान; जघ्निव &c.

§ 315. Roots which contain a radical अ between two simple radical consonants, and which do not begin with a guttural, nor with an aspirate letter, nor with व्, drop their radical अ together with the initial radical consonant, and change the vowel of the reduplicative syllable to ए in all weak forms and before the termination इथ of the 2nd Sing. Par.; (or, in other words, instead of taking reduplication they change their radical vowel to ए); e. g. rt. पच् P. Â. 'to cook,' Strong base पपच् or पपाच्, Weak base पेच्;

	Par.			Âtm.		
Sing.		Dual.	Plur.	Sing.	Dual.	Plur.
1. पपाच or पपच		पेचिव	पेचिम	पेचे	पेचिवहे	पेचिमहे
2. पपक्थ or पेचिथ		पेचथुः	पेच	पेचिषे	पेचाथे	पेचिध्वे
3. पपाच		पेचतुः	पेचुः	पेचे	पेचाते	पेचिरे

§ 316. (a) The roots वच् 'to speak,' वद् 'to say,' वप् 'to sow,' वश् 'to wish,' वस् 'to dwell,' and वह् 'to carry,' substitute उ for the reduplicative syllable व (e. g. वच् reduplicated उवच्); in the weak forms they further substitute उ also for the radical व and contract the reduplicative उ and the radical उ to ऊ (उ + उच् = ऊच्); e. g. rt. वच् P. Â., Strong base उवाच or उवच्, Weak base ऊच्;

	Par.			Âtm.		
Sing.		Dual.	Plur.	Sing.	Dual.	Plur.
1. उवाच or उवच		ऊचिव	ऊचिम	ऊचे	ऊचिवहे	ऊचिमहे
2. उवक्थ or उवचिथ		ऊचथुः	ऊच	ऊचिषे	ऊचाथे	ऊचिध्वे
3. उवाच		ऊचतुः	ऊचुः	ऊचे	ऊचाते	ऊचिरे

Perf. Par. of वह्, उवाह or उवह, उवोढ (§ 309, d) or उवहिथ, उवाह; ऊहिव &c.; Âtm. ऊहे &c.

(b) Similarly यज् 'to sacrifice,' forms its strong base इयज् or इयाज्, and its weak base ईज्; e. g. Par. इयाज or इयज, इयजिथ or इयष्ट, इयाज; ईजिव &c.

Irregular Reduplicated Perfects.

§ 317. भू P. Â. 'to be,' forms its reduplicated Perfect thus:

	Par.			Âtm.		
Sing.		Dual.	Plur.	Sing.	Dual.	Plur
1. बभूव		बभूविव	बभूविम	बभूवे	बभूविवहे	बभूविमहे
2. बभूविथ		बभूवथुः	बभूव	बभूविषे	बभूवाथे	बभूविध्वे or ढ्वे
3. बभूव		बभूवतुः	बभूवुः	बभूवे	बभूवाते	बभूविरे

§ 318. Of the Perfect of अह् 'to say,' only the following forms of the Parasmai. are in use:

	Sing.	Du.	Plur.
2.	आत्थ	आहथुः	
3.	आह	आहतुः	आहुः

All these forms convey the sense of a Present tense ('he says' &c.) and are by the Native grammarians considered as optional substitutes for the corresponding forms of the Present tense of rt. ब्रू.

Alphabetical List of other Roots which form the Reduplicated Perfect irregularly.

§ 319. 1. अश् Â. 'to pervade;' Perf. Base आनश् ; 3 Sing. आनशे ; 2 Sing. आनशिषे or आनक्षे &c.

2. ऋ P. 'to go;' Perf. B. आर् ; 3 Sing. आर ; Du. आरतुः ; Plur. आरुः ; 2 Sing. आरिथ.

3. कुट् 'to be crooked,' and certain other roots of the sixth class retain their radical vowel unchanged in the 2 Sing. Par. and optionally in the 1 Sing. Par.; *e. g.* चुकोट or चुकुट, चुकुटिथ, चुकोट. The same roots retain their vowel unchanged also in other tenses which usually require the radical vowel to be gunated.

4. ग्रन्थ् P. 'to tie,' regular; or Weak B. ग्रेथ् ; *e. g.* 3 Plur. जग्रन्थुः or ग्रेथुः.

5. ग्रह् P. Â. 'to seize ;' Weak B. जगृह् ; Par. Sing. जग्राह or जग्रह, जग्राहिथ, जग्राह ; Du. जगृहिव &c.

6. चि P. Â. 'to gather ;' Perf. B. चिचि or चिकि ; 3 Sing. Par. चिचाय or चिकाय ; Âtm. चिच्ये or चिक्ये.

7. जि P. Â. 'to conquer ;' Perf. B. जिगि ; 3 Sing. Par. जिगाय ; Âtm. जिग्ये.

8. तृ P. 'to cross;' Weak B. तेर् ; 3 Sing. ततार ; Du. तेरतुः ; Plur. तेरुः.

9. त्रप् Â. 'to be ashamed ;' Weak B. त्रेप् ; 3 Sing. त्रेपे.

10. त्रस् P. 'to tremble,' regular; or Weak B. त्रेस् ; *e. g.* 2 Sing. तत्रसिथ or त्रेसिथ ; 3 Plur. तत्रसुः or त्रेसुः.

[§ 320.] CONJUGATION OF VERBS. 117

11. दे Â., 'to guard;' Perf. दिग्ये.
12. दृश् P. 'to see;' 2 Sing. ददर्शिथ or ददृष्ठ.
13. द्युत् Â. 'to shine;' Perf. B. दिद्युत्; 3 Sing. दिद्युते.
14. प्याय् Â. 'to grow;' Perf. B. पिप्ये; 3 Sing. पिप्ये.
15. फल् P. 'to bear fruit;' Weak B. फेल्; 3 Sing. पफाल; Du. फेलतुः; Plur. फेलुः.
16. भज् P. Â. 'to share;' Weak B. भेज्; 3 Sing. Par. बभाज; Du. भेजतुः; 3 Sing. Âtm. भेजे.
17. भ्रम् P. 'to roam,' regular; or Weak B. भ्रेम्; e.g. 3 Plur. बभ्रमुः or भ्रेमुः.
18. भ्राज् Â. 'to shine,' regular; or Weak B. भ्रेज्; e.g. 3 Sing. बभ्राजे or भ्रेजे.
19. राज् P. Â. 'to shine,' regular; or Weak B. रेज्; e.g. 3 Plur. Par. रराजुः or रेजुः.
20. वे P. Â. 'to weave,' regular; or Strong B. उवय्, Weak B. ऊय् or ऊव्; e.g. 3 Sing. Par. ववौ or उवाय; 3 Du. ववतुः or ऊयतुः or ऊवतुः.
21. व्यथ् Â. 'to suffer;' Perf. B. विव्यथ्; 3 Sing. विव्यथे.
22. व्यध् P. 'to strike;' Strong B. विव्यध्; Weak B. विविध्; 3 Sing. विव्याध; 3 Plur. विविधुः.
23. व्ये P. Â. 'to cover;' Strong B. विव्यय्; Weak B. विवि. Par. विव्याय or विव्यय, विव्ययिथ, विव्याय; विवियव &c. Âtm. विव्ये.
24. श्रि P. 'to swell,' regular; or Perf. Base शुश्रु; e.g. 3 Sing. शिश्राय, or शुश्राव.
25. सृज् P. 'to dismiss;' 2 Sing. ससर्जिथ or ससृष्ठ.
26. स्वञ्ज् Â. 'to embrace;' Perf. B. सस्वञ्ज् or सस्वज्; 3 Sing. सस्वञ्जे or सस्वजे.
27. स्वप् P. 'to sleep;' Strong B. सुष्वप्; Weak B. सुषुप्; 3 Sing. सुष्वाप; Plur. सुषुपुः.
28. हि P. 'to throw;' Perf. B. जिघि; 3 Sing. जिघाय; Plur. जिघ्युः.
29. ह्वे P. Â. 'to call;' Perf. B. जुहू; 3 Sing. Par. जुहाव; Âtm. जुहुवे.

b.—The Periphrastic Perfect.

§ 320. The Periphrastic Perfect is formed by affixing आम् to the root and by adding to the base formed in this manner the Redupl. Perfect Parasmai. of अस् 'to be' (§ 312, 5) or of भू 'to be' (§ 317) or the Redupl. Perf. Parasmai. or Âtmane. of कृ 'to do' (§ 312, 13). The Red.

Perf. Parasmai. of कृ is employed after verbs which are conjugated in the Parasmaipada, the Red. Perf. Âtmane. of कृ after verbs which are conjugated in the Âtmanepada. The Perf. Par. of भस् and भू are used both after Parasmai. and after Âtmanepada verbs; *e. g.*

उन्द् P. 'to moisten,' 3 Sing. उन्दामास, or उन्दांबभूव, or उन्दांचकार.
एध् Â. 'to grow,' 3 Sing. एधामास, or एधांबभूव, or एधांचक्रे.

§ 321. *a.* उन्द् (§ 298, *c*, 1) gunates its radical उ, when आम् is affixed to it; *e. g.* ओषांचकार (or उवोष).

b. जागृ, भी, भृ, हु and ह्री (§ 298, *c*,) gunate their final vowel before आम्; *e. g.* जागरामास (or जजागार), बिभयामास (or बिभाय), बिभरामास (or बभार), &c.

Paradigms :

§ 322. The Periphrastic Perfect of उन्द् P. 'to moisten,' and of आस् Â. 'to sit.'

Par.

Sing. 1.	उन्दामास	or	उन्दांबभूव	or	उन्दांचकार or ˚चकर
2.	उन्दामासिथ		उन्दांबभूविथ		उन्दांचकर्थ
3.	उन्दामास		उन्दांबभूव		उन्दांचकार
Dual. 1.	उन्दामासिव		उन्दांबभूविव		उन्दांचक्रृव
2.	उन्दामासथुः		उन्दांबभूवथुः		उन्दांचक्रथुः
3.	उन्दामासतुः		उन्दांबभूवतुः		उन्दांचक्रतुः
Plur. 1.	उन्दामासिम		उन्दांबभूविम		उन्दांचक्रृम
2.	उन्दामास		उन्दांबभूव		उन्दांचक्र
3.	उन्दामासुः		उन्दांबभूवुः		उन्दांचक्रुः

Âtm.

Sing. 1.	आसामास	or	आसांबभूव	or	आसांचक्रे
2.	आसामासिथ		आसांबभूविथ		आसांचकृषे
3.	आसामास		आसांबभूव		आसांचक्रे
Dual. 1.	आसामासिव		आसांबभूविव		आसांचकृवहे
2.	आसामासथुः		आसांबभूवथुः		आसांचक्राथे
3.	आसामासतुः		आसांबभूवतुः		आसांचक्राते
Plur. 1.	आसामासिम		आसांबभूविम		आसांचकृमहे
2.	आसमास		आसांबभूव		आसांचकृढ्वे
3.	आसामासुः		आसांबभूवुः		आसांचक्रिरे

2.—The Aorist.

§ 323. The common characteristic of all Aorists is the augment अ, prefixed to the root (§ 229).

§ 324. The personal terminations are either added immediately to the root (*Radical Aorist*), or the letter स् is prefixed to them before they are added to the root (*S-Aorist*). There are three varieties of the radical Aorist (Forms I. II. and III.) and four varieties of the S-Aorist (Forms IV. V. VI. and VII).

a.—*The Radical Aorist.*

I.—*First Form* (only Parasmaipada).

§ 325. The personal terminations given in col. II. of § 227 are added immediately to the root; in the 3 Plur. उ: is substituted for अन्, before which a final radical vowel is dropped.

§ 326. *Paradigms*: The first form of the radical Aorist of पा P. 'to drink,' धे P. 'to suck', सो P. 'to finish' (see § 296, *a*).

Parasmaipada.

Sing. 1.	अपाम्	अधाम्	असाम्
Sing. 2.	अपाः	अधाः	असाः
Sing. 3.	अपात्	अधात्	असात्
Dual. 1.	अपाव	अधाव	असाव
Dual. 2.	अपातम्	अधातम्	असातम्
Dual. 3.	अपाताम्	अधाताम्	असाताम्
Plur. 1.	अपाम	अधाम	असाम
Plur. 2.	अपात	अधात	असात
Plur. 3.	अपुः	अधुः	असुः

§ 327. Irregular Aorists of the first Form:

(*a*) भू 'to be,' retains the termination अन् in the 3 Plur. and changes its final ऊ before vowel-terminations to उव्; *e. g.* अभूवम्, अभूः, अभूत्; 3 Plur. अभूवन्.

(*b*) इ 'to go,' forms this Aorist from गा; *e. g.* 3 Sing. अगात्.

§ 328. Only twelve roots take this form of the radical Aorist in Parasmai., viz. इ 'to go' (अगात्), घ्रा 'to smell,' छो 'to cut,' दा 'to give,'

दो 'to cut,' धा 'to place,' धे 'to suck,' पा 'to drink,' भू 'to be,' शो 'to sharpen,' सो 'to finish,' and स्था 'to stand.' Of these, ग्रा, छो, शो, and सो take also form VI. (अग्रासीत्, अच्छासीत् &c.); धे takes also forms III. and VI. (अदधत् and अधासीत्). दा, धा, and स्था take in the Âtmane. form IV. (अदित, अधित, अस्थित), and भू takes in the Âtmane. form V. (अभविष्ट).—The root इ with the prep. अधि takes in the Âtmane. form IV. (अध्यगीष्ट or अध्यैष्ट 'he has studied').

II.—*Second Form* (Parasmai., and rarely Âtmane.)

§ 329. (*a*) अ is added to the root and to the base formed in this way the personal terminations given in col. II. of § 227 are added.

(*b*) A final radical ऋ is gunated before अ; *e. g.* सृ, असरत्; a penultimate nasal is dropped; *e. g.* स्कन्द्, अस्कंदत्.

(*c*) The rules given in § 245 apply to the final अ of the base and the initial letters of the terminations; *e. g.* असिच् + अ + त् = असिचत्, असिच् + अ + अम् = असिचम्.

§ 330. *Paradigm:* The second form of the radical Aorist of सिच् P. Â. 'to sprinkle:'

	Parasmai.			Âtmane.		
	Sing.	*Dual.*	*Plur.*	*Sing.*	*Dual.*	*Plur.*
1.	असिचम्	असिचाव	असिचाम	असिचे	असिचावहि	असिचामहि
2.	असिचः	असिचतम्	असिचत	असिचथाः	असिचेथाम्	असिचध्वम्
3.	असिचत्	असिचताम्	असिचन्	असिचत	असिचेताम्	असिचन्त

§ 331. Irregular Aorists of the second Form:

1. अस् 'to throw,' 3 S. P. आस्थत्   4. शास् 'to rule,' 3 S. P. अशिषत्
2. ख्या 'to speak,' ,, ,, अख्यत्   5. श्वि 'to swell,' ,, ,, अश्वत्
3. दृश् 'to see,' ,, ,, अदर्शत्   6. ह्वे 'to call,' ,, ,, अह्वत्

§ 332. 1. The following roots must take this form of the radical Aorist in either Pada in which they may be used: अस् 'to throw', ऋ cl. 3, ख्या, शास्, and सृ cl. 3 (*e. g.* सृ cl. 3, असरत्; but सृ cl. 1, असार्षीत्).

2. The roots लिप्, सिच्, and ह्वे must take this form in Par., and in Âtm. they may take optionally this form or form IV.; *e. g.*

rt. लिप्, Par. अलिपत्; Âtm. अलिपत or अलिप्त.

CONJUGATION OF VERBS.

3. The following are the common roots which must take this form in Parasmai :—

(a) Of roots of the 1st class : कृप्, क्षुभ् (also when belonging to cl. 4 ; but when belonging to cl. 9, अक्षोभीत्), घुन्, ध्वंस्, भ्रंश् (also when belonging to cl. 4), मिद् (also when belonging to cl. 4), रुच्, वृत्, वृध्, शुभ्, शृध्, स्थित्, स्यन्द्, स्रंस्, द्विष् (also when belonging to cl. 4).

(b) Of roots of the 4th class : उच्, ऋध् (but ऋध् cl. 5 &c. आर्धीत्), कुप्, कृश्, क्रुध्, क्षम्, क्रिद्, क्षम्, शुध्, द्विद्, गृध्, तम्, तुष्, तृप् (but तृप् cl. 5 or 6 अनार्पीत् or अतार्पीत् or अनर्पीत्), नृत्, दस्, दुप्, दृप्, दुह्, नश्, पुष् (but पुष् cl. 9 or 1 अपोषीत्), भ्रम् (but भ्रम् cl. 1 अभ्रमीत्), मद्, मुह्, यस् (but यस् cl. 1 or 6 अयसीत्), रध्, रुष् (but रुष् cl. 1 अरोपीत्), लुट् (but लुट् cl. 1 अलोटीत्), लुप् (also when belonging to cl. 6), लुभ् (but लुभ् cl. 6, अलोभीत्), शक् (also when belonging to cl. 5), शाम्, शुभ्, शुष्, श्रम्, श्लिष् (except in the sense of 'to embrace'), सिध् (but सिध् cl. 1 'to govern,' असेत्सात् or असेधीत्, and सिध् cl. 1 'to go,' असेधीत्), स्निह्, हृष्.

(c) The roots आप्, गम्, यस्, विप्, मुच्, विद् cl. 6, शद्, शिष् cl. 7, सद्, सृप्.

Those of the roots enumerated under a, b, c, which are found among the 100 roots in § 366 a, 2, take in Âtm. form IV.; e. g. rt. मुच्, अमुक्त : those roots which are found among the roots enumerated in § 366 b, 2 and 3, take in Âtm. form IV. or V.; e. g. rt. स्यन्द्, अस्यन्त or अस्यन्दिष्ट; the remaining roots take in Âtm. form V.; e. g. rt. घुन्, अद्योनिष्ट.

4. (a) The roots क्षुद्, छिद्, दृश्, निज्, भिद्, युज्, रिच्, रुध्, विच्, and स्कन्द् may optionally take this form or form IV. in Par.; in Âtm. they can take only form IV.; e. g. rt. क्षुद्, Par. अक्षुदन् or अक्षौत्सीन्; Âtm. अक्षुत्त.

(b) The roots गुप्, च्युत्, हृद्, जू, तृप्, तुभ् cl. 1, स्तृ, शुच् cl. 4, क्षुत्, and स्तम् may optionally take this form or form V. in Par.; in Âtm. they can take only form V.; e. g. rt. हृद्, Par. अस्छुदत् or अस्छर्दीत्; Âtm. अस्छर्दिष्ट.

(c) श्रि takes in Par. optionally this form or form III. or form V.; अश्रत्, अशिश्रियत्, or अश्रयीत्; in Âtm. it would not take this form.

III.—*Third Form* (Parasmai. and Âtmane.).

§ 333. (a) The root is reduplicated before it takes the augment.

(b) अ is added to the root and to the base so formed the personal terminations given in col. II. of § 227 are added in the same manner in which they are added in form II.

(c) Final इ and उ are changed to इय् and उव् before अ; final आ (for ए) is dropped; *e. g.* कम्, 3 Sing. Âtm. अचकमत; श्रि, 3 Sing. Par. अशिश्रियत्; धे, 3 Sing. Par. अदधत्.

§ 334. *Paradigm*: The third form of the radical Aorist of श्रि P. Â. 'to go:'

	Sing.	Dual.	Plur.
	Parasmai.		
1.	अशिश्रियम्	अशिश्रियाव	अशिश्रियाम
2.	अशिश्रियः	अशिश्रियतम्	अशिश्रियत
3.	अशिश्रियत्	अशिश्रियताम्	अशिश्रियन्
	Âtmane.		
1.	अशिश्रिये	अशिश्रियावहि	अशिश्रियामहि.
2.	अशिश्रियथाः	अशिश्रियेथाम्	अशिश्रियध्वम्.
3.	अशिश्रियत	अशिश्रियेताम्	अशिश्रियन्त.

§ 335. श्रि P. Â. 'to go,' द्रु P. 'to run,' स्रु P. 'to flow,' and कम् Â. 'to love,' take only this form of the Aorist. श्रि P. 'to swell,' takes this form, or II. or V. (§ 332 4, c,); धे P. 'to suck,' takes this form, or I. or VI. (§ 328).

§ 336. पत् 'to fall,' forms irregularly अपप्तत्; and वच् 'to speak,' अवोचत्.

b.—The S-Aorist.

§ 337. The four forms of the S-Aorist have this in common that the letter स् or a syllable containing the letter स् (changeable to ष्) is prefixed to the personal terminations given in col. II. of § 227, before they are added to the root.

IV.—*Fourth Form* (Parasmai. and Âtmane.)

§ 338. (a) The letter स् (changeable to ष् in accordance with § 59) is prefixed to the personal terminations given in col. II. of § 227 before they are added to the root. In the 2 and 3 Pers. Sing. Par., ई is inserted

CONJUGATION OF VERBS.

between this स् or घ् and the terminations :(स्) and न् in order to prevent the loss of these terminations. In the 2 Plur. Âtm. स् is dropped before ध्वम्. In the 3 Plur. Par. and Âtm. उ: and अत are substituted for अन् and अन्त.

(*b*) Table showing the terminations of form IV. of the Aorist:

	Parasmai.			Âtmane.		
	Sing.	*Du.*	*Plur.*	*Sing.*	*Du.*	*Plur.*
1.	सम्	स्व	स्म	सि	स्वहि	स्महि
2.	सी:	स्तम्	स्त	स्था:	साथाम्	ध्वम्
3.	सीत्	स्ताम्	सु:	स्त	साताम्	सत.

§ 339. (*a*) The terminations beginning with स्त and स्थ drop their स् after short vowels and consonants except nasals and र्; *e. g.* rt. कृ, 3 Sing. Âtm. अकृ + स्त = अकृत; rt. क्षिप्, 2 Sing. Âtm. अक्षिप् + स्था : = अक्षिप्था; but rt. कृ, 2 Plur. Par. अकार् + स्त = अकार्ष्ट.

(*b*) Final radical consonants combine with the initial letters of the terminations according to the rules given in § 307 &c.; *e. g.*

rt. पच् ; 3 Sing. Par. अपच् + सीत् =अपाक्षीत्; 3 Sing. Â. अपच्+स्त =अपक्त.
rt. व्रश्च् ; ,, ,, ,, अव्रश्च् + सीत् =अव्राक्षीत्; 3 Du. P. अव्रश्च्+स्ताम् =अव्राष्टाम्
rt. प्रछ् ; ,, ,, ,, अप्राछ् + सीत् =अप्राक्षीत्; 3 Du. P. अप्राछ्+स्ताम् =अप्राष्टाम्.
rt. दह् ; ,, ,, ,, अदह् + सीत् =अधाक्षीत्; 3 Du. P. अदह्+स्ताम् =अदग्धाम्.
rt. लिह्; 1 Sing. Âtm. अलिह् + सि =अलिक्षि; 3 Sing. Â. अलिह्+स्त =अलीढ.
rt. नह्; 3 Sing. Par. अनह् + सीत् =अनात्सीत्; 3 Sing. Â. अनह् +स्त =अनद्ध.
rt. वह् ; ,, ,, ,, अवह् + सीत् =अवाक्षीत्; 3 Sing. Â. अवह् +स्त =अवोढ.
rt. वस् ; ,, ,, ,, अवस् + सीत् =अवात्सीत्; 3 Du. P. अवस् +स्ताम्=अवात्ताम्.

(*c*) The initial ध् of the termination ध्वम् is changed to ढ् after all radical vowels except अ and आ, and after र्; *e. g.*

rt. चि; 2 Plur. Âtm. अचे + ध्वम् =अचेढ्वम्.
rt. कृ; ,, ,, अकृ + ध्वम् = अकृढ्वम्.
rt. स्तृ; ,, ,, अस्तीर् + ध्वम् =अस्तीर्ढ्वम्. (§ 48.)
but rt. पच्; ,, ,, अपच् + ध्वम् = अपध्वम्.

§ 340. (a) In the Parasmaipada Vriddhi is substituted for the vowel of the root; *e. g.* rt. चि, 3 Sing. Par. अचैषीत्; rt. नी, अनैषीत्; rt. श्रु, अश्रौषीत्; rt. कृ, अकार्षीत्; rt. भज्, अभाक्षीत्; rt. भञ्ज्, अभाङ्क्षीत्; rt. भुज्, अभौक्षीत्.

(b) In the Âtmanepada Guṇa is substituted for *final* radical इ, ई, उ, and ऊ; *e. g.* rt. चि, 3 Sing. Âtm. अचेष्ट; rt. नी, अनेष्ट; rt. च्यु, अच्योष्ट; rt. सू, असोष्ट; other radical vowels remain unchanged in the Âtmanepada; *e. g.* rt. कृ, 1 Sing. Âtm. अकृषि; rt. पच्, अपक्षि.

(c) दृश् 'to see,' and सृज् 'to dismiss,' substitute रा for the Vriddhi आर् in Par., and other roots with penultimate ऋ do optionally the same; *e. g.* दृश्, 3 Sing. Par. अद्राक्षीत्; rt. कृष् 'to draw,' अकार्क्षीत् or अकृक्षीत्.

§ 341. *Paradigms:* The fourth form of the Aorist (*i. e.* the first form of the S-Aorist) of नी P. Â. 'to lead,' कृ P. Â. 'to do,' तुद् P. Â. to strike.'

		Parasmai.			Âtmane.		
Sing.	1.	अनैषम्	अकार्षम्	अतौत्सम्	अनेषि	अकृषि	अतुत्सि
	2.	अनैषीः	अकार्षीः	अतौत्सीः	अनेष्ठाः	अकृथाः	अतुत्थाः
	3.	अनैषीत्	अकार्षीत्	अतौत्सीत्	अनेष्ट	अकृत	अतुत्त
Dual.	1.	अनैष्व	अकार्ष्व	अतौत्स्व	अनेष्वहि	अकृष्वहि	अतुत्स्वहि
	2.	अनैष्टम्	अकार्ष्टम्	अतौत्तम्	अनेषाथाम्	अकृषाथाम्	अतुत्साथाम्
	3.	अनैष्टाम्	अकार्ष्टाम्	अतौत्ताम्	अनेषाताम्	अकृषाताम्	अतुत्साताम्
Plur.	1.	अनैष्म	अकार्ष्म	अतौत्स्म	अनेष्महि	अकृष्महि	अतुत्स्महि
	2.	अनैष्ट	अकार्ष्ट	अतौत्त	अनेढ्वम्	अकृढ्वम्	अतुद्ध्वम्
	3.	अनैषुः	अकार्षुः	अतौत्सुः	अनेषत	अकृषत	अतुत्सत

§ 342. Irregular Aorists of the fourth Form:

1. गम् 'to go,' drops its final म् optionally in the Âtmanepada; *e. g.* Sing. अगंसि, अगंस्थाः, अगंस्त; Du. अगंस्वहि &c. or Sing. अगसि, अगथाः, अगत; Du. अगस्वहि &c. In Par. गम् takes form II., अगमत्.

2. यम् in the sense of 'to marry,' follows the analogy of गम्; *e. g.* with prep. उप, उपयंसि or उपयसि. In Par. यम् takes form VI., अयंसीत्.

3. दा 'to give,' दे 'to protect,' धा 'to place,' स्था 'to stand' (and likewise दो 'to cut,' and धे 'to suck,' when they take the form of the

Âtmane.) change their final to इ in Âtmanepada; afterwards § 339 (a) applies to the terminations beginning with स्न् and स्थ्; e. g. Sing. अदिषि, अदिथाः, अदित; Du. अदिष्वहि &c. When used in Parasmai. these roots take form I. अदान्, अधान्, अस्थान्.

4. वृ when it takes this form, forms in the Âtm. अवृषि; वॄ, अवॄषि; similarly स्तृ, अस्तृषि; स्तॄ, अस्तीर्षि; i. e. final long ॠ is in the Âtm. changed to ईर् except when it is preceded by a labial; in the latter case it is changed to ऊर् (§ 48).

5. पद् Â. 'to go,' is regular (e. g. अपत्सि) except in the 3 Sing. Â. where it takes the passive form अपादि; बुध् (बुध्यते) 'to awaken,' does the same optionally; 3 Sing. अबुद्ध or अबोधि.

§ 343. Provided that they are not restricted to Form I. II. III. VI. or VII.—

1. All roots enumerated in § 366 a, 1 and 2, must take this form of the S-Aorist;—e. g. rt. कृ, Par. अकार्षीन्, Âtm. अकृत; rt. पच्, Par. अपाक्षीन्, Âtm. अपक्त; except—

(a) स्नु and सु 'to squeeze out,' take form V. in Par; e. g. Par. अस्नावीन्; Âtm. अस्तोष्ट.

(b) Roots in ऋ preceded by more than one consonant may take form IV. or V. in Âtm; e. g. rt. स्मृ, Par. अस्मार्षीन्; Âtm. अस्मृत or अस्मरिष्ट.

(c) क्रम् and स्तृ take form V. in Par. and IV. in Âtm.; e. g. Par. अक्रमीन्; Âtm. अक्रंस्त.

2. All roots enumerated in § 366 b, 1, 2, and 3, may optionally take this form or form V.; e. g. rt. व्रध्, Par. अव्राक्षीन् or अव्रधीन्; except—

(a) अञ्ज् takes only form V., भञ्जीन्;

(b) भू takes only form V. in Par; अभावीन्; Âtm. अभविष्ट or अभविष्ट.

3. The root वृ and all roots ending in ॠ optionally take form IV. or V. in Âtm; e. g. rt. कृ, Par. अकारीन्, Âtm. अकोष्ट or अकरिष्ट, अकरीष्ट.

V.—*Fifth Form* (Parasmai. and Âtmane.)

§ 344. (a) The terminations of this form of the S-Aorist are obtained by prefixing the intermediate इ to the terminations of form IV. (observe § 59); the terminations of the 2nd and 3rd Sing. Par. however are ईः and ईत्.

(b) Table showing the terminations of form V. of the Aorist:

	Parasmai.			Âtmane.		
	Sing.	Du.	Plur.	Sing.	Du.	Plur.
1.	इषम्	इष्व	इष्म	इषि	इष्वहि	इष्महि
2.	ईः	इष्टम्	इष्ट	इष्ठाः	इषाथाम्	इढ्वम्
3.	ईत्	इष्टाम्	इषुः	इष्ट	इषाताम्	इषत

§ 345. (a) The initial इ of these terminations may optionally be lengthened in the Âtmane. of verbs ending in ऋ and of वृ; e. g. rt. स्तृ, 3 Sing. Âtm. अस्तरिष्ट or अस्तरीष्ट; वृ 3 Sing. Âtm. अवरिष्ट or अवरीष्ट; इ *must* be lengthened in the Par. and Âtm. of ग्रह् 'to seize;' e. g. 1 Sing. Par. अग्रहीषम्; Âtm. अग्रहीषि.

(b) The ध् of the termination of the 2 Plur. Âtm. (इध्वम् or ईध्वम्) is optionally changed to ढ् when the termination is immediately preceded by one of the consonants य्, र्, ल्, व्, ह्; e. g. rt. स्तृ, 2 Plur. Âtm. अस्तरिध्वम् or अस्तरिढ्वम्; अस्तरीध्वम् or अस्तरीढ्वम्.

§ 346. (a) Vṛiddhi is substituted for final radical vowels in Parasmaipada, and Guṇa for final radical vowels in Âtmanepada; e. g. rt. लू, 1 Sing. Par. अलौ + इषम् = अलावषम्; Âtm. अलो + इषि = अलविषि.

(b) Guṇa is substituted for penultimate prosodially short radical vowels in Parasmai. and Âtmane.; e. g. rt. बुध्, 1 Sing. Par. अबोधिषम्; rt. कृप्, 1 Sing. Âtm. अकर्पिषि.

(c) The penultimate अ of roots ending in अर् and अल्, and of वद् 'to speak,' and व्रज् 'to go,' is lengthened in Parasmai., e. g. rt. जल्, 1 Sing. Par. अज्जालिषम्, rt. वद्, अवादिषम्. Other roots with penultimate अ lengthen this vowel optionally in Parasmai.; e.g. rt. पठ्, 1 Sing. Par. अपठिषम् or अपाठिषम्. But roots ending in ह्, म्, or य्, and श्वस् 'to breathe,' and some other roots do not lengthen their penultimate अ; e. g. rt. ग्रह्, 1 Sing. Par. अग्रहीषम्, rt. क्रम्, अक्रमिषम् &c.

§ 347. *Paradigms:* The fifth form of the Aorist (*i. e.* the second form of the S-Aorist) of लू P. Â. 'to cut,' स्तृ P. Â. 'to spread,' बुध् P. 'to know,' कृप् Â. 'to be fit.'

CONJUGATION OF VERBS.

Parasmai.

Sing.	1. अलाविषम्	अस्तारिषम्	अबोधिषम्
	2. अलावीः	अस्तारीः	अबोधीः
	3. अलावीत्	अस्तारीत्	अबोधीत्
Dual.	1. अलाविष्व	अस्तारिष्व	अबोधिष्व
	2. अलाविष्टम्	अस्तारिष्टम्	अबोधिष्टम्
	3. अलाविष्टाम्	अस्तारिष्टाम्	अबोधिष्टाम्
Plur.	1. अलाविष्म	अस्तारिष्म	अबोधिष्म
	2. अलाविष्ट	अस्तारिष्ट	अबोधिष्ट
	3. अलाविषुः	अस्तारिषुः	अबोधिषुः

Âtmane.

Sing.	1. अलविषि	अस्तरिषि or	अस्तरीषि	अकल्पिषि
	2. अलविष्ठाः	अस्तरिष्ठाः	अस्तरीष्ठाः	अकल्पिष्ठाः
	3. अलविष्ट	अस्तरिष्ट	अस्तरीष्ट	अकल्पिष्ट
Dual.	1. अलविष्वहि	अस्तरिष्वहि	अस्तरीष्वहि	अकल्पिष्वहि
	2. अलविषाथाम्	अस्तरिषाथाम्	अस्तरीषाथाम्	अकल्पिषाथाम्
	3. अलविषाताम्	अस्तरिषाताम्	अस्तरीषाताम्	अकल्पिषाताम्
Plur.	1. अलविष्महि	अस्तरिष्महि	अस्तरीष्महि	अकल्पिष्महि
	2. अलविध्वम् or ढ्वम्	अस्तरिध्वम् or ढ्वम्	अस्तरीध्वम् or ढ्वम्	अकल्पिध्वम्
	3. अलविषत	अस्तरिषत	अस्तरीषत	अकल्पिषत

§ 348. Irregular Aorists of the fifth Form:

1. श्वि 'to swell,' Par. अश्वयीत्; (see form II. § 332, 4, *c*.)

2. Roots of the 8th class in न् or ण् optionally drop their final consonant and substitute था: and त for the terminations इष्ठाः and इष्ट in the 2nd and 3rd Sing. Âtmane. only; *e. g.* rt. तन्, 2 Sing. Âtm. अतनिष्ठाः or अतथाः; 3 Sing. अतनिष्ट or अतत. सन् lengthens its radical vowel when न् is dropped; *e. g.* 2 Sing. Âtm. असनिष्ठाः or असाथाः.

3. The roots दीप् 'to shine,' जन् 'to be born,' पूर् 'to be full,' नाय् 'to spread,' and प्याय् 'to grow,' optionally form the 3 Sing. Âtm. like the Passive; *e. g.* अदीपिष्ट or अदीपि; अजनिष्ट or अजनि &c.

4. विज् 'to tremble,' retains its radical vowel unchanged in this form of the Aorist, and in other tenses and derivative verbal forms the terminations of which begin with the intermediate इ; *e. g.* 3 Sing. Aor. Par. अविजीत्: Simple Fut. विजिष्यति.

§ 349. All roots that are not restricted to any other form of the Aorist take this form. It is specially peculiar to those verbs that insert इ before the terminations of the Periphrastic Future. (§ 366 c).

VI.—*Sixth Form* (only Parasmaipada).

§ 350. (a) The terminations of this form of the S-Aorist are derived from the Parasmaipada-terminations of the fifth form by prefixing स् to the latter.

(b) Table showing the terminations of form VI. of the Aorist:

Parasmai.

	Sing.	Dual.	Plur.
1.	सिषम्	सिष्व	सिष्म
2.	सीः	सिष्टम्	सिष्ट
3.	सीत्	सिष्टाम्	सिषुः

§ 351. Final radical vowels remain unchanged (but observe § 296); final म् is changed to Anusvâra (§ 308, b); e.g. या 'to go,' 1 Sing. Par. अयासिषम्, नम्; 'to bend,' अनंसिषम्.

§ 352. *Paradigms:* The sixth form of the Aorist (i. e. the third form of the S-Aorist) of या P. 'to go,' गै P. 'to sing,' नम् P. 'to bend.'

Parasmaipada.

Sing. 1.	अयासिषम्	अगासिषम्	अनंसिषम्
2.	अयासीः	अगासीः	अनंसीः
3.	अयासीत्	अगासीत्	अनंसीत्
Dual. 1.	अयासिष्व	अगासिष्व	अनंसिष्व
2.	अयासिष्टम्	अगासिष्टम्	अनंसिष्टम्
3.	अयासिष्टाम्	अगासिष्टाम्	अनंसिष्टाम्
Plur. 1.	अयासिष्म	अगासिष्म	अनंसिष्म
2.	अयासिष्ट	अगासिष्ट	अनंसिष्ट
3.	अयासिषुः	अगासिषुः	अनंसिषुः

§ 353. All roots ending in आ, ए, ओ, and ऐ, which are not restricted to form I. II. or III. and the roots मि 'to throw,' मो 'to destroy,' नम्, यम्,

and रम् take this form of the S-Aorist in Par.; e.g. rt. ज्ञा 'to know,' अज्ञासीन्; rt. पा 'to protect,' अपासीन् &c. The root ली may optionally take this form or form IV. in Par., अलासीन् or अलेपीन् (cf. § 296, b). When used in Âtmane., all these roots take form IV.; e.g. ज्ञा, अज्ञास्त; नम्, अनंस्त.

VII.—*Seventh Form* (Parasmai. and Âtmane.).

§ 354. (a) The syllable स (changeable to ष by § 59) is prefixed to the personal terminations given in col. II. of § 227 before they are added to the root. The अ of स is dropped before vowel-terminations and lengthened before terminations beginning with व and म.

(b) Table showing the terminations of form VII. of the Aorist:

	Parasmai.			Âtmane.		
	Sing.	*Du.*	*Plur.*	*Sing.*	*Du.*	*Plur.*
1.	सम्	साव	साम	सि	सावहि	सामहि
2.	सः	सतम्	सत	सथाः	साथाम्	सध्वम्
3.	सत्	सताम्	सन्	सत	साताम्	सन्त

§ 355. Final radical ज्, ग् and ह् combine with the initial स् of the terminations to क्ष, (§ 308, a); afterwards initial ग् and द् of roots ending in ह become ग् and भ्(§ 53); e.g. rt. दिश् 3 Sing. Par. अदिक्षन्; द्रिप्, अद्रिक्षन्; दिह, अभिक्षन्; लिह्, अलिक्षन्.

§ 356. *Paradigm:* The seventh form of the Aorist (*i.e.* the fourth form of the S-Aorist) of दिश् P. Â. 'to show.'

	Parasmai.			Âtmane.		
	Sing.	*Du.*	*Plur.*	*Sing.*	*Du.*	*Plur.*
1.	अदिक्षम्	अदिक्षाव	अदिक्षाम	अदिक्षि	अदिक्षावहि	अदिक्षामहि
2.	अदिक्षः	अदिक्षतम्	अदिक्षत	अदिक्षथाः	अदिक्षाथाम्	अदिक्षध्वम्
3.	अदिक्षत्	अदिक्षताम्	अदिक्षन्	अदिक्षत	अदिक्षाताम्	अदिक्षन्त

§ 357. Irregular Aorists of the seventh form: The roots गुह् 'to hide,' दिह् 'to smear,' दुह् 'to milk,' and लिह् 'to lick,' may optionally drop the initial स (or सा) of the terminations of the 2nd and 3rd Sing., 1st Du. and 2 Plur. in Âtmanepada; *e. g.*

गुह् 2 Sing. अघुक्षथाः or अगूढाः; 3 Sing. अघुक्षत or अगूढ;
      1 Du. अघुक्षावहि or अगुह्वहि;
      2 Plur. अघुक्षध्वम् or अघूढ्वम्.

दुह् 2 Sing. अधुक्षथाः or अदुग्धाः; 3. Sing. अधुक्षत or अदुग्ध;
      1 Du. अधुक्षावहि or अदुह्वहि;
      2 Plur. अधुक्षध्वम् or अधुग्ध्वम्.

§ 358. All roots which take this form of the S-Aorist end with one of the consonants श्, ष् or ह्, immediately preceded by one of the vowels इ, उ or ऋ. The following roots take only this form: कृश्, दिश्, रिश्, रुश्, लिश्, विश्, त्विष्, द्विष्, विष्, दिह्, रुह्, मिह्, रुह्, and लिह्. The roots मृश्, सृश्, and कृष् take optionally this form or form IV. (*e. g.* अमृक्षन् or अमार्क्षीत् of अम्राक्षीत्). The roots क्रिश् P., गुह्, तृह्, बृह्, and स्पृह् take optionally this form or form V. (*e. g.* अक्रिक्षन् or अक्रेक्षीत्). The root श्लिष् takes this form when it means 'to embrace' (अश्लिक्षन्); otherwise it takes form II. (अश्लिषत्).

3.—THE TWO FUTURES.

§ 359. As there are two forms of the Perfect,—a Reduplicated Perf. and a Periphrastic Perf.—, and two Aorists,—a Radical Aor. and a S-Aor.,—so there exist also two forms of the Future, viz. a *Simple Future*, and a *Periphrastic Future;* unlike however what is the case in the Perfect and Aorist, neither of these Futures is restricted to a limited number or a particular class of verbal roots, but all roots may equally form both the Simple and also the Periphrastic Future.

a.—The Simple Future.

§ 360. (*a*) The syllable स्य (changeable to ष्य in accordance with § 59) is added to the root (*e. g.* rt. दा, Future base दास्य), and to the base formed in this manner the personal terminations given in col. I. of § 227 are attached in Par. and Âtm. (*e. g.* 3 Sing. Par. दास्य + ति = दास्यति). The rules laid down in § 239 apply to the vowel अ of स्य and the initial letters of the personal terminations; *c. g.* दास्य + मि = दास्यामि.

(b) Table showing the terminations of the Simple Future:

	Parasmai.			Âtmane.		
	Sing.	Du.	Plur.	Sing.	Du.	Plur.
1.	स्यामि	स्यावः	स्यामः	स्ये	स्यावहे	स्यामहे
2.	स्यसि	स्यथः	स्यथ	स्यसे	स्येथे	स्यध्वे
3.	स्यति	स्यतः	स्यन्ति	स्यते	स्येते	स्यन्ते.

§ 361. Final radical consonants combine with the initial स् of these terminations according to the rules given in § 307 &c.; *e.g.*

rt. शक्	3. Sing. Par.	शक् + स्यति = शक्ष्यति
rt. पच्	,, ,, ,,	पच् + स्यति = पक्ष्यति.
rt. बध्	,, ,, ,,	बध् + स्यति = भत्स्यति.
rt. प्रछ्	,, ,, ,,	प्रछ् + स्यति = प्रक्ष्यति.
rt. त्यज्	,, ,, ,,	त्यज् + स्यति = त्यक्ष्यति.
rt. लभ्	,, ,, Âtm.	लभ् + स्यते = लप्स्यते.
rt. विश्	,, ,, Par.	वेश् + स्यति = वेक्ष्यति.
rt. वस्	,, ,, ,,	वस् + स्यति = वत्स्यति.
rt. दह्	,, ,, ,,	दह् + स्यति = धक्ष्यति.
rt. लिह्	,, ,, ,,	लेह् + स्यति = लेक्ष्यति.
rt. नह्	,, ,, ,,	नह् + स्यति = नत्स्यति.

§ 362. (*a*) Roots which according to § 366 *must or may* insert the intermediate इ before the terminations of the Periphrastic Fut., *must or may* insert it also before the terminations स्यामि &c. of the Simple Future; *e.g.*

	Periph. Fut.	3 Sing. Simple. Fut. Par.
rt. पत्,	पतिता;	पत् + इ + स्यति = पतिष्यति.
rt. कृ,	करिता;	कर् + इ + स्यति = करिष्यति.
rt. क्रिद्,	क्रंदिता	क्रंद् + इ + स्यति = क्रंदिष्यति
	or क्रंता;	or क्रंद् + स्यति = क्रंत्स्यति.

(b) Roots ending in ऋ, and हन् 'to kill,' always insert इ in the Simple Future; e. g.

  rt. कृ, 3 Sing. Par. कर् + इ + स्यति = करिष्यति.
  rt. हन्, ,, ,, ,, हन + इ + स्यति = हनिष्यति.

(c) The roots कृत् P. 'to cut,' वृत् P. 'to kill,' छुद् P. Â. 'to play,' तृद् P. A. 'to kill,' and नृत् P. 'to dance,' insert इ optionally; e. g. rt. कृत्, 3 Sing. Par. कर्तिष्यति or कर्त्स्यति.

(d) गम् inserts इ only in Parasmai.; वृत्, वृध्, स्यन्द् and शुभ् only in Âtmane. e. g.;

  rt. गम्, 3 Sing. Par. गमिष्यति; Âtm. (with prep. सम्) संगंस्यते.
  rt. वृत्, ,, ,, ,, वर्त्स्यति; ,, वर्तिष्यते.

(e) The intermediate इ must be lengthened in the Simple Fut. of ग्रह, and it may optionally be lengthened in the Simple Fut. of वृ and of roots ending in ऋ; e. g.

  rt. ग्रह, 3 Sing. Par. ग्रहीष्यति.
  rt. कृ, ,, ,, ,, करिष्यति or करीष्यति.

§ 363. (a) Final radical इ, ई, उ, ऊ, ऋ and ॠ, and penultimate prosodially short इ, उ, ऋ and ऌ are gunated; e. g. rt. नी, 3 Sing. Par. नेष्यति; rt. भिद्, भेत्स्यति; rt. तुद्, तोत्स्यति; rt. बुध्, बोधिष्यति.

(b) दृश् 'to see,' and सृज् 'to dismiss,' must substitute र for the Guṇa अर्, and other roots with penultimate ऋ, when they do not admit the intermediate इ, may do the same optionally; e. g.

  rt. दृश्, 3 Sing. Par. द्रक्ष्यति.
  rt. तृप्, ,, ,, ,, तर्प्स्यति or त्रप्स्यति.

§ 364. *Paradigms*: The Simple Future of दा P. Â. 'to give,' भू P. Â. 'to be,' तुद् P. Â. 'to strike,' बुध् P. Â. 'to know,' गै P. 'to sing,' and जीव् P. 'to live.'

Rt. दा

	Par.	Âtm.
Sing. 1.	दास्यामि	दास्ये
2.	दास्यसि	दास्यसे
3.	दास्यति	दास्यते
Dual 1.	दास्यावः	दास्यावहे
2.	दास्यथः	दास्येथे
3.	दास्यतः	दास्येते
Plur. 1.	दास्यामः	दास्यामहे
2.	दास्यथ	दास्यध्वे
3.	दास्यन्ति	दास्यन्ते

Rt. भू

	Par.	Âtm.
Sing. 1.	भविष्यामि	भविष्ये
2.	भविष्यसि	भविष्यसे
3.	भविष्यति	भविष्यते
Dual 1.	भविष्यावः	भविष्यावहे
2.	भविष्यथः	भविष्येथे
3.	भविष्यतः	भविष्येते
Plur. 1.	भविष्यामः	भविष्यामहे
2.	भविष्यथ	भविष्यध्वे
3.	भविष्यन्ति	भविष्यन्ते

Rt. तुद्

	Par.	Âtm.
Sing. 1.	तोत्स्यामि	तोत्स्ये
2.	तोत्स्यसि	तोत्स्यसे
3.	तोत्स्यति	तोत्स्यते
Dual 1.	तोत्स्यावः	तोत्स्यावहे
2.	तोत्स्यथः	तोत्स्येथे
3.	तोत्स्यतः	तोत्स्येते
Plur. 1.	तोत्स्यामः	तोत्स्यामहे
2.	तोत्स्यथ	तोत्स्यध्वे
3.	तोत्स्यन्ति	तोत्स्यन्ते

Rt. बुध्

	Par.	Âtm.
Sing. 1.	बोधिष्यामि	बोधिष्ये
2.	बोधिष्यसि	बोधिष्यसे
3.	बोधिष्यति	बोधिष्यते
Dual 1.	बोधिष्यावः	बोधिष्यावहे
2.	बोधिष्यथः	बोधिष्येथे
3.	बोधिष्यतः	बोधिष्येते
Plur. 1.	बोधिष्यामः	बोधिष्यामहे
2.	बोधिष्यथ	बोधिष्यध्वे
3.	बोधिष्यन्ति	बोधिष्यन्ते

		Rt. गै	Rt. जीव्
		Par.	Par.
Sing.	1.	गास्यामि	जीविष्यामि
	2.	गास्यसि	जीविष्यसि
	3.	गास्यति	जीविष्यति
Dual.	1.	गास्यावः	जीविष्यावः
	2.	गास्यथः	जीविष्यथः
	3.	गास्यतः	जीविष्यतः
Plur.	1.	गास्यामः	जीविष्यामः
	2.	गास्यथ	जीविष्यथ
	3.	गास्यन्ति	जीविष्यन्ति.

b.—The Periphrastic Future.

§ 365. (*a*) The terminations of the 3 Sing. Du. and Plur. both in Par. and in Âtm. are ता, तारौ, तारः (*i. e.* the Nom. Sing. Du. and Plur. Masc. of the affix तृ; § 149); in the remaining forms ता is affixed to the root and to the base formed in this manner the corresponding forms of the Present Ind. Par. and Âtm. of अस् 'to be,' (§ 266) are added.

(*b*) Table showing the terminations of the Periphrastic Future :—

	Parasmai.			Âtmane.		
	Sing.	Dual.	Plur.	Sing.	Dual.	Plur.
1.	तास्मि	तास्वः	तास्मः	ताहे	तास्वहे	तास्महे
2.	तासि	तास्थः	तास्थ	तासे	तासाथे	ताध्वे
3.	ता	तारौ	तारः	ता	तारौ	तारः

§ 366. These terminations are either added immediately to the root, or the intermediate इ *may* optionally be prefixed to them before they are added to the root, or the intermediate *must* be prefixed to them before they are added to the root:

(*a*) The intermediate इ is *forbidden* after the following roots :—

1. All monosyllabic roots ending in vowels, except roots ending in ऋ and ॠ, and except श्रि, ष्वि, डो, शो, क्षु, ष्णु, नु, यु 'to mix,' रु, स्नु; वृ

[§ 366.] CONJUGATION OF VERBS. 135

e. g. rt. दा, 3 Sing. दाता; rt. जि, जेता; rt. नी, नेता; rt. च्यु, च्योता; rt. कृ, कर्ता; rt. धे, धाता; rt. गै, गाता; rt. सो, साता. (But rt. भू, भविता; rt. कृ, करिता; rt. श्रि, श्रयिता &c.)

2. The following **100** roots ending in consonants:* शक्, पच्, मुच्, रिच्, वच्, विच्, सिच्; प्रच्छ; त्यज्, निज्, भज्, भञ्ज्, भुज्, भ्रस्ज्, मस्ज्, यज्, युज्, रञ्ज्, सृज्, विज् 'to separate,' सञ्ज्, सृज्, स्वञ्ज्; भद्, क्षुद्, खिद्, छिद्, तुद्, नुद्, पद्, भिद्, विद्, (विद्यते 'to be found, to be,' विन्दति (?)) शाद्, सद्, स्कन्द्, सिद्, हद्; कुध्, क्षुध्, बन्ध्, बुध् (बुध्यते), युध्, राध्, रुध्, व्यध्, शुध्, साध्, सिध् (सिध्यति); मन् (मन्यते), हन्; भाप्, क्षिप्, छुप्, तप्, तिप्, लिप्, लुप्, वप्, शाप्, सुप्, स्वप्, यभ्, रभ्, लभ्; क्रम् (in Ātm.), गम्, नम्, यम्, रम्; कृश्, दंश्, दिश्, दृश्, मृश्, रिश्, रुश्, लिश्, विश्, स्पृश्; कृप्, तृप्, तिप्, दृप्, द्रिप्, विप्, पुप् (पुष्यति), विप्, शिप्, शुप्, श्रिप्; वस्, दम् (वसति 'to dwell'); दह्, दिह्, दुह्, नह्, मिह्, रुह्, लिह्, वह्. When the terminations of the Periphrastic Future are added to these roots, the rules given in § 307 &c. must be observed; *e. g.* rt. शक्, 3 Sing. शक्ता; rt. प्रच्छ, प्रष्टा; rt. त्यज्, त्यक्ता; rt. यज्, यष्टा; rt. लभ्, लब्धा; rt. दह्, दग्धा; rt. नह्, नद्धा &c.

(*b*) The intermediate इ may optionally be prefixed to the terminations after the following roots:—

---

* These roots are contained in the following memorial verses, which the student may learn by heart:—

शक् पच् मुच् रिच् वच् विच् सिच् प्रच्छि त्यज् निजभेजः ।
भञ्ज् भुज् भ्रस्ज् मस्जि यज् युज् रुज् रञ्ज् विजिर् स्वञ्जि सञ्ज् सृजः ॥ १ ॥
भद् क्षुद् खिद् छिन्नदि नुदः पद्य भिद् विद्यतिविदः ।
शाद् सदी सिद्यति: स्कान्द हदी कुध् क्षुधिबुध्यनी ॥ २ ॥
बान्ध्युभिरुधी राधि व्यभ् शुधः साधिसिध्यनी ।
मन्य हन्नाप् क्षिप् छुप् तप् तिप्स्तुप्यतितृप्यती ॥ ३ ॥
लिप् लुप् वप् शाप् स्वप् मृषि यभ् रभ् लभ् गम् नम् यमो रमिः ।
क्रुशिदंशिगदिशो दृश् मृश् रिश् रुश् लिश् विश् स्पृशः कृपिः ॥ ४ ॥
तिप् तुप् द्रिप् दुप् पुष्य विप् विप् शिप् शुप् श्रिष्यतयो वासेः ।
वसनिर्देह दिह् दृहो नह् मिह् रुह् लिह् वहिस्तथा ॥ ५ ॥

For नृ and दृ see (*b*) 3.

1. भू, सू (सूते and सूयते), and स्तृ; *e.g.* rt. सू, 3 Sing. सोता or सविता; rt. स्तृ, स्तर्ता or स्तरिता।

2. तञ्च् (तनक्ति), ब्रश्च्; अञ्ज्, मृज्; क्लिद्, स्यन्द्; सिध् (सेधति 'to govern'); क्लृप् (in Par. कल्प्ता, Âtm. कल्पिता), गुप्, लप्, क्षम्; अश् (अश्नुते), क्लिश्; अक्ष्, तक्ष् ('to cut'), त्वक्ष्; गाह्, गुह्, म्लह्, तृह्, नृह्, माह्, बृह्, स्नुह्; *e.g.* rt. तञ्च्, 3 Sing. तङ्क्ता or ताञ्चिता; rt. ब्रश्च्, व्रष्टा or व्रश्चिता; rt. क्लिद्, क्लेत्ता or क्लेदिता &c.

3. तृप्, दृप्, द्रुह, नश्, मुह्, रभ्, स्निह, स्नुह्; *e.g.* rt. तृप्, 3 Sing. तर्प्ता or तप्ता, or तर्पिता; rt. द्रुह्, द्रोग्धा or द्रोढा, or द्रोहिता।

(*c*) After all other roots the intermediate इ *must* be prefixed to the terminations of the Periphrastic Future; *e. g.* rt. लू, 3 Sing. लविता; rt. पत्, पतिता; rt. जागृ, जागरिता &c. The intermediate इ is lengthened as in the Simple Future (§ 362, *e*); *e.g.* rt. ग्रह् 3 Sing. ग्रहीता; rt. कृ, करिता or करीता.

§ 367. The rules given in § 363 apply also in the Periphrastic Future; *e. g.*

(*a*) rt. नी, 3 Sing. नेता; rt. भिद्, भेत्ता; rt. नुद्, नोत्ता; rt. बुध्, बोधिता।

(*b*) rt. दृश्, 3 Sing. द्रष्टा; rt. तृप्, तर्प्ता or तप्ता (or तर्पिता § 366, *b*, 3).

§ 368. *Paradigms:* The Periphrastic Future of दा P. Â. 'to give;' भू, P. Â. 'to be;' तुद् P. Â. 'to strike;' and गै P. 'to sing.'

		Rt. दा		Rt. भू	
		Par.	Âtm.	Par.	Âtm.
Sing.	1.	दातास्मि	दाताहे	भवितास्मि	भविताहे
	2.	दातासि	दातासे	भवितासि	भवितासे
	3.	दाता	दाता	भविता	भविता
Dual	1.	दातास्वः	दातास्वहे	भवितास्वः	भवितास्वहे
	2.	दातास्थः	दातासाथे	भवितास्थः	भवितासाथे
	3.	दातारौ	दातारौ	भवितारौ	भवितारौ
Plur.	1.	दातास्मः	दातास्महे	भवितास्मः	भवितास्महे
	2.	दातास्थ	दाताध्वे	भवितास्थ	भविताध्वे
	3.	दातारः	दातारः	भवितारः	भवितारः

	Rt. तुद्		Rt. गै
	Par.	Âtm.	Par.
Sing. 1.	तोत्तास्मि	तोत्ताहे	गातास्मि
Sing. 2.	तोत्तासि	तोत्तासे	गातासि
Sing. 3.	तोत्ता	तोत्ता	गाता
Dual. 1.	तोत्तास्वः	तोत्तास्वहे	गातास्वः
Dual. 2.	तोत्तास्थः	तोत्तासाथे	गातास्थः
Dual. 3.	तोत्तारौ	तोत्तारौ	गातारौ
Plur. 1.	तोत्तास्मः	तोत्तास्महे	गातास्मः
Plur. 2.	तोत्तास्थ	तोत्ताध्वे	गातास्थ
Plur. 3.	तोत्तारः	तोत्तारः	गातारः

§ 369. *Irregular Periphrastic Futures:*

1. इष् (इच्छति) P. 'to wish;' 3 Sing. एषिता or एष्टा.
2. रिष्   P. 'to hurt;'   „   „ रेषिता or रेष्टा.
3. रुष्   P. 'to hurt;'   „   „ रोषिता or रोष्टा.
4. लुभ्   P. 'to desire;' „   „ लोभिता or लोब्धा.
5. सह्   Â. 'to bear;'   „   „ सहिता or सोढा.

4.—THE CONDITIONAL.

§ 370. The Conditional is derived from the Simple Future by prefixing to the latter the augment and substituting for the personal terminations मि, सि, ति &c. the terminations अम् , :, त् &c. given in col. II. of § 227; *e.g.* rt. दा, Simple Fut. Par. दास्यति, Condit. अदास्यत्; Âtm. दास्यते, अदास्यत; rt. इष् 'to wish,' Simple Fut. एषिष्यति; Condit. ऐषिष्यत् &c.

§ 371. *Paradigms:* The Conditional of दा P. Â. 'to give,' भू P. Â. 'to be,' तुद् P. Â. 'to strike,' and गै P. 'to sing;'

133 SANSKRIT GRAMMAR. [§ 372—

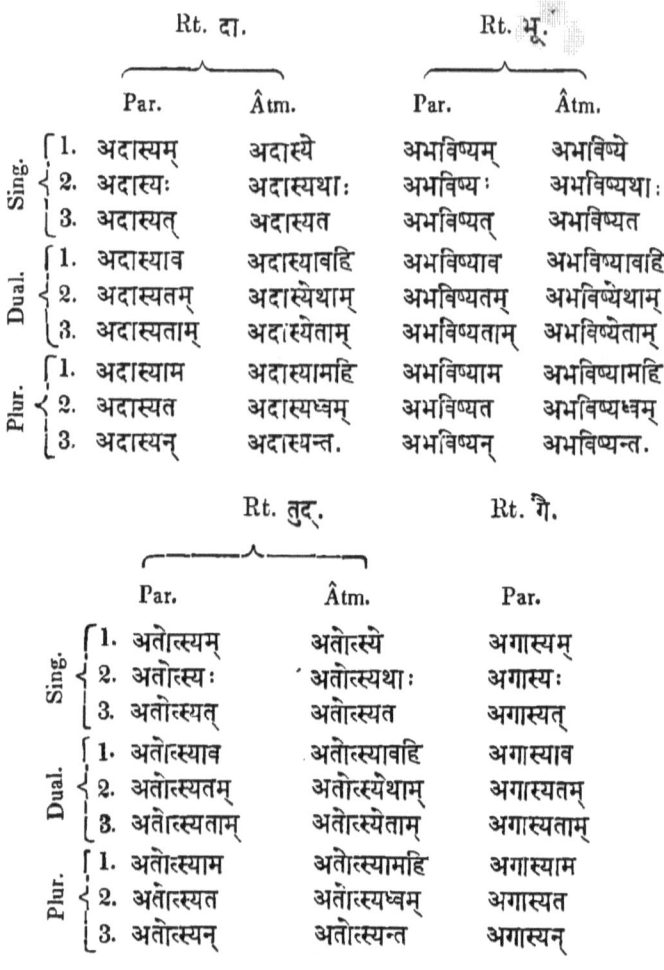

5.—THE BENEDICTIVE.

§ 372. (a) In Parasmai. यास् is affixed to the root, and to the base formed in this way the personal terminations of the Parasmai. given in col. II. of § 227 are added; in the 3rd Plur., however, उ: is substituted for अन्. In the 2nd and 3rd Sing. यास्+ : and यास्+ त् become या : and यात्.

(b) In Âtmane. सी (changeable to षी by § 59) is affixed to the root, and to the base formed in this manner the personal terminations of the

[§ 373.] CONJUGATION OF VERBS. 139

Âtmane. given in col. II. of § 227 are added; however भ is substituted for इ, रन् for अन्त, and a sibilant is prefixed to the dental of the terminations याः, त, आथाम्, and आनाम्.

(c) Table showing the terminations of the Benedictive:

	Parasmai.			Âtmane.		
	Sing.	*Du.*	*Plur.*	*Sing.*	*Du.*	*Plur.*
1.	यासम्	यास्व	यास्म	सीय	सीवहि	सीमहि
2.	याः	यास्तम्	यास्त	सीष्ठाः	सीयास्थाम्	सीध्वम्
3.	यात्	यास्ताम्	यासुः	सीष्ट	सीयास्ताम्	सीरन्

(d) The ष् of the termination सीध्वम् must be changed to ढ़ when the termination is immediately preceded by any radical vowel except अ or आ, or by र्; e.g. rt. नु, स्रोपोढ़्वम्; स्तृ, स्तोषीढ़्वम्. It may optionally be changed to ढ़ when the termination is preceded by the intermediate इ and this intermediate इ is again preceded by one of the letters य्, र्, ल्, व्, ह्; e.g. rt. लू, लविषीध्वम् or लविषीढ़्वम्.

(a).—*Parasmaipada.*

§ 373. (a) The terminations are added immediately to the root; e.g. rt. भू, 3 Sing. भूयात्; rt. नृत्, नृत्यात्.

(b) The following are the only changes that take place in the root:

1. A penultimate nasal is generally dropped; e.g. rt. दंश्, दश्यात्; rt. बन्ध्, बध्यात्.

2. Final इ and उ are lengthened; e.g. rt. चि, चीयात्; rt. स्तु, स्तूयात्.

3. Final ऋ when preceded by one radical consonant, is changed to रि; when preceded by more consonants, and in rt. ऋ 'to go,' to अर्; e.g. rt. कृ, क्रियात्; rt. स्मृ, स्मर्यात्; rt. ऋ, अर्यात्.

4. Final ॠ is changed to ईर्; but when preceded by a labial, to ऊर्; e.g. rt. कॄ, कीर्यात्; rt. पॄ, पूर्यात्.

5. The final vowel of दा 'to give,' दो, धा, धे, मा, स्था, गै, पा 'to drink,' हा 'to abandon,' and सो, must be changed to ए; and final आ and

ऐ preceded by more consonants than one may optionally be changed to ए or remain आ (§ 296, a); e. g. rt. दा, देयात्; rt. गै, गेयात्; rt. ग्लै, ग्लेयात् or ग्लायात्; but rt. पा ' to protect,' पायात् &c.

6. The roots वन्, वद्, वप्, वश्, वस् 'to dwell,' वह् and स्वप् substitute उ for व; यज्, व्यच्, and व्यध् substitute इ for य; ग्रह्, प्रच्छ्, भ्रस्ज् and व्रश्च् substitute ऋ for र; वे, ह्वे and श्वि substitute ऊ for वे and वि; व्ये and ह्या substitute ई for ये and या; शास् substitutes इ for आ; e. g. rt. वच्, उच्यात्; rt. यज्, इज्यात्; rt. ग्रह्, गृह्यात्; rt. ह्वे, हूयात्; rt. व्ये, वीयात्; rt. शास्, शिष्यात्.

7. Observe § 46; e. g. rt. दिव्, दीव्यात्.

(b).—Ātmanepada.

§ 374. (a) Those verbs which must or may prefix the intermediate इ to the terminations of the Periphrastic Future, must or may prefix it also to the Ātmane. terminations of the Benedictive before they are added to the root. But the following special rules must be observed:—

(b) Roots ending in ऋ preceded by more consonants than one, the root वृ, and roots in ॠ may prefix इ to the terminations optionally; e. g. rt. स्मृ, 3 Sing. स्मृषीष्ट or स्मरिषीष्ट; rt. स्तृ, स्तोषीष्ट or स्तरिषीष्ट.

(c) The intermediate इ is lengthened after the root ग्रह् only; e. g. ग्रहीषीष्ट.

§ 375. (a) When the intermediate इ is prefixed to the terminations, final radical vowels and penultimate prosodially short इ, उ, ऋ and ऌ are gunated; e. g. rt. लू, लविषीष्ट; rt. वृध्, वर्धिषीष्ट.

(b) When the terminations are added without the intermediate इ, final इ, ई, उ and ऊ are gunated; final ऋ is changed to ईर्, or when preceded by a labial, to ऊर्; other vowels remain unchanged (observe § 296); e. g. rt. जि, जेषीष्ट; rt. स्तृ, स्तोषीष्ट (or स्तरिषीष्ट); rt. पृ, पूर्षीष्ट (or परिषीष्ट).

(c) Final radical consonants combine with the initial स् of the terminations according to the rules in § 307 &c.; e. g. rt. भुभ्, भुक्षीष्ट; rt. युज्, युक्षीष्ट; rt. लिह्, लिक्षीष्ट &c.

§ 376. *Paradigms*: The Benedictive of जि P. Â. 'to conquer,' भू P. Â. 'to be,' बुध् cl. 1, P. Â. 'to know,' तुद् P. Â. 'to strike.'

CONJUGATION OF VERBS.

	Rt. जि		Rt. भू	
	Par.	Âtm.	Par.	Âtm.
Sing. 1.	जीयासम्	जेषीय	भूयासम्	भविषीय
Sing. 2.	जीयाः	जेषीष्ठाः	भूयाः	भविषीष्ठाः
Sing. 3.	जीयात्	जेषीष्ट	भूयात्	भविषीष्ट
Dual. 1.	जीयास्व	जेषीवहि	भूयास्व	भविषीवहि
Dual. 2.	जीयास्तम्	जेषीयास्थाम्	भूयास्तम्	भविषीयास्थाम्
Dual. 3.	जीयास्ताम्	जेषीयास्ताम्	भूयास्ताम्	भविषीयास्ताम्
Plur. 1.	जीयास्म	जेषीमहि	भूयास्म	भविषीमहि
Plur. 2.	जीयास्त	जेषीढ्वम्	भूयास्त	भविषीध्वम् or ःढ्वम्
Plur. 3.	जीयासुः	जेषीरन्	भूयासुः	भविषीरन्

	Rt. बुध्		Rt. तुद्	
	Par.	Âtm.	Par.	Âtm.
Sing. 1.	बुध्यासम्	बोधिषीय	तुद्यासम्	तुत्सीय
Sing. 2.	बुध्याः	बोधिषीष्ठाः	तुद्याः	तुत्सीष्ठाः
Sing. 3.	बुध्यात्	बोधिषीष्ट	तुद्यात्	तुत्सीष्ट
Dual. 1.	बुध्यास्व	बोधिषीवहि	तुद्यास्व	तुत्सीवहि
Dual. 2.	बुध्यास्तम्	बोधिषीयास्थाम्	तुद्यास्तम्	तुत्सीयास्थाम्
Dual. 3.	बुध्यास्ताम्	बोधिषीयास्ताम्	तुद्यास्ताम्	तुत्सीयास्ताम्
Plur. 1.	बुध्यास्म	बोधिषीमहि	तुद्यास्म	तुत्सीमहि
Plur. 2.	बुध्यास्त	बोधिषीध्वम्	तुद्यास्त	तुत्सीध्वम्
Plur. 3.	बुध्यासुः	बोधिषीरन्	तुद्यासुः	तुत्सीरन्

§ 377. *Irregular Benedictives:—*

1. इ. 'to go,' Par. ईयात्; but after prepositions, इयात्, *e. g.* समियात्: Âtm. एयेष्ट.

2. खन् 'to dig;' Par. खन्यात् or खायात्.
3. गम् 'to go;' Âtm. गंसीष्ट or गसीष्ट.
4. जन् 'to beget;' Par. जन्यात् or जायात्.
5. सन् 'to obtain;' Par. सन्यात् or सायात्.

2.—THE PASSIVE.

§ 378. With the exception of the Present Indicative, Potential, and Imperative, and of the Imperfect, the forms of the Passive are generally the same as those of the Âtmanepada or reflective voice. The Present and Imperfect of the Passive differ commonly from the Present and Imperfect Âtmane.; they are formed in one and the same manner of all primitive roots of all the nine classes.

A.—The Present (Indic., Potent., Imperat.) and Imperfect.

§ 379. *Formation of the Passive Base:*

(*a*) The syllable य is added to the root; *e. g.* rt. भू, Pass. base. भूय; rt. तुद्, तुद्य; rt. द्विष्, द्विष्य.

(*b*) Before य roots (except those ending in आ, ए, ओ and ऐ) undergo the same changes which they undergo before the terminations of the Benedictive Par. (§ 373 *b*, 1—4 and 6, 7); *e. g.* rt. बन्ध्, Pass. base बध्य; rt. चि, चीय; rt. स्तु, स्तूय; rt. कृ, क्रिय; rt. स्मृ, स्मर्य; rt. ऋ, अर्य; rt. कॄ, कीर्य; rt. पॄ, पूर्य; rt. वच्, उच्य; rt. यज्, इज्य; rt. ग्रह, गृह्य; rt. ह्वे, हूय; rt. दिव्, दीव्य.

(*c*) The final vowel of दा 'to give,' दे, दो, धा, धे, मा, स्था, गै, पा 'to drink,' हा 'to abandon,' and सो, is changed to ई; the final of other roots in आ remains unchanged, and the final of other roots in ए, ओ, ऐ becomes आ (§ 296, *a*); *e. g.* rt. दा, Pass. base दीय; rt. गै, गीय; rt. सो, सीय; but rt. ज्ञा, ज्ञाय; rt. ध्ये, ध्याय.

§ 380. The passive base is conjugated like the special base of a root of the fourth class in Âtmane.; *e. g.* rt. कृ, Pass. base क्रिय; 3 Sing. Pres. Ind. क्रियते; Pres. Pot. क्रियेत; Pres. Imperat. क्रियताम्; Imperf. अक्रियत.

§ 381. *Paradigm*: The Present and Imperfect Pass. of तुद् 'to strike:'

		Pres. Ind.	Pres. Pot.	Pres. Imper.	Imperf.
Sing.	1.	तुद्ये	तुद्येय	तुद्यै	अतुद्ये
	2.	तुद्यसे	तुद्येथाः	तुद्यस्व	अतुद्यथाः
	3.	तुद्यते	तुद्येत	तुद्यताम्	अतुद्यत
Dual.	1.	तुद्यावहे	तुद्येवहि	तुद्यावहै	अतुद्यावहि
	2.	तुद्येथे	तुद्येयाथाम्	तुद्येथाम्	अतुद्येथाम्
	3.	तुद्येते	तुद्येयाताम्	तुद्येताम्	अतुद्येताम्
Plur.	1.	तुद्यामहे	तुद्येमहि	तुद्यामहै	अतुद्यामहि
	2.	तुद्यध्वे	तुद्येध्वम्	तुद्यध्वम्	अतुद्यध्वम्
	3.	तुद्यन्ते	तुद्येरन्	तुद्यन्ताम्	अतुद्यन्त

§ 382. *Irregular Presents and Imperfects of the Passive*: The following roots are irregular so far as the formation of their Passive base is concerned :—

1. खन् 'to dig ;' Pass. Base. खन्य or खाय; Pres. Ind. खन्यते or खायते.
2. जन् 'to bring forth;' „ „ जन्य or जाय; „ „ जन्यते or जायते.
3. तन् 'to stretch ;' „ „ तन्य or ताय; „ „ तन्यते or तायते.
4. शो 'to lie down ;' „ „ शय्य ; „ „ शय्यते.
5. सन् 'to obtain ;' „ „ सन्य or साय; „ „ सन्यते or सायते.
6. उह् 'to understand' shortens its उ when a preposition is prefixed to it ; *e. g.* Pres. Ind. of समूह्, समुह्यते; but of उह्, उह्यते.

B.—The Perfect, Aorist, Future, Conditional, and Benedictive.

(*a*).—*The Perfect*.

§ 383. (α) *The Reduplicated Perfect* of the Passive is formed from the same roots and in the same manner as the Redupl. Perf. of the Âtm.; *e. g.* rt. भिद्, 3 Sing. Red. Perf. Pass. बिभिदे; rt. तुद्, तुतुदे; rt. निन्द्, निनिन्दे, rt. क्रम्, चक्रमे; rt. अञ्ज्, आनञ्जे ; rt. इष्, ईषे &c.

§ 384. (β) *The Periphrastic Perfect* of the Passive is formed from the same roots and in the same manner as the Periphrastic Perf. of the Âtm. except that all the three auxiliary verbs अस्, कृ, and भू are conjugated only in the Âtmane.; *e. g.* rt. उन्द्, 3 Sing. Periph. Perf. Pass. उन्दामासे, or उन्दाचक्रे, or उन्दाबभूवे ; rt. ईक्ष्, ईक्षामासे, or ईक्षाचक्रे, or ईक्षाबभूवे &c.

(*b*).—*The Aorist*.

1.—*Formation of the 3rd Pers. Sing.*

§ 385. The 3rd Pers. Sing. of the Aor. Pass. is formed in one and the same manner of all roots, by prefixing to the root the augment and by adding to it the termination इ; *e. g.* rt. निन्द्, 3 Sing. Aor. Pass. अनिन्दि; rt. सेव् असेवि.

§ 386. Before the termination इ the root undergoes the following changes:—

(a) Guṇa is substituted for a penultimate prosodially short vowel; *e. g.* rt. भिद्, अभेदि; rt. तुद्, अतोदि; rt. कृत्, अकर्ति.

(b) Vriddhi is substituted for a final vowel; *e. g.* rt. चि, अचायि; rt. नी, अनायि; rt. स्तु, अस्तावि; rt. लू, अलावि; rt. कृ, अकारि; rt. कॄ, अकारि.

(c) A penultimate prosodially short अ is lengthened except in roots ending in अम्; *e. g.* rt. वद्, अवादि; rt. पठ्, अपाठि; but rt. दम्, अदमि.

Exception: The penultimate अ of कम्, गम्, नम्, यम्, रम्, वम्, and of चम् when compounded with the prep. आ, is lengthened; *e. g.* अकामि, अगामि, अनामि. &c.

(d) Roots ending in आ, and roots ending in ए, ऐ and ओ (changeable to आ) insert य् between the root and the termination; *e. g.* rt. दा, अदायि; rt. धे, अधायि; rt. गै, अगायि.

§ 387. *Irregular 3rd Persons Sing. of the Aor. Pass.:*

1. जन् 'to bring forth;' अजनि.
2. भञ्ज् 'to break;' अभञ्जि or अभाजि.
3. रध् 'to kill;' अरन्धि.
4. रभ् 'to desire;' अरम्भि.
5. लभ् 'to take;' अलाभि or अलम्भि; when compounded with prepositions, only अलम्भि, *e. g.* प्रलम्भि, प्रालम्भि.

2.—*The remaining Persons of the Aorist Pass.*

(a) Rules applicable equally to all roots.

§ 388. Those roots which actually take Form IV., V., or VII. of the Aor. in Âtmane., or which, if they were used in Âtmane., would take those forms in Âtmanepada, use the same forms of the Aor. Âtmane. for the Passive; *e. g.* rt. कृ, 1 Sing. Aor. Pass. अकृषि; rt. दा, अदिषि; rt. मुच्, अमुक्षि; rt. लू, अलविषि; rt. भू, अभविषि; rt. द्विष्, अद्विक्षि.

§ 389. Forms II. and III. of the Aor. Âtmane. are not used for the Passive; the roots which in Âtmane. take Form II. or III., or which would take these forms if they were conjugated in the Âtmane., take in the Passive Form IV. or V. of the Aor. Âtmane. according as § 343 or § 349 is applicable to them; *e. g.* rt. अस् 'to throw;'

§ 391.] CONJUGATION OF VERBS. 145

1 Sing. Aor. Âtm. अर्ध्ये; Pass. आसिषि; rt. ह्वा, Âtm. अह्वे; Pass. अह्वासि; rt. श्रि, Âtm. अशिश्रिये; Pass. अश्रयिषि; rt. लु, Âtm. असुलुवे; Pass. अलावि.

(β) *Optional forms of roots ending in vowels, and of* ग्रह्, दृश् *and* हन्.

§ 390. All roots ending in vowels, and the roots ग्रह् 'to take,' दृश् 'to see,' and हन् 'to kill,' may optionally form the Passive Aorist (except in the 3 Sing.) by augmenting the root and adding to it the terminations of Form V. of the Aor. Âtmane.; before these terminations the root undergoes the same changes which it undergoes before the termination इ of the 3 Sing. Aor. Pass. The initial इ of the terminations इवि &c. is not liable to be lengthened; *e.g.* rt. चि, 1 Sing. Aor. Pass. अचायिषि (or अचेषि); rt. नी, अनायिषि (or अनेषि); rt. ग्रह्, अग्राहिषि (or अग्रहीषि); rt. दृश्, अदर्शिषि (or अदृक्षि).

§ 391. *Paradigms:* The Aorist Pass. of कृ 'to do,' तुद् 'to strike,' दृश् 'to see,' and लू 'to cut.'

		Rt. कृ.		Rt. तुद्.
Sing.	1.	अकृषि or	अकारिषि	अतुत्सि
	2.	अकृथाः	अकारिष्ठाः	अतुत्थाः
	3.		अकारि	अतोदि
Dual.	1.	अकृष्वहि	अकारिष्वहि	अतुत्स्वहि
	2.	अकृषाथाम्	अकारिषाथाम्	अतुत्सथाम्
	3.	अकृषाताम्	अकारिषाताम्	अतुत्सताम्
Plur.	1.	अकृष्महि	अकारिष्महि	अतुत्स्महि
	2.	अकृढ्वम्	अकारिध्वम् or ˚ढ्वम्	अतुद्ध्वम्
	3.	अकृषत	अकारिषत	अतुत्सत

		Rt. दृश्.		Rt. लू.	
Sing.	1.	अदृक्षि or	अदर्शिषि	अलविषि or	अलाविषि
	2.	अदृक्षाः	अदर्शिषाः	अलविष्ठाः	अलाविष्ठाः
	3.		अदर्शि		अलावि
Dual.	1.	अदृक्ष्वहि	अदर्शिष्वहि	अलविष्वहि	अलाविष्वहि
	2.	अदृक्षाथाम्	अदर्शिषाथाम्	अलविषाथाम्	अलाविषाथाम्
	3.	अदृक्षाताम्	अदर्शिषाताम्	अलविषाताम्	अलाविषाताम्
Plur.	1.	अदृक्ष्महि	अदर्शिष्महि	अलविष्महि	अलाविष्महि
	2.	अदृढ्वम्	अदर्शिध्वम्	अलविध्वम् or ˚ढ्वम्	अलाविध्वम् or ˚ढ्वम्
	3.	अदृक्षन	अदर्शिषत	अलविषत	अलाविषत

(c).—*The two Futures, the Conditional, and the Benedictive.*

(α) Rule applicable equally to all roots.

§ 392. The formation of the two Futures, the Conditional and the Benedictive of the Passive does not differ from the formation of the same forms of the Âtmanepada; *e.g.* rt. दा, 3 Sing. Simple Fut. Pass. दास्यते; rt. भू, भविष्यते; rt. तुद्, तोत्स्यते; rt. बुध्, बोधिष्यते;—rt. दा, 1 Sing. Periph. Fut. Pass. दाताहे; rt. तुद्, तोत्ताहे;—rt. जि, 3 Sing. Bened. Pass. जेषीष्ट; rt. बुध्, बोधिषीष्ट; rt. तुद्, तुत्सीष्ट.

(β) Optional forms of roots ending in vowels, and of ग्रह्, दृश्, and हन्.

§ 393. All roots ending in vowels, and the roots ग्रह्, दृश्, and हन् may optionally form the two Futures, the Conditional and the Benedictive of the Passive by adding to the root the terminations of the corresponding tenses of the Âtmanepada by means of the intermediate vowel इ, and by changing the root in the same manner in which it is changed before the termination इ of the 3 Sing. of the Aor. Pass.; *e.g.* rt. दा, 3 Sing. Simple Fut. Pass. दायिष्यते (or दास्यते); Periph. Fut. दायिता (or दाता); Condit. अदायिष्यत (or अदास्यत); Bened. दायिषीष्ट (or दासीष्ट); rt. दृश्, Simple Fut. Pass. दर्शिष्यते (or द्रक्ष्यते) &c.

Paradigm.

§ 394. Conjugation of rt. बुध् cl. 1, P. Â. 'to know,' in Parasmai., Âtmane., and Passive:

	Parasmai.	Âtmane.	Passive.
	Present Indicative.		
Sing. 1.	बोधामि 'I know.'	बोधे 'I know.'	बुध्ये 'I am known.'
Sing. 2.	बोधसि	बोधसे	बुध्यसे
Sing. 3.	बोधति	बोधते	बुध्यते
Dual. 1.	बोधावः	बोधावहे	बुध्यावहे
Dual. 2.	बोधथः	बोधेथे	बुध्येथे
Dual. 3.	बोधतः	बोधेते	बुध्येते
Plur. 1.	बोधामः	बोधामहे	बुध्यामहे
Plur. 2.	बोधथ	बोधध्वे	बुध्यध्वे
Plur. 3.	बोधन्ति	बोधन्ते	बुध्यन्ते

Present Potential.

Sing.	1. बोधेयम् 'I may know.'	बोधेय 'I may know.'	बुध्येय 'I may be known.'
	2. बोधेः	बोधेथाः	बुध्येथाः
	3. बोधेत्	बोधेत	बुध्येत
Dual.	1. बोधेव	बोधेवहि	बुध्येवहि
	2. बोधेतम्	बोधेयाथाम्	बुध्येयाथाम्
	3. बोधेताम्	बोधेयाताम्	बुध्येयाताम्
Plur.	1. बोधेम	बोधेमहि	बुध्येमहि
	2. बोधेत	बोधेध्वम्	बुध्येध्वम्
	3. बोधेयुः	बोधेरन्	बुध्येरन्

Present Imperative.

Sing.	1. बोधानि 'May I know.'	बोधै 'May I know.'	बुध्यै 'May I be known.'
	2. बोध or बोधतात्	बोधस्व	बुध्यस्व
	3. बोधतु or बोधतात्	बोधताम्	बुध्यताम्
Dual.	1. बोधाव	बोधावहै	बुध्यावहै
	2. बोधतम्	बोधेथाम्	बुध्येथाम्
	3. बोधताम्	बोधेताम्	बुध्येताम्
Plur.	1. बोधाम	बोधामहै	बुध्यामहै
	2. बोधत	बोधध्वम्	बुध्यध्वम्
	3. बोधन्तु	बोधन्ताम्	बुध्यन्ताम्

Imperfect.

Sing.	1. अबोधम् 'I knew.'	अबोधे 'I knew.'	अबुध्ये 'I was known.'
	2. अबोधः	अबोधथाः	अबुध्यथाः
	3. अबोधत्	अबोधत	अबुध्यत
Dual.	1. अबोधाव	अबोधावहि	अबुध्यावहि
	2. अबोधतम्	अबोधेथाम्	अबुध्येथाम्
	3. अबोधताम्	अबोधेताम्	अबुध्येताम्
Plur.	1. अबोधाम	अबोधामहि	अबुध्यामहि
	2. अबोधत	अबोधध्वम्	अबुध्यध्वम्
	3. अबोधन्	अबोधन्त	अबुध्यन्त

Reduplicated Perfect.

		Parasmai	Atmane	Passive
Sing.	1.	बुबोध 'I knew.'	बुबुधे 'I knew.'	बुबुधे 'I was known.'
	2.	बुबोधिथ	बुबुधिषे	Conjugated like
	3.	बुबोध	बुबुधे	the Âtmane.
Dual.	1.	बुबुधिव	बुबुधिवहे	
	2.	बुबुधथुः	बुबुधाथे	
	3.	बुबुधतुः	बुबुधाते	
Plur.	1.	बुबुधिम	बुबुधिमहे	
	2.	बुबुध	बुबुधिध्वे	
	3.	बुबुधुः	बुबुधिरे	

Aorist.

Form II. or Form V.

Sing.	1.	अबुधम्	अबोधिषम् 'I have	अबोधिषि 'I have	अबोधिषि 'I have
	2.	अबुधः	अबोधीः known.'	अबोधिष्ठाः known.'	अबोधिष्ठाः been
	3.	अबुधत्	अबोधीत्	अबोधिष्ट	अबोधि known.'
Dual.	1.	अबुधाव	अबोधिष्व	अबोधिष्वहि	अबोधिष्वहि
	2.	अबुधतम्	अबोधिष्टम्	अबोधिषाथाम्	The rest = Âtm.
	3.	अबुधताम्	अबोधिष्टाम्	अबोधिषाताम्	
Plur.	1.	अबुधाम	अबोधिष्म	अबोधिष्महि	
	2.	अबुधत	अबोधिष्ट	अबोधिध्वम्	
	3.	अबुधन्	अबोधिषुः	अबोधिषत	

Simple Future.

Sing.	1.	बोधिष्यामि 'I shall	बोधिष्ये 'I shall know.'	बोधिष्ये 'I shall be
	2.	बोधिष्यसि know.'	बोधिष्यसे	known.' Conjugated
	3.	बोधिष्यति	बोधिष्यते	like the Âtmane.
Dual.	1.	बोधिष्यावः	बोधिष्यावहे	
	2.	बोधिष्यथः	बोधिष्येथे	
	3.	बोधिष्यतः	बोधिष्येते	
Plur.	1.	बोधिष्यामः	बोधिष्यामहे	
	2.	बोधिष्यथ	बोधिष्यध्वे	
	3.	बोधिष्यन्ति	बोधिष्यन्ते	

Periphrastic Future.

		Parasmaipada	Ātmanepada	Passive
Sing.	1.	बोधितास्मि 'I shall	बोधिताहे 'I shall know.'	बोधिताहे 'I shall be known.' Conjugated like the Ātmane.
	2.	बोधितासि know.'	बोधितासे	
	3.	बोधिता	बोधिता	
Dual.	1.	बोधितास्वः	बोधितास्वहे	
	2.	बोधितास्थः	बोधितासाथे	
	3.	बोधितारौ	बोधितारौ	
Plur.	1.	बोधितास्मः	बोधितास्महे	
	2.	बोधितास्थ	बोधिताध्वे	
	3.	बोधितारः	बोधितारः	

Conditional.

Sing.	1.	अबोधिष्यम् 'I should	अबोधिष्ये 'I should	अबोधिष्ये 'I should be known.' Conjugated like the Ātmane.
	2.	अबोधिष्यः know.'	अबोधिष्यथाः know.'	
	3.	अबोधिष्यत्	अबोधिष्यत	
Dual.	1.	अबोधिष्याव	अबोधिष्यावहि	
	2.	अबोधिष्यतम्	अबोधिष्येथाम्	
	3.	अबोधिष्यताम्	अबोधिष्येताम्	
Plur.	1.	अबोधिष्याम	अबोधिष्यामहि	
	2.	अबोधिष्यत	अबोधिष्यध्वम्	
	3.	अबोधिष्यन्	अबोधिष्यन्त	

Benedictive.

Sing.	1.	बुध्यासम् 'May I	बोधिषीय 'May I know!'	बोधिषीय 'May I be known!' Conjugated like the Ātmane.
	2.	बुध्याः know!'	बोधिषीष्ठाः	
	3.	बुध्यात्	बोधिषीष्ट	
Dual.	1.	बुध्यास्व	बोधिषीवहि	
	2.	बुध्यास्तम्	बोधिषीयास्थाम्	
	3.	बुध्यास्ताम्	बोधिषीयास्ताम्	
Plur.	1.	बुध्यास्म	बोधिषीमहि	
	2.	बुध्यास्त	बोधिषीध्वम्	
	3.	बुध्यासुः	बोधिषीरन्	

§ 395. *Alphabetical list of some irregular Verbs with their principal Tenses in Parasmai., Átmane. and Passive.*

Root.	Voice.	Present.	Perfect.	Aorist.	Simple Fut.	Periph. Fut.	Benedictive.
1. अज् *cl. I. P. Par. 'to go, to throw.'		अजति	विवाय or विवाय विवियथ or विवेथ or आजिथ विवाय विविथ्व विव्युः विव्यतुः विव्यिम विव्य विव्युः	अवैषीत् IV., or आजीत् V.	वेष्यति or अजिष्यति	वेता or अजिता	वेयात्
	Pass.	वृप्यते	विव्ये	3 Sg. अवायि 1 Sg. अवेषि or आजिषि or अवाजिषि	वेष्यते or अजिष्यते or वाजिष्यते	वेता or अजिता or वाजिता	वेषीष्ट or अजिषीष्ट or वाजिषीष्ट

* In all except the Special tenses of the Parasmai. वी must be substituted for अज् before terminations beginning with a vowel or with य्, and it may optionally be substituted before terminations begining with any consonant except य्.

§ 395.] CONJUGATION OF VERBS. 151

Root.	Voice.	Present.	Perfect.	Aorist.	Simple Fut.	Periph. Fut.	Benedictive.
2. अद् cl. II. P. 'to eat.'	Par.	अत्ति	1 Sg. आद or जघस or जघास 2 ,, आदिथ or जघसिथ 3 ,, आद or जघास Du. आदिव or जघिव &c.	अघसत् II.	अत्स्यति	अत्ता	अद्यात्
	Pass.	अद्यते	आदे or जघे	3 Sg. आदि 1 Sg. आदिस			
3. इ with pre. अधि cl. II. Ā. 'to read, to study.'	Ātm.	अधीते	अधिजगे	अध्यैष्ट or अध्यगीष्ट } IV.	अध्येष्यते Cond. अध्यैष्यत or अध्यगीष्यत	अध्येता	अध्येषीष्ट
	Pass.	अधीयते					

Root.	Voice.	Present.	Perfect.	Aorist.	Simple Fut.	Periph. Fut.	Benedictive.
4. उर्णु cl. II. P. Â. 'to cover.'	Par.	उर्णौति or उर्णोति	ऊर्णुनव or उर्णुनाव ऊर्णुनविथ or ऊर्णुनविश ऊर्णुनाव ऊर्णुनुविव &c. ऊर्णुनुव	और्णवीत्, or और्णावीत्, और्णवीत्	ऊर्णविष्यति, or ऊर्णुविष्यति	ऊर्णविता, or ऊर्णुविता	ऊर्णूयात्
	Âtm.	उर्णुते	ऊर्णुनुवे	और्णविष्ट, or और्णुविष्ट	ऊर्णविष्यते, or ऊर्णुविष्यते V.	ऊर्णविता, or ऊर्णुविता	ऊर्णविषीष्ट, or ऊर्णुविषीष्ट
	Pass.	ऊर्ण्यते	ऊर्णुनुवे	3 Sg. और्णावि 1 Sg. और्णुविषि or और्णुविष्ठ or और्णाविषि	ऊर्णविष्यते, or ऊर्णुविष्यते, ऊर्णाविष्यते	ऊर्णविता, or ऊर्णुविता, ऊर्णाविता	ऊर्णविषीष्ट, or ऊर्णुविषीष्ट, ऊर्णाविषीष्ट
5. कम् cl. I. Â. 'to love,'	Âtm.	कामयते	कामयाञ्चक्रे &c. or चक्रमे	अचीकमत or अचकमत	कामयिष्यते or कमिष्यते	कामयिता or कमिता	कामयिषीष्ट or कमिषीष्ट
	Pass.	काम्यते or कम्यते	= Âtm.	3 Sg. अकामि 1 Sg. अकामिषि or अकमिषि or अकमिषि	= Âtm. or कमिष्यते	= Âtm. or कमिता	= Âtm. or कमिषीष्ट

CONJUGATION OF VERBS. [§ 395.] 153

				1 Sg. कल्पिष्यत् or कल्प्स्यत् or कर्त्सारिषम्	कल्पिष्यत्, or कल्प्स्यते, or कर्त्स्यते	अकल्पिष्ट V., or अक्लृप्त IV., or अकृपत् II.	कल्पेत or कल्प्येत or कर्त्सीत	चकॢपे चक्लृपिष or चकॢप्से	कल्पते
6. कृप् cl. I. Â. (op- Âtm. tionally P. in Aor., the two Fut.and Cond.) Par. 'to be fit.'									
7. गुप् cl. I. P. Par. 'to guard.'	गोपयिष्यति	गोपयांचकार &c. or जुगोप 2 Sg. जुगोपिथ or जुगोप्थ	अगोपायीत् V., or अगोपीत् V., or अगोपीत् IV.	गोपायिष्यति or गोपिष्यति or गोप्स्यति	अगोपायिष्यत् V., or अगोपिष्यत् V., or अगोप्स्यत् IV.	गोपायिता or गोपिता or गोप्ता	गोपायेत् or गोपेत् or गोप्यात्	जुगोपायांचकार &c. or जुगोप 2 Sg. जुगोपिथ &c. गोपायांचक्रे &c. or जुगुपे	गोपायति or गुप्यति
Pass. गोप्यते or गुप्यते									
8. गुह् cl. I. P. Â. Par. 'to hide.'	गूहति	जुगूह जुगूहिथ or जुगोढ जुगूह जुगूहिव or जुगुह्व &c.	3 Sg. अगूहत् V., or अघुक्षत् VII. 1 Sg. अगूहिषि or अगूहि or अगूहिम्	अगूहिष्यत् V., or अधुक्ष्यत् VII.	गूहिष्यति, or धुक्ष्यते	गूहिता, or गूढा	गूहिष्यति, or धुक्ष्यते	गूहित्वा, or गूढा	गूह्यात्
Âtm. गूहते	जुगूह जुगूहिषे or जुगूढषे &c.	अगूहिष्ट; the rest = Âtm.			= Âtm.			= Âtm.	गूहिविष्ट, or गूहिष्ट, or धुक्षी
Pass. गुह्यते									

20 s G

Root.	Voice.	Present.	Perfect.	Aorist.	Simple Fut.	Periph. Fut.	Benedictive.
9. जागृ cl. II. P. 'to wake.'	Par.	जागर्ति	जागरांचकार, etc. or जजागार 1 Du. जजागृिव &c.	अजागरीत् V.	जागरिष्यति	जागरिता	जाग्यात्
10. दरिद्रा cl. II. Par. P. 'to be poor.'	Par.	दरिद्राति	दरिद्रांचकार &c. or ददरिद्रौ	अदरिद्रासीत् VI., or अदरिद्रीत् V.	दरिद्रिष्यति	दरिद्रिता	दरिद्र्यात्
11. दी cl. IV. Â. Âtm. 'to perish.'	Âtm.	दीयते	दिदीये	अदास्त IV.	दास्यते	दाता	दासीष्ट
12. द्युत् cl. I. Â. (optionally P. in Aor.) 'to shine.'	Âtm.	द्योतते	दिद्युते	अद्योतिष्ट V. or अद्युतत् II.	द्योतिष्यते	द्योतिता	द्योतिषीष्ट
13. नश् cl. IV. P. 'to perish.'	Par.	नश्यति	ननश or ननाश ननंश् or नेशिथ नेमश नेशिव or नेश्म &c.	अनशत् II.	नशिष्यति, or नङ्क्ष्यति	नशिता, or नंष्टा	नश्यात्

[§ 395.] CONJUGATION OF VERBS. 155

14. भृज्ज् cl. VI. P. A. 'to fry.'	Par. भृज्जति	बभर्ज or बभर्ज्ज बभर्जिथ or बभर्ष्ठ बभृज्ज or बभर्ज बभृज्जिव or बभर्जिव &c.	अभ्राक्षीत् or अभार्क्षीत् } IV. अभ्राष्टीत् or अभार्ष्टीत्	भर्क्ष्यति or भर्ष्यति = Ātm.	भ्रष्टा, or भर्टा	भ्रक्ष्यात्, or भर्ष्यात्
	Ātm. भृज्जते	बभृज्जे or बभर्जे = Ātm.	अभ्रष्ट or } IV. अभर्ष्ट 3 Sg. अभ्रक्षिष्ट or अभर्षि the rest = Ātm.	भर्क्ष्यते or भर्ष्यते = Ātm.	भ्रष्टा or भर्टा = Ātm.	भर्क्षीष्ट, or भर्षीष्ट = Ātm.
	Pass. भृज्ज्यते					
15. मज्ज् cl. VI P. 'to dive.'	Par. मज्जति	ममज्ज ममज्जिथ or ममङ्क्थ ममज्ज &c.	अमाङ्क्षीत् IV.	मङ्क्ष्यति	मङ्क्ता	मज्ज्यात्
16. मि cl. V. P. Ā. 'to throw.'	Par. मिनोति	ममि ममिथ or ममाथ ममि मिमिव मिम्यतुः &c.	अमासीत् VI.	मास्यति	माता	मायात्
	Ātm. मिन्वे	मिम्ये मिम्ये	अमास्त IV. 3 Sg. अमासि 1 Sg. अमासि or अमायिषि	मास्यते मास्यते or मायिष्यते	माता माता or मायिता	मासीष्ट मासीष्ट or मायिषीष्ट
	Pass. मीयते					

156 SANSKRIT GRAMMAR. [§ 395—

Root.	Voice.	Present.	Perfect.	Aorist.	Simple Fut.	Periph. Fut.	Benedictive.
17. मी cl. IX.P. Â. 'to destroy.'	Par. Âtm.	मिनोति मिनीते } the rest like जि.					
18. मृ cl. VI. Â. (but P. in Perf., the two Fut. and Cond.) 'to die.'		म्रियते	ममर or ममार	अमृत IV.	मरिष्यति	मर्ता	मृषीष्ट
19. मृज् cl. II. P. 'to wipe off.'	Par.	मार्ष्टि	ममार्ज ममार्जिथ or ममार्ष्ठ ममार्ज ममार्जिव or ममृजिव or ममृज्व ममार्जथुः or ममृजथुः or ममृष्टुः ममार्जतुः or ममृजतुः or ममृष्टुः ममार्जिम or ममृजिम or ममृज्म ममार्ज or ममृज ममार्जुः or ममृजुः or ममृजुः ममार्ज or ममृज	अमार्जीत् V. or अमार्क्षीत् IV.	मार्जिष्यति, or मार्क्ष्यति	मार्जिता or मार्ष्टा	मृज्यात्
	Pass.	मृज्यते		3 Sg. अमार्जि 1 Sg. अमार्जिषि or अमृक्षि	मार्जिष्यते, or मार्क्ष्यते	मार्जिता, or मार्ष्टा	मार्जिषीष्ट, or मृक्षीष्ट.

§ 395.] CONJUGATION OF VERBS. 157

20. ली cl. IX.P. 'to attain; cl. IV. Â. 'to adhere.'	Par. लिनाति	लिलय or लिलाय लिलयिथ or लेथ लिलाय or लिलय लिलिय्य लिलिय्यु: &c.	}or ललौ ललयिथ or ललिथ ललौ	अलेषीत् IV., or अलासीत् VI.	लेष्यति or लास्यति	लेता, or लाता	लेष्टि, or लाष्टि
	Âtm. लीयते	लिलिये		अलेष्ट IV., अलास्त IV. 3 Sg. अलाषि 1 Sg. अलेषि or अलासि or अलायिषि	लेष्यते, or लास्यते लेष्यते or लास्यते or लायिष्यते	लेता, or लाता लेता, or लाता or लायिता	लेष्टि, or लाषीष्ट लेष्टि, or लाषीष्ट, or लायिषीष्ट
	Pass. लीयते	लिलिये					
21. वृ cl. I. Â. Âtm. वर्ते (optionally P. in Aor., Simple Fut. and Cond.) 'to be.'		वव्रे		अवर्तिष्ट V., or अवृत्तू II.	वर्तिष्यते or वर्स्यति	वर्तिता	वर्तिषीष्ट
22. वृष् 'to grow,' conjugated like वृत्.							

Root.	Voice.	Present.	Perfect.	Aorist.	Simple Fut.	Periph. Fut.	Benedictive.
23. स्यन्द् cl. I. Â. Âtm. (optionally P. in Aor. Simple Fut. and Cond.) 'to flow, to drop.'	Âtm.	स्यन्दते	सस्यन्दे सस्यन्दिषे or सस्रन्त्से	अस्यन्दिष्ट V., or अस्यन्त IV. or अस्यदत् II.	स्यन्द्यते, or स्यन्त्स्यते, or स्यन्त्स्यति	स्यन्दिता, or स्यन्ता	स्यन्दिषीष्ट or स्यन्सीष्ट
24. हन् cl. II. P. Par. (with prep. sometimes Â.) 'to strike.'		हन्ति	जघान or जघन जघनिथ or जघन्थ जघ्निव &c.	अवधीत् V.	हनिष्यति	हन्ता	व्यात्
	Âtm.	हते	जघ्ने	अवधिषि, V. or अहसि IV. अवधिष्ठाः or अहथाः अवधिष्ट or अहत अवधिष्वहि or अहस्वहि &c.	हनिष्यते	हन्ता	वधिषीष्ट
	Pass.	हन्यते	जघ्ने	3 Sg. अवधानि or अवधि 1 Sg. अवधानिषि or अवधिषि or अवधि	हनिष्यते, or घानिष्यते	हन्ता or घानिता	वधिषीष्ट or घानिषीष्ट

II.—CONJUGATION OF DERIVATIVE VERBAL BASES.

1. CONJUGATION OF THE ROOTS OF THE TENTH CLASS AND OF THE CAUSAL OF ALL ROOTS.

(A.)—Conjugation of the Roots of the Tenth Class.

§ 396. The Conjugation of the roots contained in the *tenth class* (denominated चुरादि, *i. e.* 'commencing with चुर्') of the native grammarians differs in this respect from that of the primitive roots collected in the first nine classes, that the personal terminations and the characteristic marks of the various tenses and moods are not added immediately to the root, but to a *derivative* base previously derived from the root. This derivative base appears not merely in the special tenses, but it remains, with few exceptions, throughout the whole conjugation; *e. g.* rt. चुर् 'to steal;' Derivative base चोरि; Pres. Ind. Par. चोरयति *choray-ati;* Perf. चोरयामास *choray-âmâsa;* Simple Fut. चोरयिष्यति *choray-ishyati;* Periph. Fut. चोरयिता *choray-itâ;* Bened. Par. चोर्यात् *chor-yât;* Bened. Âtm. चोरयिषीष्ट, *choray-ishîshṭa;* Pass. Pres. Ind. चोर्यते *chor-yate,* &c.

(a) *Formation of the Derivative Base:*

§ 397. 1. The vowel इ is added to the root; *e. g.* rt. चिन्त्, Der. Base चिन्ति; rt. पीड्, पीडि; rt. अर्थ्, अर्थि.

2. The root undergoes the following changes:—

(*a*) Guṇa is substituted for a penultimate prosodially short vowel; *e. g.* rt. चिन्त्, चेति; rt. चुर्, चोरि; rt. पृथ्, वर्धि.

(*b*) Vṛddhi is substituted for a final vowel; *e. g.* rt. जि, जायि: rt. ग्री, ग्रायि; rt. यु, यावि; rt. भू, भावि; rt. गॄ, गारि; rt. पॄ, पारि.

(*c*) A penultimate prosodially short अ is lengthened; *e. g.* rt. कण्, काणि; rt. मन्, मानि.

(*d*) Penultimate ऋ is changed to ईर्; *e. g.* rt. कॄत्, कीर्ति.

§ 398. The following are the common roots in which the radical vowel (against § 397 2, a, c) remains unchanged: rt. मृग् (Der. Base मृगि), सुव्, स्पृह्; कथ् (Der. Base कथि), गण्, ध्वन्, मह्, रच्, रम्, रह्, वर्, स्तन्, स्वर्. Rt. कल् forms optionally कलि or कालि.

§ 399. Some roots may optionally add आपि to the root, instead of इ; e. g. rt. अर्थ्, अर्थि or अर्थापि; rt. गण्, गणि or गणापि.

(b) *Conjugation of the Derivative Base:*

§ 400. Roots of the tenth class are like roots of the first nine classes conjugated in three voices, the Parasmaipada, the Âtmanepada, and the Passive voice, and the remarks made in § 224, 225 apply to them as they apply to primitive roots.

1.—THE PARASMAIPADA AND ÂTMANEPADA.

A.—THE PRESENT (INDIC., POTENT., IMPERAT.) AND IMPERFECT.

§ 401. The Derivative Base is conjugated like a primitive root in इ of the first class; e. g. rt. चुर्, Derivat. Base चोरि; Special Base चोरय; Pres. Ind. Par. चोरयति, Âtm. चोरयते; Pres. Pot. Par. चोरयेत्, Âtm. चोरयेत; Pres. Imper. Par. चोरयतु or चोरयतात् ; Âtm. चोरयताम्; Imperf. Par. अचोरयत्, Âtm. अचोरयत.

B.—THE PERIPHRASTIC PERFECT, THE TWO FUTURES, THE CONDITIONAL, AND THE BENEDICTIVE.

§ 402. Roots of the tenth class must form the Perfect from their derivative base by means of the auxiliary verbs अस्, भू, or कृ, according to the rule given in § 320. The final इ of the derivative base is gunated before आम्; e. g. rt. चुर्, Periphrastic Perf. Par. चोरयामास, or चोरयाम्बभूव, or चोरयाञ्चकार; Âtm. चोरयामास, or चोरयाम्बभूव, or चोरयाञ्चक्रे.

§ 403. In the two Futures the terminations given in § 360 b, and § 365 b, are added to the derivative base by means of the intermediate इ, before which the final इ of the derivative base is gunated; e. g. rt. चुर्, Simple Fut. Par. चोरयिष्यति; Âtm. चोरयिष्यते; Periphr. Fut. 1 Sing. Par. चोरयितास्मि; Âtm. चोरयिताहे.

§ 404. The Conditional is derived from the Simple Future according to the rule given in § 370; *e. g.* rt. चुर्; Condit. Par. अचोरयिष्यन्; Âtm. अचोरयिष्यन.

§ 405. In the Bened. Par. the Parasmai. terminations given in § 372, (c), are added to the derivat. base the final इ of which is dropped; *e. g.* rt. चुर्, चोर्यात्. In the Âtmane. the Âtmane. terminations given in § 372 (c) are added to the derivat. base by means of the intermediate इ, before which the final इ of the derivative base is gunated; *e. g.* rt. चुर्, चोरयिषीष्ट.

C.—THE AORIST.

§ 406. Roots of the tenth class always take the *third* or *reduplicated form* of the Aorist. The derivative base is reduplicated, and the augment is prefixed to the reduplicated form. The terminations are the same as those of the third form of the radical Aorist of primitive roots (§ 333 *b*), and before them the final इ of the derivative base must be dropped; *e. g.* rt. चिन्त्, Deriv. Base चिन्ति; with redupl. and augment अचिचिन्ति; with termination of the 1 Sing. Par. अचिचिन्ति + अम् = अचिचिन्तम्; Âtm. अचिचिन्ते. rt. सूच्, 3 Sing. Par. असूसुचन्; rt. कथ्, अचकथत्.

Note: It will be convenient to call in the following rules the deriv. base, after its final vowel इ has been dropped, the *base-syllable; e. g.* चिन्न will be called the base-syllable of चिन्ति, चोर् the base-syllable of चोरि (derivative base of rt. चुर्).

§ 407. The vowel of the *base-syllable* undergoes in the reduplicated Aorist the following changes:—

(a) A penultimate आ is shortened; penultimate ई, ए, and ऐ are changed to इ; penultimate ऊ, ओ and औ are changed to उ; *e. g.*

rt.	ज्ञि;	Deriv. B.	ज्ञायि;	Aor. Par.	अजिज्ञयत्.
rt.	यु;	,, ,,	यावि;	,, Âtm.	अयीयवत.
rt.	पॄ;	,, ,,	पारि;	,, Par.	अपीपरत्.
rt.	चित्;	,, ,,	चेति;	,, Âtm.	अचीचितत.
rt.	सूद्;	,, ,,	सूदि;	,, Par.	असूसुदत्.
rt.	चुर्;	,, ,,	चोरि;	,, ,,	अचूचुरत्.

(b) The penultimate vowel of पीड़् and certain other roots may optionally follow (a) or remain unchanged; e. g.

rt. पीड्; Deriv. B. पीडि; Aor. Par. अपीपिडत् or अपिपीडत्.

(c) The penultimate vowel of the base-syllable of सूच्, स्तेन्, लोक्, लोच् and certain other roots must (against a) remain unchanged; e. g.

rt. सूच्; Deriv. B. सूचि; Aor. Par. असुसूचत्.
rt. स्तेन्; „ „ स्तेनि; „ „ अतिस्तेनत्.
rt. लोच्; „ „ लोचि; „ „ अलुलोचत्.

(d) Penultimate अर्, आर्, ईर्, (and अल्) of the base-syllable, being substitutes for original radical ऋ, ॠ, (or ऌ), remain either unchanged, or अर्, आर्, and ईर् are changed to ऋ, (and अल् to ऌ); e. g.

rt. पृथ्; Deriv. B. पर्थि; Aor. Par. अपपर्थत् or अपीपृथत्.
rt. कृत्; „ „ कीर्ति; „ „ अचिकीर्तत् or अचीकृतत्.

§ 408. When the rules given in the preceding paragraph have been applied to the *base-syllable*, the following rules must be applied to the vowel of the *reduplicative* syllable:—

(a) The vowels इ and उ of the reduplicative syllable are lengthened, if the base-syllable is prosodially short and commences with only one consonant; e. g.

rt. नुर्; Deriv. B. चोरि; reduplicated चुचोरि; changed by § 407 (a) to चुचुर्; becomes चूनुर्; Aor. Par. अनूनुरत्.

rt. चित्; Deriv. B. चेति; reduplicated चिचेति; changed to चिचित्; becomes चीचित्; Aor. Âtm. अचीचितत.

But rt. सूच्; Deriv. B. सूचि; Red. सुसूचि; remains सुसूच्; Aor. Par. असुसूचत्.
rt. स्तेन्; „ „ स्तेनि; „ तिस्तेनि; „ तिस्तेन्; „ „ अतिस्तेनत्.
rt. पीड्; „ „ पीडि; „ पिपीडि; when remaining पिपीड्, „ अपिपीडत्.
„ „ „ „ „ „ „ changed to पिपिड्, „ अपीपिडत्.

(b) The vowel अ of the reduplicative syllable is changed to इ, if the base-syllable is prosodially short and begins with only one consonant, and to इ, if the base-syllable is prosodially short and begins with more consonants than one; e. g.

Rt.	Deriv. B.	Red.	Changed to	becomes		Aor.
मन् ;	मानि ;	ममानि ;	ममन् ;	मीमन् ;	Ātm.	अमीमनत.
पृ ;	पारि ;	पपारि ;	पपर् ;	पीपर् ;	Par.	अपीपरत्.
ज्रि ;	ज्रायि ;	जज्रायि ;	जज्रय् ;	जिज्रय् ;	,,	अजिज्रयत्.
पृथ् ;	पर्थि ;	पपर्थि ;	पपृथ् ;	पीपृथ् ;	,,	अपीपृथत् ;

but when it remains पपृथ्, the base-syllable is prosodially long, and the अ of the reduplicated syllable remains unchanged; Aor. Par. अपपृथन्.

Rt. लक्ष् ; Aor. Par. अलललक्षन् &c.

(c) The vowel अ of the reduplicative syllable of कथ्, रह्, स्वर्, प्रथ् and certain other roots remains unchanged; that of गण् remains अ or it is changed to इ; e. g.

rt. कथ् ; Aor. Par. अचकथत् ; rt. प्रथ्, अपप्रथत् ; rt. गण्, अजगणत् or अजीगणत्.

§ 409. Derivative bases commencing with vowels are reduplicated in the following manner :

(a) When the initial vowel is followed by one consonant or by a conjunct the first part of which is neither a nasal nor one of the consonants द् or र्, the consonant which immediately follows the initial vowel (or the substitute of that consonant, see § 231), together with the vowel इ, is inserted after the initial vowel; e. g.

rt. इल् ; deriv. base एलि ; without इ, एल् ; with reduplic. एलिल् ; with augment ऐलिल् ; Aor. Par. ऐलिलत्.

(b) When the initial vowel is followed by a conjunct the first part of which is either a nasal or one of the consonants द् or र्, the second consonant of the conjunct or its substitute together with the vowel इ is inserted after the first consonant of the conjunct ; e. g.

rt. अन्ज्; deriv. base आर्जि; without इ, अर्ज्; with reduplic. आर्जंज्; with augment आर्जिज्ञ्; Aor. Par. आर्जिजत्.

rt. अद्द् (for अद्दट्); Aor. Par. आदिदटत् (for आदटिटत्).

(c) The roots ऊन्, अर्थ्, अन्भ्, अङ्क् and certain other roots substitute the vowel अ for the इ of the reduplicative syllable; e. g.

rt. ऊन्, Aor Par. औननत्; rt. अन्भ्, आन्दधत्; rt. अङ्क्, आञ्चकत्; rt. अर्थ् Aor. Âtm. आर्तयत.

2.—THE PASSIVE.

A.—The Present (Indic., Potent., Imperat.) and Imperfect.

§ 410. The Present in its three moods and the Imperfect are formed from the derivative base in the same manner in which the Present and Imperfect of the Passive of a primitive root are formed from the root; the final इ of the derivative base, however, is dropped before the characteristic syllable य of the Passive; e.g. rt. चुर्, deriv. Base चोरि; Pres. Ind. Pass. चोर्यते; Pres. Pot. चोर्येत; Pres. Imper. चोर्यताम्; Imperf. अचोर्यत;—rt. पृ, deriv. Base पारि; Pres. Ind. Pass. पार्यते;—rt. कृत्, deriv. Base कीर्ति; Pres. Ind. Pass. कोर्त्यते.

B.—The Perfect, Aorist, Future, Conditional, and Benedictive.

(a).—The Perfect.

§ 411. The Perfect of the Passive is formed in the same manner as the Perf. Âtmane., except that all the three auxiliary verbs भस्, भू and कृ must be conjugated in the Âtmane.; e. g. rt. चुर्, Perf. Pass. चोरयामासे, or चोरयांबभूवे, or चोरयाचक्रे.

(b).—The Aorist.

§ 412. *Formation of the 3 Pers. Sing.*

(a) The 3 Pers. Sing. of the Aor. Pass. of roots of the tenth class is formed by prefixing the augment to the derivative base; e. g. rt. चुर्, deriv. B. चोरि; 3 Sing. Aor. Pass. अचोरि; rt. पीड्, अपीडि; rt. अर्थ्, आर्थि; rt. पृ, अपारि.; rt. मन्, अमानि.

§ 414.]   CONJUGATION OF VERBS.   165

(b) The vowel अ of रह् and certain other roots which do not lengthen their अ in the derivative base may optionally be lengthened in the 3 Sing. Aor. Pass; *e. g.* अरहि or अराहि.

§ 413. The remaining persons of the Aor. Pass. are formed optionally either by augmenting the derivative base and by the addition to it of the Âtmanepada terminations of the fifth form of the Aorist (§ 344 *b*) before which the final इ of the deriv. base is gunated,—or by adding the same terminations, without their initial इ, to the 3 Sing. of the Aor. Pass.; *e. g.*

rt. चुर्; Deriv. Base. चोरि; 1 Sg. Aor. Pass. अचोरयिषि; or अचोरिषि.
rt. पीड्;   ,,   ,,   पीडि;   ,,   ,,   ,,   अपीडयिषि; or अपीडिषि.
rt. पृ;   ,,   ,,   पारि;   ,,   ,,   ,,   अपारयिषि; or अपारिषि.
rt. रह्;   ,,   ,,   रहि;   ,,   ,,   ,,   अरहयिषि; or अरहिषि;
                                          or अराहिषि.

(c).—*The two Futures, the Conditional, and the Benedictive.*

§ 414. The Âtmanepada forms of these tenses are likewise used for the Passive. But the Passive may also be formed from the corresponding forms of the Âtmane. by leaving out the syllable अय् of the latter, and by changing the vowel of the derivative Base in the same manner in which it is changed in the 3 Sing. of the Aor. Pass.; *e. g.*

rt. चुर् Simple Fut. Pass. चोरयिष्यते or चोरिष्यते;
       Periph. Fut.   ,,   चोरयिता   or चोरिता;
       Condit.   ,,   अचोरयिष्यत or अचोरिष्यत;
       Bened.   ,,   चोरयिषीष्ट or चोरिषीष्ट.
rt. रह् Simple Fut.   ,,   रहयिष्यते or रहिष्यते or राहिष्यते;
       Periph. Fut.   ,,   रहयिता   or रहिता   or राहिता;
       Condit.   ,,   अरहयिष्यत or अरहिष्यत or अराहिष्यत;
       Bened.   ,,   रहयिषीष्ट or रहिषीष्ट or राहिषीष्ट.

Paradigm:

§ 415. Conjugation of rt. चुर् cl. 10 'to steal,' in Parasmai., Âtmane., and Passive :

	Parasmai.	Âtmane.	Passive.

Present Indicative.

		Parasmai.	Âtmane.	Passive.
Sing.	1.	चोरयामि	चोरये	चोर्ये
	2.	चोरयसि	चोरयसे	चोर्यसे
	3.	चोरयति	चोरयते	चोर्यते
Dual.	1.	चोरयावः	चोरयावहे	चोर्यावहे
	2.	चोरयथः	चोरयेथे	चोर्येथे
	3.	चोरयतः	चोरयेते	चोर्येते
Plur.	1.	चोरयामः	चोरयामहे	चोर्यामहे
	2.	चोरयथ	चोरयध्वे	चोर्यध्वे
	3.	चोरयन्ति.	चोरयन्ते	चोर्यन्ते

Present Potential.

		Parasmai.	Âtmane.	Passive.
Sing.	1.	चोरयेयम्	चोरयेय	चोर्येय
	2.	चोरयेः	चोरयेथाः	चोर्येथाः
	3.	चोरयेत्	चोरयेत	चोर्येत
Dual.	1.	चोरयेव	चोरयेवहि	चोर्येवहि
	2.	चोरयेतम्	चोरयेयाथाम्	चोर्येयाथाम्
	3.	चोरयेताम्	चोरयेयाताम्	चोर्येयाताम्
Plur.	1.	चोरयेम	चोरयेमहि	चोर्येमहि
	2.	चोरयेत	चोरयेध्वम्	चोर्येध्वम्
	3.	चोरयेयुः	चोरयेरन्	चोर्येरन्

Present Imperative.

		Parasmai.	Âtmane.	Passive.
Sing.	1.	चोरयाणि	चोरयै	चोर्यै
	2.	चोरय or ˚यतात्	चोरयस्व	चोर्यस्व
	3.	चोरयतु or ˚यतात्	चोरयताम्	चोर्यताम्
Dual.	1.	चोरयाव	चोरयावहै	चोर्यावहै
	2.	चोरयतम्	चोरयेथाम्	चोर्येथाम्
	3.	चोरयताम्	चोरयेताम्	चोर्येताम्
Plur.	1.	चोरयाम	चोरयामहै	चोर्यामहै
	2.	चोरयत	चोरयध्वम्	चोर्यध्वम्
	3.	चोरयन्तु	चोरयन्ताम्	चोर्यन्ताम्

Imperfect.

	Sing.	Dual	Plur.
1.	अचोरयम्	अचोरये	अचोर्ये
2.	अचोरयः	अचोरयथाः	अचोर्ययथाः
3.	अचोरयत्	अचोरयत	अचोर्ययत
1.	अचोरयाव	अचोरयावहि	अचोर्ययावहि
2.	अचोरयतम्	अचोरयेथाम्	अचोर्ययेथाम्
3.	अचोरयताम्	अचोरयेताम्	अचोर्ययेताम्
1.	अचोरयाम	अचोरयामहि	अचोर्ययामहि
2.	अचोरयत	अचोरयध्वम्	अचोर्ययध्वम्
3.	अचोरयन्	अचोरयन्त	अचोर्ययन्त

Periphrastic Perfect.

	Parasmai.	Par. or Âtm.	
Sing. 1.	चोरयांचकार or °चक्रर	चोरयामास	चोरयांबभूव
2.	चोरयांचकर्थ	चोरयामासिथ	चोरयांबभूविथ
3.	चोरयांचकार	चोरयामास	चोरयांबभूव
Dual 1.	चोरयांचकृव	चोरयामासिव	चोरयांबभूविव
2.	चोरयांचक्रथुः	चोरयामासथुः	चोरयांबभूवथुः
3.	चोरयांचक्रतुः	चोरयामासतुः	चोरयांबभूवतुः
Plur. 1.	चोरयांचकृम	चोरयामासिम	चोरयांबभूविम
2.	चोरयांचक्र	चोरयामास	चोरयांबभूव
3.	चोरयांचक्रुः	चोरयामासुः	चोरयांबभूवुः

Periphrastic Perfect (continued).

	Âtm. or Pass.	Passive.	
Sing. 1.	चोरयांचक्रे	चोरयामासे	चोरयांबभूवे
2.	चोरयांचकृषे	चोरयामासिषे	चोरयांबभूविषे
3.	चोरयांचक्रे	चोरयामासे	चोरयांबभूवे
Dual 1.	चोरयांचक्रवहे	चोरयामासिवहे	चोरयांबभूविवहे
2.	चोरयांचक्राथे	चोरयामासाथे	चोरयांबभूवाथे
3.	चोरयांचक्राते	चोरयामासाते	चोरयांबभूवाते
Plur. 1.	चोरयांचकृमहे	चोरयामासिमहे	चोरयांबभूविमहे
2.	चोरयांचकृढ्वे	चोरयामासिध्वे	चोरयांबभूविध्वे or ढ्वे
3.	चोरयांचक्रिरे	चोरयामासिरे	चोरयांबभूविरे

Aorist.

		Parasmai.	Âtmane.	Passive.	
Sing.	1.	अचूचुरम्	अचूचुरे	अचोरयिषि	or अचोरिषि
	2.	अचूचुरः	अचूचुरथाः	अचोरयिष्ठाः	अचोरिष्ठाः
	3.	अचूचुरत्	अचूचुरत		अचोरि
Dual.	1.	अचूचुराव	अचूचुरावहि अचोरयिष्वहि		अचोरिष्वहि
	2.	अचूचुरतम्	अचूचुरेथाम् अचोरयिषाथाम्		अचोरिषाथाम्
	3.	अचूचुरताम्	अचूचुरेताम् अचोरयिषाताम्		अचोरिषाताम्
Plur.	1.	अचूचुराम	अचूचुरामहि अचोरयिष्महि		अचोरिष्महि
	2.	अचूचुरत	अचूचुरध्वम् अचोरयिध्वम् or ढ्वम्		अचोरिध्वम् or ढ्वम्
	3.	अचूचुरन्	अचूचुरन्त अचोरयिषत		अचोरिषत

Simple Future.

		Parasmai.	Âtm. or Pass.	Passive.
Sing.	1.	चोरयिष्यामि	चोरयिष्ये	चोरिष्ये
	2.	चोरयिष्यसि	चोरयिष्यसे	चोरिष्यसे
	3.	चोरयिष्यति	चोरयिष्यते	चोरिष्यते
Dual.	1.	चोरयिष्यावः	चोरयिष्यावहे	चोरिष्यावहे
	2.	चोरयिष्यथः	चोरयिष्येथे	चोरिष्येथे
	3.	चोरयिष्यतः	चोरयिष्येते	चोरिष्येते
Plur.	1.	चोरयिष्यामः	चोरयिष्यामहे	चोरिष्यामहे
	2.	चोरयिष्यथ	चोरयिष्यध्वे	चोरिष्यध्वे
	3.	चोरयिष्यन्ति	चोरयिष्यन्ते	चोरिष्यन्ते.

Periphrastic Future.

		Parasmai.	Âtm. or Pass.	Passive.
Sing.	1.	चोरयितास्मि	चोरयिताहे	चोरिताहे
	2.	चोरयितासि	चोरयितासे	चोरितासे
	3.	चोरयिता	चोरयिता	चोरिता
Dual.	1.	चोरयितास्वः	चोरयितास्वहे	चोरितास्वहे
	2.	चोरयितास्थः	चोरयितासाथे	चोरितासाथे
	3.	चोरयितारौ	चोरयितारौ	चोरितारौ
Plur.	1.	चोरयितास्म	चोरयितास्महे	चोरितास्महे
	2.	चोरयितास्थ	चोरयिताध्वे	चोरिताध्वे
	3.	चोरयितारः	चोरयितारः	चोरितारः

Conditional.

	Parasmai.	Âtm. or Pass.	Passive.
Sing. 1.	अचोरयिष्यम्	अचोरयिष्ये	अचोरिष्ये
2.	अचोरयिष्यः	अचोरयिष्यथाः	अचोरिष्यथाः
3.	अचोरयिष्यत्	अचोरयिष्यत	अचोरिष्यत
Dual. 1.	अचोरयिष्याव	अचोरयिष्यावहि	अचोरिष्यावहि
2.	अचोरयिष्यतम्	अचोरयिष्येथाम्	अचोरिष्येथाम्
3.	अचोरयिष्यताम्	अचोरयिष्येताम्	अचोरिष्येताम्
Plur. 1.	अचोरयिष्याम	अचोरयिष्यामहि	अचोरिष्यामहि
2.	अचोरयिष्यत	अचोरयिष्यध्वम्	अचोरिष्यध्वम्
3.	अचोरयिष्यन्	अचोरयिष्यन्त	अचोरिष्यन्त

Benedictive.

	Parasmai.	Âtm. or Pass.	Passive.
Sing. 1.	चोर्यासम्	चोरयिषीय	चोरिषीय
2.	चोर्याः	चोरयिषीष्ठाः	चोरिषीष्ठाः
3.	चोर्यात्	चोरयिषीष्ट	चोरिषीष्ट
Dual. 1.	चोर्यास्व	चोरयिषीवहि	चोरिषीवहि
2.	चोर्यास्तम्	चोरयिषीयास्थाम्	चोरिषीयास्थाम्
3.	चोर्यास्ताम्	चोरयिषीयास्ताम्	चोरिषीयास्ताम्
Plur. 1.	चोर्यास्म	चोरयिषीमहि	चोरिषीमहि
2.	चोर्यास्त	चोरयिषीध्वम् or ०ढ्वम्	चोरिषीध्वम् or ०ढ्वम्
3.	चोर्यासुः	चोरयिषीरन्	चोरिषीरन्

(B.)—The Causal.

§ 416. A causal form, conjugated in all the tenses and moods of the three voices, may be derived from any root of the ten classes. It conveys the notion that a person or thing causes or makes or orders another person or thing to perform the action or to undergo the state denoted by the root; *e. g.*

Rt.	Pres. Ind. Par.	Pres. Ind. Caus. Par.
बुध् 'to know;'	बोधति 'he knows;'	बोधयति 'he causes to know.'
द्विष् 'to hate;'	द्वेष्टि 'he hates;'	द्वेषयति 'he causes to hate.'
भू 'to be;'	भवति 'he is;'	भावयति 'he causes to be.'
पत् 'to fall;'	पतति 'he falls;'	पातयति 'he causes to fall, he fells.'

22 s g

§ 417. The conjugation of the Causal agrees almost entirely with the conjugation of roots of the tenth class; it differs from the latter mainly in this, that causal forms are derivative both in form and in meaning, and that they may be formed of all roots. The Causal of roots of the tenth class does generally not differ from the simple verb; *e. g.*

rt. चुर् 'to steal;' Pres. Ind. Par. चोरयति 'he steals;' Pres. Ind. Caus. Par. चोरयति 'he causes to steal.'

§ 418. To express the notion of causality a *causal base* is derived from the root, to which base the terminations of the tenses and moods are attached in the same manner in which they are attached to the derivative base of a root of the tenth class; *e. g.*

rt. बुध्; Causal base बोधि; Pres. Ind. Caus. Par. बोधयति; Imperf. अबोधयत्; Perf. बोधयामास &c.

(*a*)—*Formation of the Causal Base.*

§ 419. The Causal base is formed like the derivative base of a root of the tenth class (§ 397, 1 and 2); *e. g.*

1. Rt. भाष् 'to speak;' Caus. B. भाषि 'to cause to speak;'—rt. जीव् 'to live;' Caus. B. जीवि 'to cause to live;'—rt. बन्ध् 'to bind;' Caus. B. बन्धि 'to cause to bind.'

2. (*a*) Rt. भिद् 'to split;' Caus. B. भेदि 'to cause to split;'—rt. बुध् 'to know;' Caus. B. बोधि 'to cause to know;'—rt. वृध् 'to grow;' Caus. B. वर्धि 'to cause to grow;'—rt. कॢप् 'to be fit;' Caus. B. कल्पि 'to make fit.'

(*b*) Rt. हि 'to send;' Caus. B. हायि 'to cause to send;'—rt. नी 'to lead;' Caus. B. नायि 'to cause to lead;'—rt. स्तु 'to praise;' Caus. B. स्तावि 'to cause to praise;'—rt. लू 'to cut;' Caus. B. लावि 'to cause to cut;'—rt. कृ 'to do,' or rt. कॄ 'to scatter;' Caus. B. कारि 'to cause to do,' or 'to cause to scatter.'

(*c*) Rt. पत् 'to fall;' Caus. B. पाति 'to cause to fall.'

(*d*) Rt. स्तृह् 'to strike;' Caus. B. स्तोहि 'to cause to strike.'

§ 420. Exceptions to § 397, 2, (*b*): Guṇa is substituted, instead of Vṛiddhi, for the final vowel of जृ 'to grow old,' when it belongs to cl. 4, and of स्मृ in the sense of 'to regret, or remember with tenderness;' Causal bases जरि 'to cause to grow old,' स्मरि 'to cause to regret.' But जृ cl. 9. &c. forms regularly जारि, and स्मृ 'to remember,' स्मारि.

§ 421. Exceptions to § 397, 2, (*c*): The following are the most common roots that do not lengthen their penultimate अ in the Causal:

(*a*) rt. घट् 'to strive;' Caus. B. घटि 'to cause to strive.'

rt. चल् when it means 'to shake or tremble;' Caus. B. चलि; otherwise चालि.

rt. जन् 'to be born;' Caus. B. जनि 'to beget, to bring forth.'

rt. ज्वर् 'to be diseased, as with fever;' Caus. B. ज्वरि.

rt. त्वर् 'to hurry;' Caus. B. त्वरि.

rt. ध्वन् when it means 'to sound;' Caus. B. ध्वनि 'to cause to sound, to ring (a bell);' but ध्वानि 'to articulate indistinctly.'

rt. नट् when it means 'to dance;' Caus. B. नटि; but when it means 'to act,' Caus. B. नाटि.

rt. प्रथ् 'to be famous;' Caus. B. प्रथि.

rt. मद्, when it means 'to rejoice;' Caus. B मदि; otherwise मादि.

rt. स्वद् 'to rub;' Caus. B. स्वदि.

rt. व्यथ् 'to suffer pain;' Caus. B. व्यथि.

rt. ज्वल् 'to shine,' when compounded with a preposition, forms in the Causal ज्वलि; when not compounded with a preposition, it forms optionally ज्वलि or ज्वालि.

(*b*) Roots ending in अम् (except those mentioned under *c* below); *e. g.* rt. गम् 'to go;' Caus. B. गमि 'to cause to go.'

rt. क्रम् 'to stride;' Caus. B. क्रमि 'to cause to stride.'

(*c*) The roots भ्रम् 'to go,' &c., कम् 'to love,' and चम् 'to eat,' &c. follow the general rule; Caus. bases भ्रामि, कामि, and चामि. The roots नम्

'to bend,' and वम् ' to vomit,' when compounded with a preposition, form in the Causal नमि, वमि; when not compounded with a preposition they form optionally नामि or नमि, वमि or वामि. The rt. यम् when meaning ' to eat,' forms in the Causal यमि, otherwise it forms यामि. The rt. ज्ञम् in the sense of ' to see,' forms in the Causal ज्ञमि; in other senses it forms ज्ञामि.

(d) Exceptions to the above rules are found in the works of the best writers.

§ 422. (a) Most roots ending in आ or in one of the diphthongs ए, ऐ or ओ, and the roots मि ' to throw,' मी ' to destroy,' दो ' to perish,' the final of which is changeable to आ by § 296, insert the letter य् between their final radical vowel and the vowel इ of the causal base; *e. g.*

    rt. दा ' to give;' Caus. B. दापि ' to cause to give.'
    rt. धे ' to suck;' Caus. B. धापि ' to cause to suck.'
    rt. गै ' to sing;' Caus. B. गापि ' to cause to sing.'
    rt. दो ' to cut;' Caus. B. दापि ' to cause to cut.'
    rt. मि ' to throw;' Caus. B. मापि ' to cause to throw.'

(b) The roots पा ' to drink,' वे ' to weave,' व्ये ' to cover,' ह्वे ' to call,' सै ' to waste,' छो ' to cut,' शो ' to sharpen,' and सो ' to finish,' insert the letter य् between their final radical vowel (changeable to आ) and the vowel इ of the causal base; *e. g.*

    rt. पा ' to drink;' Caus. B. पायि ' to cause to drink.'
    rt. ह्वे ' to call;' Caus. B. ह्वायि ' to cause to call.'
    rt. छो ' to cut;' Caus. B. छायि ' to cause to cut.'

(c) Some roots ending in आ and ऐ (changeable to आ) shorten their radical vowel before the inserted य् of the causal base:

    rt. ज्ञा forms ज्ञपि in the sense of ' to cause to see, to exhibit; to slay; to gratify;' but ज्ञापि ' to cause to know;' &c.

    rt. श्रा or श्रै ' to cook,' Caus. B. श्रपि.

    rt. ग्ला or ग्लै ' to be languid,' and rt. स्ना ' to bathe,' form optionally ग्लापि or ग्लपि and स्नापि or स्नपि; but when compounded with prepositions, only ग्लापि and स्नापि.

§ 423.] CONJUGATION OF VERBS.

§ 423. The following roots form their Causal Base irregularly

1. इ 'to go,' forms its Caus. B. from गम्, गमि; *e. g.* 3 Sing. Pres. Ind. Caus. Par. गमयति 'he causes to go;' but when it means 'to understand,' it forms regularly आयि (*e. g.* Caus. of इ with प्रति, प्रत्याययति 'he causes to understand'); and when it is compounded with अधि in the sense of 'to read,' it forms आपि (*e. g.* अध्यापयति 'he causes to read or study, he teaches).'

Root.	Caus. Base.	3 Sing. Pres. Ind. Caus.
2. ऋ 'to go;'	अर्पि; Par.	अर्पयति 'he causes to go, he moves.'
3. क्रुप् 'to be wet' &c.;	क्रोपि; ,,	क्रोपयति 'he makes wet,' &c.
4. क्री 'to buy;'	क्रापि; ,,	क्रापयति 'he causes to buy.'
5. क्ष्माय् 'to tremble;'	क्ष्मापि; ,,	क्ष्मापयति 'he causes to tremble.'
6. गुह् 'to hide;'	गूहि; ,,	गूहयति 'he causes to hide.'
7. चि cl. 5. 'to gather';	चायि or ,, / चापि; ,,	चाययति / चापयति } 'he causes to gather.'
cl. 10. ,, ,, ;	चयि or ,, / चपि; ,,	चययति / चपयति } ,, ,, ,, ,,
8. जागृ 'to wake;'	जागरि; ,,	जागरयति 'he rouses.'
9. जि 'to conquer;'	जापि; ,,	जापयति 'he causes to conquer.'
10. दरिद्रा 'to be poor;'	दरिद्रि; ,,	दरिद्रयति 'he makes poor.'
11. दुष् 'to sin;'	दूषि; ,,	दूषयति 'he causes to sin;' in the

sense of 'to make depraved' it forms optionally दूषि or दोषि (दूषयति or दोषयति).

Root.	Caus. Base.	3 Sing. Pres. Ind. Caus.
12. धू 'to shake;'	धूनि; Par.	धूनयति 'he causes to shake.'
13. पा 'to protect;'	पालि; ,,	पालयति 'he protects.'
14. प्री 'to delight;'	प्रीणि; ,,	प्रीणयति 'he causes to delight.'
15. भी 'to fear;'	भायि; ,, / भापि; Ātm. / भीषि; ,,	भाययति 'he frightens with.' / भापयते / भीषयते } 'he inspires fear.'
16. भ्रज्ज् 'to fry;'	भ्रज्जि; Par. / भर्जि; ,,	भ्रज्जयति / भर्जयति } 'he causes to fry.'
17. मृज् 'to wipe off;'	मार्जि; ,,	मार्जयति 'he causes to wipe off.'
18. रञ्ज् 'to colour;'	रञ्जि; ,,	रञ्जयति 'he colours;' but in the

sense of 'to hunt deer,' it forms रंजि, रजयति.

Root.	Caus. Base.		3 Sing. Pres. Ind. Caus.
19. रभ् 'to perish;'	रन्भि ;	Par.	रन्भयति 'he subdues.'
20. रभ् 'to desire ;'	रम्भि ;	,,	रम्भयति 'he makes desirous.'
21. री 'to go,' &c.	रेपि ;	,,	रेपयति 'he causes to go.'
22. रुह् 'to grow ;'	रोहि ; or ,,		रोहयति } 'he causes to grow.'
	रोपि ; ,,		रोपयति
23. लभ् 'to obtain ;'	लाभि ;	,,	लम्भयति 'he causes to obtain.'
24. ली 'to attain;'	लायि or ,,		लाययति ⎫
	लोनि or ,,		लोनयति ⎪ used in various senses,
	लापि or ,,		लापयति ⎬ for which see the Dic-
	लालि ; ,,		लालयति ⎭ tionary.
25. वा 'to blow ;'	वापि or ,,		वापयति 'he causes to blow,' &c.
	वाजि ; ,,		वाजयति 'he shakes.'
26. वो 'to conceive ;'	वायि or ,,		वाययति } 'he causes to conceive ;'
	वापि ; ,,		वापयति

in other senses it forms regularly वायि, वाययति.

Root.	Caus. Base.		3 Sing. Pres. Ind. Caus.
27. व्लो 'to select;'	व्लेपि ;	Par.	व्लेपयति 'he causes to select.'
28. शद् 'to fall ;'	शाति ;	,,	शातयति 'he causes to fall.'
	शादि ;	,,	शादयति 'he causes to go.'
29. सिध् 'to be ac-	साधि ;	,,	साधयति 'he accomplishes, he pre-
complished,' &c.			pares.'
	सेधि ;	,,	सेधयति 'he makes perfect' (only
			used of sacred things).
30. स्फाय् 'to swell;'	स्फावि ;	,,	स्फावयति 'he causes to swell.'
31. स्फुर् 'to shine ;'	स्फोरि or ,,		स्फोरयति } 'he causes to shine.'
	स्फारि ; ,,		स्फारयति
32. स्मि 'to smile ;'	स्मायि ; ,,		स्माययति 'he causes a smile by.'
	स्मापि ; Átm.		स्मापयते 'he astonishes.'
33. हन् 'to strike ;'	घाति ;	Par.	घातयति 'he causes to strike.'
34. ह्री 'to be ashamed;'	ह्रेपि ;	,,	ह्रेपयति 'he makes ashamed.'

(b).—*Conjugation of the Causal Base.*

§ 424. The Causal Base is conjugated like the Derivative Base of a root of the tenth class in all the tenses and moods of the Parasmaipada, Átmanepada, and Passive; *e. g.* rt. कृ 'to do,' Caus. B. कारि ; Pres. Ind. Par. कारयति

[§ 426.] CONJUGATION OF VERBS. 175

'he causes (a person) to do (something for somebody else);' Âtm. कारयते 'he causes (a person) to do (something for himself);' Pass. कार्यते 'he is made to do.'

§ 425. *Paradigm*: The 3 Sing. of all the tenses and moods in Par., Âtm., and Pass., of the Causal of rt. बुध् 'to know,' Causal Base बोधि.

	Parasmai.	Âtmane.	Passive.
Pres. Ind.	बोधयति	बोधयते	बोध्यते.
Pres. Pot.	बोधयेत्	बोधयेत	बोध्येत.
Pres. Imp.	बोधयतु or 'तात्	बोधयताम्	बोध्यताम्.
Imperf.	अबोधयत्	अबोधयत	अबोध्यत.

	Par.	Par. or Âtm.	Âtm. or Pass.	Pass.
Per. Perf.	बोधयांचकार	बोधयामास, बोधयांबभूव	बोधयांचक्रे	बोधयामासे, बोधयांबभूवे.

	Par.	Âtm.	Pass.
Aor. 1 Sing.	अबूबुधम्	अबूबुधे	अबोधयिषि or अबोधिषि.
,, 3 Sing.	अबूबुधत्	अबूबुधत	अबोधि.

	Par.	Âtm. or Pass.	Pass.
Simple Fut.	बोधयिष्यति	बोधयिष्यते	बोधिष्यते.
Periph. Fut.	बोधयिता	बोधयिता	बोधिता.
Condit.	अबोधयिष्यत्	अबोधयिष्यत	अबोधिष्यत.
Bened.	बोध्यात्	बोधयिषीष्ट	बोधिषीष्ट.

(c)—*Further Illustrations of the Rules concerning the Formation of the Aorist (§ 406) and some additional Rules:*

§ 426. (a) Examples of § 407 (a):

rt. पत्; Caus. B. पाति; Aor. Par. अपीपतत्.
rt. नी; ,, ,, नायि; ,, ,, अनीनयत्.
rt. लू; ,, ,, लावि; ,, ,, अलोलवत्.
rt. कृ; ,, ,, कारि; ,, ,, अचीकरन्.
rt. भिद्; ,, ,, भेदि; ,, ,, अबीभिदन्.
rt. नुद्; ,, ,, नोदि; ,, ,, अनूनुदन्.

(b) The penultimate vowel of the base-syllable of जीव् 'to live,' दीप् 'to shine,' पीड् 'to press,' भाष् 'to speak,' भास् 'to shine,' भ्राज् 'to shine,' मील् 'to close the eyes,' कण् 'to sigh,' रण् 'to sound,' भण् 'to speak,' लुप् 'to break' and some other roots may optionally follow (a) or remain unchanged; e.g.

    rt. जीव् ;   Caus. B. जीवि ;   Aor. Par. अजीजिवत्   or   अजिजीवत्.
    rt. भाष् ;   ,,   ,, भाषि ;   ,,   ,, अबीभषत्   or   अबभाषत्.
    rt. भ्राज् ;   ,,   ,, भ्राजि ;   ,,   ,, अबिभ्रजत्   or   अबभ्राजत्.
    rt. भण् ;   ,,   ,, भणि ;   ,,   ,, अबीभणत्   or   अबभाणत्.
    rt. लुप् ;   ,,   ,, लोपि ;   ,,   ,, अलूलुपत्   or   अललोपत्.

(c) The penultimate vowel of the base-syllable of शास् 'to govern,' बाध् 'to hurt,' याच् 'to ask,' दौक् 'to approach' and some other roots remains unchanged; e.g.

    rt. शास् ;   Caus. B. शासि ;   Aor. Par. अशशासन्.
    rt. दौक् ;   ,,   ,, दौकि ;   ,,   ,, अदुदौकत्.

(d) Examples of § 407 (d):

    rt. कृत् ;   Caus. B. कर्ति ;   Aor. Par. अचकर्तत्   or   अचीकृतत्.
    rt. स्तृह् ;   ,,   ,, स्तर्हि ;   ,,   ,, अतिस्तीर्हत् or अतिस्तृहत्.
    rt. मृज् ;   ,,   ,, मार्जि ;   ,,   ,, अममार्जत्   or   अमीमृजत्.
    rt. कृप् ;   ,,   ,, कल्पि ;   ,,   ,, अचकल्पत्   or   अचीकृपत्.

§ 427. (a) Examples of § 408 (a):

    rt. भिद् ;   Caus. B. भेदि ;   Aor. Par. अबीभिदत्.
    rt. तुद् ;   ,,   ,, तोदि ;   ,,   ,, अनूतुदत्.

(b) Examples of § 408 (b):

    rt. पठ् ;   Caus. B. पाठि ;   Aor. Par. अपीपठत्.
    rt. नी ;   ,,   ,, नायि ;   ,,   ,, अनीनयत्.
    rt. कृ ;   ,,   ,, कारि ;   ,,   ,, अचीकरत्.
    rt. त्यज् ;   ,,   ,, त्याजि ;   ,,   ,, अतित्यजत्.

(c) The roots जु 'to hasten,' पू 'to purify,' भू 'to be,' मू 'to bind,' यु 'to bind,' &c. ह्रु 'to sound,' and लू 'to cut' take regularly the vowel ई in the reduplicative syllable; e.g.

    rt. भू ;   Caus. B. भावि ;   Aor. Par. अबीभवत्.

[§ 429.] CONJUGATION OF VERBS. 177

The roots च्यु 'to move,' द्रु 'to run,' म्रु 'to go,' प्लु 'to swim,' श्रु 'to hear,' and स्रु 'to flow' take in the reduplicative syllable optionally इ or उ; e. g.

   rt. च्यु ; Caus. B. च्यावि ; Aor. Par. अचिच्यवत् or अचुच्यवत्.

Other roots in उ or ऊ take in the reduplicative syllable ऊ if the root begins with one consonant, and उ, if it begins with more than one consonant; e. g.

   rt. दु ; Caus. B. दावि ; Aor. Par. अदूदवत्.
   rt. द्यु ; "   " द्यावि ; "   " अदुद्यवत्.

(d) The vowel अ of the reduplicative syllable of त्वर् 'to hurry,' दृ 'to burst,' प्रथ् 'to be famous,' म्रद् 'to rub,' स्तृ 'to spread,' स्पश 'to restrain,' and स्मृ 'to remember,' remains unchanged; e. g.

   rt. त्वर् ; Caus. B. त्वरि ; Aor. Par. अतत्वरत्.
   rt. स्तृ ; "   " स्तारि ; "   " अतस्तरत्.

§ 428. (a) Examples of § 409 (a):

   rt. अट् ; Caus. B. आटि ; Aor. Par. आटिटत्.
   rt. अश् ; "   " आशि ;   "   "   आशिशत्.
   rt. इष् ; "   " एषि ;   "   "   ऐषिषत्.
   rt. ईक्ष् ; "   " ईक्षि ; "   "   ऐचिक्षत्.

(b) Examples of § 409 (b):

   rt. उन्द् ;   Caus. B. उन्दि ; Aor. Par. औन्ददत्.
   rt. अञ्ज् ;   "   " अञ्जि ; "   "   आञ्जिजत्.
   rt. अर्च् ;   "   " अर्चि ;   "   "   आर्चिचत्.
   rt. उन्ज् ; (for उद्ज्) "   " उञ्जि ;   "   "   औञ्जिजत्.
   rt. ऋ ;   "   " अर्पि ;   "   "   आर्पिपत्.

§ 429. Alphabetical list of roots, the Aor. of the Causal of which is formed irregularly:

1. rt. इ with prep. अधि 'to study;' Caus. B. अध्यापि ; Aor. Par. अध्यापिपत् or अभ्यजीगपत्.
2. rt. ईर्ष्य् 'to envy;' Caus. B. ईर्षि ; Aor. ऐर्षिष्यत् or ऐर्षियत्.
3. rt. ऊर्णु 'to cover;' "   " ऊर्णावि ; "   और्णुनवत्.

4.	rt. घ्रा 'to smell;'	Caus.	B.	घ्रापि;	Aor.	अजिघ्रपत् or अजिघ्रिपत्.
5.	rt. चेष्ट् 'to stir;'	,,	,,	चेष्टि;	,,	आचिचेष्टत् or अचचेष्टत्.
6.	rt. द्युत् 'to shine;'	,,	,,	द्योति;	,,	अदिद्युतत्.
7.	rt. पा 'to drink;'	,,	,,	पायि;	,,	अपीप्यत्.
8.	rt. वेष्ट् 'to surround;'	,,	,,	वेष्टि;	,,	अविवेष्टत् or अववेष्टत्.
9.	rt. श्रि 'to grow;'	,,	,,	श्रायि;	,,	आशिश्रयत् or अशुश्रावत्.
10.	rt. स्था 'to stand;'	,,	,,	स्थापि;	,,	अतिष्ठिपत्.
11.	rt. स्फुर् 'to shine;'	,,	,,	स्फोरि or स्फारि;	,,	अपुस्फुरत् / अपुस्फरत्.
12.	rt. स्वप् 'to sleep;'	,,	,,	स्वापि;	,,	असूषुपत्.
13.	rt. ह्वे 'to call;'	,,	,,	ह्वायि;	,,	अजूहवत् or अजुहावत्.

§ 430. *The 3 Sing. Aor. Passive:*

(a) Examples of § 412 (a):

rt. भिद्; Caus. B. भेदि; 3 Sing. Aor. Pass. अभेदि.
rt. बुध्; ,, ,, बोधि ,, ,, ,, ,, अबोधि.
rt. दा; ,, ,, दापि;,, ,, ,, ,, अदापि.

(b) The radical vowel अ of roots which retain this vowel unchanged in the Causal base (§ 421 a, b, c,), while according to the general rule they ought to lengthen it, and the short अ of the Causal bases of the roots enumerated in § 422 (c), is optionally lengthened in the 3 Sing. of the Aor. Pass. of the Causal; *e. g.*

rt. घट्; Caus. B. घटि; 3 Sing. Aor. Pass. अघटि or अघाटि.
rt. श्रा; ,, ,, श्रपि ,, ,, ,, ,, अश्रपि or अश्रापि.

2.—THE DESIDERATIVE.

§ 431. A desiderative form which is likewise conjugated in all the tenses and moods of the three voices, may be derived from any primitive root of the first nine classes, from the derivative base of any root of the tenth class, and from any causal base. It conveys the notion that a person or thing wishes or is about to perform the action or to undergo the state expressed by the root or the derivative base; *e. g.*

	Pres. Ind. Par.	Pres. Ind. Des. Par.
rt. कृ 'to do;'	करोति 'he does;'	चिकीर्षति 'he wishes to do.'
rt. भू 'to be;'	भवति 'he is;'	बुभूषति 'he wishes to be.'
rt. बुध् 'to know;'	बोधति 'he knows;'	बुबोधिषति 'he wishes to know.'
rt. गम् 'to go;'	गच्छति 'he goes;'	जिगमिषति 'he wishes to go.'

Deriv. B. चोरि (of rt. चुर् cl. 10.) 'to steal.'

  Pres. Ind. Par. चोरयति 'he steals.'

  Pres. Ind. Des. Par. चुचोरयिषति 'he wishes to steal.'

Caus. B. बोधि (from rt. बुध्) 'to cause to know;'

Pres. Ind. Caus. Par. बोधयति 'he causes to know.'

Pres. Ind. Desid. Par. of Caus. बुबोधयिषति 'he wishes to cause to know.'

§ 432. In order to impart to a root or base the peculiar sense of wishing, desiring &c., which is denoted by the Desiderative, a *desiderative base* has to be derived from it, to which base the terminations of the tenses and moods are attached according to certain rules which will be given further on; e. g. rt. भू; Desid. Base बुभूष, Pres. Ind. Des. Par. बुभूषति; Impf. अबुभूषन्; Perf. बुभूषामास, &c.

  (*a*)—*Formation of the Desiderative Base.*

§ 433. The Desiderative Base is formed by adding to the root or base the syllable स (changeable to ष by § 59), and by at the same time reduplicating the root or base; e. g.

rt. भिद् 'to split;'	Desid. B. बिभित्स 'to wish to split.'
rt. भुज् 'to enjoy;'	,, ,, बुभुक्ष 'to wish to enjoy.'
rt. भू 'to be;'	,, ,, बुभूष 'to wish to be.'

Caus. B. बोधि 'to cause to know;' Desid. B. बुबोधयिष 'to wish to cause to know.'

§ 434. In the application of the preceding general rule it is necessary to observe the following special rules, which will show (1) when the intermediate vowel इ must or may be inserted before the syllable स (or ष);

(2) when the letters of the root or base undergo any change; and (3) when the general rules of reduplication (§ 230) are modified in the formation of the desiderative base.

1.—*Addition to the root or base of the syllable* स (*or* ष).

§ 435. The syllable स is added *without* the intermediate इ—

(*a*) To the roots enumerated in § 366 (*a*) 1 and 2, except those to which any of the following special rules apply; *e. g.*

    rt. पा ' to drink;' Desid. B. पिपास ' to desire to drink, to thirst.'
    rt. नी ' to lead;'   „   „ निनीष ' to wish to lead.'
    rt. पच् ' to cook;'   „   „ पिपक्ष ' to wish to cook.'

(*b*) To all roots ending in ऋ or ॠ, except those to which any of the following special rules apply; *e. g.*

    rt. नु ' to praise;' Desid. B. नुनूष ' to wish to praise.'
    rt. लू ' to cut;'   „   „ लुलूष ' to wish to cut.'

(*c*) To the roots गुह् ' to hide,' and ग्रह् ' to seize' (Desid. Bases: जुघुक्ष and जिघृक्ष).

(*d*) To the five roots कृप् ' to be fit,' वृत् ' to be,' वृध् ' to grow,' शृध् and स्यन्द् ' to drop,' in Parasmai. In Âtmane. the first four roots must insert इ, and स्यन्द् may do so optionally; *e. g.*

    rt. वृत्; Desid. B. in Par. विवृत्स; Pres. Ind. विवृत्सति;
       „   „   Âtm. विवर्तिष;   „   „ विवर्तिषते.
    rt. स्यन्द्; „   „   Par. सिस्यन्त्स;   „   „ सिस्यन्त्सति;
       „   „   Âtm. सिस्यन्त्स or „   सिस्यन्त्सते or
                   सिस्यन्दिष   सिस्यन्दिषते.

§ 436. The syllable स may be added optionally *with* or *without* the intermediate इ—

(*a*) To the roots enumerated in § 366 (*b*) 1, 2, 3, except अञ्ज्, अश्, गुह् and except स्यन्द् in Parasmai.; *e. g.*

    rt. व्रश्च् ' to tear;' Desid. B. विव्रक्षिष or विव्रक्ष ' to wish to tear.'
    rt. तृप् ' to enjoy;' „   „ तितर्पिष or तितृप्स ' to wish to enjoy.'

CONJUGATION OF VERBS.

(b) To the root वृ, and to all roots ending in ऋ except कृ and वृ; the intermediate इ may optionally be lengthened after these roots; e. g.
rt. वृ 'to choose;' Desid. B. विवरिष or विवरीष or वुवूर्ष 'to wish to choose.'
rt. तॄ ' to cross;'   ,,   ,, तितरिष or तितरीष or तितीर्ष 'to wish to cross.'

(c) To roots ending in इव्; when स is added without इ, the final इव् of these roots is changed to यू; e. g.

rt. दिव् 'to play;' Desid. B. दिदेविष or दुद्यूष 'to wish to play.'

(d) To ऊर्णु 'to cover,' ऋध् 'to prosper,' कृत् 'to cut,' चृत् 'to kill,' छुर् 'to play,' ज्ञपि (deriv. B. of rt. ज्ञप् cl. 10 and optional causal B. of rt. ज्ञा,) तन् 'to stretch,' तॄ 'to kill,' दम्भ् 'to deceive,' दरिद्रा 'to be poor,' नृत् 'to dance,' पत् 'to fall,' भृ 'to bear,' भ्रज्ज् 'to fry,' यु 'to join,' श्रि 'to go,' सन् 'to honour;' e. g.

rt. कृत् 'to cut;' Desid. B. चिकर्तिष or चिकृत्स 'to wish to cut.'
rt. श्रि 'to go;'   ,,   ,, शिश्रयिष or शिश्रीष 'to wish to go.'

(e) स is added with इ in Parasmai., but without इ in Âtmane., to the roots क्रम् 'to stride,' गम् 'to go,' and स्रु 'to flow;' e. g.

rt. क्रम्; in Par. चिक्रमिष ; Pres. Ind. चिक्रमिषति ;
          in Âtm. चिक्रंस ;   ,,   ,, चिक्रंसते.

§ 437. The syllable स is added *with* the intermediate इ—

To the roots अञ्ज् 'to anoint,' अश् to 'pervade,' ऋ 'to go,' कॄ 'to scatter,' गॄ 'to devour,' दृ 'to respect,' धृ 'to hold,' पू (cl. 1.) 'to purify,' प्रच्छ् 'to ask,' स्मि 'to smile,' to all roots which do not fall under § 435 and 436, and to all derivative bases of roots of the tenth class and all causal bases (except ज्ञपि); e.g. rt. कृ ; Desid B. चिकरिष.

rt. स्मि ;   ,,   ,, सिस्मयिष.
rt. क्रीड ;   ,,   ,, चिक्रीडिष 'to wish to play.'

Note: The intermediate इ cannot be lengthened in the Desid. B. of कृ and गृ.

2.—*Changes of the root or base before* स (*or* ष).

§ 438. Vowels of roots and bases undergo the following changes before the syllable स (or ष):

(*a*) Final इ and उ are lengthened, and final ऋ and ॠ are changed to ईर् or, after labials, to ऊर्, when the syllable स is added without intermediate इ; *e. g.*

rt. जि	'to conquer;'	Desid. B.	जिगीष	'to wish to conquer.'
rt. द्रु	'to run;'	,,	,, दुद्रूष,	'to wish to run.'
rt. कृ	'to do;'	,,	,, चिकीर्ष	'to wish to do.'
rt. तृ	'to cross;'	,,	,, तितीर्ष	'to wish to cross.'
rt. मृ	'to die;'	,,	,, मुमूर्ष	'to wish to die.'
rt. पृ	'to fill;'	,,	,, पुपूर्ष	'to wish to fill.'

(*b*). Final इ, ई, उ, ऊ, ऋ, and ॠ, are gunated, when the syllable स is added to the root or base with the intermediate इ; *e. g.*

rt. स्मि	'to smile;'	Desid. B.	सिस्मयिष	'to wish to smile.'
rt. यु	'to join;'	,,	,, युयविष	'to wish to join.'
rt. पू (cl. 1.)	'to purify;'	,,	,, पिपविष	'to wish to purify.'
rt. दृ	'to respect;'	,,	,, दिदरिष	'to wish to respect.'
rt. तृ	'to cross;'	,,	,, तितरिष or तितरीष	'to wish to cross.'

Caus. B. बोधि 'to cause to know;' बुबोधयिष ' to wish to cause to know.

(*c*). Penultimate prosodially short इ, उ, ऋ and ऌ are gunated, when स is added to the root with the intermediate इ; *e. g.*

rt. इष्	'to wish;'	Desid. B.	एषिषिष	'to desire to wish.'
rt. वृत्	'to be;'	,,	,, विवर्तिष	'to wish to be.'
rt. कॢप्	'to be fit;'	,,	,, चिकल्पिष	'to wish to be fit.'

The same vowels remain unchanged when स is added to the root without इ (Desid. B. विवृत्स, चिकृप्स &c.).

(*d*) Penultimate prosodially short इ and उ of roots beginning with consonants and ending with any consonant except व् are *optionally* gunated, and penultimate इ of roots in इव् *must* be gunated, when स is added to the root with the intermediate इ; *e. g.*

rt. द्युत् ' to shine ;' Desid. B. दिद्युतिष or दिद्योतिष ' to wish to shine.'
rt. क्लिद् ' to be moist ;' ,, ,, चिक्लिदिष or चिक्लेदिष ' to wish to be moist.'
rt. दिव् ' to play ;' ,, ,, दिदेविष ' to wish to play.'

The same vowels remain unchanged when स is added without इ Desid. B. चिक्लित्स).

Exception: The radical vowel of विद् ' to know,' मुष् ' to steal,' and रुद् ' to weep' remains unchanged ; Desid. B. विविदिष, मुमुषिष, रुरुदिष.

§ 439. Radical vowels of roots which do not fall under any of the rules given in the preceding paragraph, remain unchanged (final ए, ऐ and ओ being changed to आ by § 296 a) ; *e. g.*

rt. पच् ' to cook ;' Desid. B. पिपक्ष ' to wish to cook.'
rt. पठ् ' to read ;' ,, ,, पिपठिष ' to wish to read.'
rt. जीव् ' to live ;' ,, ,, जिजीविष ' to wish to live.'
rt. घ्रा ' to smell ;' ,, ,, जिघ्रास ' to wish to smell.'
rt. गै ' to sing ;' ,, ,, जिगास ' to wish to sing.'
rt. दो ' to perish ;' ,, ,, दिदोष ' to wish to perish.'

3.—*Special rules of Reduplication.*

§ 440. *Roots or bases beginning with consonants* after they have undergone the changes required by the preceding paragraphs, are reduplicated according to the general rules laid down in § 230 &c.; afterwards the vowel इ is substituted for the vowel अ of the reduplicative syllable; *e. g.*

rt. पठ् ; by § 437 & 439   पठिष ; by § 231, e पपठिष, Desid. B. पिपठिष
rt. पा ; ,, § 435 a & 439   पास ; ,, § ,, पपास ; ,, ,, पिपास.
rt. स्यज् ; ,, § ,,   त्यक्ष ; ,, § ,, तत्यक्ष ; ,, ,, तित्यक्ष.
rt. नृ ; ,, § 436, b & 438, a तीर्ष ; ,, § ,, तितीर्ष.
rt. मृ ; ,, § 435, a & 438, a मूर्ष ; ,, § ,, मुमूर्ष.
rt. दिव् ; ,, § 436, c   द्यूष ; ,, § ,, दुद्यूष.

Deriv. B. चोरि (of rt. चुर् cl. 10.) ; by §437 & 438, *b* चोरयिष; Desid. B. चुचोरयिष.

Caus. B. नायि (from rt. नी); by § 437 & 438, b नाययिष; by § 231, e ननाययिष; Desid. B. निनाययिष.

§ 441. Causal Bases in आवि, derived from roots in उ or ऊ, are slightly irregular as far as the vowel of the reduplicative syllable of the Desid. Base is concerned (see § 427 c):

(a) The causal bases of जु, पू, भू, मू, यु, रु, and लू, follow the general rule (§ 440); e. g. Caus. B. भावि (from rt. भू); Desid. B. of the Caus. बिभावयिष.

(b) The causal bases of च्यु, द्रु, प्रु, म्रु, श्रु, and स्रु follow the general rule or take the vowel उ in the reduplicative syllable; e. g.

Caus. B. द्रावि (from rt. द्रु); Desid. B. of the Caus. दिद्रावयिष or दुद्रावयिष.

(c) The causal bases of other roots in उ or ऊ take the vowel उ in the reduplicative syllable; e. g.

Caus. B. दावि (from rt. दु); Desid. B. of the Caus. दुदावयिष.

§ 442. *Roots or bases beginning with vowels*, after having undergone the changes required by the preceding paragraphs, are reduplicated according to the rules in § 409 a and b (not c); e. g.

rt. अट् 'to go;' Desid. B. अटिटिष 'to wish to go.'
rt. इष्; by § 437 and 438 (c) एषिष; Desid. B. एषिषिष.
rt. ईक्ष; 'to see;' Desid. B. ईचिक्षिष.
rt. ऋ 'to go;' by § 437 and 438, (b.) अरिष; Desid. B. अरिरिष.
rt. अञ्जू 'to anoint;' Desid. B. अञ्जिजिष.
rt. ऋज् 'to go;' by § 437 and 438 (c) अर्जिष; Desid. B. अर्जिजिष.

Caus. B. एषि (fr. rt. इष्) by § 437 and 438 (b.) एषयिष; Desid. B. एषिषयिष.

§ 443. The following roots and bases form their desiderative Base irregularly:

1. अद् 'to eat,' forms its Desid. B. from घस्, जिघत्स; 3 Sing. Pres. Ind. Par. जिघत्सति 'he wishes to eat.'

2. आप् 'to obtain,' Desid. B. ईप्स; 3 Sing. Pres. Ind. Par. ईप्सति 'he wishes to obtain.'

3. इ 'to go,' forms its Desid. B. from गम्; e.g. 3 Sing. Pres. Ind. Par. जिगमिषति, Âtm. जिगांसते 'he wishes to go.' But when it means 'to understand,' it is regular; e.g. Desid. of इ with प्रति, प्रतीषिषति 'he wishes to understand.' When इ is compounded with अधि in the sense of 'to read,' it forms जिगांसते; e.g. अधिजिगांसते 'he wishes to read.'—The root गम् 'to go,' when it is not a substitute for इ, forms in Âtm. regularly जिगंसते; e.g. संजिगंसते 'he wishes to meet.'

The Desid. of the Causal of इ with prep. अधि, is either अध्यापिपयिषति or अधिजिगापयिषति 'he wishes to teach.'

4. ईर्ष्य् 'to envy;' Desid. B. ईर्ष्यियिष or ईर्ष्यिषिष; 3 Sing. Pres. Ind. Par. ईर्ष्यियिषति or ईर्ष्यिषिषति 'he wishes to envy.'

	Desid. B.	3 Sing. Pres. Ind.	
5. ऊर्णु 'to cover;'	ऊर्णुनुव or ऊर्णुनुविष or ऊर्णुनविष;	ऊर्णुनुवति ऊर्णुनुविषति ऊर्णुनविषति	'he wishes to cover.'
6. ऋध् 'to prosper;'	ईर्त्स or अर्दिधिष;	ईर्त्सति अर्दिधिषति	'he wishes to prosper.'
7. गॄ 'to swallow;'	जिगरिष or जिगलिष;	जिगरिषति जिगलिषति	'he wishes to swallow.'
8. ग्रह् 'to seize;'	जिघृक्ष;	जिघृक्षति	'he wishes to seize.'
9. चि 'to gather;'	चिचीष or चिकीष;	चिचीषति चिकीषति	'he wishes to gather.'
10. जि 'to conquer;'	जिगीष	जिगीषति	'he wishes to conquer.'
11. ज्ञप् base of cl. 10. or optional Caus. of ज्ञा; but ज्ञापि opt. Caus. of ज्ञा;'	ज्ञीप्स or जिज्ञपयिष; जिज्ञापयिष;	ज्ञीप्सति; जिज्ञपयिषति. जिज्ञापयिषति.	
12. तन् 'to stretch;'	नितंस; or तितांस; or तितनिष;	नितंसति तितांसति तितनिषति	'he wishes to stretch.'
13. तृंह् 'to kill;'	तितृक्ष; or तितृंहिष;	तितृक्षति तितृंहिषति	'he wishes to kill.'
14. दम्भ् 'to deceive;'	धिप्स; or धीप्स; or दिदम्भिष;	धिप्सति धीप्सति दिदम्भिषति	'he wishes to deceive.'

15. दरिद्रा 'to be poor;'	दिदरिद्रास; or दिदरिद्रिष;	दिदरिद्रासति दिदरिद्रिषति	'he wishes to be poor.'
16. दा 'to give;'	दित्स;	दित्सति	'he wishes to give.'
17. दे 'to protect;'		दित्सते	'he wishes to protect.'
18. दो 'to cut;'		दित्सति	'he wishes to cut.'
19. द्युत् 'to shine;'	दिद्युतिष; or दिद्योतिष;	दिद्युतिषते दिद्योतिषते	'he wishes to shine.'
20. धा 'to place;'	धित्स;	धित्सति	'he wishes to place, or to suck.'
21. धे 'to suck;'			
22. नश् 'to perish;'	निनङ्क्ष or निनशिष;	निनङ्क्षति निनशिषति	'he is about to perish.'
23. पत् 'to fall;'	पित्स; or पिपतिष;	पित्सति पिपतिषति	'he wishes or is about to fall.'
24. पद् 'to go;'	पित्स;	पित्सते	'he wishes to go.'
25. प्रच्छ् 'to ask;'	पिपृच्छिष;	पिपृच्छिषति	'he wishes to ask.'
26. भ्रज्ज् 'to fry;'	बिभ्रक्ष; or बिभर्क्ष; or बिभ्रज्जिष; or बिभर्जिष;	बिभ्रक्षति बिभर्क्षति बिभ्रज्जिषति बिभर्जिषति	'he wishes to fry.'
27. मज्ज् 'to dive;'	मिमङ्क्ष;	मिमङ्क्षति	'he wishes to dive.'
28. मा 'to measure;'	मित्स;	मित्सति	'he wishes to measure.'
29. मि 'to throw;'		मित्सति	'he wishes to throw.'
30. मी 'to destroy;'		मित्सति	'he wishes to destroy.'
31. मे 'to exchange;'		मित्सते	'he wishes to exchange.'
32. मुच् when used intransitively; otherwise only	मुमुक्ष; or मोक्ष; मुमुक्ष;	मुमुक्षते मोक्षते मुमुक्षति	'he longs for final liberation.' 'he wishes to free.'
33. मृज् 'to wipe off;'	मिमृक्ष; or मिमार्जिष;	मिमृक्षति मिमार्जिषति	'he wishes to wipe off.'
34. रभ् 'to desire;'	रिप्स;	रिप्सते	'he wishes to desire.'
35. राध् in the sense of 'to injure;' otherwise	रित्स; रिरात्स;	रित्सति रिरात्सति	'he wishes to injure.' 'he wishes to favour.'
36. लभ् 'to take;'	लिप्स;	लिप्सते	'he wishes to take.'
37. शक् 'to be able;'	शिक्ष;	शिक्षति	'he wishes to be able.'
38. श्राप्, Caus. B. of श्रि 'to swell;'	शिश्रापयिष; or शुश्रावयिष;	शिश्रापयिषति शुश्रावयिषति	'he wishes to cause to swell.'
39. सन् 'to honour;'	सिषास; or सिसनिष;	सिषासति सिसनिषति	'he wishes to honour.'

40. स्फारि optional Caus. B. of स्फुर् 'to shine;'	पुस्फारयिष;	पुस्फारयिषति	'he wishes to cause to shine.'
41. स्वप् 'to sleep;'	सुषुप्स;	सुषुप्सति	'he wishes to sleep.'
42. स्वापि, Caus. B. of स्वप् 'to sleep;'	सुष्वापयिष;	सुष्वापयिषति	'he wishes to cause to sleep.'
43. हन् 'to kill;'	जिघांस;	जिघांसति	'he wishes to kill.'
44. हि 'to send;'	जिघीष;	जिघीषति	'he wishes to send.'
45. ह्वायि, Caus. B. of ह्वे 'to call;'	जुह्वावयिष;	जुह्वावयिषति	'he wishes to cause to call.'
46. ह्वे 'to call;'	जुहूष;	जुहूषति	'he wishes to call.'

§ 444. A Desiderative Base, which however does not convey a desideratvie sense, is derived from the following roots:

rt. गुर्	Desid. B.	जुगुप्स 'to blame;'	Pres. Ind.	जुगुप्सते.
rt. निज्	,,	,,	निनिक्ष 'to endure;'	,,	निनिक्षते.
rt. किन्	,,	,,	चिकित्स 'to heal;' &c.	,,	चिकित्सति, ˚ते.
rt. मान्	,,	,,	मीमांस 'to investigate;'	,,	मीमांसते.
rt. बध्	,,	,,	बीभत्स 'to become angry;'	,,	बीभत्सते.
rt. दान्	,,	,,	दीदांस 'to straighten;'	,,	दीदांसते.
rt. शान्	,,	,,	शीशांस 'to sharpen;'	,,	शीशांसते.

As these seven desiderative bases are considered, as it were, primitive verbs, new desiderative bases may be derived from them; from other desiderative bases no new Desideratives can be derived; *e. g.* Desid. of जुगुप्स, जुगुप्सिषते ' he wishes to blame.'

(*b*)—*Conjugation of the Desiderative Base.*

§ 445. The Desiderative Base, after it has been prepared in the manner described in the preceding section, may, like a primitive root, be conjugated in all the three voices; as regards however the Parasmaipada and Âtmanepada, the Desiderative Base is restricted to the same voice to which the root or base from which it is derived, is restricted (provided there be such restriction) : *e. g.*

Rt. यज् ' to sacrifice;' Pres. Ind. Par. यजति 'he sacrifices' (for somebody else);

,, ,, Âtm. यजते 'he sacrifices' (for himself);

,, ,, Pass. इज्यते.

Desid. B. यियक्ष ' to
wish to sacrifice ;' ,, ,, Par. यियक्षति 'he wishes to sacrifice' (for somebody else);

,, ,, Âtm. यियक्षते 'he wishes to sacrifice' (for himself);

,, ,, Pass. यियक्ष्यते.

Rt. एध् ' to grow;' ,, ,, Âtm. एधते 'he grows.'

Desid. B. एदिधिष ' to
wish to grow ;' ,, ,, Âtm. एदिधिषते ' he wishes to grow.'

§ 446. Exceptions: (a) The Desid. Base of ज्ञा ' to know' (unless it be compounded with the prepos. अनु), श्रु ' to hear' (unless it be compounded with the prepos. प्रति, or with आ), स्मृ ' to remember,' and दृश् ' to see,' is conjugated only in the Âtmanepada; e. g.

Pres. Ind. of Desid. of ज्ञा, जिज्ञासते ' he wishes to know.'

,, ,, ,, ,, ,, श्रु, शुश्रूषते ' he wishes to listen to, he is obedient.'

(b) The Desid. Base of कृप्, वृत्, वृध्, शृध्, and स्यन्द् (§ 435, d) may optionally be conjugated in the Parasmaipada; e. g.

rt. वृध् ' to grow ;' Pres. Ind. (only) Âtm. वर्धते ' he grows,' Pres. Ind. of Desid. Par. and Âtm. विवृत्सति or विवर्धिषते ' he wishes to grow.'

§ 447. In the three moods of the Present tense and in the Imperf. Par. and Âtm. the Desid. Base is conjugated like the special base of a root of the sixth class. In the remaining tenses of the Par. and Âtm. and in the Passive the final अ of the Desid. Base is dropped; subsequently the tenses are formed from the base as remaining after the loss of its final अ, in the manner stated below. It must, however, be borne in mind, that wherever the characteristic स (or ष) of the Desiderative is added to a root or base by means of the intermediate इ or ई, this इ or ई is liable to no change whatever.

1.—THE PARASMAI. AND ÂTMANE.

(*a*) The Perfect is formed by means of auxiliary verbs अस्, कृ and भू according to § 320.

(*b*) In the Aorist the Desid. B. takes the terminations of form V. (§ 344, *b*).

(*c*) In the Simple and Periphrastic Futures the terminations given in § 360, *b* and § 365, *b* are added to the Desid. Base with the intermediate इ.

(*d*) The Conditional is formed according to § 370.

(*e*) In the Benedictive the terminations given in § 372, *c*, are added to the Desid. Base, those of the Âtmane. by means of the intermediate इ.

2.—THE PASSIVE.

(*a*) The Present and Imperfect are formed from the Desid. Base according to the rules in § 379, *a*, and § 380.

(*b*) The Perfect is formed by means of the auxiliary verbs अस्, कृ, and भू according to § 384.

(*c*) The 3rd Sing. of the Aor. is formed from the Desid. B. according to the rule given in § 385.

(*d*) The remaining forms of the Aorist and all the other tenses of the Passive do not differ from the corresponding forms of the Âtmanepada.

§ 448. *Paradigm:* The 3 Sing. of all the tenses and moods in Par. Âtm., and Pass. of the Desider. of rt. बुध् 'to know,' Desid. Base बुबोधिष or बुबुधिष. (*Note:* It will be sufficient to give the forms of only one of these two bases, because those of the other base are formed in exactly the same manner.)

	Parasmai.	Âtmane.	Passive.
Pres. Ind.	बुबोधिषति	बुबोधिषते	बुबोधिष्यते.
Pres. Pot.	बुबोधिषेत्	बुबोधिषेत	बुबोधिष्येत.
Pres. Imper.	बुबोधिषतु or तात्	बुबोधिषताम्	बुबोधिष्यताम्.
Imperf.	अबुबोधिषत्	अबुबोधिषत	अबुबोधिष्यत.

	Par.	Par. or. Ātm.	
Periph. Perf.	बुबोधिषांचकार,	बुबोधिषामास, बुबोधिषांबभूव,	
	Ātm. or. Pass.	Pass.	
Periph Perf.	बुबोधिषांचक्रे	बुबोधिषामासे, बुबोधिषांबभूवे.	
	Par.	Ātm.	Pass.
Aor. 1 Sing.	अबुबोधिषिषम्	अबुबोधिषिषि	अबुबोधिषिषि.
,, 3 Sing.	अबुबोधिषीत्	अबुबोधिषिष्ट	अबुबोधिषि.
	Parasmai.	Ātmane. or Passive.	
Simple Fut.	बुबोधिषिष्यति	बुबोधिषिष्यते·	
Periphr. Fut.	बुबोधिषिता	बुबोधिषिता.	
Condit.	अबुबोधिषिष्यत्	अबुबोधिषिष्यत.	
Bened.	बुबोधिष्यात्	बुबोधिषिषीष्ट.	

3.—THE FREQUENTATIVE.

§ 449. A Frequentative may be derived from any primitive root of the first nine classes, which begins with a consonant and consists of only one syllable. It conveys the notion, that a person or thing performs the action or undergoes the state which is expressed by the root, repeated or intensely ; *e. g.*

Rt.	Pres. Ind. Par.	Frequent.
कृ 'to do;'	करोति 'he does;'	चेक्रीयते or चर्करीति 'he does repeatedly.'
भू 'to be;'	भवति 'he is;'	बोभूयते or बोभवीति 'he is repeatedly.'

But no Frequent. can be derived *e. g.* from जागृ 'to wake,' because this root consists of two syllables.

§ 450. (*a*) Exceptionally a Frequentative may likewise be formed from the roots अट् 'to go,' ऋ 'to go,' अश् 'to pervade,' ऊर्णु 'to cover,' सूच् cl. 10. 'to indicate,' मूल cl. 10., and सूत्र cl. 10. ' to string together.'

(*b*) The Frequentative of a root signifying motion conveys always the import of tortuous motion ; *e. g.* Frequ. of rt. व्रज् 'to walk,' वाव्रज्यते 'he walks tortuously' (not 'he walks repeatedly'). The Frequentatives of the roots लू 'to cut,' सद् 'to sit,' चर् 'to go,' जप् 'to mutter,' जभ् 'to yawn,' दह् 'to burn,' दंश् 'to bite,' and गृ 'to swallow,' convey the notion of reproach &c ; e. g. Frequ. of लू, लोलुप्यते 'he cuts disgracefully.'

§ 451. In order to impart to a root the peculiar meaning which is denoted by the Frequentative, a *frequentative base* has to be derived from it, to which base the terminations of the various tenses and moods are attached ; e. g.

at. भू Freq. Base. बोभूय; Pres. Ind. Freq. Âtm. बोभूयते ; Impf. अबोभूयत &c.
or ,, बोभू ; ,, ,, ,, Par. बोभोति ; ,, अबोभोत्
             or बोभवीति; ,, अबोभवीत्&c:

§ 452. *The Frequentative Base* has two forms; both agree with each other in a peculiar reduplication of the root; they differ from each other in this, that one form ends in य, and is conjugated in the Âtmanepada only, whereas the other form does not end in य, and is conjugated in the Parasmaipada only.* It will be convenient to call the one frequentative Base the Âtmanepada frequentative Base, and the other the Parasmaipada frequentative Base ; e. g.

  rt. भू, Âtmanepada Frequ. B. बोभूय.
      Parasmaipada Frequ. B. बोभू.
  rt. भिद्, Âtmanepada Frequ. B. बेभिद्य.
      Parasmaipada Frequ. B. बेभिद्.

I. (*a*)—*Formation of the Âtmanepada Frequentative Base.*

§ 453. (*a*) The syllable य is added to the root ; e. g. rt. नी, नीय; rt. भू, भूय ; rt. भिद्, भिद्य ; rt. व्रज्, व्रज्य.

(*b*) Before य the root undergoes the following changes :—

1. Final इ, उ, ऋ and ॠ are changed as they are changed before the syllable य of the Passive (§ 379), except that final ऋ when preceded by only one radical consonant is changed to री (not to रि); e. g. rt. श्रि, श्रीय ; rt. दु, दूय ; rt. कृ, क्रीय ; rt. रम्, रम्य ; rt. कृ, कीर्य ; rt. पृ, पूर्य.

---

* Some grammarians admit also the Âtmanepada.

2. The final vowel of दा 'to give,' दे, दो, धा, धे, मा, स्था, गै, पा 'to drink,' हा 'to abandon,' सो, and of घ्रा 'to smell,' and ध्मा 'to blow,' is changed to ई. The final of other roots in आ remains unchanged, and the final vowel of other roots in ए, ऐ and ओ is changed to आ (see however 4); *e. g.* rt. दा, दोय; rt. धे, धोय; rt. गै, गोय; rt. सो, सोय; rt. ज्ञा, ज्ञाय rt. ग्ले, ग्लाय; rt. छो, छाय.

3. A penultimate nasal is generally dropped; *e. g.* rt. बन्ध्, बध्य.

4. The roots व्यच्, व्यध् and स्यम् substitute इ for य; ज्या and व्ये substitute ई for या and ये; स्वप् substitutes उ for व; ह्वे substitutes ऊ for वे; ग्रह्, मृछ्, भ्रस्ज् and व्रश्च, substitute ऋ for र; and शास् substitutes इ for आ; *e. g.* rt. व्यच्, विच्य; rt. ज्या, जीय; rt. स्वप्, सुप्य; rt ह्वे, हूय; rt. ग्रह्, गृह्य; rt. शास्, शिष्य.

5. Observe § 46; *e. g.* rt. दिव्, दीव्य.

§ 454. The form in य, derived from the root according to the rules of the preceding paragraph, is reduplicated according to the general rules of reduplication (§ 230); subsequently the vowels इ and उ of the reduplicative syllable are gunated, and the vowel अ of the reduplicative syllable is lengthened ; *e. g.*

rt. दा;	by § 453,	दीय;	by § 231	दिदीय ;	Â. Freq. Base.		देदीय
rt. ज्ञा;	,, ,,	,, ज्ञाय;	,, ,,	जज्ञाय ;	,,	,,	जाज्ञाय
rt. धे ;	,, ,,	,, धीय;	,, ,,	दिधीय ;	,,	,,	देधीय
rt. भू ;	,, ,,	,, भूय;	,, ,,	बुभूय ;	,,	,,	बोभूय
rt. कृ ;	,, ,,	,, क्रीय;	,, ,,	चिक्रीय ;	,,	,,	चेक्रीय
rt. पृ ;	,, ,,	,, पूर्य;	,, ,,	पुपूर्य ;	,,	,,	पोपूर्य
rt. जीव्;	,, ,,	,, जीव्य;	,, ,,	जिजीव्य ;	,,	,,	जेजीव्य
rt. दैक्;	,, ,,	,, दैक्य;	,, ,,	दुदैक्य ;	,,	,,	दोदैक्य
rt. व्यच्;	,, ,,	,, विच्य;	,, ,,	विविच्य ;	,,	,,	वेविच्य
rt. स्वप्;	,, ,,	,, सुप्य;	,, ,,	सुषुप्य ;	,,	,,	सोषुप्य
rt. शास्;	,, ,,	,, शिष्य;	,, ,,	शिशिष्य ;	,,	,,	शोशिष्य

§ 455. (*a*) When a root ends in a nasal preceded by the vowel अ, the vowel अ of the reduplicative syllable is (against § 454) not lengthened, but Anusvâra or the nasal of that class to which the first radical consonant belongs, is inserted between the vowel अ of the reduplicative syllable and the first radical consonant; this rule applies, however, only when the final radical nasal remains unchanged before the syllable य of the frequent. base; *e. g.*

    rt. भम्; by § 453 भम्य; by 231 बभम्य; Â. Freq. B. बंभम्य or बम्भम्य.
    rt. यम्; ,, ,, ,, यम्य; ,, ,, ययम्य; ,, ,, ,, यंयम्य or यंय्यम्य.
    rt. जन्; ,, ,, ,, जन्य; ,, ,, जजन्य; ,, ,, ,, जंजन्य or जञ्जन्य.

But when जन् combined with य becomes जाय, the Â. Frequ. Base is जाजाय.

(*b*) The same rule applies to the roots जन्, जभ्, दह्, दंश्, (see § 450, *b*) भञ्ज् 'to break,' and पच् cl. 1, 'to restrain'; *e. g.*

    rt. दह्; by § 453 दह्य; by § 231 दरह्य; Â. Freq. B. दंदह्य or दन्दह्य.

(*c*) The syllable नी is inserted between the vowel अ of the reduplicative syllable (which against § 454 remains short) and the first radical consonant in the frequentative base of वच् 'to go,' ह्लंस् 'to fall,' ध्वंस् 'to fall,' भ्रंस् 'to fall,' कस् 'to go,' पन् 'to fall,' पद् 'to go,' and स्कन्द् 'to step;' *e. g.*

    rt. वच्; by § 453 वच्य; by § 231 ववच्य; Â. Freq. B. वनीवच्य.
    rt. पन्; ,, ,, ,, पन्य ,, ,, पपन्य ,, ,, ,, पनीपन्य.

§ 453. The syllable री is inserted between the vowel अ of the reduplicative syllable (which against § 454 remains short) and the first radical consonant in the Âtmane. frequentative base of roots which, after the addition of य to them, contain a medial ऋ. Similarly ली is inserted in the frequentative base of rt. कृ; *e. g.*

    rt. वृत्; by § 453 वृत्य; by § 231 ववृत्य; Â. Freq. B. वरीवृत्य.
    rt. प्रछ्; ,, ,, ,, पृछ्य; ,, ,, पपृछ्य; ,, ,, ,, परीपृछ्य.
    rt. कृ; ,, ,, ,, कृय्य; ,, ,, चकृय्य; ,, ,, ,, चलीकृय्य.

Note :—A list of irregular Âtmanepada Frequentative Bases will be given below.

1. (*b*).—*Conjugation of the Âtmanepada Frequentative Base.*

§ 457. In the three moods of the Present tense and in the Imperfect of the Âtmanepada, the Âtm. Frequent. Base is conjugated like the special base of a root of the fourth class in Âtmanepada. In the remaining tenses of the Âtmanepada, and in all the tenses of the Passive, the base loses its final अ when the final य is preceded by a vowel, and it loses its final य, when य is preceded by a consonant; e. g. बोभूय becomes बोभूय्; बोबुध्य becomes बोबुध्. The base, changed in this way, can undergo no further changes, and the Perfect and the remaining tenses are formed from it thus:

1. *The Âtmanepada.*

(a) The Perfect is formed by means of the auxiliary verbs अस्, कृ and भू, according to § 320.

(b) In the Aorist the frequentative base takes the Âtmanepada terminations of form V. (§ 344, b).

(c) In the Simple and Periphrastic Futures the Âtmanepada terminations given in § 360, b, and § 365, b, are added to the frequent. Base with the intermediate इ.

(d) The Conditional is formed according to § 370.

(e) In the Benedictive the Âtmanepada terminations given in § 372, c, are added to the frequent. Base by means of the intermediate इ.

2. *The Passive.*

(a) The Present and Imperfect are formed from the Frequent. Base according to the rules in § 379, (a), and § 380.

(b) The Perfect is formed by means of the auxiliary verbs अस्, कृ and भू, according to § 384.

(c) The 3 Sing. Aor. is formed from the frequent. Base according to the rules given in § 385.

(d) The remaining forms of the Aorist and all the other tenses of the Passive do not differ from the corresponding forms of the Âtmanepada.

§ 459. *Paradigms*: The 3 Sing. of all the tenses and moods in Âtmane. and Passive of the Âtmanepada Frequentative of rt. बुध् 'to know,' Â. Frequent. Base बोबुध्य ; and भू 'to be,' Â. Frequent. Base बोभूय.

Ātmanepada.

Pres. Ind.	बोबुध्यते	बोभूयते
Pres. Pot.	बोबुध्येत	बोभूयेत
Pres. Imper.	बोबुध्यताम्	बोभूयताम्
Imperf.	अबोबुध्यत	अबोभूयत
Periph. Perf.	बोबुधामास &c.	बोभूयामास &c.
Aorist. 1 Sing.	अबोबुधिषि	अबोभूयिषि
„ 3 Sing.	अबोबुधिष्ट	अबोभूयिष्ट
Simple Fut.	बोबुधिष्यते	बोभूयिष्यते
Periph. Fut.	बोबुधिता	बोभूयिता
Condit.	अबोबुधिष्यत	अबोभूयिष्यत
Benedict.	बोबुधिषीष्ट	बोभूयिषीष्ट.

Passive.

Pres. Ind.	बोबुध्यते	बोभूय्यते
Pres. Pot.	बोबुध्येत	बोभूय्येत
Pres. Imper.	बोबुध्यताम्	बोभूय्यताम्
Imperf.	अबोबुध्यत	अबोभूय्यत
Periph. Perf.	बोबुधामासे &c.	बोभूयामासे &c.
Aorist. 1 Sing.	अबोबुधिषि	अबोभूयिषि
„ 3. Sing.	अबोबुधि	अबोभूयि.

Simple Fut.
Periph. Fut. } like Ātmanepada.
Condit.
Benedict.

2 (a).—Formation of the Parasmaipada Frequentative Base.

§ 459. The root is reduplicated according to the general rules of reduplication; subsequently the vowels इ and उ of the reduplicative syllable are gunated, and the vowel अ of the reduplicative syllable is lengthened; e. g.

rt. दा 'to give;'	by	§ 231	ददा;	Par. Frequ. B.	दादा.
rt. ज्ञा 'to know;'	,,	,, ,,	जज्ञा;	,, ,,	,, जाज्ञा.
rt. शि 'to go;'	,,	,, ,,	शिश्रि;	,, ,,	,, शेश्रि.
rt. नी 'to lead;'	,,	,, ,,	निनी;	,, ,,	,, नेनी.
rt. दु 'to agitate;'	,,	,, ,,	दुदु;	,, ,,	,, दोदु.
rt. भू 'to be;'	,,	,, ,,	बुभू;	,, ,,	,, बोभू.
rt. कृ 'to scatter;'	,,	,, ,,	चकृ;	,, ,,	,, चाकृ.
rt. गै 'to sing;'	,,	,, ,,	जगै;	,, ,,	,, जागै.
rt. भिद् 'to split;'	,,	,, ,,	बिभिद्;	,, ,,	,, बेभिद्.
rt. बुध् 'to know;'	,,	,, ,,	बुबुध्;	,, ,,	,, बोबुध्.

§ 460. The rules given in § 455, (a), (b), and (c), apply likewise to the Parasmai. Frequ. base; e. g.

rt. भ्रम्;	by § 231	बभ्रम्;	Par. Freq. B.	बंभ्रम् or बम्भ्रम्.
rt. दह्;	,, ,, ,,	ददह्;	,, ,, ,,	देदह् or दन्दह्.
rt. वञ्च्;	,, ,, ,,	ववञ्च्;	,, ,, ,,	वनीवञ्च्.

§ 461. The letter र्, or the syllable रि, or the syllable री, is inserted between the vowel अ of the reduplicative syllable (which against § 459 remains short) and the first radical consonant in the Parasmai. Frequentative base of roots which end with short ऋ or which have short ऋ as their penultimate letter; similarly ल् or लि or ली is inserted in the Par. Frequ. Base. of rt. कॢप्; e. g.

rt. कृ;	by § 231	चकृ;	Par. Freq. B.	चर्कृ,	or चरिकृ,	or चरीकृ.
rt. वृत्;	,, ,,	,, ववृत्;	,, ,, ,,	वर्वृत्,	or वरिवृत्,	or वरीवृत्.
rt. कॢप्;	,, ,,	,, चकॢप्:	,, ,, ,,	चलकॢप्,	or चालिकॢप्,	or चलीकॢप्.

2 (b).—Conjugation of the Parasmaipada Frequentative Base.

§ 462. In the three moods of the Present and in the Imperfect Par. the Parasmai. Frequent. base is conjugated like the special base of a root of the third class. The terminations of the Singular Pres. Ind., of the 2 and 3 Sing. Imperf., and of the 3 Sing. Pres. Imper. may be attached to the base with or without इ; when they are added with इ, a penulti-

[§ 464.] CONJUGATION OF VERBS. 197

mate short vowel of the base cannot be gunated; *e. g.* 3 Sing. Pres. Ind. Freq. Par. of rt. भू, (Par. Freq. B. बोभू) बोभोति or बोभवीति; of rt. बुध् (Par. Freq. B. बोबुध्) बोबोद्धि or बोबुधीति; of rt. दा (Par. Freq. B. दादा) दादाति or दादेति; of rt. वृन् (Par. Freq. B. वर्वृन्, or वरिवृन्, or वरीवृन्) वर्वार्ति, or वरिवर्ति, or वरोवर्ति, or वर्वृतीति, or वरिवृतीति, or वरीवृतीति; of rt. कृ (Par. Freq. B. चर्कृ, or चरिकृ, or चरोकृ), चर्कर्ति, or चरिकर्ति, or चरोकर्ति, or चर्करीति, or चरिकरीति, or चरोकरीति.

§ 463. About the formation of the Perfect and the remaining tenses grammarians do not always agree, the chief cause of all difficulties being the doubt, whether the rules which apply to a primitive root, apply also to its Parasmaipada Frequentative Base. As this form of the verb is of very rare ocurrence, it will be sufficient to conjugate one paradigm throughout all its tenses and moods. For special and detailed information on this subject the student must consult the works of the native grammarians.

§ 464. *Paradigm*: The Parasmaipada Frequentative of rt. भू 'to be,' Par. Freq. B. बोभू.

Parasmaipada.

		Pres. Ind.	Pres. Pot.	Pres. Imper.	Imperf.
Sing.	1.	बोभोमि or बोभवीमि	बोभूयाम्	बोभवानि	अबोभवम्
	2.	बोभोषि or बोभवीषि	बोभूयाः	बोभूहि	अबोभोः or अबोभवीः
	3.	बोभोति or बोभवीति	बोभूयात्	बोभोतु or बोभवीतु	अबोभोत् or अबोभवीत्
Dual.	1.	बोभूवः	बोभूयाव	बोभवाव	अबोभूव
	2.	बोभूथः	बोभूयातम्	बोभूतम्	अबोभूतम्
	3.	बोभूतः	बोभूयाताम्	बोभूताम्	अबोभूताम्
Plur.	1.	बोभूमः	बोभूयाम	बोभवाम	अबोभूम
	2.	बोभूथ	बोभूयात	बोभूत	अबोभूत
	3.	बोभुवति	बोभूयुः	बोभुवतु	अबोभवुः

Perfect.

Sing.	1. बोभवांचकर or °चकार &c. or	बोभव or	बोभाव or	बोभूव
	2. बोभवांचकर्थ	बोभविथ		बोभूविथ
	3. बोभवांचकार	बोभाव		बोभूव
Du.	1. बोभवांचकृव	बोभुविव		बोभूविव
	&c.	&c.		&c.

Aorist.

Sing.	1. अबोभाविषम् or अबोभूवम्			
	2. अबोभावीः	अबोभूः or अबोभूवीः or अबोभोः or अबोभवीः
	3. अबोभावीत्	अबोभूत् or अबोभूवीत् or अबोभोत् or अबोभवीत्
Du.	1. अबोभाविष्व	अबोभूव
Pl.	3. अबोभाविषुः	अबोभूवुः	..	..	or अबोभवुः

	Simple Fut.	Periph. Fut.	Condit.	Bened.
Sg. 1.	बोभविष्यामि	बोभवितास्मि	अबोभविष्यम्	बोभूयासम्

	Âtmanepada.	Passive.
Pres. Ind. 3 Sg.	बोभूते	बोभूयते
„ Pot. „ „	बोभुवीत	बोभूयेत
„ Imp. „ „	बोभूताम्	बोभूयताम्
Impf. „ „	अबोभूत	अबोभूयत
Perfect. „ „	बोभवांचक्रे &c.	बोभवांचक्रे &c.
Aorist. „ „	अबोभाविष्ट	अबोभावि
Simple. Fut. „ „	बोभविष्यते	बोभविष्यते or बोभाविष्यते
Periph. Fut. „ „	बोभविता	बोभविता or बोभाविता
Condit. „ „	अबोभविष्यत	अबोभविष्यत or अबोभाविष्यत
Bened. „ „	बोभविषीष्ट	बोभविषीष्ट or बोभाविषीष्ट

§ 465. The four roots अट्, ऋ, अश्, and ऊर्णु mentioned in § 450, a, form their Frequentative thus:

rt. अट् 'to go;'	Â. अटाट्यते;
rt. ऋ 'to go;'	„ अरार्यते; P. अरर्ति or अरिर्यर्ति &c.
rt. अश् 'to pervade;'	„ अशाइयते;
rt. ऊर्णु 'to cover;'	„ ऊर्नोनूयते.

§ 466. The following roots form their Frequentative irregularly:

Root.		Âtm. Frequ.	Par. Frequ.
1. कु cl. 1.	'to sound;'	कोकूयते.	
2. खन्	'to dig;'	चङ्खन्यते or चंखन्यते or चाखायते;	चङ्खनीति or चङ्खन्ति &c.
3. गृ	'to swallow;'	जेगिल्यते;	जागर्ति.
4. चर्	'to walk;'	चञ्चूर्यते or चंचूर्यते;	चञ्चुरीति or चञ्चूर्ति &c.
5. याय्	'to worship;'	चेकायते;	चेकयीति or चेकेति.
6. जन्	'to be born;'	जञ्जन्यते or जंजन्यते or जाजायते;	जञ्जनीति or जञ्जन्ति &c.
7. द्युत्	'to shine;'	देद्युत्यते;	देद्युतीति or देद्योत्ति.
8. फल्	'to burst;'	पम्फुल्यते or पंफुल्यते;	पम्फुलीति or पम्फुल्ति &c.
9. श्वी	'to lie down;'	शाश्वय्यते;	शाशयीति or शाश्वेति.
10. श्वि	'to swell;'	शेश्वीयते or शोश्रूयते;	शेश्वयीति or शेश्वेति.
11. सन्	'to obtain;'	संसन्यते or सासायते;	संसनीति or संसन्ति.
12. हन् in the sense of 'to injure;' otherwise:		जेघ्नीयते; जङ्घन्यते or जंघन्यते;	जङ्घनीति or जङ्घन्ति. &c.

4.—NOMINAL VERBS.

§ 467. Verbs may be formed from nominal bases either by adding to the latter merely the characteristic marks of the tenses and moods and the personal terminations, or by previously deriving a verbal base from the nominal base with the help of some derivative affix, and by adding the characteristic marks of the tenses and moods and the personal terminations to the derivative verbal base formed in this manner. Thus from the nominal base वि 'a bird,' we may form वयति 'he behaves like a bird,' by adding to वि the personal termination ति and by changing वि before this termination just as a root of the first class would be changed in the

Pres. Indic.; or we may form, e. g. from मधु 'honey,' मधुस्यति 'he longs vehemently for honey,' by deriving with the help of the affix स्य from the nominal base मधु 'honey,' the derivative verbal base मधुस्य ' to long vehemently for honey,' and by forming from this base a Pres. Indic. just as it would be formed from the special base of a root of the first class. Verbs thus derived from nominal bases are called *nominal verbs*; they generally convey the notion that a person or thing behaves or is like, or treats a person or thing like, or wishes for, that which is expressed by the nominal base. As these verbs are of comparatively rare occurrence, all the special rules for their formation and conjugation need not be given here; it will suffice to indicate generally the manner in which, and to point out the principal affixes by which, verbal bases are derived from nominal bases and to illustrate the formation and conjugation of the various classes of nominal verbs by a few examples.

Nominal Verbs derived from Nominal Bases

(a.)—*Without a derivative affix, and conjugated in the Parasmaipada.*

§ 468. Nominal verbs may be derived from nominal bases without any special derivative affix, *i. e.* the characteristic signs of the tenses and moods and the personal terminations may be added immediately to the nominal base. The penultimate vowel of a nominal base that ends in a nasal must be lengthened. The verbal bases formed in this manner are conjugated in the Parasmaipada, and convey the notion that a person or thing behaves or is like that which is expressed by the nominal base. In the special tenses the nominal base is treated like a root of the first class; if it contain more than one vowel, its last vowel only undergoes the changes which the vowel of a root of the first class has to undergo. A final अ of a nominal base is dropped before the अ which is added to it in the special tenses; *e. g.*

Nominal Base.	Derivat. Verbal Base.	Pres. Ind. Par.
वि 'a bird;'	वि ' to behave like a bird;'	वयति 'he behaves like a bird.' (Perf. विवाय; Aor. अवायीत्‌ or अवयीत्‌; Bened. वेयात्‌.)

कवि 'a poet;'	कवि 'to behave like a poet;'	कवयति 'he behaves like a poet.'
श्री 'Lakshmî;'	श्री 'to behave like L.'	श्रयति 'she behaves like L.'
भू 'the earth;'	भू 'to behave like the earth;'	भवति 'she behaves like the earth.' (Perf. बुभाव; Aor. अभावीत्.)
पितृ 'a father;'	पितृ 'to behave like a father;'	पितरति 'he behaves like a father.'
कृष्ण 'Krishṇa;'	कृष्ण 'to behave like K;'	कृष्णति 'he behaves like Krishṇa.'
माला 'a garland;'	माला 'to be like a garland;'	मालाति 'it is like a garland.' (Perf. मालांचकार; Aor. अमालासीत्.)
राजन् 'a king;'	राजान् 'to behave like a king;'	राजानति 'he behaves like a king.'

(b).—*By means of the affix य, and conjugated in the Parasmaipada.*

§ 469. Nominal verbs may be derived from nominal bases (except those that end in म् and those that are indeclinable) by adding to the latter the affix य and by conjugating the derivative verbal base, formed in this manner, in the Parasmaipada only. Before the affix य final letters of nominal bases undergo the following changes:—

	Nom. Base.	Deriv. Verb. Base.
Final अ and आ are changed to ई; *e. g.*	पुत्र;	पुत्रीय.
Final इ and उ are lengthened; *e. g.*	कवि;	कवीय.
Final ऋ is changed to री; *e. g.*	कर्तृ;	कर्तरीय.
Final ओ and औ are changed to अव् and आव् respectively; *e. g.*		

Nom. Base. गो; Deriv. Verb. Base. गव्य.
„ „ नौ; „ „ „ नाव्य.

A final nasal is dropped and the preceding vowel changed as an originally final vowel would be changed; *e. g.* Nom. Base राजन्; Deriv. Verb. Base राजीय. Other final consonants remain unchanged; *e. g.*

Nom. Base वाच्; Deriv. Verb. Base वाच्य.
„ „ समिध्; „ „ „ समिध्य.

Penultimate इ and उ of nominal bases in र् or व् are generally lengthened; *e. g.*

Nom. Base गिर्; Deriv. Verb. Base गीर्य
„ „ पुर्; „ „ „ पूर्य.

§ 470. Derivative verbal bases formed in this manner convey the notion that a person wishes for that, or treats a person or thing like that, or looks upon a person or thing as upon that, which is expressed by the nominal base; *e. g.*

Nom. Base.	Deriv. Verb. Base.	Pres. Ind. Par.
पुत्र 'a son;'	पुत्रीय 'to wish for a son;'	पुत्रीयति 'he wishes for a son.' (Perf. पुत्रीयाञ्चकार; Periph. Fut. पुत्रीयिता.)
कवि 'a poet;'	कवीय 'to wish for a poet;'	कवीयति 'he wishes for a poet.'
गो 'a cow;'	गव्य 'to wish for a cow;'	गव्यति 'he wishes for a cow.' (Perf. गव्याञ्चकार; Periph. Fut. गव्यिता.)
राजन् 'a king;'	राजीय 'to wish for a king;'	राजीयति 'he wishes for a king.'
समिध् 'fuel;'	समिध्य 'to wish for fuel;'	समिध्यति 'he wishes for fuel.' (Periph. Fut. समिध्यिता or समिधिता.)
विष्णु 'Vishṇu;'	विष्णूय 'to treat like V.;'	विष्णूयति 'he treats (somebody) like V.'
प्रासाद 'a palace;'	प्रासादीय 'to look upon (anything) as upon a palace;'	प्रासादीयति 'he looks upon (a hut &c.) as upon a palace.'

§ 471. In the following instances the verbal base formed by य conveys a different meaning:

Nom. Base.	Deriv. Verb. Base.	Pres. Ind. Par.
तपस् 'penance;'	तपस्य 'to practise penance;'	तपस्यति 'he practises penance.'
नमस् 'adoration;'	नमस्य 'to adore;'	नमस्यति 'he adores.'

(c).—*By means of the affix* काम्य, *and conjugated in the Parasmaipada.*

§ 472. To express the notion of wishing for that which is denoted by a nominal base, a verbal base may be derived from the latter by adding to it the affix काम्य and by conjugating the derivative verbal base, so formed, in the Parasmai.; *e. g.*

[§ 474.]

Nom. Base.	Deriv. Verb. Base.	Pres. Ind. Par.
पुत्र 'a son;'	पुत्रकाम्य 'to wish for a son;'	पुत्रकाम्यति 'he wishes for a son.' (Perf. पुत्रकाम्याञ्चकार; Periph. Fut. पुत्रकाम्यिता.)
यशस् 'fame;'	यशस्काम्य 'to wish for fame;'	यशस्काम्यति 'he wishes for fame.'

(d).—By means of the affixes स्य or अस्य, and conjugated in the Parasmaipada.

§ 473. Verbal bases are also derived from nominal bases by the addition to the latter of the affixes स्य or अस्य. They are conjugated in the Parasmaipada only and convey the notion of wishing ardently for that which is expressed by the nominal base; *e. g.*

Nom. Base.	Deriv. Verb. Base.	Pres. Ind. Par.
मधु 'honey;'	मधुस्य or मध्वस्य 'to wish ardently for honey;'	मधुस्यति or मध्वस्यति 'he wishes ardently for honey.'
अश्व 'a horse;'	अश्वस्य 'to long ardently for the horse;'	अश्वस्यति '(the mare) longs for the horse.'

(e).—By means of the affix य, and conjugated in the Âtmanepada.

§ 474. By adding to nominal bases the affix य and by conjugating the derivative verbal bases so formed in the Âtmane., nominal verbs are formed which convey the notion of behaving like that which is expressed by a nominal base. Before the affix य of this class of nominal verbs, the final अ of a nominal base is lengthened; आ remains unchanged; other final letters undergo the same changes which they undergo before the affix य in § 469. The final अम् of अप्सरस् and ओजस् must, the final अस् of other nominal bases may optionally, be changed to आ. When the affix य is added to a feminine base, the corresponding masculine base is generally substituted for the latter; *e. g.*

Nom. Base.	Deriv. Verb. Base.	Pres. Ind. Âtm.
कृष्ण 'Krishna;'	कृष्णाय 'to behave like K.;'	कृष्णायते 'he behaves like K.'
अप्सरस् 'an Apsaras;'	अप्सराय 'to behave like an A.;'	अप्सरायते 'she behaves like an A.'

यशस् 'fame,' or 'famous;'	यशस्य or यशस्य	'to behave like one famous;'	यशस्यते or यशस्यते	'he behaves like one who is famous.'
कुमारी 'a girl;'	कुमाराय 'to behave like a girl;'		कुमारायते 'he behaves like a girl.'
युवति 'a maiden;'	युवाय 'to behave like a maiden;'		युवायते 'he behaves like a maiden.'

§ 475. The same affix य is also added to a few nominal bases such as भृश 'frequent,' मन्द 'slow,' पण्डित 'wise,' सुमनस् 'benevolent,' उन्मनस् 'agitated,' &c., to convey the notion of becoming like that, or becoming that, which is expressed by the nominal base. A final consonant of nominal bases to which य may be added in this sense, is dropped; *e. g.*

Nom. Base.	Deriv. Verb. Base.	Pres. Ind. Âtm.
भृश 'frequent;'	भृशाय 'to become frequent;'	भृशायते 'it becomes frequent.'
उन्मनस् 'agitated;'	उन्मनाय 'to become agitated;'	उन्मनायते 'he becomes agitated.'
		(Imperf. उदमनायत.)

§ 476. The following are a few instances in which the affix य conveys a different meaning:—

Nom. Base.	Deriv. Verb. Base.	Pres. Ind. Âtm.
दुःख 'pain;'	दुःखाय 'to suffer pain;'	दुःखायते 'he suffers pain.'
रोमन्य 'ruminating;'	रोमन्याय 'to ruminate;'	रोमन्यायते 'he ruminates.'
वाष्प 'tear;'	वाष्पाय 'to shed tears;'	वाष्पायते 'he sheds tears.'
शब्द 'a sound;'	शब्दाय 'to make a sound;'	शब्दायते 'he makes a sound.'
सुख 'pleasure;'	सुखाय 'to show one's pleasure;'	सुखायते 'he shows his pleasure.'

(*f.*)—*By means of the affix* इ *or* आपि.

§ 477. Some verbal bases are formed from nominal bases by the addition to the latter of the affix इ or आपि; they convey various meanings and are conjugated like the derivative bases in इ or आपि of roots of the tenth class or of Causals. When the affix इ or आपि is added to the bases of adjectives, the latter generally undergo the same changes which they undergo before the Comparative and Superlative affixes ईयस् and इष्ठ ; when it is added to a feminine base, the corresponding masculine base is substituted for the latter ; e. g.

Nom. Base.	Deriv. Verb. Base.	Pres. Ind.
मुण्ड ' shaven;'	मुण्डि ' to shave ;'	मुण्डयति 'he shaves.'
सत्य ' true ;'	सत्यापि ' to declare as true ;'	सत्यापयति 'he declares as true.'
पृथु ' broad ;'	प्रथि 'to declare as broad ;'	प्रथयति 'he declares (anything) broad.'
एनी (Fem. of एत) 'variegated;'	एति 'to declare as variegated ;'	एतयति ' he declares (her) variegated.'

CHAPTER VIII.

PREPOSITIONS AND OTHER VERBAL PREFIXES.

§ 473. The following are the prepositions which are commonly prefixed to verbal roots and their derivatives :—

अति ' over, beyond;' e. g. अति-क्रम् ' to overstep, to go beyond, to transgress, to surpass.'

अधि ' over, above, on ;' e. g. अधि-कृ ' to place over, to appoint ;' अधि-रुह् ' to rise above, to ascend.'

अनु ' after, along, near to ;' e. g. अनु-गम् ' to go after or along ;' अनु-कृ ' to do after, to imitate.'

अप ' away, off;' e. g. अप-गम् ' to go away ;' अप-नी ' to lead off.'

अपि (sometimes पि) ' near to, on ;' e. g. अपि-गम् ' to approach ;' अपि-धा or पि-धा ' to put on, to shut.'

अभि ' towards, to, upon ;' e. g. अभि-गम् ' to go towards or to ;' अभिपत् ' to fall upon.'

अव ' away, off, down ;' e. g. अव-छिद् 'to cut off;' अव-नृ ' to descend.'

आ ' towards, to, at ;' e. g. आ-कृष् ' to draw towards, to attract ;' आ-क्रन्द् ' to shout at.'

उद् ' up, on, out ;' e. g. उद्-इ ' to go up, to rise ;' उद्-सृज् ' to pour out.'

उप ' near to, under ;' e. g. उप-गम् ' to go near to ;' उप-स्था ' to stand near or under.'

नि ' down, into ;' e. g. नि-पद् ' to sit down ;' नि-ग्रह ' to hold down, to suppress.'

निः ' out of, forth from ;' e. g. निर्-गम् ' to go out ;' निष्-पद् ' to spring from.'

परा ' away, back ;' e. g. परा-वृत् ' to turn away or back.'

परि ' round, about ;' e. g. परि-इ ' to go round ;' परि-भ्रम् ' to roam about.'

प्र ' forth, forward, pro- ;' e. g. प्र-क्रम् ' to step forth, to proceed.'

प्रति ' back, re- ;' e. g. प्रति-हन् ' to repel ;' प्रति-वद् ' to respond.'

वि ' apart, dis- ;' e. g. वि-ग्रह ' to take a part ;' वि-धा ' to dispose.'

सम् ' together, con- ;' सं-गम् ' to go together, to assemble ;' सं-चि ' to collect.'

समुपा (i. e. सम् + उप + आ) — गम् ' to come together near to ;' अभिसमा (i. e. अभि + सम् + आ) — गम् ' to approach together,' &c.

§ 479. (a) The initial स् of the roots स्था ' to stand,' and स्तम्भ ' to support,' is dropped when it is immediately preceded by the preposition उद् ; e. g. Periph. Fut. of स्था with उद्, उत्थाता, but Pres. Ind. Par. उत्तिष्ठामि ; Perf. Par. उत्तस्थौ.

(b) The sibilant स् (changeable to ष्) is prefixed to the rt. कृ ' to do,' after the preposition सम्, and after the prepositions उप and परि in the sense of ' to decorate, ornament,' &c. ; likewise to the rt. कृ ' to scatter,' after the prepositions उप and प्रति in the sense of ' to cut, to hurt.' (See § 229, d.)

§ 480. The following words are prefixed to certain roots only; and they share in the peculiarities of prepositions (§ 229, c, and § 504) when they are so prefixed :—

1. अच्छ is prefixed to वद् and to roots which mean ' to go ;' e. g. अच्छ-गम् ' to go towards,' Gerund अच्छगम्य or अच्छगत्य ; अच्छ-वद् ' to salute,' Gerund अच्छोद्य.

2. अन्तर् is prefixed to इ, गम्, धा, भू and similar roots; *e. g.* अन्तर्-इ or अन्तर्-गम् 'to go between, to disappear;' अन्तर्-धा 'to conceal;' अन्तर्-भू 'to be within;' Gerund अन्तरित्य, अन्तर्गम्य or अन्तर्गत्य &c.

3. अलम्, सन्, असन्, ऊरी, खान् and certain other words that are imitative of sound, are prefixed to rt. कृ; *e. g.* अलं-कृ 'to decorate,' सन्-कृ 'to treat with respect,' असन्-कृ 'to treat with disrespect;' ऊरी-कृ 'to promise;' खान्-कृ 'to make the sound which is produced in clearing one's throat;' Gerund अलंकृत्य, सत्कृत्य &c.

4. अस्तम् is prefixed to इ, गम्, या, नी and similar roots; *e. g.* अस्तम्-इ 'to go down, to set;' अस्तं-नी 'to lead down, to cause to set;' Gerund अस्तमित्य &c.

5. आविः and प्रादुः are prefixed to कृ, भू &c.; *e. g.* आविष्-कृ 'to make manifest;' प्रादुर्-भू 'to become manifest;' Gerund आविष्कृत्य, प्रादुर्भूय. See 8.

6. निरः is prefixed to भू, धा &c., and optionally to कृ when it denotes disappearance; *e. g.* निरो-भू 'to disappear', Gerund तिरोभूय. तिरस्-कृ or तिरः-कृ, or in two separate unconnected words तिरः कृ 'to cover, conceal,' Gerund निरस्कृत्य, or तिरःकृत्य, or तिरः कृत्वा.

7. पुरः is prefixed to कृ, भू, गम् &c.; *e. g.* पुरस्-कृ 'to place before;' Gerund पुरस्कृत्य; पुरो-गम् 'to go before,' Gerund पुरोगम्य or पुरोगत्य.

8. साक्षात्, मिथ्या, वशे, प्रादुः, नमः, and certain other words may optionally either be prefixed to the root कृ or remain separate; *e. g.* वशे-कृ or वशे कृ 'to subdue,' Gerund वशेकृत्य or वशे कृत्वा.

§ 481. (*a*) Nouns substantive and adjective may be prefixed to the roots कृ 'to make,' अस् 'to be,' and भू 'to become,' to express the meaning that somebody makes a person or thing, or that a person or thing becomes, that which is denoted by the noun prefixed to कृ, अस्, or भू; *e. g.* कृष्णी-कृ 'to make (that which is not black) black,' कृष्णी-भू 'to become black,' गङ्गीभू 'to become the Ganges.' The roots कृ, अस्, and भू are in this connection treated as they are treated when prepositions are prefixed to them; *e. g.* Gerund of कृष्णी-कृ, कृष्णीकृत्य.

(b) The final letters of nouns which are so prefixed to कृ, अस्, and भू, undergo the following changes:

1. अ and आ are changed to ई, except when final letters of indeclinables; इ and उ are lengthened; and ऋ is changed to री; *e. g.* कृष्णी-भू (from कृष्ण and भू), गङ्गी-भू (from गङ्गा and भू); शुची-भू (from शुचि and भू), गुरू-भू (from गुरु and भू); पितरी-भू (from पितृ and भू). But दोषा-भू (from the indecl. दोषा and भू) 'to become evening.'

2. A final न् is dropped and afterwards the preceding rule is applied to the penultimate vowel; *e. g.* राजी-भू (from राजन् and भू) 'to become a king;' भस्मी-कृ (from भस्मन् and कृ) 'to reduce to ashes.'

3. Nouns with two bases assume their weak base, nouns with three bases their middle base; their finals are first changed as in the Loc. Plur., and afterwards the Sandhi-rules in § 27 &c. are applicable; *e. g.* तिर्यक्-कृ (from तिर्यच् and कृ) 'to put aside.'

§ 482. To express the sense that a person or thing becomes completely that, or that somebody changes a person or thing altogether to that, which is expressed by a certain noun, the affix सात् (the initial स् of which is never changed to ष्) may be added to that noun, and the roots कृ, अस्, and भू, or the root पद् with the preposition सम्, may be added to the derivative so formed; *e. g.* अग्निसाद्भू or अग्निसात्संपद् 'to be changed completely to fire,' भस्मसात्कृ 'to change completely to ashes.' Sometimes the affix सात् conveys the notion that a person or thing becomes, or that somebody makes a person or thing, dependent or the property of that which is denoted by a certain noun; *e. g.* राजसाद्भू 'to become dependent on, or the property of, a king;' राजसात्कृ 'to make (a person or thing) dependent on, or the property of, a king.' The derivatives in सात् which are formed in accordance with this paragraph remain independent words and do not share in the properties of prepositions; therefore the Gerund of कृ after भस्मसात् is कृत्वा (*not* कृत्य) भस्मसात्कृत्वा.

CHAPTER IX.

FORMATION OF NOMINAL BASES.

§ 483. There are a few verbal roots which without undergoing any change may be used also as nominal bases; *e. g.* the root दृश् 'to see,' may also be used as a feminine noun in the sense of 'sight,' or 'an eye;' similarly मुद् as a verbal root means 'to rejoice,' as a feminine noun 'joy;' युभ् as a verbal root 'to fight,' as a feminine noun 'a fight, a battle;' दिश् as a verbal root 'to point out,' as a feminine noun 'a region of the compass.' In the same way the verbal root पद् when the preposition आ is prefixed to it, means 'to go to, to befall,' and आपद् as a feminine noun means 'what befalls a person, misfortune;' the root सद् with the preposition सम् prefixed to it means 'to sit together,' the feminine noun संसद् 'an assembly;' the root नह् with the prepositions उप and आ conveys the sense of 'to bind on to,' the word उपानह् as a feminine substantive that of 'a sandal, a shoe' (that which is bound to the foot).

§ 484. (*a*) Nearly all roots may without undergoing any change be used as the last members of compound nouns, and when employed thus, they convey generally the sense of a Present Participle of the Active; *e. g.* धर्मवुध् 'knowing the law, one who knows the law' (from धर्म and बुध्), वेद-विद् 'knowing the Vedas, one who knows the Vedas' (from वेद and विद्).

(*b*) When a root that ends in a short vowel is used in this manner, the letter त् is affixed to it; *e. g.* विश्वजित् 'conquering all, one who conquers all' (from विश्व and जि); चित्रकृत् 'making pictures,' 'a painter' (from चित्र and कृ). But विश्वपा 'protecting all, one who protects all' (from विश्व and पा) &c..

§ 485. In general, however, nominal bases are derived by means of *affixes* from verbal roots or derivative verbal bases, and from the nominal bases so formed other nominal bases are derived by means of other affixes; or nominal bases are formed by composition. Nominal bases derived from roots or from other nominal bases by means of affixes are called *Derivative Nominal Bases*; nominal bases formed by composition are called *Compound Nominal Bases* or *Compounds*.

I.—DERIVATIVE NOMINAL BASES.

§ 486. The affixes by which nominal bases are derived from roots or derivative verbal bases are called *primary* or *kṛit* affixes, and the nominal bases formed by them *primary nominal bases*. Those affixes by which nominal bases are derived from other nominal bases, are called *secondary* or *taddhita* affixes, and the nominal bases formed by them *secondary nominal bases*; *e. g.* the bases कर्तृ 'a doer,' मति 'intelligence,' बोधयितृ 'one who causes to know,' are primary nominal bases, the first derived by the primary or kṛit affix तृ from rt. कृ 'to do,' the second derived by the kṛit affix ति from the root मन् 'to think,' and the third derived by the kṛit affix तृ from the causal base बोधि 'to cause to know' (from rt. बुध्). But the bases कर्तृत्व 'the state of a doer,' मतिमत् 'possessed of intelligence,' अपुत्रता 'childlessness,' are secondary nominal bases, derived, the first by the secondary or taddhita affix त्व from the primary nominal base कर्तृ 'a doer,' the second by the taddhita affix मत् from the primary nominal base मति 'intelligence,' and the third by the taddhita affix ता from the compound nominal base अपुत्र 'childless.'

§ 487. There is a peculiar class of primary or kṛit affixes to which the native grammarians have applied the technical denomination of *Uṇâdi*-affixes, *i. e.* a list of affixes headed by the affix उण् (or उ with the mute or indicatory letter ण् attached to it). They form, like other kṛit affixes, primary nouns from verbal roots, but are given in special lists because their application is rare and because the nouns derived by them are either formed very irregularly or the connection between the meanings of the nouns derived by them and the roots from which they are supposed to have been derived, is not so clearly discernible as it is in the case of other primary nouns. Instances of nouns formed by means of Uṇâdi-affixes are अश्व 'a horse,' from अश् 'to pervade,' उष्ट्र 'a camel,' derived from उष् 'to burn,' &c.

§ 488. The rules of Sandhi which apply to the final letters of roots or derivative verbal bases and the initial letters of primary or kṛit affixes are generally those stated in § 44 &c. and § 307 &c. The same rules apply also to the final letters of nominal bases and initial vowels or initial य् of secondary or taddhita affixes. Before taddhita affixes which begin with any other consonant than य्, nominal bases that end in consonants must first undergo the same changes which they undergo in their Loc. Plur., afterwards the rules given in § 27 &c. are applied; there are, however, exceptions.

§ 489. The only primary nouns, the formation of which will be taught here, are the Participles, the Gerund, the Infinitive, and the Verbal Adjectives. In § 530 the student will find a list of the most common Secondary or Taddhita affixes.

1.—PARTICIPLES.

(a)—Participles of the Present tense.

§ 490. (a) The *Participle of the Present Parasmai.* is formed by the addition of the affix अत् to the special base of the Pres. Ind. Par.; when the special base is changeable, अत् is added to the special weak base. Final letters of the special base undergo before अत् the same changes which they undergo before the termination अन्ति or अति of the 3 Plur. Pres. Ind. Par.; *e. g.*

Root.	Special B.	3 Pl. Pres. Ind. Par.	Partic.
भू cl. 1.	भव;	भवन्ति;	भवत् 'being.'
दिव् cl. 4.	दीव्य;	दीव्यन्ति;	दीव्यत् 'playing.'
तुद् cl. 6.	तुद;	तुदन्ति;	तुदत् 'striking.'
	Weak B.		
द्विष् cl. 2.	द्विष्;	द्विषन्ति;	द्विषत् 'hating.'
या cl. 2.	या;	यान्ति;	यात् 'going.'
हु cl. 3.	जुह्;	जुह्वति;	जुह्वत् 'sacrificing.'
सु cl. 5.	सुन्व्;	सुन्वन्ति;	सुन्वत् 'squeezing out.'
आप् cl. 5.	आप्नु;	आप्नुवन्ति;	आप्नुवत् 'obtaining.'
रुध् cl. 7.	रुन्ध्;	रुन्धन्ति;	रुन्धत् 'obstructing.'
तन् cl. 8.	तन्व्;	तन्वन्ति;	तन्वत् 'stretching.'
क्री cl. 9.	क्रीणी;	क्रीणन्ति;	क्रीणत् 'buying.'

	Root.	Special B.	3 Pl. Pres. Ind. Par.	Partic.
	चुर् cl. 10.	चोरय ;	चोरयन्ति ;	चोरयत् 'stealing.'
	बुध् Causal.	बोधय ;	बोधयन्ति ;	बोधयत् 'causing to know.'
	,, Desiderat.	बुबोधिष ;	बुबोधिषन्ति ;	बुबोधिषत् 'wishing to know.'

(b) The Declension and formation of the feminine base of this participle has been treated of in § 101 &c.

(c) विद् cl. 2. 'to know,' forms its Pres. Partic. Par. either regularly विदत्, or it forms by means of the affix of the Partic. of the Red. Perf. Par. विद्वस् (declined § 124).

§ 491. (a) The *Participle of the Present Âtmane.* is formed by the addition of the affix मान (changeable to माण by § 58, Fem. माना or माणा) to the special base of the Present; but when the special base is changeable, आन (instead of मान) is added to the special weak base. Final अ of the special base remains unchanged before मान ; final letters of the special weak base undergo before आन the same changes which they undergo before the termination अते of the 3 Plur. Pres. Ind. Âtm. ; *e. g.*

Rt. भू cl. 1. Spec. B. भव ; Partic. भवमान.
Rt. दिव् cl. 4. ,, ,, दीव्य ; ,, दीव्यमान.
Rt. तुद् cl. 6. ,, ,, तुद ; ,, तुदमान.

	Root.	Sp. Weak B.	3 Plur. Pres. Ind. Âtm.	Partic.
	द्विष् ; cl. 2.	द्विष् ;	द्विषते	द्विषाण.
	हु cl. 3.	जुह् ;	जुह्वते ;	जुह्वान.
	सु cl. 5.	सुन् ;	सुन्वते ;	सुन्वान.
	आप् cl. 5.	आप्नु ;	आप्नुवते ;	आप्नुवान.
	रुध् cl. 7.	रुन्ध् ;	रुन्धते ;	रुन्धान.
	तन् cl. 8.	तनु ;	तन्वते ;	तन्वान.
	क्री cl. 9.	क्रीणी ;	क्रीणते ;	क्रीणान.
	चुर् cl. 10. Special Base	चोरय ;	Partic.	चोरयमाण.
	बुध् ; Spec. B. of the Caus.	बोधय ;	,,	बोधयमान.
	,, ,, ,, ,, Desid.	बुबोधिष ;	,,	बुबोधिषमाण.

(b) This Participle is declined according to § 131

(c) आस् cl. 2. 'to sit,' forms its Pres. Partic. Âtm. irregularly आसीन 'sitting.'

§ 492. The *Participle of the Present Passive* is formed by the addition of the affix मान (changeable to माण by § 59) to the passive base in य. For its declension see § 131; *e.g.*

Rt.	Passive B.	Partic.	
तुद्;	तुद्य;	तुद्यमान	'who or what is struck.'
चि;	चीय;	चीयमान	'who or what is gathered.'
श्रु;	श्रूय;	श्रूयमाण	'who or what is heard.'
कृ;	क्रिय;	क्रियमाण	'who or what is done.'
दा;	दीय;	दीयमान	'who or what is given.'
चुर् cl. 10.	चोर्य;	चोर्यमाण	'who or what is stolen.'
बुध् Caus.	बोध्य;	बोध्यमान	'who or what is caused to know.'
Desid.	बुबोधिष्य;	बुबोधिष्यमाण	'who or what is desired to know.'

(b).—*Particples of the Simple Future.*

§ 493. The *Participle of the Simple Future in Parasmai.* is formed by the addition of the affix अत् to the base of the Simple Fut. Par. in स्य or ष्य; the participle of the Simple Future in *Âtmane.* and in *Passive* by the addition of the affix मान to the base of the Simple Fut. Âtm. and Pass. in स्य or ष्य. Before the affix अत् the final अ of the Future base is dropped, before the affix मान it remains unchanged. For the declension and the formation of the Feminine of these particples see § 101 and § 131; *e. g.*

Base of the Simple Fut.		Future Partic.		
rt. दा; in Par. and Âtm.	दास्य;	Par. दास्यन् Âtm. दास्यमान	}	'one who will give.'
", " in Pass.	{ दास्य or दायिष्य;	Pass. दास्यमान " दायिष्यमाण	}	'who or what will be given.'

Base of the Simple Fut.		Future Partic-	
rt. भू; in Par. and Âtm.	भविष्य;	Par. भविष्यत् Âtm. भविष्यमाण	} 'who or what will be.'
,, ,, in Pass.	{ भविष्य or भाविष्य;	Pass. भविष्यमाण ,, भाविष्यमाण	
rt. बुध्; in Par. Âtm. and Pass.	बोधिष्य;	Par. बोधिष्यत् Âtm. बोधिष्यमाण	} 'who or what will know.'
		Pass. बोधिष्यमाण	{ 'who or what will be known.'
rt. चुर्; in Par. and Âtm.	चोरयिष्य;	Par. चोरयिष्यत् Âtm. चोरयिष्यमाण	} 'who or what will steal.'
,, ,, in Pass.	{ चोरयिष्य or चोरिष्य;	Pass. चोरयिष्यमाण ,, चोरिष्यमाण	} 'who or what will be stolen.'

(c).—*Participles of the Perfect.*

§ 494. (a) *The Participle of the Reduplicated Perfect Parasmai.* is generally formed by the addition of the affix वस् to the weak base of the Red. Perfect. This affix is added by means of the intermediate vowel इ to all reduplicated weak bases which consist of only one syllable (except those of जन् and खन् in § 314); and it may be added with or without the intermediate इ to the reduplicated weak bases of the roots गम् 'to go,' हन् 'to kill,' दृश् 'to see,' विश् 'to enter,' and विद् cl. 6 'to find;' *e. g.*

Rt.	Red. Weak B.	Partic. of the Red. Perf. Par.	
भिद्;	बिभिद्;	बिभिद्वस्	'who or what has split.'
तुद्;	तुतुद्;	तुतुद्वस्	'who or what has struck.'
नी;	निनी;	निनीवस्	'who or what has led.'
स्तु;	तुष्टु;	तुष्टुवस्	'who or what has praised.'
कृ;	चक्कृ;	चक्रृवस्	'who or what has done.'
अस्;	आस्;	आसिवस्	'who or what has thrown.'
इष्;	ईष्;	ईषिवस्	'who or what has wished.'
दा;	दद्;	ददिवस्	'who or what has given.'
घस्;	जक्ष्;	जक्षिवस्	'who or what has eaten.'
पच्;	पेच्;	पेचिवस्	'who or what has cooked.'

वच्;	ऊच्;	अचिवस्	'who or what has spoken.'
यज्;	ईज्;	ईजिवस्	'who or what has sacrificed.'
But अञ्ज्;	आनञ्ज्;	आनञ्जिवस्	'who or what has anointed.'
तॄ;	तेर्;	तितीर्वस्	'who or what has crossed.'
गम्;	Ptc. जग्मिवस् or जगन्वस्	(§ 307, b)	'who or what has gone.'
हन्;	,, जघ्निवस् or जघन्वस्		'who or what has killed.'
दृश्;	,, ददृशिवस् or ददृश्वस्		'who or what has seen.'

(b) The declension and formation of the Feminine of this Participle has been treated of in § 122—125.

§ 495. The *Participle of the Red. Perfect Âtmane.* is generally formed by the addition of the affix आन (changeable to आण) to the weak base of the Red. Perfect; final letters of the base undergo before आन the same changes which they undergo before the termination इरे of the 3 Plur. Âtm. For the declension of this participle see § 131; *e. g.*

Rt.	Red. Weak B.	3 Plur. Âtm.	Partic. Red. Perf. Âtm.
भिद्;	बिभिद्;	बिभिदिरे;	बिभिदान.
नी;	निनी;	निन्यिरे;	निन्यान.
स्तु;	तुष्टु;	तुष्टुविरे;	तुष्टुवान.
कृ;	चकृ;	चक्रिरे;	चक्राण.
दा;	दद्;	ददिरे;	ददान.
यज्;	ईज्;	ईजिरे;	ईजान.
But हृ;	चकॄ;	चकरिरे;	चिकिराण.

§ 496. The *Participles of the Periphrastic Perfect in Parasmai. and Âtmane.* are formed by the addition of the Participles of the Redupl. Perf. of the auxiliary verbs अस्, भू, or कृ to the base in आम्; *e. g.*

Rt.	Partic. of the Periph. Perf.
उन्द्;	उन्दामासिवस् or उन्दांबभूवस् or उन्दांचकृवस्.
आस्;	आसामासिवस् or आसांबभूवस् or आसांचक्राण.
चुर्; Par.	चोरयामासिवस् or चोरयांबभूवस् or चोरयांचकृवस्.
Âtm.	चोरयामासिवस् or चोरयांबभूवस् or चोरयांचक्राण.

(d).—*The Past Participles.*

§ 497. (a) The *Past Passive Participle* is generally formed by the addition to the root or to the derivative verbal base, of the affix त (Fem. base ता) ; sometimes by the addition to the root of the affix न (changeable to ण by § 58; Fem. base ना or णा); *e. g.*

rt. स्ना 'to bathe;'	Past Pass. Ptc.			स्नात 'bathed.'
rt. चि 'to gather;'	,,	,,	,,	चित 'gathered.'
rt. नी 'to lead;'	,,	,,	,,	नीत 'led.'
rt. स्तु 'to praise;'	,,	,,	,,	स्तुत 'praised.'
rt. भू 'to become;'	,,	,,	,,	भूत 'become.'
rt. कृ 'to do;'	,,	,,	,,	कृत 'done.'
rt. मुच् 'to loosen;'	,,	,,	,,	मुक्त 'loosened.'
But rt. कॄ 'to scatter;'	,,	,,	,,	कीर्ण 'scattered.'
rt. भिद् 'to split;'	,,	,,	,,	भिन्न 'split.'
Causal B. बोधि (of rt. बुध्),	,,	,,	,,	बोधित 'made to know.'
Desider. B. चिकीर्ष (of rt. कृ),	,,	,,	,,	चिकीर्षित 'desired to do.'

(*b*) For the declension of this Participle see § 131.

§ 498. (*a*) The affix न is generally added to roots ending in ऋ (changeable to इर्, or, after a labial letter, to ऊर्), in र्, and in द्; to those roots ending in आ, ए, ऐ, and ओ (changeable to आ) which begin with a conjunct consonant and contain a semivowel; and to certain other roots such as भुज् 'to bend,' वृ 'to grow,' हा 'to go,' हा 'to abandon,' लू 'to cut,' लो 'to adhere' &c. It is always added immediately to the root; *e. g.*

rt. कृ 'to scatter;'	Past Pass. Ptc.			कीर्ण 'scattered.'
rt. तूर् 'to strike;'	,,	,,	,,	तूर्ण 'struck.'
rt. भिद् 'to split;'	,,	,,	,,	भिन्न 'split.'
rt. ग्लै 'to fade;'	,,	,,	,,	ग्लान 'faded.'
rt. भुज् 'to bend;'	,,	,,	,,	भुग्न 'bent.'
rt. व्रश्च् 'to tear;'	,,	,,	,,	वृक्ण 'torn.'
rt. हा 'to go;'	,,	,,	,,	हान 'gone.'
rt. हा 'to abandon;'	,,	,,	,,	हीन 'abandoned.'
rt. लू 'to cut;'	,,	,,	,,	लून 'cut.'
rt. सद् 'to sit;'	,,	,,	,,	सन्न (with prep. नि &c. निषण्ण &c.)

§ 499.] FORMATION OF NOMINAL BASES.

(b) The following are common exceptions to this rule: rt. मद् 'to become intoxicated,' P. P. Ptc. मत्त ' intoxicated;' rt. ख्या ' to name,' ख्यात 'named, known;' ध्यै 'to think,' ध्यात 'thought.'

(c) Some roots take optionally त or न; rt. उन्द् 'to moisten,' P. P. Ptc. उत्त or उन्न 'moistened;' rt. नुद् 'to strike,' नुत्त or नुन्न 'struck;' rt. घ्रा 'to smell,' घ्रात or घ्राण 'smelt;' rt. लै 'to protect,' लात or लाण 'protected;' rt. ह्री 'to be ashamed,' ह्रीत or ह्रीण 'ashamed.' Rt. दिव् 'to play,' generally forms द्यून 'played,' but when it means 'to gamble,' it forms द्यून. Rt. विद् 'to know,' forms विदित 'known;' in other senses it forms वित्त or विन्न, &c.

§ 499. (a) The affix त is added to many roots without intermediate इ, to other roots it must be added by means of the intermediate इ, and to a few roots it may be added optionally with or without the intermediate इ. In general त is added without the intermediate इ to all those roots ending in vowels which take त, and to those monosyllabic roots ending in consonants to which any other affix must or may be added without intermediate इ; e.g.

rt. श्रि	'to go;'	Past Pass. Ptc.	श्रित 'gone.'
rt. भू	'to become;'	,, ,, ,,	भूत 'become.'
rt. सिच्	'to sprinkle;'	,, ,, ,,	सिक्त 'sprinkled.'
rt. युज्	'to join;'	,, ,, ,,	युक्त 'joined.'
rt. गुह्	'to cover;'	,, ,, ,,	गूढ 'covered.'
rt. वृध्	'to grow;' (§ 362, d)	,, ,, ,,	वृद्ध 'grown.'

(b) When त is added without intermediate इ to roots ending in consonants, the rules given in § 307 &c. must be observed; e.g.

rt. मुच्	'to loosen;' Past Pass. Ptc.	मुक्त 'loosened.'
rt. त्यज्	'to abandon;' ,, ,, ,,	त्यक्त 'abandoned.'
rt. प्रछ्	'to ask;' ,, ,, ,,	पृष्ट 'asked.'
rt. सृज्	'to dismiss;' ,, ,, ,,	सृष्ट 'dismissed.'
rt. लभ्	'to obtain;' ,, ,, ,,	लब्ध 'obtained.'
rt. वृध्	'to grow;' ,, ,, ,,	वृद्ध 'grown;'

rt. इष्	' to wish;'	Past Pass. Ptc.			इष्ट	'wished.'
rt. दह्	' to burn;'	,,	,,	,,	दग्ध	'burnt.'
rt. लिह्	' to lick;'	,,	,,	,,	लीढ	'licked.'
rt. मुह्	' to faint;'	,,	,,	,,	मुग्ध or मूढ	'faint.'
rt. नह्	' to bind;'	,,	,,	,,	नद्ध	'bound.'
rt. सह्	' to bear;'	,,	,,	,,	सोढ	'borne.'

(c) त may be added optionally with or without the intermediate इ to rt. क्लिश्, P. P. Ptc. क्लिष्ट or क्लिशित 'afflicted;' rt. त्वर्, P. P. Ptc. त्वरित or तूर्ण ' swift;' rt. पू cl. 1, P. P. Ptc. पवित or पून ' purified;' and to certain other roots provided the Past Pass. Ptc. is used impersonally or conveys the sense of ' beginning' to perform the action or to undergo the state which is expressed by the root; e. g. rt. स्विद् forms स्विदित (or स्वेदित) or स्विन्न in the sense of ' beginning to perspire,' or when the Partic. is used impersonally (स्विदितमनेन or स्विन्नमनेन ' he has perspired').

(d) To all other roots, and to all derivative verbal bases except those which end in इ, त must be added by means of the intermediate इ; likewise (against the general rule under (a)) to क्षुध् ' to be hungry' (P. P. Ptc. क्षुधित), पत् ' to fall' (पतित), वस् ' to dwell' (उषित), शी ' to lie down,' (शयित) &c. After ग्रह ' to seize,' the intermediate इ must be lengthened (P. P. Ptc. गृहीत); e. g.

rt. शङ्क् ' to suspect;' Past Pass. Ptc. शङ्कित ' suspected.'

rt. निन्द् ' to blame;' ,, ,, ,, निन्दित ' blamed.'

rt. चुर् ' to steal;' Deriv. Base. चोरि; Past P. Ptc. चोरित 'stolen.'

rt. बुध् ' to know;' Caus. Base बोधि; Past P. Ptc. of Caus. बोधित 'made to know.'

,, ,, Desid. Base. बुबोधिष; Past P. Ptc. Desid. बुबोधिषित ' desired to know.'

,, ,, ,, Ātm. Freq. Base. बोबुध्य; Past P. Ptc. Freq. बोबुधित.

rt. भू ' to be;' ,, ,, ,, बोभूय; ,, ,, ,, बोभूयित.

§ 500. Before the affixes of the Past Passive Participle roots undergo the following changes:—

(a) The roots mentioned in § 373, b, 6, are changed in the same manner in which they are changed in the Benedictive Par.; e. g.

rt. वच् 'to speak;' Past Pass. Ptc. उक्त 'spoken.'
rt. वद् 'to speak;' ,, ,, ,, उदित 'spoken.'
rt. वह् 'to carry;' ,, ,, ,, ऊढ 'carried.'
rt. यज् 'to sacrifice;' ,, ,, ,, इष्ट 'sacrificed.'
rt. व्यध् 'to pierce;' ,, ,, ,, विद्ध 'pierced.'
rt. प्रछ् 'to ask;' ,, ,, ,, पृष्ट 'asked.'
rt. ह्वे 'to call;' ,, ,, ,, हूत 'called.'
rt. श्वि 'to swell;' ,, ,, ,, शून 'swollen.'
rt. ज्या 'to decay;' ,, ,, ,, जीन 'decayed.'
rt. शास् 'to rule;' ,, ,, ,, शिष्ट 'ruled.'

(b) A penultimate radical nasal is generally dropped; e. g.

rt. वन्ध् 'to bind;' Past Pass. Ptc. बद्ध 'bound.'
rt. इन्ध् 'to kindle;' ,, ,, ,, इद्ध 'kindled.'
rt. दंश् 'to bite;' ,, ,, ,, दष्ट 'bitten.'
rt. ग्रन्थ् 'to tie;' ,, ,, ,, ग्रथित 'tied.'
rt. भञ्ज् 'to break;' ,, ,, ,, भग्न 'broken.'

(c) The penultimate vowel of roots that end in a nasal is generally lengthened before त (without the intermediate इ); e. g.

rt. क्रम् 'to step;' Past Pass Ptc. क्रान्त 'stepped.'
rt. शम् 'to grow calm;' ,, ,, ,, शान्त 'calm.'

(d) The roots गम् 'to go,' नम् 'to bend,' यम् 'to restrain,' रम् 'to sport,' मन् 'to think', हन् 'to kill', वन् cl. 1, 'to serve,' and all roots of the eighth class that end in a nasal, drop their final nasal before त; e. g.

rt. गम् 'to go;' Past Pass. Ptc. गत 'gone.'
rt. हन् 'to kill;' ,, ,, ,, हत 'killed.'
rt. तन् 'to stretch;' ,, ,, ,, तत 'stretched.'

(e) The roots खन् 'to dig,' जन् 'to bear,' and सन् 'to obtain,' drop their final न् and lengthen at the same time their penultimate vowel before त; e. g.

    rt. खन् 'to dig;' Past Pass. Ptc. खात 'dug.'

(f) A final radical व् is changed to ऊ before त (without intermediate इ) and न; but when preceded by र, it is dropped; e. g.

    rt. सिव् 'to sew;' Past Pass. Ptc. स्यूत 'sewn.'
    rt. दिव् 'to play;' ,, ,, ,, द्यूत or द्यून (§ 498, c).
    rt. उर्व् 'to hurt;' ,, ,, ,, ऊर्ण 'hurt' (§ 46).

(g) Roots of the first class with penultimate उ may optionally substitute Guṇa for their radical vowel before the affix त (when added with intermediate इ), provided the Past Pass. Ptc. is used impersonally or conveys the sense of 'beginning' to perform the action or to undergo the state expressed by the root; e. g. rt. मुद् 'to delight,' forms usually मुदित 'delighted;' but in the sense of 'beginning to delight,' or when the Past Pass. Ptc. is used impersonally, it forms मुदित or मोदित. In a few other roots, such as स्विद् cl. 1, to which the affix of the Past Pass. Ptc. may under certain conditions (§ 499, c) optionally be added with the intermediate इ, Guṇa *must* be substituted for the radical vowel when त is added with इ; e. g. स्वेदित or स्विन्न; but of rt. स्विद् cl. 4, स्विदित or स्विन्न.

§ 501. The following roots form their Past Passive Partic. irregularly:

(a) दो 'to cut;'   Past Pass. Ptc.   दित 'cut.'
    धा 'to place;'   ,, ,, ,,   हित 'placed.'
    मा 'to measure;' \
    मे 'to barter;' } ,, ,, ,,   मित 'measured,' 'bartered.'
    सो 'to finish;'   ,, ,, ,,   सित 'finished.'
    स्था 'to stand;'   ,, ,, ,,   स्थित 'standing.'
    गै 'to sing;'   ,, ,, ,,   गीत 'sung.'
    धे 'to suck;'   ,, ,, ,,   धीत 'sucked.'
    पा 'to drink;'   ,, ,, ,,   पीत 'drunk.'
    छो 'to split;'   ,, ,, ,,   छात or छित 'split.'
    शो 'to sharpen;'   ,, ,, ,,   शात or शित 'sharpened.'
    वे 'to weave;'   ,, ,, ,,   उत 'woven.'
    दरिद्रा 'to be poor;' ,, ,, ,,   दरिद्रित 'poor.'

(b) The roots दा 'to give,' and दे 'to protect,' form in the Past Pass. Ptc. दत्त 'given,' 'protected;' this participle may drop its initial द, when a preposition that ends in a vowel is prefixed to it; e. g. प्रदत्त or प्रत्त; when द has thus been dropped a preceding इ or उ is lengthened; e. g. निदत्त or नीत्त.

(c) Alphabetical list of some other roots which form their Past Pass. Ptc. irregularly and have not yet been mentioned in the preceding rules:—

rt. अद् 'to eat;'	Past Pass. Ptc.	जग्ध 'eaten.'
rt. अव् 'to protect;'	,, ,, ,,	ऊत 'protected.'
rt. क्षि 'to destroy;'	,, ,, ,,	क्षित or क्षीण 'destroyed.'
rt. ज्वर् 'to be ill;'	,, ,, ,,	जूर्ण 'ill' (as with fever).
rt. धाव् 'to cleanse;'	,, ,, ,,	धौत 'cleansed.'
rt. प्याय् 'to grow;'	,, ,, ,,	प्यान or पीन 'grown.'
rt. मज्ज् 'to dive;'	,, ,, ,,	मग्न 'immersed.'
rt. मुर्छ 'to faint;'	,, ,, ,,	मूर्त or मूर्छित 'fainting.'
rt. ट्यै	,, ,, ,,	श्यान 'contracted.' / शीन 'coagulated.' / शित 'cold.'
rt. श्रा 'to cook;'	,, ,, ,,	श्राण or शृत 'cooked.'
rt. स्फाय् 'to grow;'	,, ,, ..	स्फीत 'grown.'
rt. ह्लाद् 'to delight;'	,, ,, ,,	हृन्न 'delighted.'

§ 502. A few roots cannot form the Past Pass. Ptc. in त or न; its meaning however is expressed by certain adjectives derived from the roots; e. g. rt. क्षै 'to waste,' क्षाम 'wasted;' rt. पच् 'to cook,' पक्व 'cooked, ripe;' rt. शुष् 'to become dry,' शुष्क 'dry;' rt. कृश् 'to emaciate,' कृश 'emaciated' (but e. g. with prep. प्र, प्रकृशित); rt. फल् 'to burst open,' फुल्ल 'blown' (but e. g. with prep. प्र, प्रफुल्ल or प्रफुल्ल) &c.

§ 503. A *Past Active Ptc.* is derived from the Past Pass. Ptc. in त or न by the addition to the latter of the affix वत् ; e. g.

Rt.	Past Pass. Ptc.	Past Active Ptc.
स्ना 'bathe;'	स्नात 'bathed;'	स्नातवत् 'one who has bathed.'
कृ 'to do;'	कृत 'done;'	कृतवत् 'one who has done.'
भिद् 'to split;'	भिन्न 'split;'	भिन्नवत् 'one who has split.'

For the declension and the formation of the Feminine of this participle see § 111 &c.

2.—THE GERUND.

§ 504. (a) The Gerund is generally formed either by the addition of the affix त्वा, or by the addition of the affix य, to the root or derivative verbal base. The affix त्वा is added to roots or derivative verbal bases to which no preposition (nor any of the words mentioned in § 480, 481) is prefixed; य is added to roots or derivative verbal bases to which a preposition or one of the words mentioned in § 480, 481, is prefixed; e. g.

rt. नी ' to lead ;' Ger. नीत्वा ' having led.'

rt. चुर् ' to steal ;' Deriv. Base. चोरि ; Ger. चोरयित्वा ' having stolen.'

rt. बुध् 'to know;' Deriv. Caus. B. बोधि, Ger. बोधयित्वा 'having caused to know.'

Ger. of rt. नी with prep. वि, विनीय ' having trained.'

Ger. of the Caus. of rt. बुध् with prep. प्र, प्रबोध्य 'having informed.'

(b) The negative prefix अ 'not' may be prefixed to either form of the Gerund; e. g.

अ + नीत्वा = अनीत्वा 'not having led.'

अ + चोरयित्वा = अचोरयित्वा 'not having stolen.'

अ + विनीय; = अविनीय; अ + प्रबोध्य = अप्रबोध्य.

(c) The meaning of the Sanskrit Gerund may sometimes in English be rendered by prepositions or prepositional phrases; e. g. नीत्वा or गृहीत्वा or आदाय 'having led or taken,' i. e. 'together with;' मुक्त्वा or विहाय 'having left or abandoned,' i. e. ' without,' &c.

(a).—*Formation of the Gerund by means of the affix* त्वा.

§ 505. The affix त्वा is added to many roots without intermediate इ; to some roots it may be added optionally with or without intermediate इ; to other roots and to derivative verbal bases it is added with the intermediate इ.

(a) त्वा is added without intermediate इ to all monosyllabic roots ending in vowels (except श्रि, डो, श्रो, पू and जॄ), to ऊर्णु 'to cover,' and to those roots mentioned in § 366, a, 2, which do not fall under rules (b) and (c) below; e. g.

rt.	ज्ञा	'to know;'	Ger.	ज्ञात्वा.
rt.	जि	'to conquer;'	,,	जित्वा.
rt.	नी	'to lead;'	,,	नीत्वा.
rt.	यु	'to join;'	,,	युत्वा.
rt.	भू	'to become;'	,,	भूत्वा.
rt.	कृ	'to do;'	,,	कृत्वा.
rt.	तॄ	'to cross;'	,,	तीर्त्वा.
rt.	वे	'to protect;'	,,	वात्वा.
rt.	मुच्	'to loosen;'	,,	मुक्त्वा.
rt.	छिद्	'to split;'	,,	छित्त्वा.

(b) त्वा may be added optionally with or without intermediate इ, to the roots enumerated in § 366, b, 2 and 3 (except ब्रश्च), to इष् (इच्छति) 'to wish,' रिष् 'to hurt,' रुष् 'to hurt,' लुभ् 'to desire,' सह् 'to bear,' पू 'to purify,' to many roots ending in भन् and अम् (e. g. to खन्, तन्, मन्, कम्, क्रम्, दम्, भ्रम्, श्रम्), and to some other roots such as वृन् 'to be,' स्तम्भ् 'to support,' &c. ; e. g.

rt.	अञ्ज्	'to anoint;'	Ger.	अञ्जित्वा, or अङ्क्त्वा or अक्त्वा.
rt.	इष्	'to wish;'	,,	एषित्वा, or इष्ट्वा.
rt.	खन्	'to dig;'	,,	खनित्वा, or खात्वा.
rt.	दम्	'to tame;'	,,	दमित्वा, or दान्त्वा.
rt.	वृन्	'to be;'	,,	वर्तित्वा, or वृत्त्वा.

(c) त्वा must be added with intermediate इ to क्षुध् 'to be hungry,' जृ 'to become old,' स्रंस् 'to tear,' वस् 'to dwell,' to all roots that do not fall under (a) and (b), and to derivative verbal bases ; e.g.

    rt. क्षुध् ' to be hungry ;' Ger. क्षुधित्वा or क्षोधित्वा.
    rt. जीव् ' to live ;'   ,, जीवित्वा.
    rt. बुध् Caus. B. बोधि ; ,, बोधयित्वा.
    Desid. B. बुबोधिष ,, बुबोधिषित्वा.

(d) The intermediate इ must be lengthened after the rt. ग्रह् 'to seize' (Ger. गृहीत्वा), and it may optionally be lengthened after rt. जृ 'to become old' (Ger. जरित्वा or जरीत्वा).

§ 506. When त्वा is added to a root without intermediate इ, § 48, and 296, a, must be observed; final radical consonants combine with the initial त् of त्वा as they combine with the initial त् of the affix त (§ 499 b); moreover the root is liable to all the changes described in § 500 (a) —(f); e.g.

    rt. तृ ' to cross ;'   Ger. तीर्त्वा.
    rt. पृ ' to fill ;'   ,, पूर्त्वा.
    rt. त्रै ' to protect ;'   ,, त्रात्वा.
    rt. वच् ' to speak ;'   ,, उक्त्वा.
    rt. यज् ' to sacrifice ;' ,, इष्ट्वा.
    rt. बन्ध् ' to bind ;'   ,, बद्ध्वा.
    rt. शम् ' to grow calm ;' ,, शान्त्वा.
    rt. गम् ' to go ;'   ,, गत्वा.
    rt. खन् ' to dig ;'   ,, खात्वा.
    rt. दिव् ' to play ;'   ,, द्यूत्वा.

§ 507. When त्वा is added to a root by means of the intermediate इ, the following rules apply to the root:

(a) Guṇa is generally substituted for penultimate short vowels, and for final radical vowels. Penultimate nasals are not dropped; e. g.

[§ 508.] FORMATION OF NOMINAL BASES. 225

rt. दिव् 'to play;' Ger. देविद्वा (or द्यूत्वा).
rt. वृत् 'to be;' ,, वर्तित्वा (or वृत्त्वा).
rt. शी 'to lie down;' ,, शयित्वा.
rt. पू 'to purify;' ,, पविद्वा (or पूत्वा).
rt. जॄ 'to grow old;' ,, जरित्वा or जरीत्वा.
rt. स्रंस् 'to fall;' ,, स्रंसित्वा (or स्रस्त्वा).

(b) Guṇa may optionally be substituted for penultimate इ and उ of roots which begin with consonants and end in any other consonant than व्; likewise for the penultimate ऋ of तृष् 'to thirst,' मृष् 'to bear,' and कृश् 'to emaciate;' e.g.

rt. द्युत् 'to shine;' Ger. द्युतित्वा or द्योतित्वा.
rt. लिख् 'to write;' ,, लिखित्वा or लेखित्वा.
rt. क्लिद् 'to be moist;' ,, क्लिदित्वा or क्लेदित्वा (or क्लित्त्वा).
rt. तृष् 'to thirst;' ,, तृषित्वा or तर्षित्वा.

(c) Guṇa is (against a and b) not substituted for the radical vowel of कुष् 'to extract,' क्लिश् 'to torment,' गुह् 'to put on' (clothes), मुष् 'to steal,' मृड् 'to delight,' मृज् 'to rub,' रुद् 'to weep,' विद् 'to know,' and of विज् 'to tremble,' and certain other roots. The roots ग्रह् 'to seize,' वद् 'to speak,' and वस् 'to dwell,' are changed as in the Past Pass. Ptc.; e. g.

rt. क्लिश् 'to torment;' Ger. क्लिशित्वा (or क्लिष्ट्वा).
rt. विद् 'to know;' ,, विदित्वा.
rt. वद् 'to speak;' ,, उदित्वा.
rt. वस् 'to dwell;' ,, उषित्वा.

(d) A penultimate nasal of roots ending in थ् or फ्, and the penultimate nasal of व्रश्च् 'to roam about,' and लुञ्च् 'to tear out,' may (against a) be dropped; e. g.

rt. ग्रन्थ् 'to tie;' Ger. ग्रथित्वा or ग्रन्थित्वा.
rt. वञ्च् 'to roam;' ,, वचित्वा or वञ्चित्वा (or वक्त्वा).

§ 509. The final इ of derivative verbal bases in इ is guṇated;

other derivative verbal bases undergo before the intermediate इ of the Gerund the same changes which they undergo before the intermediate इ of the Future &c.; *e. g.*

 rt. चुर् 'to steal;' Deriv. Base चोरि   Ger. चोरयित्वा.
 rt. बुध् 'to know;' Caus. Base बोधि;   ,, बोधयित्वा.
       Desid. Base बुबोधिष;   ,, बुबोधिषित्वा.
       Ātm. Frequ. B. बोबुध्य; ,, बोबुधित्वा.

§ 509. The following roots form their Gerund in त्वा irregularly:

(*a*) The roots enumerated in § 501 (*a*) and (*b*) are changed in the Gerund in त्वा as they are changed in the Past Pass. Ptc.; *e. g.*

 rt. दो 'to cut;' Past Pass. Ptc. दित; Ger. दित्वा.
 rt. धा 'to place;' ,, ,, हित; ,, हित्वा.
 rt. स्था 'to stand;' ,, ,, स्थित; ,, स्थित्वा.
 rt. पा 'to drink;' ,, ,, पीत; ,, पीत्वा.
 rt. वे 'to weave;' ,, ,, उत; ,, उत्वा.
 rt. दा 'to give;' ,, ,, दत्त; ,, दत्त्वा.

(*b*) Roots in ज् preceded by a nasal optionally drop the latter when त्वा is added to them without intermediate इ; *e. g.*

 rt. भञ्ज् 'to break;' Ger. भङ्क्त्वा or भक्त्वा.
 rt. अञ्ज् 'to anoint;' ,, अङ्क्त्वा or अक्त्वा (or अञ्जित्वा).

(*c*) Alphabetical list of some other roots that form their Gerund in त्वा irregularly:

 rt. अद् 'to eat;' Ger. जग्ध्वा.
 rt. क्रम् 'to stride;' ,, क्रान्त्वा or क्रन्त्वा or क्रमित्वा.
 rt. गुह् 'to hide;' ,, गुहित्वा or गूहित्वा or गूढ्वा.
 rt. नश् 'to perish;' ,, नंष्ट्वा or नष्ट्वा or नशित्वा.
 rt. मज्ज् 'to dive;' ,, मङ्क्त्वा or मक्त्वा.
 rt. मृज् 'to wipe off;' ,, मार्जित्वा or मृष्ट्वा.
 rt. स्कन्द् 'to descend;' ,, स्कन्त्वा.
 rt. स्यन्द् 'to flow;' ,, स्यन्त्वा or स्यन्दित्वा.
 rt. हा 'to abandon;' ,, हित्वा; (but Ger. of हा 'to go,' हात्वा).

(b).—*Formation of the Gerund by means of the affix* य.

§ 510. (a) The affix य is added immediately to the root ; *e. g.*

आ + rt. दा ;   Ger. आदाय.
वि + rt. नी ;   ,,   विनीय.
प्र + rt. भू ;   ,,   प्रभूय.
वि + rt. छिद् ; ,,   विच्छिद्य (§ 39, *a*).
अप + rt. नुद् ; ,,   अपनुद्य.

(*b*) The affix य is changed to त्य when it is preceded by a short radical vowel. This rule applies even then when the short radical vowel combines with the final vowel of a preceding preposition to a long vowel ; *e. g.*

वि + rt. जि ;   Ger. विजित्य.
प्र + rt. स्तु ; ,,   प्रस्तुत्य.
प्र + rt. कृ ;   ,,   प्रकृत्य.
अधि + rt. इ ; ,,   अधीत्य.
प्र + rt. इ ;   ,,   प्रेत्य.

§ 511. The rules given in § 373 (*b*), 1, 4, 6 and 7, apply to the root also in the Gerund in य ; *e. g.*

नि + rt. बन्ध् ; Ger. निबध्य.
प्र + rt. कॄ ;   ,,   प्रकीर्य.
प्र + rt. पॄ ;   ,,   प्रपूर्य.
प्र + rt. वच् ; ,,   प्र + उच्य = प्रोच्य.
प्र + rt. वस् ; ,,   प्र + उष्य = प्रोष्य.
नि + rt. ग्रह् ; ,,   निगृह्य.
आ + rt. प्रछ् ; ,,   आपृच्छय.
आ + rt. ह्वे ;   ,,   आहूय.
प्र + rt. दिव् ; ,,   प्रदीव्य.

§ 512. Final radical आ remains unchanged, final ए, ऐ and ओ, and the इ and ई of मि, दो, and मी are changed to आ ; the final ई of ली is optionally changed to आ (§ 296) ; *e. g.*

आ + rt. दा ;   Ger. आदाय.
परि + rt. वै ; ,,   परिवाय
उप + rt. दी ; ,,   उपदाय.
वि + rt. ली ; ,,   विलाय or विलीय.

§ 513. The roots गम् 'to go,' नम् 'to bend,' यम् 'to restrain,' रम् 'to rejoice,' may drop their final म् before य (which by § 510, b, must be changed to त्य when स् is dropped); the roots of the eighth class which end in a nasal (except सन्), and the roots हन् and मन् cl. 4 must drop their final nasal; *e. g.*

आ + rt. गम्;	Ger.	आगम्य or आगत्य.	
वि + rt. तन्;	,,	वितत्य.	
प्र + rt. हन्;	,,	प्रहत्य.	
अव + rt. मन्;	,,	अवमत्य.	

§ 514. Alphabetical list of roots which form the Gerund in य irregularly:

rt.	अद्	'to eat;'	Ger.	°जग्ध्य;	*e.g.*	प्रजग्ध्य.
rt.	क्षि	'to destroy;'	,,	°क्षीय;	,,	प्रक्षीय.
rt.	खन्	'to dig;'	,,	°खन्य;	,,	निखन्य.
			or	°खाय;	,,	निखाय.
rt.	जागृ	'to wake;'	,,	°जागर्य;	,,	प्रजागर्य.
rt.	जन्	'to bear;'	,,	°जन्य;	,,	प्रजन्य.
			or	°जाय;	,,	प्रजाय.
rt.	ज्या	'to grow old;'	,,	°ज्याय;	,,	प्रज्याय.
rt.	मे	'to barter;'	,,	°माय;	,,	अपमाय.
			or	°मित्य;	,,	अपमित्य.
rt.	वे	'to weave;'	,,	°वाय;	,,	प्रवाय.
rt.	व्ये	'to surround;'	,,	°व्याय;	,,	उपव्याय.
	(with prep. परि, परिव्याय or परिवीय).					
rt.	शी	'to lie down;'	,,	°शय्य;	*e.g.*	निशय्य.
rt.	सन्	'to obtain;'	,,	°सन्य;	,,	प्रसन्य.
			or	°साय;	,,	प्रसाय.

§ 515. (*a*) When the affix य is added to derivative verbal bases of roots of the tenth class or to causal bases, the final इ of these bases is

§ 517.] FORMATION OF NOMINAL BASES. 229

dropped; but if the syllable which immediately precedes the final इ of the base is prosodially short, the final इ of the base is changed to अय् before य; e.g.

rt. चुर्;	Deriv. Base	चोरि;	Ger.	°चोर्य;	e.g.	प्रचोर्य.
rt. बुध्;	Caus. Base	बोधि;	,,	°बोध्य;	,,	प्रबोध्य.
rt. नी;	,,	,,	नायि;	,,	°नाय्य;	,,	आनाय्य.
rt. कृ;	,,	,,	कारि;	,,	°कार्य;	,,	प्रकार्य.
But rt. गण्;	Deriv. Base	गणि;	,,	°गणय्य;	,,	विगणय्य.
rt. गम्;	Caus. Base	गमि;	,,	°गमय्य;	,,	अपगमय्य.

(b) The causal base आपि (of rt. आप् 'to obtain') may either drop its final इ or change it to अय्; e.g. Ger. of the Causal of प्र + आप्, प्राप्य or प्रापय्य.

§ 516. Desiderative bases drop their final अ before य; frequentative bases in य drop their final य when it is preceded by a consonant; but when it is preceded by a vowel, they drop only their final अ; e.g.

rt. बुध्;	Desid. Base	बुबोधिष;	Ger.	°बुबोधिष्य;	e.g.	प्रबुबोधिष्य.
	Ātm. Frequ. B.	बोबुध्य;	,,	°बोबुध्य;	,,	प्रबोबुध्य.
rt. भू;	,,	,,	,,	बोभूय;	,,	°बोभूय्य;	,,	प्रबोभूय्य.

(c).—*The Gerund in* अम्.

§ 517. (a) The affix अम् is added immediately to the root or the derivative verbal base, which before अम् generally undergo the same changes which they undergo before the final इ of the 3 Sing. Aor. of the Passive; e.g.

rt. भिद्;	3 Sing. Aor. Pass.	अभेदि;	Ger.	भेदम्	'having split.'
rt. चि;	,, ,, ,, ,,	अचायि;	,,	चायम्	'having gathered.'
rt. लू;	,, ,, ,, ,,	अलावि;	,,	लावम्	'having cut.'
rt. वद्;	,, ,, ,, ,,	अवादि;	,,	वादम्	'having spoken.'
rt. दा;	,, ,, ,, ,,	अदायि;	,,	दायम्	'having given.'
rt. गम्;	3 Sing. Aor. Pass. of the Causal.	अगामि; or अगामि;	,,	गमम् or गामम्	'having caused to go.'

(b) The Gerund in अम् occurs only rarely. It is mostly repeated to denote reiteration or repetition of the action or the state which is expressed by the root; e. g. स्मारंस्मारम् 'having repeatedly remembered,' पायंपायम् 'having drunk repeatedly.' It may also be employed after the adverbs अग्रे, पूर्वम्, प्रथमम्, e. g. प्रथमं भोजं व्रजति 'having first eaten he goes.' Sometimes it is used as the last member of a compound in peculiar idiomatic constructions; e.g. एवंकारं भुङ्क्ते 'he eats doing (it) thus;' i. e. 'he eats thus;' ब्राह्मणवेदं भोजयति 'he feeds as many Brâhmans as he knows,' &c.

3.—THE INFINITIVE.

§ 518. The Infinitive is formed by the affix तुम् which is added to roots and to derivative verbal bases in the same manner in which the termination ता of the 3 Sing. of the Periph. Future is added to them; e. g.

rt. दा;	Periph. Fut.	दाता;	Infin.	दातुम्	'to give.'
rt. जि;	,,	,, जेता;	,,	जेतुम्	'to conquer.'
rt. नी;	,,	,, नेता;	,,	नेतुम्	'to lead.'
rt. भू;	,,	,, भविता;	,,	भवितुम्	'to be.'
rt. कृ;	,,	,, कर्ता;	,,	कर्तुम्	'to do.'
rt. तृ;	,,	,, तरिता; or तरीता;	,, ,,	तरितुम् तरीतुम् }	'to cross.'
rt. गै;	,,	,, गाता;	,,	गातुम्	'to sing.'
rt. पच्;	,,	,, पक्ता;	,,	पक्तुम्	'to cook.'
rt. बभ्र्;	,,	,, बर्भिता; or बष्टा;	,, ,,	बर्भितुम् बष्टुम् }	'to tear.'
rt. जीव्;	,,	,, जीविता;	,,	जीवितुम्	'to live.'
rt. चुर्;	,,	,, चोरयिता;	,,	चोरयितुम्	'to steal.'
rt. बुध्; of Causal.	Periph. Fut.	बोधयिता;	,,	बोधयितुम्	'to cause to know.'
of Desid.		बुबोधिषिता;	,,	बुबोधिषितुम्	'to wish to know.'
of Âtm. Frq.		बोबुधिता;	,,	बोबुधितुम्	'to know often.'

4.—VERBAL ADJECTIVES.

§ 519. There are three common verbal adjectives which may be derived from every root or derivative verbal base; they convey the notion that the action or the state expressed by the root or derivative base must or ought to be done of undergone. One of these verbal adjectives is formed by means of the affix तव्य (*masc.* and *neut.*; तव्या *fem.*), one by means of the affix अनीय (*masc.* and *neut.*; अनीया *fem.*), and the third by means of the affix य (*masc.* and *neut.*; या *fem.*); *e. g.*

बुध् 'to know;' बोधितव्य or बोधनीय or बोध्य 'what must or ought to be known.'
कृ 'to do;' कर्तव्य or करणीय or कार्य 'what must or ought to be done.'

(a).—The Verbal Adjective in तव्य.

§ 520. The affix तव्य is added to roots and derivative bases in the same manner in which the affix तुम् of the Infin. is added to them; *e. g.*

Root.	Infin.	Verb. Adj.	
दा;	दातुम्;	दातव्य	'what must or ought to be given.'
जि;	जेतुम्;	जेतव्य	' ,, ,, ,, ,, conquered.'
भू;	भवितुम्;	भवितव्य	'what must or ought to be.'
मुच्;	मोक्तुम्;	मोक्तव्य	'what must or ought to be loosened.'
चुर्;	चोरयितुम्;	चोरयितव्य	' ,, ,, ,, ,, stolen.'
बुध्; Caus.	बोधयितुम्;	बोधयितव्य	' ,, ,, ,, made to know.'

(b).—The Verbal Adjective in अनीय.

§ 521. The vowels of primitive roots are before the affix अनीय (changeable to अणीय by § 58) liable to the same changes to which they are liable in the Simple or Periph. Future; penultimate ऋ, however, is always changed to अर् (not to र्); in मृज् it is changed to आर्; *e. g.*

Root.	Verb. Adj.	
दा;	दा+अनीय=दानीय	'what must or ought to be given.'
गै;	गा+अनीय=गानीय	' ,, ,, ,, ,, sung.'

Root.	Verb. Adj.						
जि ;	जे+अनीय=जयनीय	'what must or ought to be conquered.'					
नी ;	ने+अनीय=नयनीय '	,,	,,	,,	,,	,,	led.'
श्रु ;	श्रो+अनीय=श्रवणीय '	,,	,,	,,	,,	,,	heard.'
कृ ;	कर+अनीय=करणीय '	,,	,,	,,	,,	,,	done.'
पच् ;	पचनीय 'what must or ought to be cooked.'						
भिद् ;	भेदनीय '	,,	,,	,,	,,	split.'	
सृज् ;	सर्जनीय '	,,	,,	,,	,,	dismissed.'	
निन्द् ;	निन्दनीय 'blamable.'						
गुह् ;	गूहनीय 'what must or ought to be hidden.'						
मृज् ;	मार्जनीय '		,,		,,	,, wiped off.'	
भ्रज्ज् ;	भ्रज्जनीय or भर्जनीय	' ,,		,,		,, fried.'	

§ 522. The final इ of derivative bases of roots of the tenth class and of causal bases, and the final अ of desiderative bases is dropped before अनीय; the final अ of Âtmanepada Frequent. bases is dropped when their final य is preceded by a vowel; but when it is preceded by a consonant, the whole final य is dropped; *e. g.*

Rt.	Deriv. Base.	Verb. Adj.		
चुर् ;	चोरि ;	चोरणीय	'what must or ought to be stolen.'	
	Caus. Base.			
बुध् ;	बोधि ;	बोधनीय	' ,, ,,	made to know.'
	Desid. Base.			
	बुबोधिष ;	बुबोधिषणीय	' ,, ,,	desired to know.'
	Âtm. Frequ. B.			
	बोबुध्य ;	बोबुधनीय	' ,, ,,	known frequently.'
भू ;	बोभूय ;	बोभूयनीय	'what must or ought frequently to be.'	
	Caus. Base.			
दा ;	दापि ;	दापनीय	'what must or ought to be made to give.'	

(c).—*The Verbal Adjective in* य.

§ 523. When the affix य is added to roots ending in vowels, the final radical vowels undergo the following changes:—

(a) Final आ, ए, ऐ, and ओ are changed to ए; *e. g.*

rt. दा; Verb. Adj. देय 'what must or ought to be given.'
rt. धे; ,, ,, धेय ' ,, ,, ,, sucked.'
rt. गै; ,, ,, गेय ' ,, ,, ,, sung.'
rt. सो; ,, ,, सेय ' ,, ,, ,, finished.'

(b) Final इ and ई are gunated; *e. g.*

rt. जि; Verb. Adj. जेय 'what must or ought to be conquered.'
rt. नी; ,, ,, नेय ' ,, ,, ,, led.'

(c) For final ऋ and ॠ Vṛiddhi is substituted; *e. g.*

rt. हृ; Verb. Adj. हार्य 'what must or ought to be seized.'
rt. तॄ; ,, ,, तार्य ' ,, ,, ,, crossed.'

(d) अव् is substituted for final उ and ऊ; but when the verbal adjective is to convey the notion of necessity, आव् is substituted for final उ and ऊ; *e. g.*

rt. नु; Verb. Adj. नव्य 'what must or ought to be praised.'
,, ,, ,, ,, नाव्य 'what must necessarily be praised.'
rt. लू; ,, ,, लव्य 'what must or ought to be cut.'
,, ,, ,, ,, लाव्य 'what must necessarily be cut.'

§ 524. When the affix य is added to roots with penultimate prosodially short इ, उ, ऋ, or ऌ, the following rules apply to the penultimate radical vowels:

(a) Penultimate इ, उ, and ऌ, are gunated; *e. g.*

rt. भिद्; Verb. Adj. भेद्य 'what must or ought to be split.'
rt. बुध्; ,, ,, बोध्य ' ,, ,, ,, known.'

(b) Penultimate ऋ remains unchanged; *e. g.*

rt. तृद्; Verb. Adj. तृद्य 'what must or ought to be destroyed.'

§ 525. To roots with penultimate prosodially short अ, the affix य is added thus:

(a) When the root with penultimate अ ends in a labial letter, the penultimate अ remains unchanged; but when the root ends in any other than a labial letter, the penultimate अ is lengthened; e.g.

rt. शप्; Verb. Adj. शाप्य 'what must or ought to be cursed.'
rt. क्षम्;   ,,   ,,   क्षम्य ' ,,   ,, ,, ,, ,, ,, borne.'
rt. पठ्;   ,,   ,,   पाठ्य ' ,,   ,, ,, ,, ,, ,, read.'
rt. वद्;   ,,   ,,   वाद्य ' ,,   ,, ,, ,, ,, ,, said.'
rt. वच्;   ,,   ,,   वाच्य ' ,,   ,, ,, ,, ,, ,, spoken.'

(b) The penultimate अ of the roots त्रप् 'to be ashamed,' रप् 'to speak,' लप् 'to speak,' वप् 'to sow,' and चम् 'to sip' is lengthened, although these roots end in labial letters; on the other hand the penultimate अ of the roots चन् 'to ask,' जन् 'to bear', तक् 'to laugh' &c., यत् 'to endeavour,' शक् 'to be able,' शस् 'to hurt', and सह् 'to bear' remains short. The penultimate अ of गद् 'to speak' and of some other roots remains short when no preposition is prefixed to them; e. g.

rt. वप्; Verb. Adj. वाप्य 'what must or ought to be sown.'
rt. सह्;   ,,   ,,   सह्य ' ,,   ,, ,, ,, ,, ,, borne.'
rt. गद्;   ,,   ,,   गद्य ' ,,   ,, ,, ,, ,, ,, spoken.'

(But when compounded with prep. प्र, प्रगाद्य.)

§ 526. Prosodially long vowels of roots ending in consonants remain unchanged when य is added to the roots; e. g.

rt. निन्द्; Verb. Adj. निन्द्य 'what must or ought to be blamed.'
rt. पूज्;   ,,   ,,   पूज्य ' ,,   ,, ,, ,, ,, ,, honoured.'
rt. बन्ध्;   ,,   ,,   बन्ध्य ' ,,   ,, ,, ,, ,, ,, bound.'

§ 527. (a) Final radical च् and ज् of roots to which the affix of the Past Pass. Ptc. is added without intermediate इ, are changed to क् and ग् respectively before the affix य; e. g.

FORMATION OF NOMINAL BASES.

Rt.	P.P.Ptc.	Verb. Adj.	
सिच्;	सिक्त;	सेक्य	'what must or ought to be sprinkled.'
पच्;	पक्क;	पाक्य	' ,, ,, ,, ,, ,, ,, cooked.'
अन्ज्;	अक्त;	अङ्ग्य	' ,, ,, ,, ,, ,, ,, anointed.'
But गर्ज्;	गर्जित;	गर्ज्य.	

(b) The finals of वच् 'to speak,' त्यज् 'to abandon,' and यज् 'to sacrifice,' remain unchanged; likewise the final of युज् in प्रयोज्य, and नियोज्य, that of भुज् in भोज्य when it means 'what must be eaten,' and the final च् or ज् of any root when अवश्य is prefixed to the Verbal Adjective; e. g.

rt. वच्; Verb. Adj. वाच्य 'what must or ought to be spoken.'
rt. त्यज्; ,, ,, त्याज्य ' ,, ,, ,, ,, ,, abandoned.'
rt. पच्; ,, ,, अवश्यपाच्य ' ,, ,, necessarily to be cooked.'

§ 528. Alphabetical list of some roots that form the Verb. Adj. in य irregularly:

rt. इ 'to go;' Verb. Adj. इत्य.
rt. ऋच् 'to praise;' ,, ,, अर्च्य.
rt. कृ 'to do;' ,, ,, कृत्य or कार्य.
rt. खन् 'to dig;' ,, ,, खेय.
rt. गुह् 'to hide;' ,, ,, गुह्य or गोढ्य.
rt. चर् 'to go,' when without prepos., or with prepos. आ, Verb. Adj. चर्य; otherwise चार्य; (आचर्य 'to be gone to;' आचार्य 'an instructor').
rt. जुष् 'to be pleased;' Verb. Adj. जुष्य.
rt. दुह् 'to milk;' ,, ,, दुह्य or दोह्य.
rt. दृ 'to respect;' ,, ,, दृत्य.
rt. भृ 'to support;' ,, ,, भृत्य; (with prep. सम्, संभृत्य or संभार्य).
rt. मृज् 'to wipe off;' ,, ,, मृज्य or मार्ज्य.
rt. यु 'to mix;' ,, ,, याव्य.
rt. लभ् 'to take' (with prep. आ) ,, ,, आलम्भ्य; (otherwise लभ्य).

rt. वृ 'to select;'   Verb. Adj. वृह्य or वार्य.
rt. वृष् 'to rain;'   ,,   ,, वृष्य or वर्ष्य.
rt. शंस् 'to praise;'   ,,   ,, शस्य or शंस्य.
rt. शास् 'to rule;'   ,,   ,, शिष्य.
rt. सु 'to press out'
     (with prep. आ)   ,,   ,, आसाव्य; (otherwise सव्य or
                                     साव्य).
rt. स्तु 'to praise;'   ,,   ,, स्तुत्य.
rt. हन् 'to slay;'   ,,   ,, वध्य or घात्य.

§. 529. When the affix य is added to derivative verbal bases, the final letters of the latter undergo the same changes which they undergo before the affix अनीय (§ 522); *e. g.*

rt. चुर्; Deriv. Base चोरि; V. Adj. चोरणीय; चोर्य.
rt. बुध्; Caus. Base बोधि;   ,,   ,, बोधनीय; बोध्य.
rt. दा;   ,,   ,,   दापि;   ,,   ,, दापनीय; दाप्य.
rt. कृत्; Deriv. Base कीर्ति;   ,,   ,, कीर्तनीय; कीर्त्य.

5.—A LIST OF THE MOST COMMON SECONDARY OR TADDHITA AFFIXES.

§ 530. 1. अ forms substantives and adjectives with various significations; *e. g.* शौच *n.* (from शुचि) 'purity;' यौवन *n.* (from युवन्) 'youth;' सौहार्द *n.* (from सुहृद्) 'friendship;' पार्थव *n.* (from पृथु) 'breadth;' काक *n.* (from काक) 'a collection of crows;' पौत्र *m.* (from पुत्र) 'a son's son, a grandson;' पौर *m.* (from पुर) 'a citizen;' पार्थिव *m.* (from पृथिवी) 'a lord of the earth, a king;' पौरव *m.* (from पुरु) 'a descendant of Puru;' औपगव *m.* (from उपगु) 'a descendant of Upagu;' वैयाकरण *m.* (from व्याकरण) 'a grammarian;' दैव (from देव) 'divine;' काषाय (from कषाय) 'coloured red;' चाक्षुष (from चक्षुस्) 'visible;' आश्म (from अश्मन्) 'made of stone,' &c.*

---

* The examples will show that Vṛiddhi is often substituted for the first vowel of a noun to which the affix अ or य is added. When the first vowel of a primitive word is preceded by य् or व्, being both the finals of a word, these semivowels are first changed to इय् and उव् respectively before Vṛiddhi can be substituted; *e. g.* वैयाकरण from व्याकरण (changed first to वियाकरण); सौवश्व 'a descendant of Svaśva,' (from स्वश्व, changed first to सुवश्व). The same rule is observed in regard to some other words in which य् and व् are not finals of a word; *e. g.* सौवर, 'treating of accents' (from स्वर, changed to सुवर;) &c.

2. य is similarly employed; e. g. दारिद्र्य n. (from दरिद्र) 'poverty;' पाण्डित्य n. (from पण्डित) 'wisdom;' शौर्य n. (from शूर) 'bravery;' वाणिज्य n. (from वणिज्) 'trade;' औत्सुक्य n. (from उत्सुक) 'eagerness;' राज्य n. (from राजन्) 'sovereignty;' वीर्य n. (from वीर) 'manliness;' सख्य n. (from सखि) 'friendship;' सैनाप्य n. (from सेनापति) 'generalship;' राजन्य m. (from राजन्) 'a member of the regal caste;' गार्ग्य m. (from गर्ग) 'a descendant of Garga;' दैव्य (from देव) 'divine;' दिव्य (from दिव्) 'celestial;' गव्य (from गो) 'bovine;' ग्राम्य (from ग्राम) 'rustic;' दन्त्य (from दन्त) 'dental, suitable for the teeth,' &c.

3. त्व n. and ता f. form abstract nouns; e. g. गोत्व n. or गोता f. (from गो) 'cowhood, the nature of a cow;' दृढत्व n. or दृढता f. (from दृढ) 'firmness;' भीरुत्व n. or भीरुता f. (from भीरु) 'cowardice;' निःसारत्व n. or निःसारता f. (from निःसार) 'worthlessness;' भृत्यत्व n. or भृत्यता f. (from भृत्य) 'servitude,' &c. The affix ता sometimes denotes a collection of the objects expressed by the noun to which it is added; e. g. जनता f. (from जन) 'a collection of men, mankind.'

4. इमन् m. is added to adjectives denoting a colour and to some other adjectives, to form abstract nouns; the adjectives to which it is attached undergo before it the same changes which they undergo before the comparative and superlative affixes ईयस् and इष्ठ (§ 173); e. g. शुक्लिमन् m. (from शुक्ल) 'whiteness;' महिमन् m. (from महत्) 'greatness;' वरिमन् m. (from उरु) 'width;' द्रढिमन् m. (from दृढ) 'firmness;' प्रथिमन् m. (from पृथु) 'breadth;' गरिमन् m. (from गुरु) 'heaviness.' Nouns formed by this affix are always masculine and must be carefully distinguished from primary neuter nouns in मन्, such as कर्मन् n. 'action,' &c.

5. मत् and वत् (Decl. VIII.) form possessive adjectives; e. g. श्रीमत् (from श्री) 'possessed of intelligence, intelligent,' विद्यावत् (from विद्या) 'possessed of knowledge, wise.' The affix वत् is added to nouns the final or penultimate letter of which is अ, आ or म, and to nouns that end in a hard or soft unaspirate or aspirate Guttural, Palatal, Lingual, Dental, or Labial; e. g. ज्ञानवत् (from ज्ञान) 'possessed of knowledge;' विद्यावत्; किंवत् (from किम्) 'possessed of what?;' कामवत् (from काम) 'loving;' पयस्वत् (from पयस्) 'possessed of milk, milky;' भास्वत् (from भास्) 'possessing light.'

मरुत्वत् (from मरुत्) 'possessed of, or accompanied by, the Maruts;' दृषद्वत् (from दृषद्) 'containing stones.' To other nouns मत् is generally added; e.g. अग्निमत् (from अग्नि) 'possessed of fire,' &c. Final त् and स् undergo before possessive affixes the same changes which they undergo before vowel-terminations in weak cases; e.g. मरुत्वत् (from मरुत्; *not* मरुद्वत्), पयस्वत् (from पयस्; *not* पयोवत्); ज्योतिष्मत् (from ज्योतिस्; *not* ज्योतिमंत्) 'possessed of light;' विद्वसुमत् (from विद्वस्; *not* विद्वन्मत्) 'containing learned men;' so also यशस्विन्, &c. (see No. 6).

6. इन्, विन्, and मिन् (Decl. IV.) likewise form possessive adjectives. इन् is mostly added to nouns ending in अ which is dropped before इन्; विन् mostly to nouns ending in अस्, (see No. 5); मिन् appears only in a few derivatives; e. g. धनिन् (from धन) 'wealthy,' मन्त्रिन् m. (from मन्त्र) 'one who posesses or gives advice, a minister;' तेजस्विन् (from तेजस्) 'splendid;' तपस्विन् (from तपस्) 'ascetic;' मेधाविन् (from मेधा) 'intelligent;' वाग्मिन् (from वाच्) 'talkative.'

7. इत forms adjectives which denote 'containing' that which is expressed by the nouns to which इत is added; e.g. पुष्पित (from पुष्प) 'containing or bearing flowers;' कण्टकित (from कण्टक) 'thorny;' व्याधित (from व्याधि) 'afflicted with a disease, diseased.'

8. मय (*fem.* मयी) forms adjectives which denote 'made of, consisting of, abounding in' that which is expressed by the nouns to which मय is added. Before मय and मात्र final क्, ट्, त् and प् *must* be changed to the corresponding nasal; e. g. अइमंमय (from अइमन्) 'made of stone;' आम्रमय (from आम्र) 'consisting of mango trees;' अन्नमय (from अन्न) 'abounding in food;' दारुमय from दारु) 'made of wood;' चिन्मय (from चित्, *not* चिद्मय), 'consisting of intelligence.' Nouns in मय are sometimes used as neuter substantives to denote 'abundance of' that which is expressed by the noun to which मय is added; e. g. अन्नमय n. 'abundance of food.'

9. मात्र (*fem.* मात्री) forms adjectives which denote 'measuring as much as, or reaching as far as' that which is expressed by the noun to which मात्र is added; e. g. ऊरुमात्र (from ऊरु) 'as high as the thigh.'

10. वत् *indecl.* forms adverbs which denote the sense of 'like that' which is denoted by the noun to which वत् is added, provided the likeness referred to be an action; *e. g.* ब्राह्मणवत् *indecl.* (from ब्राह्मण) 'like a Brâhman' (ब्राह्मणवदधीते 'he studies like a Brâhman').

II.—COMPOUND NOMINAL BASES OR COMPOUNDS.

§ 531. Primary and secondary nominal bases, adverbs, prepositions, and particles may be compounded with primary and secondary nominal bases, and the compound bases formed in this manner have the power to express various relations that exist between the objects or ideas denoted by their several members, or between that which they denote as a whole and other objects or ideas not denoted by their members— relations which, if no composition had taken place, would have had to be expressed by two or more inflected words or by subordinate sentences; *e. g.*

राजन् 'a king' + पुरुष 'a man' = राजपुरुष 'a king's man' (राज्ञः पुरुषः) ;

नील 'blue' + उत्पल 'a lotus' = नीलोत्पल 'a blue lotus' (नीलमुत्पलम्);

त्रि 'three' + भुवन 'world' = त्रिभुवन 'the three worlds' taken collectively (त्रयाणां भुवनानां समाहारः);

दीर्घ 'long' + बाहु 'an arm' = दीर्घबाहु 'a person possessed of long arms' (दीर्घौ बाहू यस्य सः) ;

ब्राह्मण 'a Brâhman' + क्षत्रिय 'a Kshatriya' = ब्राह्मणक्षत्रिय 'a Brâhman and a Kshatriya' (ब्राह्मणश्च क्षत्रियश्च) ;

आ 'unto' + मुक्ति 'final liberation' = आमुक्ति 'unto final liberation' (आ मुक्तेः).

§ 532. Nominal bases when employed as *first members*, or when they form any but the last member of a compound, take in general no case-terminations, but retain (except in so far as they are subject to the rules of Sandhi) their crude form unchanged. Nouns with two bases

(§ 94) assume their weak base, nouns with three bases (§ 95) their middle base, pronouns the pronominal bases given in § 177, &c. Feminine adjectives that qualify a following member in the same compound, generally assume their masculine base; *e. g.*

चोर 'a thief' + भय 'fear'=चोरभय 'fear from thieves' (चोरेभ्यो भयम्);

रूपवत् 'beautiful' (§ 109) + पति 'a husband' = रूपवत्पति 'a beautiful husband' (रूपवान्पति:);

विद्वस् 'wise' (§ 122) + पुरुष 'a man' = विद्वत्पुरुष 'a wise man' (विद्वान्पुरुष:);

अस्मद् 'our' + पितृ 'father' = अस्मत्पितृ 'our father' (अस्माकं पिता);

पञ्चम 'the fifth' + भार्या 'a wife' = पञ्चमभार्या 'the fifth wife' (पञ्चमो भार्या);

रूपवत् 'beautiful' + भार्या 'a wife' = रूपवद्भार्य 'a person who has a beautiful wife' (रूपवतो भार्या यस्य स:).

§ 533. Final vowels of preceding members of compounds combine with the initial letters of succeeding members according to the rules in § 19—39. Preceding members that end in consonants first change their final consonants as they would be changed before the termination सु of the Loc. Plur., and combine afterwards with succeeding members likewise according to the rules laid down in § 19—39; *e. g.*

दैत्य 'a Daitya'+ अरि 'enemy'=दैत्यारि (§ 19) 'an enemy of the Daityas.'
श्री 'Lakshmî'+ ईश 'a lord'=श्रीश (§ 19) 'the lord of Lakshmî.'
गङ्गा 'the Ganges'+उदक 'water'=गङ्गोदक (§ 20) 'the water of the Ganges.'
देव 'a god'+ऐश्वर्य 'sovereignty'=देवैश्वर्य (§20) 'the sovereignty of the gods.'
मधु 'Madhu'+ अरि 'an enemy'=मध्वरि (§ 21) 'the enemy of Madhu.'
वृक्ष 'a tree' +छाया 'shade' = वृक्षच्छाया (§ 38, *a*) 'the shade of a tree.'
लक्ष्मी 'Lakshmî'+छाया 'shade'= लक्ष्मीछाया or लक्ष्मीच्छाया (§ 38, *b*).
मरुत् 'a Marut' + पति 'a lord' = मरुत्पति (§ 28, *a*) 'the lord of the Maruts.'
                + गण 'a troup'= मरुद्गण (§ 28, *b*) 'the troup of the Maruts.'

क्षुध् (§ 73, 3) 'hunger' + पिपासा 'thirst' = क्षुत्पिपासा (§ 29, a) 'hunger and thirst.'

+रोग 'a disease' = क्षुद्रोग (§ 28, b.) 'hunger-disease.'

वाच् (§ 76, 2, a) 'speech' + पारुष्य 'harshness' = वाक्पारुष्य (§ 27, a.) 'harshness of speech.'

+ मुख 'beginning' = वाङ्मुख (§ 27, c) 'the beginning of a speech.'

मनस् (§ 89, 4) 'mind' + गत 'gone' = मनोगत (§ 35, a) 'gone or seated in the mind.'

राजन् (§ 115, 3) 'a king' + पुरुष 'a man' = राजपुरुष 'a king's man.'

+ईश्वर 'a king' = राजेश्वर (§ 20) 'a king of kings.'

§ 534. There are a few exceptions. When the bases ओतु 'a cat' or ओष्ठ 'lip' are preceded in the same compound by a word in अ or आ, these vowels may unite with the initial ओ of ओतु and ओष्ठ optionally to ओ or to औ; बिम्बोष्ठ or बिम्बौष्ठ 'one who has bimba-like lips.' When the word गो is followed in the same compound by a word beginning with अ, both the final of गो and the initial अ may remain unchanged; according to some the ओ of गो may before all vowels be changed to अव; e. g. गो + अग्र = गोग्र or गोअग्र or गवाग्र. Final इस् and उस् of first members of compounds before initial क्, ख्, प्, फ् are changed to इष् and उष्; final अम् of first members remains before certain words unchanged; e. g. सर्पिस् + कुण्डिका = सर्पिःकुण्डिका 'a butter-jar;' अयस् + पात्र = अयस्पात्र 'an iron vessel.' These and other specialities are best learnt from the dictionary.

§ 535. Nouns employed as *last members* of compounds generally retain their bases unchanged; occasionally however the latter are liable to undergo slight changes, the most important of which will be enumerated in the following paragraphs. Some compounds are peculiar in requiring certain affixes to be added to them, either necessarily or optionally; these affixes convey no new meaning beyond what is already expressed by the compound as such. For examples see below.

§ 536. (a) When a feminine noun which ends with one of the feminine affixes आ, ई, or ऊ, forms the last member of a Tatpurusha compound in which the first member governs the second member (§ 541 *a, b*), or of a Dvigu-compound which conveys a derivative meaning such as is usually denoted by a Taddhita affix (§ 551), or of a Bahuvrîhi-compound, its final vowel is shortened (see, however, § 557 *b*). Under the same conditions the final ओ of गो is changed to उ. For examples see below.

(*b*) When a nominal base which ends in a long vowel forms the last member of a compound word of the neuter gender or of an adverbial compound, its final long vowel must be shortened (final ए be changed to इ, final ओ and औ to उ).

§ 537. All compound nominal bases have by the native grammarians been divided into four classes, *Tatpurusha, Bahuvrîhi, Dvandva,* and *Avyayîbhâva*.

1. A *Tatpurusha*-compound may, in general, be described as a compound which denotes that which is expressed by its second member determined or qualified by what is expressed by its first member. When the first member of a Tatpurusha stands in apposition to the second, so that, if the compound were dissolved, it would have to be expressed by a substantive or adjective agreeing in case with the second member, the Tatpurusha-compound is called a *Karmadhâraya*. Again, a Karmadhâraya-compound, the first member of which is a cardinal number, is called a *Dvigu*-compound. It will appear, then, that a Tatpurusha-compound to which neither the term Karmadhâraya nor the term Dvigu is applicable, must in general be a compound the first member of which, if the compound were dissolved, would be governed by the second member, and would have to be expressed by a word in an oblique case. *E. g.*

Tatpurusha only : राजपुरुष 'the king's man' (राज्ञः पुरुषः); Compare the English 'house-top,' &c.

Karmadhâraya : नीलोत्पल 'a blue lotus' (नीलमुत्पलम्); Compare the English 'low-land' &c.

Dvigu : त्रिभुवन 'the three worlds collectively' (त्रयाणां भुवनानां समाहारः); Compare the English 'fortnight,' etc.

§ 537.] FORMATION OF NOMINAL BASES. 243

Tatpurusha-compounds in general may be called *Determinative* compounds; those Tatpurusha-compounds which are neither Karmadhâraya nor Dvigu, *Dependent determinative* compounds. Karmadhâraya-compounds may be called *Appositional determinative* compounds, and Dvigu-compounds *Numeral determinative* compounds.

2. A *Bahuvrîhi*-compound is a compound which denotes something else than what is expressed by its members. It generally attributes that which is expressed by its second member, determined or qualified by what is denoted by its first member, to something denoted by neither of its members. When dissolved, it must be expressed by more than two inflected words, viz. by the two words which are its members generally standing both in the Nominative case, and by a relative or demonstrative pronoun in any except the Nominative case. A Bahuvrîhi-compound has the nature of an adjective and assumes the gender of the word which expresses that of which the Bahuvrîhi-compound forms an attribute; *e. g.*

Bahuvrîhi: पीताम्बर 'a person that has a yellow garment' (पीतमम्बरं यस्य सः).
रूपवद्भार्य 'one who has a beautiful wife' (रूपवती भार्या यस्य सः).

Compare the English 'blue-beard,' 'noble-minded,' &c.

Bahuvrîhi-compounds may be called *Attributive* compounds.

3. A *Dvandva*-compound is a compound which denotes all the person or things &c. denoted by its several members; when dissolved, its members must be connected with each other by the particle च 'and.' Whereas Tatpurusha and Bahuvrîhi-compounds always consist of only two members (either of which may be a simple or a compound word), Dvandva-compounds may consist of two or three or more members; *e. g.*

Dvandva: ब्राह्मणक्षत्रिय 'a Brâhman and a Kshatriya' (ब्राह्मणश्च क्षत्रियश्च).
ब्राह्मणक्षत्रियविट्शूद्र 'a Brâhman, a Kshatriya, a Vais'ya, and a S'ûdra.'

Dvandva-compounds may be called *Copulative* compounds.

4. An *Avyayîbhâva*-compound is a compound which is indeclinable; its first member is generally a preposition or adverb which, if the compound were dissolved, would govern the second member. There are some Avyayîbhâva-compounds the sense of which cannot be expressed by their members, when uncompounded, but requires for its expression other words than those actually compounded; *e. g.*

Avyayîbhâva: प्रत्यग्नि 'towards the fire' (अग्निं प्रति).
यथाशक्ति 'according to one's ability' (शक्तिमनतिक्रम्य 'not going beyond one's powers').

Avyayîbhâva-compounds may be called *Adverbial* compounds.

1.—TATPURUSHA OR DETERMINATIVE COMPOUNDS.

(a)—*Dependent Determinative Compounds.*

§ 538. The second member is determined or qualified by the first member which, if the compound were dissolved, would have to stand:

1. In the *Accusative* case; *e. g.*

कृष्णश्रित (N. Sing. Masc. °त:) 'one who has had recourse to Krishna' (कृष्णं श्रित:).

दुःखातीत (N. Sing. Masc. °त:) 'one who has overcome pain' (दुःखमतीत:).

मुहूर्तसुख (Neut., N. Sing. °खम्) 'pleasure that lasts a moment' (मुहूर्तं सुखम्).

2. In the *Instrumental* case; *e. g.*

धान्यार्थ (Masc., N. Sing. °र्थ:) 'wealth acquired by grain' (धान्येनार्थ:).
मातृसदृश (N. Sing. Masc. °श:) 'like his mother' (मात्रा सदृश:).
हरित्रात (N. Sing. Masc. °त:) 'protected by Hari' (हरिणा त्रात:).
नखभिन्न (N. Sing. Masc. °न्न:) 'split with the nails' (नखैर्भिन्न:).

3. In the *Dative* case; *e. g.*

यूपदारु (Neut., N. Sing. °रु) 'wood for a sacrificial post' (यूपाय दारु).
गोहित (N. Sing. Masc. °त:) 'good for cattle' (गवे हित:).
द्विजार्थ (Masc. and Neut.; °र्था Fem.) 'intended for a Brâhman;' *e. g.*

द्विजार्यः सूपः 'broth for a Br.,' द्विजार्थी यवागूः 'gruel for a Br.,' द्विजार्थे पयः 'milk for a Br.' (Though compounded of द्विज + अर्थ, the sense of द्विजार्थ is, when no composition takes place, not expressed by the two words द्विज and अर्थ; *e. g.* द्विजार्थः सूपः is dissolved into द्विजायार्थं सूपः).

4. In the *Ablative* case; *e. g.*

चौरभय (Neut., N. Sing. °यम्) 'fear from a thief' (चौराद्भयम्).

वृकभीत (N. Sing. Masc. °तः) 'afraid of a wolf' (वृकाद्भीतः).

स्वर्गपतित (N. Sing. Masc. °तः) 'fallen from heaven' (स्वर्गात्पतितः).

5. In the *Genitive* case; *e g.*

राजपुरुष (Masc., N. Sing. °षः) 'the king's man' (राज्ञः पुरुषः).

तत्पुरुष (Masc., N. Sing. °षः) 'the man of him' *i. e.* 'his man' (तस्य पुरुषः).

गिरिनदी (Fem., N. Sing. °दी) 'a mountain-torrent' (गिरेर्नदी).

मूर्खशत (Neut., N. Sing. °तम्) 'a hundred fools' (मूर्खाणां शतम्).

6. In the *Locative* case; *e. g.*

अक्षशौण्ड (N. Sing. Masc. °ण्डः) 'skilled in dice' (अक्षेषु शौण्डः).

ईश्वराधीन (N. Sing. Masc. °नः) 'dependent on god' (from ईश्वर and the preposition अधि, with the affix ईन added to the whole compound).

स्थालीपक्व (N. Sing. Masc. °क्वः) 'cooked in a pot' (स्थाल्यां पक्वः).

पूर्वाह्णकृत (N. Sing. Neut. °तम्) 'done in the forenoon' (पूर्वाह्णे कृतम्).

7. Sometimes the first member is an *indeclinable*; *e. g.*

स्वयंकृत (N. Sing. Neut. °तम्) 'done by one's self' (स्वयं कृतम्).

सामिकृत (N. Sing. Neut. °तम्) 'half done' (सामि कृतम्).

तत्रभुक्त (N. Sing. Neut. °क्तम्) 'eaten there' (तत्र भुक्तम्).

§ 539. There is a class of Tatpurusha-compounds, the sense of which cannot be expressed by their members, when uncompounded, because the last member, which may be a root or a primary noun, is either not used alone, or does when used by itself not convey the meaning which it conveys in the compound; *e. g.*

कुम्भकार (N. Sing. Masc. °र:) 'a pot-maker;' (not कुम्भं कार:. It is usual to dissolve this and similar compounds by means of such phrases as कुम्भं करोतीति कुम्भकार:).

सामग (N. Sing. Masc. °ग:) 'one who sings a verse of the Sâmaveda' (साम गायतीति सामग:).

अंशहर (N. Sing. Masc. °र:) 'one who takes a share' (अंशं हरतीत्यंशहर:).

वृत्रहन् (N. Sing. Masc. °हा) 'one who kills Vritra' (वृत्रं हन्तीति वृत्रहा).

सर्वजित् (N. Sing. Masc. °त्) 'one who conquers all' (सर्वञ्जयतीति सर्वजित्).

§ 540. In certain Tatpurushas the first member retains (against § 532) its case-termination; many of the compounds in which this is the case are proper names or have otherwise a restricted meaning; e. g.

ओजसाकृत (N. Sing. Neut. °तम्) 'done with strength' (ओजसा कृतम्)

जनुषान्ध (N. Sing. Masc. °न्ध:) 'blind by nature' (जनुषा+अन्ध:).

आत्मनापञ्चम (N. Sing. Masc. °म:) 'fifth with one's self;' i. e. 'himself and four others.'

परस्मैपद (Neut., N. Sing. °दम्) 'voice for another' (परस्मै पदम्).

आत्मनेपद (Neut., N. Sing. °दम्) 'voice for one's self' (आत्मने पदम्).

दूरादागत (N. Sing. Masc. °त:) 'come from afar' (दूरात्+आगत:).

दास्या:पुत्र or दासी:पुत्र (Masc., N. Sing °त्र:) 'the son of a slave,' used as a term of contempt.

युधिष्ठिर (Masc., N. Sing. °र:) 'Yudhishthira' i. e. firm in battle (युधि स्थिर:).

हृदिस्पृश् (N. Sing. Masc. °क्) 'touching the heart' (हृदि स्पृशतीति हृदिस्पृक्).

शरदिज (N. Sing. Masc. °ज:) 'born in autumn' (शरदि जायत इति शरदिज:).

§ 541. (a) Some compounds of which the first member would govern the second member, if no composition had taken place, are likewise considered Tatpurusha-compounds by the native grammarians; e. g.

पूर्वकाय (Masc., N. Sing. °य:) 'the fore-part of the body' (पूर्वे कायस्य).

मध्याह्न (Masc., N. Sing. °ह्न:) 'mid-day' (मध्यमह्न:).

प्राप्तजीविक (N. Sing. Masc. °क:) 'one who has found a livelihood' (प्राप्तो जीविकाम्); also जीविकाप्राप्त:.

मासजात (N. Sing. Masc. °त:) 'born a month ago' (मासो जातस्य यस्य स:).

(b) Similar are compounds the first member of which is a preposition, the sense of which, when the compound is dissolved, must be expressed by the Past Pass. Participle of certain roots to which that preposition is prefixed; *e. g.*

अतिमाल (N. Sing. Masc. °ल:) 'surpassing a garland' (अतिक्रान्तो मालाम्).

निष्कौशाम्बि (N. Sing. Masc. °म्बि:) 'departed from Kaus'âmbî' (निष्क्रान्तः कौशाम्ब्याः).

(c) Compounds like अब्राह्मण (Masc., N. Sing. °ण:) 'one who is not a Brâhman' (न ब्राह्मण:) 'अनश्व (Masc., N. Sing. °श्व:) 'not a horse' (न+अश्व:) are likewise called Tatpurusha.

§ 542. (*a*) Dependent and Appositional determinative compounds assume mostly the gender of their final member. Dependent determinative compounds like प्राप्तजीविक however (§ 541, *a*) and the compounds described in § 541, *b*, such as अतिमाल, take the gender of the noun which they qualify.

(*b*) There are a few exceptions to this rule. Dependent determinative compounds (provided their first member be not the negative prefix अ), the last member of which is one of the nouns सेना, सुरा, छाया, शाला, or निशा, may optionally be feminine or neuter; *e. g.* ब्राह्मणसेना *fem.* or ब्राह्मणसेन *neut.*, 'a host of Brâhmans;' but there are Tatpurusha-compounds ending in छाया and सभा that must be neuter, *e. g.* इक्षुच्छाय *neut.*, 'the shade of (many) sugar-canes;' ईश्वरसभ *neut.* 'an assembly of princes.' Tatpurusha-compounds ending in रात्र (for रात्रि) 'night,' and अह्न or अह (for अहन्) 'day,' are generally masc.; *e. g.* पूर्वरात्र *masc.*, 'the first part of the night,' पूर्वाह्ण *masc.* 'the fore-noon;' on the other hand सुदिनाह 'a clear day' and others are neuter.

§ 543. The power of composition, although great, is not unlimited, and the native grammarians have given many rules stating not merely when it is permitted to compound two words, but also when it is forbidden to do so. Here, a few examples must suffice. The two nouns अक्षि 'an eye' and काण 'blind' cannot be compounded to express the sense 'blind of an eye' (अक्ष्णा काण:) because in general an adjective is compounded with a preceding Instr. case (or, rather, with a noun which if no composition were to take place would stand in the Instr. case) only when that which is expressed by the adjective is caused by what is expressed by the noun in the Instr. case, whereas in the present instance 'blindness' is not caused by 'the eye.' Again, in phrases like नृणां द्विज: श्रेष्ठ: 'the Bráhman is the best of men' it is not permitted to form a compound of the two words नृ and श्रेष्ठ. An ordinal number cannot be compounded with a noun in the Genit. case; (*e. g.* सर्वां षष्ठ: 'the sixth of those present;') a Present Participle not with a noun dependent on it (*e. g.* द्विजस्य कुर्वन् or द्विजस्य कुर्वीणः 'a workman of the Bráhman'). Nominal bases in नृ or अक, denoting an agent, are, with some exceptions, not compounded with a noun in the Genit. case (*e. g.* अपां स्रष्टा 'the creator of the waters,' ओदनस्य पाचक: 'one who cooks rice;' but देवपूजक 'a worshipper of the gods').

(*b*).—*Appositional Determinative Compounds (Karmadháraya).*

§ 544. The following are instances of appositional determinative compounds given by the native grammarians:

नीलोत्पल (Neut., N. Sing. °लम्) ' a blue lotus' (नीलमुत्पलम्).

एकनाथ (Masc., N. Sing. °थ:) 'an only lord.'

पुराणमीमांसक (Masc., N. Plur. °का:) 'the old Mímánsakas;' *i. e.* the old school of the Mímánsakas.

सद्विज (Masc., N. Sing.) 'a good Vedic scholar.'

स्नातानुलिप्त (N. Sing. Masc. °प्त:) 'first bathed and afterwards anointed' (पूर्वं स्नातः पश्चादनुलिप्तः).

कृताकृत (N. Sing. Neut. °तम्) 'done and not done,' *i. e.* badly done (कृतं च तदकृतं च).

कृष्णसारङ्ग (N. Sing. Neut. °ङ्गम्) 'blackish-variegated.'

सदृशश्वेत (N. Sing. Neut. °तम्) 'of similar white colour.'
युवखलति (N. Sing. Masc. °ति:) 'a young bald-headed person.'
(युवा खलतिः).

इषत्पिङ्गुल (N. Sing. Neut. °लम्) 'a little brown.'
सुपुरुष (Masc., N. Sing. °ष:) 'a good man.'
प्राचार्य (Masc., N. Sing. °र्य:) 'an excellent teacher.' (प्रगत आचार्यः).
पूगकृत (N. Sing. Neut. °तम्) 'made into a heap.'
घनश्याम (N. Sing. Masc. °मः) 'black like a cloud.' (घन इव श्यामः).
देवब्राह्मण (Masc., N. Sing. °णः) 'a Brâhman who worships the gods.'
(देवपूजको ब्राह्मणः).

§ 545. In some Karmadhâraya-compounds the qualifying member takes the second place; e. g.

पुरुषव्याघ्र (Masc., N. Sing. °घ्र:) 'a tiger-like man' (व्याघ्र इव पुरुष:).
राजकुञ्जर (Masc., N. Sing. °र:) 'an elephant-like king;' i. e. an excellent king (कुञ्जर इव राजा).
इभयुवति (Fem., N. Sing. °ति:) 'a young female elephant.'
गोवशा (Fem., N. Sing. °शा) 'a barren cow.'
राजान्तर (Neut., N. Sing. °रम्) 'another king' (अन्यो राजा).

§ 546. (a) महत्, when used as first member of Karmadhâraya and Bahuvrîhi-compounds, is changed to महा; e. g.

Karmadhâraya: महादेव (Masc., N. Sing. °व:) 'the great god,' a name of S'iva.

Bahuvrîhi: महाबाहु (N. Sing. Masc. °हुः) 'a person possessed of great arms.'

(b) The base of the interrogative pronoun किम्, or कु (§ 194), sometimes also का, and before words beginning with vowels and a few words beginning with consonants कद्, are used as first members of Karmadhâraya-compounds to express censure or contempt; e. g.

किंराजन् (Masc., N. Sing. °जा) 'a bad king' (literally 'what sort of a king?' कुत्सितो राजा).

कुपुरुष or कापुरुष (Masc., N. Sing. °ष:) 'a bad man, a coward' (कुत्सितः पुरुषः).

कदश्व (Masc., N. Sing. °श्व:) 'a bad horse' (कुत्सितोऽश्वः).

§ 547. Words which denote a point of the compass (like पूर्व 'eastern,' उत्तर 'northern' &c.) and the cardinal numbers द्वि 'two', त्रि 'three' &c. cannot enter into composition with other words to form with them Karmadhâraya-compounds, except when the Karmadhâraya-compound is a proper name; *e. g.* it is forbidden to compound the two words उत्तरा वृक्षाः 'northern trees,' or पञ्च ब्राह्मणाः 'five Brâhmans;' but the two words सप्तन् 'seven' and ऋषि 'a Rishi' are compounded in the word सप्तर्षि (Masc., N. Plur. ° षय:) 'the seven Rishis,' because this compound is a proper name for the constellation of the Great Bear.

§ 548. (*a*) Contrary to this rule a word denoting a point of the compass and a cardinal number may form a Karmadhâraya-compound with another noun, provided the compound so formed is not used by itself but has a Taddhita affix added to it, or conveys at least besides the sense which it would convey as a Karmadhâraya, a derivative meaning such as is usually denoted by a Taddhita affix, or provided the compound so formed becomes the first member of another compound. *E. g.* It is allowable to compound पूर्व 'eastern' + शाला 'a hall' = पूर्वशाला 'the eastern hall,' provided this compound is not used by itself, but has a Taddhita-affix added to it, पूर्वशाला + Taddh. अ = पौर्वशाल 'being in the eastern hall.' Similarly षष् + मातृ = षण्मातृ 'six mothers' (not used by itself) + Taddh. अ = षाण्मातुर 'one who has six mothers' (*i. e.* Kârttikeya). द्वि + गो = द्विगो 'two cows,' not used in this sense but, changed to द्विग, in the sense of 'bartered for two cows.' पञ्च + गो = पञ्चगो 'five cows,' not used by itself, but as first member in the Bahuvrîhi-compound पञ्चगवधन 'one whose wealth consists in five cows.'

(*b*) Moreover a cardinal number is compounded with another noun when the whole compound so formed denotes an aggregate; *e. g.* त्रि

'three' + भुवन 'world' = त्रिभुवन (Neut., Nom. Sing. नम्) 'the aggregate of the three worlds' or 'the three worlds collectively.'

(c).—*Numeral Determinative Compounds* (*Dvigu*).

§ 549. A Karmadhâraya-compound formed by § 548 is called a Dvigu, when its first member is a cardinal number. Dvigu-compounds that have not entered into composition with other words, and have neither received a Taddhita affix nor convey a meaning such as is usually denoted by a Taddhita affix, must, as will appear from § 548 *b*, always denote an aggregate; *e. g.*

त्रिभुवन (Neut., N. Sing. °नम्) 'the three worlds collectively.'

चतुर्युग (Neut., N. Sing. °गम्) 'the four Yugas collectively.'

§ 550. Dvigu-compounds that denote an aggregate, are commonly neuter. When the final member of a Dvigu-compound ends in अ, the feminine affix ई is generally added to it; some nouns in अ, however, retain their final अ and in this case the Dvigu-compound is neuter. Feminine nouns in आ shorten their final आ, or substitute ई for it. Nouns in अन् either drop their final न्, or substitute ई for अन्; *e. g.*

पञ्चमूली (Fem., N. Sing. °ली) from पञ्चन् + मूल (Neut.), 'an aggregate of five roots.'

पञ्चपात्र (Neut., N. Sing. °त्रम्) from पञ्चन् + पात्र (Neut.), 'an aggregate of five dishes.'

पञ्चखट्वं (Neut., N. Sing. °ट्वम्) or पञ्चखट्वी (Fem., N. Sing. °ट्वी) from पञ्चन् + खट्वा (Fem.) 'an aggregate of five beds.'

पञ्चतक्ष (Neut., N. Sing. °क्षम्) or पञ्चतक्षी (Fem., N. Sing. °क्षी) from पञ्चन् + तक्षन् (Masc.) 'five carpenters.'

§ 551. Dvigu-compounds which, although no Taddhita affix is added to them, express a meaning usually denoted by a Taddhita affix, assume the gender of the nouns which they qualify, and their last members are subject to § 536; *e. g.* पञ्चकपाल in the sense of 'prepared in five dishes' may be masc., fem., or neut.; पञ्चगु (from पञ्चन् + गो) 'bartered for five cows,' &c.

§ 552. **General rule for all Determinative Compounds:—**

The following is an alphabetical list of the more common nominal bases that undergo slight changes when they form the last members of Determinative compounds:

1. अङ्गुलि 'a finger' is changed to अङ्गुल after numerals and indeclinables; *e. g.* द्व्यङ्गुल 'two fingers long.'

2. अञ्जलि 'a handful' may optionally be changed to अञ्जल in Dvigu-compounds (except those described in § 551) after द्वि and त्रि; *e. g.* द्व्यञ्जल *neut.*, or द्व्यञ्जलि *neut.*, 'two handfuls;' but only द्व्यञ्जलि 'bought for two handfuls.'

3. अहन् 'a day,' is changed to अह; *e. g.* उत्तमाह *masc.*, 'a holy day,' द्व्यह *masc.* 'an aggregate of two days;' but it is changed to अह्न after indeclinables, सर्व, and words denoting parts of the day; *e. g.* सर्वाह्न *masc.* 'the whole day,' पूर्वाह्न *masc.'* (see § 542, *b*).

4. गो 'a bull, a cow,' is changed to गव except in the Dvigu-compounds described in § 551; *e. g.* परमगव 'an excellent bull,' पञ्चगव *neut.*, 'a collection of five cows;' but द्विगु 'bartered for two cows.'

5. नौ 'a ship,' is changed to नाव after अर्ध, and in Dvigu-compounds, except those described in § 551. अर्धनाव *neut.* 'half a ship;' द्विनाव *neut.* 'two ships;' but पञ्चनौ 'bartered for two ships.'

6. पथिन् 'a road' is at the end of all compounds changed to पथ; *e. g.* धर्मपथ *masc.* 'the path of religion;' रम्यपथ (Bahuvrīhi) a country &c. 'in which the roads are lovely.'

7. राजन् 'a king' is changed to राज; *e. g.* परमराज *masc.*, 'an excellent king.'

8. रात्रि 'night' is changed to रात्र after numerals, indeclinables, सर्व, words denoting parts of the night, संख्यात, and पुण्य; *e. g.* सर्वरात्र *masc.* 'the whole night,' पूर्वरात्र *masc.*, 'the first part of the night;' द्विरात्र *neut.*, 'two nights' (see § 542, *b*).

9. सक्थि 'a thigh' is changed to सक्थ after उत्तर, पूर्व, मृग, and after a word which denotes an object with which a thigh is compared; e. g. मृगसक्थ, neut., 'the thigh of a deer;' फलकसक्थ neut., 'a thigh like a plank.'

10. सखि 'a friend' is changed to सख; e. g. कृष्णसख masc., 'a friend of Kṛishṇa.'

But these changes do generally not take place in Tatpurusha-compounds the first member of which is सु, or किम् (§ 546, b), or the negative prefix अ; e. g. सुराजन् masc. (N. Sing. सुराजा) 'a good king,' किंसखि masc. (N. Sing. किंसखा) 'a bad friend;' अराजन् masc. (N. Sing. अराजा) 'one who is not a king.'

2.—Bahuvrîhi or Attributive Compounds.

§ 553. (a) The following are instances of attributive compounds:

पीताम्बर (N. Sing. Masc. °रः) 'one who has a yellow garment' (पीतम्बरं यस्य सः).

दीर्घबाहु (N. Sing. Masc. °हुः) 'long-armed' (दीर्घौ बाहू यस्य सः).

प्राप्तोदक (N. Sing. Masc. °कः) a village &c., 'which water has approached' (प्राप्तमुदकं यं सः).

उढरथ (N. Sing. Masc. °थः) 'one by whom a car is drawn' (उढो रथो येन सः).

उपहृतपशु (N. Sing. Masc. °शुः) 'one to whom cattle are offered' (उपहृताः पशवो यस्मै सः).

उद्धृतौदन (N. Sing. Masc. °नः) a pot, &c., 'from which boiled rice has been taken out' (उद्धृतमोदनं यस्मात्सः).

वीरपुरुष (N. Sing. Masc. °षः) a village, &c., 'in which the men are heroes' (वीराः पुरुषा यस्मिन्सः).

कृतकृत्य (N. Sing. Masc. °त्यः) 'one who has done his work' (कृतं कृत्यं येन सः).

देवदत्तनामन् (N. Sing. Masc. °मा) 'one whose name is Devadatta' (देवदत्तो नाम यस्य सः).

नलाभिध (N. Sing. Masc. °ध:) 'one whose name is Nala' (नलो ऽभिधा यस्य स:).

धर्मप्रधान (N. Sing. Masc. °न:) 'one whose chief (aim) is justice' (धर्मः प्रधानं यस्य स:).

चिन्तापर (N. Sing. Masc. °र:) 'one whose highest (occupation) is thinking,' 'thoughtful' (चिन्ता परं यस्य स:).

इन्द्रादि (N. Plur. Masc. °दय:) the gods 'of whom Indra is the first' *i. e.* Indra and the others (इन्द्र आदिर्येषां ते).

(*b*) As the preceding may in general be considered to have been appositional determinative compounds which, by changing their original sense so as to make it become the attribute of some other subject and by assuming the gender of the noun which they qualify, have been changed into attributive compounds, so the following compounds may be looked upon as dependent determinative compounds that have undergone a similar change:

विद्युत्प्रभ (N. Sing. Masc. °भ:) 'one who has the brightness of lightning' (विद्युत् इव प्रभा यस्य स:).

देवाकृति (N. Sing. Masc. °ति:) 'of godlike shape' (देवस्येवाकृतिर्यस्य स:).

In some compounds of this kind the dependent member is placed last; *e. g.*

असिपाणि (N. Sing. Masc. °णि:) 'one who has a sword in his hand' (असि: पाणौ यस्य स:).

दण्डहस्त (N. Sing. Masc. °स्त:) 'one who bears a staff in his hand' (दण्डो हस्ते यस्य स:).

(*c*) Attributive compounds the first member of which is a cardinal number must not be confounded with numeral determinative or Dvigu-compounds. Instances of attributive compounds of this kind are:

त्रिलोचन (N. Sing. Masc. °न:) 'one who has three eyes,' a name of S'iva, (त्रीणि लोचनानि यस्य स:).

चतुर्मुख (N. Sing. Masc. °ख:) 'one who has four faces,' a name of Brahman (चत्वारि मुखानि यस्य स:).

§ 554. The following attributive compounds may be compared with the Tatpurusha-compounds described in § 541 *b, c:*

प्रपर्ण or प्रपतितपर्ण (N. Sing. Masc. °र्णः) a tree &c. 'from which the leaves have fallen down' (प्रपतितानि पर्णानि यस्मात्सः).

निस्तेजस् (N. Sing. Masc. °जाः) 'devoid of energy' (निर्गतं तेजो यस्मात्स :).

उन्नस (N. Sing. Masc. °सः) 'high-nosed' (उन्नता नासिका यस्य सः).

अपुत्र (N. Sing. Masc. °त्रः) 'one who has no son' (पुत्रो यस्य नास्ति सः).

§ 555. (*a*) महत् when used as the first member of Bahuvrîhi-compounds is changed to महा (§ 546, *a*); *e. g.*

महाबाहु (N. Sing. Masc. °हुः) 'one who has great arms' (महान्तौ बाहू यस्य सः).

(*b*) The indeclinable सह 'with,' when used as the first member of Bahuvrîhi-compounds, is often changed to स; *e. g.*

सपुत्र or सहपुत्र (N. Sing. Masc. °त्रः) 'with one's son,' or 'accompanied by one's son' (पुत्रेण सह).

§ 556. The general rule concerning feminine nouns which has been given in § 532 applies also to feminine nouns which form the first members of Bahuvrîhi-compounds, provided those feminines do not end in ऊ, and provided the second member of the compound is any other feminine noun, than an ordinal number, and is not one of the words प्रिया, मनोज्ञा, कल्याणी &c.; *e. g.*

चित्रगु (N. Sing. Masc. °गुः) 'one who has a brindled cow' (चित्रा गौर्यस्य सः ; गो is changed to गु by § 536, *a*).

रूपवद्भार्य (N. Sing. Masc. °र्यः) 'one who has a beautiful wife' (रूपवती भार्या यस्य सः); the final आ of भार्या is shortened by § 536, *a*).

But कल्याणीप्रिय (N. Sing. Masc. °यः) 'one to whom a virtuous woman is dear' (कल्याणी प्रिया यस्य सः); the first member retains here its feminine form, in order that this compound may be distinguished from कल्याण-प्रिय 'one to whom a virtuous man is dear.' For similar reasons the feminine forms are retained in other compounds, such as पाणिनीभार्य, ब्राह्मणीभार्य &c.

§ 557. (*a*) The word गो, and feminine nouns in आ, when they are the last members of Bahuvrîhi-compounds, are subject to § 536; *e. g.* चिलगु, रूपवद्भार्यं.

(*b*) Bahuvrîhi-compounds the last member of which is a feminine noun in ई or ऊ, or a noun ending in ऋ, assume the affix क्. Many other Bahuvrîhi-compounds assume the same affix क्, either necessarily or optionally. Bahuvrîhi-compounds in इन् must take the affix क् in the Feminine; *e. g.*

बहुनदीक (N. Sing. Masc. क:) a country &c. 'in which there are many rivers.'

गतभर्तृक (N. Sing. Fem. °का) a woman 'whose husband has died.'

बहुमाल or बहुमाल्क or बहुमालाक (N. Sing. Masc. °ल: or °क:) 'one who has many garlands' (माला).

महायशस्क (N. Sing. Masc. °स्क:) or महायशास् (N. Sing. Masc. °शा:) 'one who possesses great fame.'

बहुस्वामिन्, N. Sing. Fem. बहुस्वामिका, a woman 'who has many masters.'

§ 558. The following are some specimens of compounds which likewise are considered Bahuvrîhi-compounds by the native grammarians:

उपदश (N. Plur. Masc. °शा:) 'about ten' ('nine' or 'eleven').

आसन्नविंश (N. Plur. Masc. °शा:) 'near twenty.'

द्वित्र (N. Plur. Masc. °त्र:) 'two or three.'

द्विदश (N. Plur. Masc. °शा:) 'twice ten' (*i. e.* 'twenty.')

दक्षिणपूर्वी (Fem., N. Sing. °र्वी) 'south-east.'

केशाकेशि indecl., 'seizing each other by the hair.'

दण्डादण्डि indecl., 'beating each other with sticks.'

§ 559. Some nouns undergo slight changes when forming the last members of Bahuvrîhi-compounds; the most common of them are:

1. अक्षि 'an eye' is changed to अक्ष; when used literally for the eye of an animal, the Bahuvrîhi-compound takes in the Feminine the feminine affix ई; *e. g.* लोहिताक्ष, Fem. लोहिताक्षी 'red-eyed.'

2. गन्ध 'smell' is changed to गन्धि after सु, सुरभि &c.; e. g. सुगन्धि 'having a good smell, fragrant;' पद्मगन्धि 'smelling like a lotus.'

3. जाया 'a wife' is changed to जानि; e. g. युवजानि 'having a young wife.'

4. दन्त 'a tooth' is changed to दत् after सु and after numerals when the Bahuvrîhi-compound is intended to indicate a certain age; e. g. द्विदत् (N. Sing. Masc. द्विदन्, Fem. द्विदती) 'having two teeth.'

5. धनुस् 'a bow' is changed to धन्वन्; e. g. शार्ङ्गधन्वन् (N. Sing. Masc. °न्वा) 'having a bow made of horn.'

6. धर्म 'law' is changed to धर्मन् when it is preceded by only one word in the same compound; e. g. विदितधर्मन् 'one who knows the law.'

7. नासिका 'a nose' is changed to नस chiefly after prepositions; e. g. उन्नस 'high-nosed.'

8. पाद 'a foot' is changed to पाद् after numerals, after सु, and in certain other compounds; e. g. द्विपाद् 'biped;' व्याघ्रपाद् 'having feet like a tiger's.'

9. प्रजा 'offspring' and मेधा 'understanding,' are changed to प्रजस् and मेधस् after सु, दुः, and the negative prefix अ; e. g. अप्रजस् (N. Sing. Masc. °जाः) 'without offspring;' दुर्मेधस् 'stupid.'

10. सक्थि 'a thigh' is changed to सक्थ when used literally for the thigh of an animal; e. g. दीर्घसक्थ 'having long thighs.' (For पथिन् see § 552, 6.)

3.—DVANDVA OR COPULATIVE COMPOUNDS.

§ 560. A Dvandva-compound denotes either the mutual conjunction of the objects denoted by its several members, or it denotes their aggregate. In the former case the Dvandva-compound assumes the gender of its final member and the terminations of the Dual or Plural according as it denotes two or more objects; in the latter case it always is neuter and assumes the terminations of the Singular; e. g.

युधिष्ठिरार्जुनौ (Masc. Du.) 'Yudhishthira and Arjuna.'
अर्थधर्मौ or धर्मार्थौ (Masc. Du.) 'wealth and religion.'

ब्राह्मणक्षत्रियविट्शूद्राः (Masc. Plur.) 'a Bráhman, and a Kshatriya, and a Vais'ya, and a S'ûdra.'

मयूरीकुक्कुटौ (Masc. Du.) 'a pea-hen and a cock;' but कुक्कुटमयूर्यौ (Fem. Du.) 'a cock and a pea-hen.'

पाणिपादम् (Neut. Sing.) 'hand and foot.'

अहिनकुलम् (Neut. Sing) 'the snake and the ichneumon' (as an instance of two natural enemies).

सुखदुःखे (Neut. Du.) or सुखदुःखम् (Neut. Sing.) 'pleasure and pain.'

शीतोष्णे (Neut. Du.) or शीतोष्णम् (Neut. Sing.) 'cold and heat.'

There are exceptions; *e. g.* अश्ववडवौ (Masc. Du.) 'a horse and a mare;' अहोरात्रः (Masc. Sing.) 'day and night.'

§ 561. The order in which the various members of a Dvandva-compound are arranged depends partly on their meaning and partly on their form. Words denoting various castes should be placed in the order of the castes, beginning from the highest; the name of an elder should precede that of his younger brother, and, in general, the more important word should be placed first. Words ending with इ or उ should precede others (*e. g.* हरिहरौ); likewise words which begin with a vowel and end in अ (*e. g.* ईशकृष्णौ), and words which contain fewer syllables (*e. g.* शिवकेशवौ).

§ 562. (*a*) When two nouns in ऋ expressive of relationship, or two nouns in ऋ that are designations of sacrificial priests, form a Dvandva-compound, the final ऋ of the first member is changed to आ; the same change takes place when a noun in ऋ expressive of relationship forms a Dvandva together with पुत्र; *e. g.*

मातापितरौ (Masc. Du.) 'father and mother.'
पितापुत्रौ (Masc. Du.) 'father and son.'
होतापोतारौ (Masc. Du.) 'the Hotṛi and the Potṛi' (two priests).

(*b*) When the names of two deities that are usually mentioned together, form a Dvanda-compound, the final vowel of the first member is mostly lengthened, *e. g.*

मित्रावरुणौ (Masc. Du.) 'Mitra and Varuṇa.'
अग्नीषोमौ (Masc. Du.) 'Agni and Soma.'

Similar changes take place in similar compounds; *e. g.*

द्यावाभूमी or द्यावाक्षमे or द्यावापृथिव्यौ or दिवस्पृथिव्यौ (Fem. Du.) 'heaven and earth.'

§ 563. When the last member of an aggregative Dvanda-compound ends either in a palatal consonant, or in द्, ष्, or ह्, the vowel अ is added to it; *e. g.*

त्वक्स्रज (Neut., N. Sing. °जम्) 'a skin and a garland' (from त्वच् + स्रज्).

छत्रोपानह (Neut., N. Sing °हम्) 'an umbrella and a shoe' (from छत्र + उपानह्).

But प्रावृट्शरदौ (N. Du. of प्रावृट्शरद्) 'the rains and the autumn.'

§ 564. It is allowable to use instead of the compound मातापितरौ (§ 562, *a*) simply the Dual of पितृ; पितरौ 'father and mother;' similarly श्वश्रूश्वशुरौ or श्वशुरौ 'father and mother-in-law;' भ्रातरौ 'brother and sister;' पुत्रौ 'son and daughter,' &c.

4.—AVYAYÎBHÂVA OR ADVERBIAL COMPOUNDS.

§ 565. The final letters of nouns that form the final member of an Avyayîbhâva-compound, are subject to the following changes:

(*a*) Final long vowels are shortened (as in the neuter), final ए changed to इ, and final ओ and औ changed to उ.

(*b*) Final अ, whether it be original or substituted for आ in accordance with (*a*), is changed to अम् (*i. e.* it receives the termination of the Nom. or Acc. Sing. of a neuter noun in अ).

(*c*) Final अन् of masc. and fem. nouns is changed to अम्; final अन् of neuter nouns may be changed to अ or to अम्.

(*d*) The termination अम् must be added to शरद्, मनस्, उपानह्, दिव्, दिश् and to certain other nouns.

(*e*) अम् may optionally be added to all nouns which end in a hard or soft unaspirate or aspirate Guttural, Palatal, Lingual, Dental, or Labial.

§ 566. The following are instances of adverbial compounds: अधिहरि 'upon Hari;' अधिगोपम् 'on the cow-herd' (अधि + गोपा, § 565, a and b); अध्यात्मम् 'on the soul' (अधि + आत्मन्, § 565, c); उपराजम् 'under the king' (उप + राजन्, § 565, c); उपशरदम् 'near the autumn' (उप + शरद्, § 565, d); उपसमिधम् or उपसमित् 'near fuel' (उप + समिध्, § 565, e); उपचर्मम् or उपचर्म 'near the skin' (उप + चर्मन्, § 565, c); उपनदम् or उपनदि 'near the river;' उपगिरम् or उपगिरि 'near the mountain;' अनुविष्णु 'after Vishṇu;' अनुगङ्गम् 'along the Ganges;' अनुज्येष्ठम् 'according to seniority;' अनुरूपम् 'in a corresponding manner;' प्रत्यग्नि 'towards the fire;' प्रतिनिशम् 'every night;' प्रत्यक्षम् or समक्षम् 'before one's eyes;' परोक्षम् 'out of sight;' निर्मक्षिकम् 'free from flies;' अतिनिद्रम् 'beyond sleep' *i. e.* wakefully; यथाशक्ति 'in accordance with one's strength;' यावज्जीवम् 'as long as life lasts,' *i. e.* 'all one's life;' सहरि 'like Hari;' सतृणम् 'with the grass,' *i. e.* including even the grass (तृणेन सह, the latter word being usually changed to स in Avyayîbhâva-compounds).

§ 567. Compounds may be compounded again with other simple or compound words, the compounds so formed may become the members of new compounds, and so on. This repeated composition may theoretically be carried to any extent. In practice, however, we find that the further we follow back the current of Sanskrit literature to the time when Sanskrit was really a living and spoken language, the more sparing is the employment of compound words and the more limited the length of the compounds actually used. The student, when writing, therefore, should remember that long and unwieldy compounds are by no means characteristic of a good style. When dissolving a long compound he should, unless it be a Dvandva, always dissolve it first into its two main parts, and should dissolve the latter afterwards again, and so on, until at last none but simple words remain.

THE END.

BOMBAY: PRINTED AT THE EDUCATION SOCIETY'S PRESS, BYCULLA.

www.ingramcontent.com/pod-product-compliance
Lightning Source LLC
Chambersburg PA
CBHW031941230426
43672CB00010B/2010